ADMINISTRATIVE LAW
IN CENTRAL
AND
EASTERN
EUROPE

ADMINISTRATIVE LAW IN CENTRAL AND EASTERN EUROPE 1996–1998

Denis J. Galligan and Daniel M. Smilov

CEU PRESS

Central European University Press
Budapest

Published by

Central European University Press

Október 6. utca 12
H-1051 Budapest
Hungary

400 West 59th Street
New York, NY 10019
USA

Distributed by
Plymbridge Distributors Ltd., Estover Road, Plymouth PL6 7PZ, United Kingdom
Distributed in the United States by
Cornell University Press Services, 750 Cascadilla Street, Ithaca, New York 14851-6525, USA

ISBN 963-9116-40-8 Cloth
ISBN 963-9116-39-4 Paperback

Library of Congress Cataloging in Publication Data
A CIP catalog record for this book is available upon request

Printed in Hungary by Akaprint Budapest

CONTENTS

LIST OF TABLES

ACKNOWLEDGEMENTS

This book was made possible by the financial support of the Open Society Institute. The editors wish to express their appreciation for that support and for the helpful advice of Mr Peter Komives of the Constitutional and Legal Policy Institute in Budapest.

The material for each chapter was collected by a person or persons native to the respective country. Their names are recorded in this volume, and I am most grateful to them for their good work. It is gratifying to note that several of them are former students whom I taught at the Central European University since its creation in 1992.

A major contribution to the editing of the chapters was made by a small group of Oxford students. They are Shaheed Fatme, Michael Likosky, and Francesca Galligan. I also wish to thank Ms Charlotte Barrow for her work as copy editor.

My warmest thanks go to Mr Daniel Smilov who is a graduate of the Central European University and one of my doctoral students in Oxford. Daniel has been responsible for overseeing the assembly, production, and publication of this book. He has done a very fine job in enlisting contributors, commenting on their drafts, and ensuring the quality of the final product. He has also borne a large part of the editorial work and has shepherded the book through each stage of production.

Finally, I would like to thank my colleagues at the Oxford Centre for Socio-Legal Studies, especially my secretary, Mrs Ann Hawes, who helped in a multitude of ways.

Denis J. Galligan
Wolfson College, Oxford

INTRODUCTION

I

Following the constitutional and political reforms that have marked the last decade in Central and Eastern Europe, the time has now come for the whole-scale reform of public administration. That involves several parts: the creation of a professional civil service; a clear sense of the objectives to be achieved by the administration; and the provision of adequate resources to perform the tasks of public administration.

In addition, and perhaps most importantly of all, there must be a sound legal basis for public administration. This has a particular and a general aspect. The particular aspect means clear and well-drafted laws stating the powers and responsibilities of each part of the administration, whether it be a minister of state, a government department, or a special agency. The general part itself has several directions. It is important that the administration should become imbued with fundamental constitutional notions of administration according to law, openness and transparency, respect for the rights of individuals and groups, and a general concern for fair and reasonable decision-making.

The general part also involves creating a structured environment which aids and assists the administrator in achieving those constitutional goals. This has many practical dimensions, but in particular it requires two main developments: one is a general and stable system of administrative procedures, and the other is an effective system of administrative oversight.

Administrative procedures provide a pattern of order and consistency in the way administrative bodies behave. This facilitates the achievement of the statutory objectives; it also allows citizens who are affected by administrative action to know that decisions will be made according to a predictable pattern rather than at the will of the administrator. Administrative procedures go farther than just contributing to order; they also protect important values such as participation by interested parties, openness and transparency, the giving of reasons, and the availability of recourse.

Oversight mechanisms, for their part, help to ensure that primary decision-makers perform their tasks properly and in accordance with constitutional and administrative law values. Such mechanisms include internal administrative appeals, external appeals, judicial scrutiny, external complaints procedures or ombudsmen as they are often called, inspectorates, the prosecutor, and parliamentary committees. The general idea is that there is a range of functions that supervisory bodies ought to perform and that certain kinds of institutions are best suited to those functions.

II

The programme needed to achieve a public administration that is not only stable, professional, and effective, but also conducted in accordance with the values that derive from principles of democracy and legality, is obviously a massive one. Nevertheless, the countries of the region recognise the importance of these reforms, and most have made considerable efforts towards achieving them. Progress of course varies according to historical and cultural factors, as well as current commitment and determination.

The time has arrived for these changes and developments to be recorded in a readily available form. A great deal of writing and commentary is now becoming available in the region through books, journals, reports, and various other media. The idea behind this volume is to make a contribution to that literature by recording the state of administrative law in the countries of the region. Our hope is that this will be the first of a series of annual publications which will report changes and developments in the field of administrative law. Our longer term objective is to move from an annual publication to a more frequent review.

The launch of this first volume on administrative law in the region is intended to serve a number of purposes. The first is simply to record what is happening. The second is to provide the countries of the region with easily accessible information on what is happening in neighbouring countries. In working in countries of the region, I often discover that each knows more about ideas and developments in the West than in their immediate neighbourhood. Each country is of course different and each must create laws and institutions compatible with its history and culture; at the same time, there is a shared experience across the region and the problems confronting each country have much in common.

Our third purpose is to enable legislators, courts, and administrative officials in any one country to learn from the experience of other countries. Some countries, for instance, have well-developed codes of administrative procedure, while to many others the idea is novel. Much time and effort can be saved if, in matters like this, each can draw on the experience of others.

III

Our main goals in this first volume are twofold: one is to give a snapshot of the administrative law system of each country as it was at the end of 1997; the other is to record the main changes and developments that have occurred in each country during the period 1996-7. Each chapter deals with these two issues. The approach taken in this first volume is descriptive and presentational, the idea being to create a base of information that is of interest in itself and that will be a reference point in future volumes. Accordingly, we do not offer an analysis or critique of the material. Our intention is that in future volumes the description of current developments in each country will be accompanied by analysis and comment, so that in time the annual volume will be an important forum for discussion of administrative law issues in the region.

Each chapter is structured along the following lines:

Part I: Here an account is provided of the main features of the system of administrative law in each country. The presentation begins with a brief account of the historical background to administrative law and institutions. This includes a description of the main institutions of government and administration, the nature and structure of the executive branch, and relations between central and local government. The power of the government and other officials to make subordinate legislation or normative acts is examined. Then the focus turns to the judicial bodies dealing with administrative matters.

The next issue is administrative procedures. Where there is a code of administrative procedures, its main features are described; where there is no code, an outline is given of the general procedural approach. The forms of appeal and other methods of recourse are then described; these include internal administrative appeals, judicial scrutiny, and other complaints procedures where they exist. In most of the chapters, the grounds on which judicial scrutiny is based are described in detail. A very brief account is then given of other forms of administrative supervision, including the audit commission or court, inspectorates, and parliamentary committees.

Part II: Here a summary is given of the main changes that have occurred in administrative law during the period 1996-7. This in turn has two parts. The more general part includes constitutional changes that have direct implications for administrative law. It deals with major changes to the nature and structure of government, the executive, and the administration. It also includes changes to general codes of procedure and to the judicial system insofar as they relate to administrative supervision. Where new institutions are created, such as an ombudsman or an administrative court, these are noted and briefly described.

The second section of Part II gives an outline of the major legislative changes that have occurred during the period. Substantive reforms in a range of areas are of interest because they usually include creating or adjusting administrative authorities to oversee the particular area of regulation. A fair amount of this legislation occurs within the privatisation process, but it often extends to such varied fields as welfare, the environment, national security, citizenship and immigration, and taxation.

This is followed by notes on the most important pieces of secondary legislation during the period. In the next section the focus is on the major judicial decisions concerning administrative law. This covers relevant decisions of the constitutional court as well as the administrative or civil courts (where applicable). The account of judicial decisions, it is hoped, will be especially useful as a point of reference for courts across the region.

The last section of Part II offers some empirical information on the workings of the various supervisory institutions. The range and quality of this information varies greatly from country to country, depending partly on whether such information is recorded and partly on its accessibility. In many cases, enough is available to give some indication of the activities and effectiveness of the different institutions.

D. J. Galligan
Wolfson College, Oxford

CHAPTER ONE
BULGARIA

I. GENERAL DESCRIPTION OF THE ADMINISTRATIVE LEGAL SYSTEM

1. THE EVOLUTION OF THE BULGARIAN ADMINISTRATIVE SYSTEM

1.1 The Constitution of 1991

Although the Bulgarian Grand National Assembly adopted a new democratic constitution on July 12, 1991–fairly soon after the breakdown of the communist regime–the country's administrative legal system is still in transformation. At present, its major characteristic is the coexistence of new laws with acts and regulations inherited from the socialist past.

The major state institutions were established in their present form after the new Bulgarian Constitution was adopted in 1991. According to the constitutional texts, power in Bulgaria is divided among five major institutions: Parliament (National Assembly or Grand National Assembly); the Cabinet (Council of Ministers); the President of the Republic; the Constitutional Court; and the Judiciary (Supreme Judicial Council, Supreme Court of Cassation, Supreme Administrative Court, Chief Prosecutor and Investigation).

The new Constitution introduced a number of new features into the judicial system. First, it established a Constitutional Court, empowered to rule on the constitutionality of acts passed by Parliament and to interpret the constitutional provisions. The Constitutional Court consists of 12 justices–four elected by the National Assembly, one third is appointed by the President and four elected by a joint meeting of the justices of the Supreme Court of Cassation and the Supreme Administrative Court.[1] The justices of the court are appointed for a term of nine years and are not eligible for re-election or re-appointment. The Court is to be renewed every three years from each quota, on a rotating basis. The justices of the Constitutional Court enjoy the same immunity as the members of Parliament, and only by the vote of (two-thirds of all justices of the Court can the immunity of a justice be lifted. No authority of the Constitutional Court can be vested or suspended by a law. The first six years of democratic experience have shown that the Court is a counterbalance to the power of Parliament: on several occasions the Court has been the only obstacle to the introduction of oppressive majoritarian legislation. Second, the Constitution provided for the establishment of the Supreme Administrative Court and the Supreme Court of Cassation.[2] Before the adoption of the new basic law, the judicial system of Bulgaria was headed by a single Supreme Court dealing with administrative, civil, and criminal law issues. Finally, the drafters of the Constitution ensured the independence of the judicial branch of power by the introduction of the Supreme Judicial Council. It is responsible for the administration of personnel matters within the Judiciary and is elected by Parliament and the organs of the Judiciary according to a quota principle.

1.2 Adoption of the major administrative acts and codes

Several major procedural laws were inherited from the socialist regime. The basic procedural law, the Administrative Procedure Act (APA), was first promulgated in Official Gazette No. 90/1979 and was later amended in 1988, 1990, 1992 and 1995. The major law regulating administrative offences, the Administrative Offences and Sanctions Act, was first promulgated in *Official Gazette* No. 92/1969, and later amended several times, with the most important amendments introduced in 1992. Some other laws of general importance for every legal branch are also still valid, even though they were adopted some 25 years ago. For instance, the Law on Normative Acts, regulating the procedures for adoption of normative acts, was first promulgated in *Official Gazette* No. 27/1973 and was amended only once (in 1995) after the regime transition in 1989.

Apart from these old laws, a number of new legal acts were passed after the adoption of the Constitution. Following its provisions, a law regulating the structure and the prerogatives of the different judicial authorities was passed: the Law on Judicial Power, promulgated in *Official Gazette* No. 59/1994 (later on two amendments to the law were made following the decisions of the Constitutional Court–amendments were promulgated in Official Gazette No. 64/1996 and in *Official Gazette* No. 104/1996).

The procedural laws still do not correspond to the constitutional prescriptions for the organisation of the judicial power. The new Bulgarian Constitution includes an explicit requirement for passing a number of new procedural laws within pre-set time limits (§ 4 of the Transitional and Concluding Provisions of the Constitution). These laws are the Law on the Supreme Administrative Court, the Law on the Supreme Court of Cassation, and procedural laws regulating the three-instance legal procedure, which is constitutionally prescribed to replace the current two-instance system.[3] The time limit set for the adoption of these laws was three years after the promulgation of the Constitution (i.e. July 1991): three years after that deadline passed, the laws had still not been passed by Parliament.

In 1996 the Constitutional Court was asked to decide whether the establishment of the Supreme Administrative Court and of the Supreme Court of Cassation, as well as the appointment of judges and other staff could start before the new procedural laws had been passed. The issue was at the centre of a major political controversy. Parliament and the Government were controlled by the Bulgarian Socialist Party, while the Supreme Judicial Council was staffed by judges and lawyers who were appointed at the time of the previous parliamentary majority and who were believed to be generally sympathetic to the Union of Democratic Forces and other opposition parties. For this reason, Parliament delayed off the adoption of procedural laws until the expiration of the term of the Supreme Judicial Council. Parliament's intention was to ensure that the new Supreme Judicial Council (to be appointed at the time of the Socialist majority) would change the balance in the judicial branch and appoint judges to the new Supreme Courts more sympathetic to the party in power.

To prevent this development, the Supreme Judicial Council tried to speed up the process of appointing judges before the adoption of procedural laws, only on the basis of the constitutional provisions. In order to achieve this, a lawsuit was brought in the Constitutional Court challenging the constitutionality of an amendment to the Law on Judicial Power (passed by the Socialist-controlled Parliament) according to which the three-instance judicial system was to be built after the procedural laws were passed.

The Constitutional Court ruled that this amendment hindered the Supreme Judicial Council in exercising its constitutional prerogatives to nominate chairmen of the Supreme Administrative Court and the Supreme Court of Cassation (the appointment being made by the President of the Republic) and to appoint judges, prosecutors and examining magistrates.[4] According to the Constitutional Court's decision, the new text of the law restricted the prerogatives of the Supreme Judicial Council and improperly gave the power to interpret constitutional provisions. This amendment was declared an interference in the domain of the judicial power. Thus, after the decision of the Constitutional Court, the reform of the administrative system continued despite the lack of some important procedural laws.

2. STRUCTURE OF THE EXECUTIVE

According to the new Bulgarian Constitution, the highest executive body in the country is the Council of Ministers. Article 105(2) of the Constitution stipulates that "the Council of Ministers shall ensure the public order and national security and shall exercise overall guidance over the state administration and the armed forces".[5] The National Assembly exercises parliamentary control over the intentions, legal acts and activities of the Cabinet as a whole as well as over each individual minister. Members of the National Assembly have the prerogative to address questions and interpellations to the Council of Ministers and to individual ministers, who are obliged to respond. In the practice of the Bulgarian Parliament, questions and interpellations are a commonly used mechanism to keep the Council of Ministers accountable for all administrative acts. Parliamentary control is directly related to the mechanism for holding the Cabinet politically responsible for its actions. A motion for a vote of no confidence in the Council of Ministers may be initiated by at least one-fifth of the members of the National Assembly. The motion of no confidence can pass only with an absolute majority (more than half of the 240 elected members voting in favour). The Council of Ministers may also request a vote of confidence in its program, its overall policy or any particular issue. In other words, the Cabinet is given the chance to ask for and receive immediate and unambiguous support for its policy. A motion of confidence may pass with a simple majority, i.e. more than half of the present members voting in favour of the cabinet. According to the Constitution, if a vote of no confidence is rejected or a motion of confidence is supported, a new motion requesting a no-confidence vote cannot be made during the following six months.

3. RELATIONS BETWEEN THE CENTRAL AND THE LOCAL ADMINISTRATION

The new Bulgarian Constitution includes a separate chapter concerning the autonomy of the local governments. The municipality is the basic administrative territorial unit at the level of which self-government is practised. The region is an administrative territorial unit entrusted with the implementation of state government on a local level. It is governed by a regional governor who is appointed by the Council of Ministers and who is vested with the prerogative to exercise administrative control over the municipalities' activities. As provided by Article 144, the central bodies of state as well as their local representatives can exercise control over the legality of the acts of the local-government bodies only if authorised to do so by a law. In turn, any local-government body is free to challenge before a court any act that encroaches on its rights. The Law on Local Government[6] further specifies the constitutional provisions in attributing to the municipalities a wide range of prerogatives.

4. NORMATIVE REGULATIONS OF THE GOVERNMENT AND THE DEPARTMENTS

According to Article 114 of the Constitution, pursuant to and in implementation of the laws, the Council of Ministers shall adopt decrees, ordinances and resolutions. The Council of Ministers shall promulgate rules and regulations by decree. Within the prerogatives vested in him, the President of the Republic can issue decrees, addresses and messages.[7]

The President of the Republic has no power to pass normative decrees. All decrees issued by the President shall be countersigned by the Prime Minister or the minister concerned.[8] The cases for which no countersigning procedure is required are listed in the constitutional provision of Article 102 (3). One of the most important Constitutional Court decisions in 1996 was related to the prerogatives of the President. The Constitutional Court gave an interpretation as to whether all presidential decrees should be countersigned by a representative of the executive power, whether the list of the acts that do not need countersigning is exhaustive, and what the consequences are if a decree is not countersigned. The Constitution does not provide for any special provisions for delegating legislative powers by Parliament to the President or the Government.

5. SYSTEM OF COURTS DEALING WITH ADMINISTRATIVE LAW ISSUES

5.1 Structure of the judicial system

Until 1991, when the new Constitution was passed, the judicial system consisted of regional, district, and military courts and the Supreme Court. First-instance courts were the regional and district courts; second-instance courts were the district courts and the Supreme Court. The new Constitution provides for a three-instance judicial system. Article 119 (1) stipulates that "Justice shall be administrated by the Supreme Court of Cassation, the Supreme Administrative Court, courts of appeal, courts of district courts, courts-martial and county courts".[9] According to Part 2 of the same article, specialised courts may be set up by virtue of a law.[10] The Law on Judicial Power[11] has further specified the above-mentioned constitutional provisions. According to Article 9 the courts exercise control over the legality of all acts and actions of the administrative bodies: the citizens and all legal entities have the right to challenge before a court any administrative act that affects their rights and legitimate interests, except those listed expressly by a law.[12] According to Article 58 (1) the district courts have administrative departments–they are first instance for administrative cases.[13] Although the courts of appeal are second-instance courts, no decision of the district courts under the Administrative Procedure Act can be appealed before them.[14]

5.2 Scope of jurisdiction of the different courts

The Supreme Administrative Court is vested with the prerogative to "exercise supreme judicial oversight as to the precise and equal application of the law in administrative justice".[15] The Court can rule on all challenges to the legality of acts of the Council of Ministers and the individual ministers, and of other acts established by a law. According to Article 124 of the Constitution, the Supreme Court of Cassation exercises supreme judicial oversight as to the precise and equal application of the law by all courts.[16]

5.3 Special quasi-judicial bodies for adjudicating cases requiring professional expertise

In Bulgaria a number of quasi-judicial bodies are designed to adjudicate on questions requiring professional expertise. They are established as special units at different administrative departments. Such bodies include the Central Conscription Commission at the Ministry of Defence adjudicating on conflicts in relation to the obligatory military service, and the Central Labour-Expert Medical Commission at the Ministry of Health Care. Insofar as they act as jurisdictional bodies, these units are independent of the administration. According to the Bulgarian administrative law doctrine, the quasi-jurisdictional bodies have the following characteristics.

First, they are explicitly defined as jurisdictions by a law. Second, they act upon a complaint and not ex officio. Third, they are independent in the adjudication process. Fourth, they follow elementary adversarial procedures, in which the two parties have similar rights.

6. PROCEDURAL LAWS OR CODES OF ADMINISTRATIVE LAW AND GENERAL ADMINISTRATIVE PROCEDURES

The major codes for administrative procedure in Bulgaria are: the Administrative Procedure Act, the Administrative Offences and Sanctions Act, and the Law on Normative Acts.

6.1 Internal administrative appeal

According to the Administrative Procedure Act, control over the administration and its acts is carried out through procedures of appeal and judicial review. The judicial supervision over administrative acts requires, as a prerequisite, their appeal before the immediately superior authority of the organ that has issued the contested act. The acts of ministers, of directors of departments directly subordinated to the government or of district governors are not subject to appeal. The concerned citizens and organisation may appeal the legality and the correctness (appropriateness) of the act through complaint (Article 21[2]). The public prosecutor may appeal against the legality of an administrative act by filing a "protest".[17] If the concerned party has not signed a written declaration that he will not appeal the administrative act, it is not executed until the end of the term in which the concerned party and the public prosecutor may contest it–seven days after the announcement of the administrative act.[18] The exceptions to this principle are set by law. The authority that has issued the act has the opportunity to reconsider the appealed act–to cancel or to modify it, or to issue the act or the document it has refused to issue. Otherwise it has to send the complaint or protest to the immediately superior authority within seven days (14 days if the organ is collective). If this period is exceeded, a copy of the complaint may be sent to the higher authority. It pronounces its decision after taking into consideration the explanations and objections of the concerned party. The reasoned decision of the competent higher authority may cancel (repeal) in part or as a whole the appealed act or reject the complaint. If the lower authority has to issue another act to replace the cancelled one, the higher authority gives binding instructions or decides on the substance of the case if the circumstances and the facts related to the case are clear. If the higher authority exceeds the term defined by the law the matter could be referred directly to the competent court. The judicial review of administrative acts[19] guarantees the legality of the way the administration exercises its prerogatives, and protects the citizens and the private legal entities in cases of malfeasance.

Bulgarian administrative law provides for another form of internal appeal of administrative acts: this form is regulated by the Law on Proposals, Signals, Complaints and Requests.[20] According to this law, citizens have the right to file a complaint or to make a proposal or a signal to the organs that control and supervise the organ against whose decision they are appealing. The complaint must be considered within a month (two months for a collective organ), and the appellant must be notified within seven days after a decision is taken. The decision must be reasoned unless all the demands of the complaint have been met and no rights of other citizens are affected. The Law provides similar procedures for the consideration of the signals, proposals, and requests.

Some administrative lawyers have argued that the existence of the Law on Proposals, Signals, Complaints and Requests causes unnecessary ambiguity in the internal appeal regulations. On the other hand, however, this law is an attempt to facilitate the out-of-court settlements of administrative disputes.

6.2 Judicial review of administrative action

Judicial control over the administrative actions is carried out by courts and administrative jurisdictions, stipulated in special laws for cases when the judgement of the legality of an act requires special knowledge. These special jurisdictions are a part of the executive power. Their decisions were previously controlled by the Supreme Court; now such control is conferred to the Supreme Administrative Court. The tendency is to limit the number of administrative jurisdictions so that judicial control over the administration lies within the prerogative of the Court. According to its purpose and consequences, judicial control is direct and indirect. The latter concerns civil or criminal cases when the legality of an administrative act is a preliminary question. In that case the court cannot cancel the illegal act–it refuses to recognise its effect.

Judicial review of the administrative acts concerns only their legality and is carried out by the initiative of the concerned citizens and organisations (through complaint) and of the prosecutor (through protest). The opportunity for judicial review may be used when the competent administrative authority has pronounced its decision or has exceeded the time limits for it. The judicial review hinders the execution of the contested act. The complaint or the protest is lodged through the authority that has issued the act–it is obliged to send it to the competent court in a limited term. If the time limit is exceeded, a copy of the complaint or the protest may be sent directly to the competent court. In its decision it rules on the competence of the authority which has issued it; the required form; and its accordance with the substantive law, with the procedure and the purpose of the law.

6.3 Exceptions from the scope of judicial review

Some administrative acts are not submitted to judicial review: acts related to the defence and security of the country, monetary and currency control, and others. The judgement of the legality of administrative acts of ministers or directors of departments directly subordinated to the Government, or of regional governors, is in the competence of the Supreme Administrative Court. All the other administrative acts (those not excluded by a special law) are judicially reviewable by the district courts.

6.4 Judicial remedies

The court cancels the act as a whole or in part; modifies it or rejects it. If the concerned administrative authority has no right of freedom of judgement in the particular situation before issuing the act (has no legally granted discretion in taking the decision), the court looks to the substance of the matter and decides the case on its merits. In case of an illegal refusal to issue an act or a document, the court binds the authority to issue it but cannot give instructions about its content.

6.5 Exceptions from the general procedure provided by the Administrative Procedural Code or the general procedural laws

According to Article 3 of the Administrative Procedure Act, exceptions from the general procedure are all acts of the President of the Republic and the Council of Ministers; all acts on planning of the economic development of the country; all acts on setting up prices; and all acts issued for the purpose of granting rights or obligations on organs or organisations that are subordinated to the body issuing the act.[21]

7. OMBUDSMAN

No such institution is provided for by the current Bulgarian Constitution.

8. OTHER FORMS OF SUPERVISION OF THE ADMINISTRATION

8.1 The Accountancy Chamber

As provided in the Constitution, the Parliament elects an Accountancy Chamber to control the state expenditures.[22] The Law on Accountancy Chamber[23] regulates the organisation, activity and prerogatives of control over the implementation of the budget. It is independent from the executive power. The Accountancy Chamber has prerogatives in examining the legality and appropriateness of the spending of the state budget, the budget of the municipalities and other budgets passed by the Parliament; in checking the use of budget funds; current reporting of budget revenues and expenses; quarterly and annual account reports; the reports of the Bulgarian National Bank (BNB); and the interrelations of the BNB with other state authorities. The Accountancy Chamber controls all organisations and institutions supported by the budget, including the security services. It has prerogatives to approach the public prosecutors with the results of the audit or when state officials refuse to co-operate.[24] The Accountancy Chamber consists of 11 members elected (and dismissed) by the National Assembly for a term of nine years. The president of the Accountancy Chamber cannot be re-elected for another term of office.[25] The law sets down rigid restrictions on who can be elected a member of the Accountancy Chamber: no former members of the Cabinet or former directors of any Cabinet departments who served during the last three years before the date of the election are eligible.[26] No member of the Accountancy Chamber can be engaged in paid activities other than some academic research.[27] The officials of the Accountancy Chamber draw up acts of findings. The concerned parties may state their explanations and objections to the director of the particular territorial department.[28] Its decision may be appealed before the president of the Accountancy Chamber, whose decisions are peremptory.[29] The directors of the territorial departments and the president have the prerogative to issue orders for ceasing actions harming the state property or in cases of illegal expenses of budgetary funds. They are subject to appeal, but the objection does not cease their execution.[30] The decision of the Accountancy Chamber is peremptory. The president of the Accountancy Chamber issues a report to the Minister of Finance about the results of the inspections and makes suggestions for the elimination of all infringements found.[31] The Accountancy Chamber also reports to the Parliament about the account reports of the outcome of the state budget and the budget expenses of BNB.[32]

8.2 Public prosecutors

The public prosecutors are not a part of the executive power, but they have prerogatives to control the legality of the administrative acts and actions. They do not directly interfere in the process of administering; they only approach other authorities. The prosecutors' supervision over the administration was regulated by a special law that was abrogated by the Law on Judicial Power. The prosecutors examine the issued administrative acts; protest against illegal administrative acts; make suggestions about the reasons and the conditions for the illegal actions of the administration; and demand the issuing of administrative acts. They exercise their prerogatives ex officio and when approached by complainants.

9. THE ROLE OF THE SYSTEM OF PARLIAMENTARY COMMITTEES IN THE SUPERVISION OVER THE ADMINISTRATION

According to the Rules of Organisation and Procedure of the 37th National Assembly,[33] two different standing committees are granted special prerogatives in supervising the administration: The Government Authorities Committee reports on bills and drafts resolutions relating to the organisation and activities of judicial authorities and the organisation and activities of other government authorities and administration,[34] and the Anti-Corruption Committee reviews the existing legislation for any provisions capable of creating conditions conducive to corruption and reports to the Assembly accordingly.[35] According to the Constitution, the National Assembly may establish ad hoc committees to conduct inquiries and investigations.[36] So far, the practice of the parliamentary committees has shown that it is far from effective in cases when the ruling party holds an absolute majority within the Parliament. The composition and leadership of the standing committees is based on the principle of proportional representation of the parliamentary groups.[37]

II. DEVELOPMENTS IN ADMINISTRATIVE LAW DURING 1996-1997

In 1996, two major factors determined the overall legislative activity in Bulgaria. The first was that the ruling Bulgarian Socialist Party had an absolute majority in the Parliament, so there were no obstacles preventing the Council of Ministers from passing all its bills in the National Assembly. Second, the beginning of 1996 Bulgaria faced a critical deterioration of its economic situation, and thus most legislative activity addressed the urgent need of re-organising and stabilising the economy. Thus, almost 70 per cent of all passed bills referred to economic and budgetary issues. A major focus of the Cabinet's legislative activity was the attempt to extend its prerogatives within the process of privatisation.[38] Because the organisation of the judicial system is constantly seen as a political issue, the ruling majority has tried to amend the Law on Judicial Power by introducing a clause prohibiting the Supreme Judicial Council from appointing the chairmen of the Supreme Administrative Court and the Supreme Court of Cassation.[39] After a parliamentary crisis arose in December 1996, the 37th National Assembly was dissolved on February 12, 1997, by a presidential decree. A caretaker cabinet was appointed the same day.

A. THE CONSTITUTION

In 1996 and the first four months of 1997 constitutional amendments were passed.

B. LEGISLATION

1. PROCEDURAL AND GENERAL ORGANISATIONAL LAWS

1.1 Organisation of the judicial system

As already mentioned, in 1996 an attempt to amend the Law on Judicial Power provoked a serious political scandal. The Supreme Judicial Council made an unprecedented decision to appoint chairmen of the Supreme Administrative Court and the Supreme Court of Cassation, though the necessary legislative basis was nonexistent. The decrees for the appointment of the two chairmen were signed by the President (who was authorised to do so), but not promulgated, as the Minister of Justice refused to countersign them.

The next step was the amendment of the Law on Judicial Power, passed by the parliamentary majority on July 4.[40] The opposition refused to participate in the voting. The amendment stipulated that the Supreme Judicial Council can appoint the chairmen of the two supreme courts only after the passage of the respective laws. The deputy who introduced the bill referred to the provisions of the Constitution, stipulating that the new organisational structure of the judicial system could begin to function only after the enactment of the new organisational laws. On July 18 the President vetoed the law, arguing that it annulled the appointment of the two chairmen, which was already an accomplished fact. But the two presidential decrees were not yet promulgated in the Official Gazette (the Minister of Justice had refused to sign them). On July 23 the parliament overruled the presidential veto (by a vote of 127-93). Meanwhile the Prosecutor General appealed to the Constitutional Court, which on July 25 decided that the presidential decree appointing the chairmen of the two supreme courts did not need the countersignature of the Minister of Justice. The amended law was also appealed to the Constitutional Court.[41]

2. SUBSTANCE

2.1 The management of economy

2.1.1 LAWS ON PRIVATISATION

In 1996 an amendment to the Law on Privatisation was promulgated in Official Gazette No. 68/1996, as part of the governmental programme to increase the Cabinet's control over the privatisation processes. It introduced a number of changes in the statute of the Privatisation Agency, namely a decrease in the number of Supervisory Board members from 11 to five, and a substantial modification of the election procedure: instead of having six of the current 11 members elected by Parliament and five by the Cabinet, now all five members of the reduced board are elected by the Cabinet. The candidates are nominated by the Minister of Economic Development, and are then voted on by the Cabinet. The Minister also approves the Agency's budget and its annual report and oversees the implementation of the privatisation program. Furthermore, the amendment removes the ban on market privatisation of the enterprises included in the lists of firms for mass privatisation and changes the method of distribution of the funds raised through privatisation—now the majority of privatisation income is allocated for payments on internal and external state debt.

2.1.2 LAWS ON THE OWNERSHIP AND MANAGEMENT OF (AGRICULTURAL) LANDS

The Law on Protection of Agricultural Land[42] introduces some restrictions on the usage of agricultural land. The Ministry of Agriculture is to produce a register of all cultivated lands classified in 10 groups. The Ministry is authorised to prescribe obligatory requirements and measures for protection of the land against erosion. The law provides for the establishment of Protection and Improvement of Agricultural Land Fertility Fund (on the national and municipal level) and a Committee on Agricultural Land, chaired by the Minister of Agriculture.

2.1.3 LAWS ON FINANCE AND PROPERTY

The Amendment to the Bulgarian National Bank Law[43] was seen as strengthening the control of Parliament over the National Bank by introducing a procedure for early dismissal of the Bank governor and the members of the Board of Directors. The National Bank governor is given the right to propose pre-term dismissal of the members of the Board of Directors from the presidential quota. But the restriction on the checking powers of the President envisaged in the draft version of the act was not introduced.

After the Constitutional Court declared unconstitutional the Cabinet decree updating the scale for local taxes and duties, the legislative procedure for the amendment of the Law on Local Taxes[44] was speeded up. The Constitutional Court decision stated that changes in the amounts of local taxes are to be introduced by a legislative act. The decree itself was annulled by a decision of the Supreme Court. The law was vetoed by the President. The main criticism of the proposed law was that the amendment should not be enforced retroactively (from the beginning of the financial year—January 1, 1996).

The Law on State Property[45] regulates the purchase, management, and disposition of real estate and movable property belonging to the state. In accordance with the Constitution, state property is divided into public and private; the law regulates the differences in the disposal and management of the two types of state property. The state may forcibly expropriate property, provided that the respective needs cannot otherwise be met and after a fair compensation has been ensured in advance–in cash/pecuniary on market prices or with real estate of equal value. In cases when the sides cannot reach an agreement, the regional governor issues an order for expropriation, and the owner has the right to appeal the order to the court within a month period. The law also specifies the terms for cancellation of the expropriation. The surveillance and certification of state property is regulated. A special Office of State Property is established within the regional governors' offices.

The Law on State Protection of Deposits and Accounts with Commercial Banks Subject to Bankruptcy Proceedings Initiated on BNB Petition[46] was submitted by the Cabinet and voted on urgently because of the severe crisis in the banking system and growing popular distrust in the banks. It guarantees in full the accounts of natural persons and stipulates that the state will guarantee the accounts of juridical persons for up to half of their value. A special fund for state protection of deposits and accounts is established under the supervision of the Minister of Finance. When a claim for opening a bankruptcy procedure is made, the Minister of Finance places mandatory restrictions upon the property of the members of the governing bodies of the respective bank. The Bulgarian National Bank is obliged to approach the prosecution for the opening of a preliminary investigation of the officials who have contributed to the bank's failure. The law shall apply until a special law for protection of deposits and accounts is passed and enacted.

The Law on the Financial Recovery of State Enterprises[47] establishes a legal framework for the unprofitable state enterprises' financial recovery. The law concentrates more power in the hands of the Cabinet, allowing it to intervene directly in the management of such enterprises and even make management decisions. A recovery program for such firms will be prepared for a term of not longer than 12 months. The program will serve as a basis for negotiating delaying payments to creditors, and if an enterprise reaches an agreement with its creditors, this agreement is to be approved by the Minister of Finance. If within three months there is no improvement in the situation, creditors may require the liquidation of the enterprise. A special Recovery Fund is to be established for financing the programs. It is subsidised by the budget, the State Fund for Reconstruction and Development, charity, and credits from international institutions. The fund is directed by the Minister of Finance. No efficient control mechanism for the program was provided in the law.

The Law on Commodity Exchanges and Market-Places[48] aims at setting stable rules and regulations for spot and futures contracts between independent traders. The law regulates the organisational structure and activities of the State Commission on Commodity Exchanges and Market-Places. The Commission consists of a chairman, vice-chairman, and three members, and is appointed and dismissed by the Council of Ministers with a mandate of five years. The organisation of each exchange should be based on regulations passed at a general meeting of shareholders; all disputes and conflicts should be brought to a special body, the Exchange Arbitration, established at each commodity exchange, authorised to resolve such cases. Market-places are also licensed and supervised by a special state commission.

The Law on the Measures against Money Laundering[49] is the legislative consequence of Bulgaria's ratification of an international convention. The law criminalises all money-laundering activities, regardless of the nature of the initial transgression, but has no retroactive force. A specialised agency is to be established within the structures of the Ministry of the Interior.

2.2 Laws on the media

The Law on Radio and Television[50] established procedures for election of the National Radio and TV Council; the licensing of the radio and TV channels (which is done not by the National Radio and TV Council, but by the Cabinet, as regulated by the Law on Concessions); and the powers of the National Council to suspend private radio and TV programs, while awaiting for a decision of the Supreme Administrative Court, among others. The law was challenged before the Constitutional Court, which struck down most of its provisions.[51]

2.3 Laws on the environment

The Clean Ambient Air Act[52] regulates the indicators and norms for the quality of the ambient air. It also defines the sources of pollution subject to the law. The municipalities have the right to introduce more rigid restrictions than those approved by the national authorities. The act defines the competent control and sanction agencies.

2.4 Other laws

The Law on Notary[53] regulates the institution of notary, its organisation and the notary fees and charges; it also decentralises and updates the current notary activities. The institute of private notary is introduced, and notaries are no longer part of the Ministry of Justice. Notaries are to be appointed by competition. The law envisages the establishment of a Notary Chamber and Register of the Notary Chamber, which never beforeexisted in Bulgarian judicial practice.

The Law on Referendum[54] is intended to replace the outdated 1983 law that is still in force. The necessity of such a law derives from the enactment of the Law on the Administrative and Territorial System: it empowers the majority in the municipal councils to call a local referendum for the dismissal of the mayors (directly elected) and the citizens to introduce changes in the territorial division (to establish autonomous municipalities) through referenda. The law envisages several possibilities for direct participation of the citizens: national or local referenda, general assembly of the population, and citizens' petitions. These are regulated in separate chapters of the law. The national referendum provides the opportunity for the "citizens to directly solve basic issues within the sphere of competencies of the National Assembly."[55] The issues that cannot be solved through referenda are explicitly enumerated in Article 5: "1. on the amendment of the Constitution; 2. those within the competencies of the Grand National Assembly; 3. on the state budget and the taxation; 4. within the competencies of the judiciary; 5. within the competencies of the Constitutional Court; 6. other questions that are to be solved in a manner specified by law." The referenda are to be proposed by at least one-fourth of the members of the Parliament, by the Council of Ministers, or by the President, but the decision for calling a referendum is taken only by the National Assembly.[56] A referendum is valid when at least half of the voters have participated in it, and the respective decision is considered approved when at least half of the valid votes are in favour. In the event of a successful referendum, the Parliament takes a decision to implement the referendum decision. Local referenda are qualified to decide only on issues of local importance within the powers of the local government. They are to be called on the level of the municipality, district, towns or villages. The local referendum cannot decide on questions referring to the local budget, local taxation, or other local issues to be decided in a procedure regulated by law. General assemblies are to be called for towns and villages with populations of up to 2000 inhabitants. If the mayor disagrees with the referendum decisions he may block its implementation and ask the municipal council to confirm it. The council is to decide within a month. The petition is a means of initiating a number of procedures by appealing to the municipal councils.

C. REGULATION

No statistical information is available for the year 1996 regarding normative acts of the head of state (President). In 1996 the Council of Ministers issued 319 decrees, 527 ordinances and 46 resolutions. For the period of its activity (from February 12, 1997 until May 20, 1997), the caretaker Cabinet issued 14 decrees, 13 ordinances and 13 resolutions. It is difficult to assess the importance of the "informal rules" in a country like Bulgaria, where the activity of the administration is not properly regulated—the country still lacks a Law on Public Service.

D. JUDICIAL DECISIONS

INTRODUCTION

The judicial decision has two parts: motives (reasons) and disposition. The motives are written considerations grounding the decision. They include the judgement on the evidence, factual findings, and legal conclusions of the court. The cogency, the control of the regularity and the interpretation of the decision are based on them.

The disposition is what the court has enacted and the way it has decided the case (sentence, verdict). The court announces the decision in the same session in which the trying of the case has been finished. If the case is complicated, the court may postpone the announcement of the decision, but it also must be reported at a public sitting. The decision is registered in a special book published periodically. The date of the registration is the date of the decision. The judicial decisions are published by the authority that has enacted them. The decisions of the Supreme Court are published in the Bulletin of the Supreme Court. The courts–regardless of their level, do not make law: the judicial decisions are result of exercising jurisdictional, not legislative prerogatives.

1. THE CONSTITUTIONAL COURT

This is an institution without precedent in Bulgarian legal tradition. It is vested with broad powers: to provide binding interpretations of the Constitution; to rule on challenges to the constitutionality of the laws and other acts passed by the Assembly and the acts passed by the President; to rule on competency suits between the Assembly, the President and the Cabinet, and between bodies of local government and the central executive branch of the Government; to rule on the compatibility of the Constitution and the international instruments concluded by the Republic of Bulgaria prior to their ratification and on the compatibility of the domestic laws with the universally recognised norms of international law and the international instruments to which Bulgaria is a party; to rule on challenges to the constitutionality of political parties and associations; to rule on challenges to the legality of the election of the President, the Vice-President and of any member of the Parliament; and to rule on impeachment by the National Assembly against the President or the Vice-President.[57] By way of decisions, the Constitutional Court interprets texts of the Constitution, judges the constitutionality of laws and other normative acts passed by the Parliament and of acts of the President and judges their accordance with the international conventions ratified by the country. The Constitutional Court is not a part of the judicial system. Its decisions are binding for all public authorities and for the Constitutional Court itself. They are published in the *Official Gazette*.

One of the Constitutional Court's most important decisions[58] in 1996 was related to the prerogatives of the President. The Constitutional Court gave an opinion as to whether all of the President's decrees should be countersigned by a representative of the executive power, whether the list of the acts which do not need countersigning is exhaustive, and what the consequences are if a decree is not countersigned. The Constitution does not define the countersigning as a legal act. According to the Constitutional Court no conclusions could be made from the discussions in the Parliament when the new Constitution was voted. Therefore, in its decision it made a historical review of the institute of countersigning; its development in different countries and its accordance with the Constitution and its principles. On the basis of this analysis, the decision of the Constitutional Court was that the countersigning of the President's decrees by a representative of the executive power is necessary only when he extends his prerogatives towards and interfere with the executive power. The countersigning is a form of political control as the president is not responsible to Parliament. The Prime Minister or the member of the Government who has countersigned the decree is politically responsible; the countersigning expresses their consent about the constitutionality, legality and advisability of the act. By countersigning, these parties accept the political responsibility and the obligation to carry it out. If the decree is not countersigned, it is invalid. The list of cases stipulated in the Constitution in which a presidential decree need not be countersigned is not exhaustive; it does not include all of the President's decrees, which are not related to the executive authorities.

In an important 1995 decision,[59] the Constitutional Court ruled on the prerogative of the Government to organise the management of state property and the sequences of its exercise for the material conditions and the premises for the functioning of the other public authorities. The Government has at its disposal state property used by other institutions. The legislative, executive and judicial powers have a constitutional status, which must not be violated not only by interfering or subordinating but also by infringement of their prestige. The acts of the Government concerning the properties used by the state authorities are not to be justified only by arguments of advisability. They cannot be determinant; in exercising this prerogative the constitutional principle of division of powers should be taken into consideration. The interrelations between their powers require that acts of organising the management of such properties be the result of mutual consent between the Government and the concerned institutions. According to the Constitutional Court, the Government organises the management of state properties used by the other public authorities in accordance with their hierarchy and competence; its acts must not infringe their independence, importance, or representativeness.

Two of the Constitutional Court's landmark 1996 decisions concern freedom of speech and information as basic individual rights and media regulation. The first decision[60] interprets three texts of the Constitution which are systematically and functionally connected. They proclaim the rights to express and disseminate opinions, as well as to seek out, receive, and disseminate information; they also stipulate restrictions of these rights. According to the Constitutional Court these constitutional provisions protect the personal right of everyone to express his nature and dignity as a member of society, guarantee his right to be informed about social realities and to develop his plans taking into account the opinion of the others, formed as a result of the freedom to exchange different views. These rights are basic for the development of one's personality and of the society. The public authorities should restrain from interfering in their exercising. The rights of information and of expressing opinions are limited only in the interest of protecting other constitutional rights and values such as personal dignity and honour, good reputation, legality, social decency and national security. The limitations should be interpreted restrictively. The press and the other media are free. The public authorities have no right to interfere in their activity. Their organisational and financial structures should be regulated by a special law assuring their independence. The personal and social right to receive complete, pluralistic and balanced information defines the limits of the legislative competence. Any influence exerted over the media by public institutions, or representatives of political or private interests is a form of censorship according to the Constitution. The constitutional right to seek out and receive information includes the obligation of the public authorities to assure access to information of public importance and to publish official information. The right to receive such information may be limited only by a law, defining circumstances and reasons related to national security or public order or cases when the information is an official secret.

During 1996 the Parliament passed a Law on Television and Radio which attracted public attention. The Constitutional Court was approached to judge the constitutionality of some of its texts. In its decision[61] it confirmed the sovereign right of the legislator to set limitations on the freedom to create and disseminate television and radio programs, justified by reasons of protecting basic individual rights, public order, national security, and people's health. It also confirmed its right to define the cases in which only the Bulgarian language must be used. According to the law all television and radio programs must be in Bulgarian. That does not exclude the constitutional right of everyone to use his mother tongue and the right to express his opinions in every language. But according to the Constitution a law may stipulate limitations of these rights. The Constitutional Court has ruled that some of the principles of creating and disseminating television and radio programs, as proclaimed by the law, are unconstitutional. Among these are the principle of requiring the radio and television programs to conform to a constitutional form of government (the Constitution does not exclude the possibility of criticising the form of government, politicians, government officials and important figures in political and social life); the principle of exclusion of programs with immoral and slanderous character (the term "slanderous" refers to criminal law; it presupposes judicial qualification and cannot be used as a preliminary criterion). The law created a specialised authority–the National Council of Television and Radio, with prerogatives to govern and control these media. The Court ruled that the text is in contradiction with the constitutional principles of independence of the media and of non-interference in their activities, since the Council was to be appointed in practice by the governing party.

One of the most important decisions of the Constitutional Court to date concerns judicial review of the administrative acts interpreting the text of the Constitution proclaiming the prerogative of the courts to control the administrative acts.[62] The principle is that all administrative acts are subject to judicial review, including those which are normative. It guarantees the legality of the activities of the executive branch. The public authorities exercise their prerogatives in conformity with the Constitution and the laws. The judicial control over the administrative acts protects the interests of the state and the public authority and at the same time expresses the principle of judicial protection of the individual rights and legal interests. According to the Constitutional Court, the judicial protection is against administrative acts concerning citizens and private legal entities–this is the condition *sine qua non* for the procedural interest of judicial review. "Concerning" means infringement or endangering individual rights or legal interests, or the contravention of an act with an act of a higher rank.

All administrative acts are subject to judicial review, without reference to their character or theoretical classification. Only a law may exclude an administrative act from the category subject to judicial review. The constitutional principle of judicial control over the administration requires, as a prerequisite, an administrative act which concerns rights and legal interests of citizens and private legal entities and which is not excluded by law from the administrative acts subject to judicial review. The legislator stipulates the exceptions in accordance with the constitutional principles–administrative acts concerning basic individual rights are not to be excluded. According to Bulgarian legal doctrine, some administrative acts create rights and obligations only for organisations and institutions subordinated to the authorities that have issued them. Such acts, as some scholars, argued, do not concern rights and interests of citizens and private legal entities and were to be appealed only through administrative channels; they are not judicially controlled. The Court held that where acts of interpreting legal texts of higher rank or instructing subordinated institutions infringe or endanger individual rights or legal interests, they are not to be excluded from the scope of judicial review, regardless of their theoretical classification. The concerned physical persons and private legal entities may exercise their right of judicial protection against the eventual illegality of the act.

2. THE SUPREME ADMINISTRATIVE COURT

In the new structure of the judicial power set up by the Law on Judicial Power, the Supreme Administrative Court exercises supreme supervision for precise and equal application of the administrative laws. It is an instance of cassation of all contested judicial acts about the legality of administrative acts and the only instance which addresses, the legality of acts of the Government and ministers. The interpretative decisions of the Supreme Administrative Court are binding on the public authorities of the executive and judicial branches. They are not normative acts–through interpretation the substance of the laws is revealed in order to bring about their uniform application. As an instance of cassation, the plenary session consists of three judges; as an instance judging the legality of government and ministerial acts, it consists of five. Because the Supreme Administrative Court has existed only for several months, it has no interpretation decisions. In 1996 it tried 1,741 administrative cases as a first and second instance and 7,241 cases of special procedures for supervision.

3. ORDINARY ADMINISTRATIVE COURTS

As already mentioned, there are no ordinary administrative courts in the Bulgarian judicial system. Statistical information on the operation of the district courts as a first instance for administrative cases is published in the Bulletin of the Ministry of Justice (BMJ). In 1995 the district courts tried 23,426 cases, 9,594 or 40.95 per cent of them administrative. The cases related to the territorial planning are 3167 or 13.50 per cent; to the ownership and utilisation of agricultural land - 2,220 or 9.48 per cent; to taxation procedures - 1,755 or 7.49 per cent; to the ownership of nationalised and expropriated real estate - 1,244 or 5.31 per cent of cases. For the first half of 1996, the number of all cases of the district courts is 11,912; of them 4,366 or 36.6 per cent administrative. The cases related to the territorial planning are 1,659; to the ownership and utilisation of agricultural land 580; to taxation procedures - 1,145; to the ownership of nationalised and expropriated real estate - 326. The statistical data for the second half of 1996 have not yet been published.

The Chapter has been prepared on the basis of information provided by Katya Hristova

NOTES

1 Article 147(1).
2 Article 119(1).
3 Article 119(1).
4 Article 129 (2).
5 Article 105(2).
6 *Official Gazette* No. 77, 1991.
7 Article 102(1) of the Constitution.
8 Article 102(2) of the Constitution.
9 Article 119 (1).
10 Article 119 (2).
11 *Official Gazette* No. 59, 1994.
12 Article 9.
13 Article 58 (1).
14 Article 72 (2), Law on Judicial Power.
15 Article 125 (1) of the Constitution.
16 Article 124.
17 Article 21(3).
18 Article 23 (1).
19 Chapter II of the Administrative Procedure Act.
20 *Official Gazette* No. 54, 1988, with amendments.
21 Article 3.
22 Article 91 (2).
23 Passed in 1995 and promulgated in *Official Gazette* No. 71/1995.
24 Article 4 (3).
25 Article 6 of the Law on Accountancy Chamber.
26 Article 7(1).
27 Article 10 (2).
28 Article 25.

29 Article 25 (4).
30 Article 26.
31 Article 27 (1).
32 Article 30.
33 Promulgated in the *Official Gazette* No. 13/ 1995.
34 Article 18 (1).
35 Article 18 (3).
36 Article 79(3).
37 Article 20 (1) of the Rules of Organisation and Procedure of the 37th National Assembly.
38 For detailed information, see part B2.
39 A description of the case is given in part B1.
40 128 "for" and 4 abstained, out of 240 MPs.
41 See the explanation given in Part I.
42 Promulgated on April 24, 1996, in *Official Gazette* No. 35, 1996.
43 Promulgated on April 16, 1996, in *Official Gazette* No. 32, 1996.
44 Promulgated in *Official Gazette* No. 37, 1996.
45 Promulgated on May 21, 1996, in *Official Gazette* No. 44, 1996 enacted on June 1, 1996.
46 Promulgated in *Official Gazette* No. 46, 1996.
47 Promulgated on August 9, 1996, *Official Gazette* No. 68, 1996.
48 Promulgated on November 1, 1996, in *Official Gazette* No. 93, 1996.
49 Promulgated on June 4, 1996, in *Official Gazette* No. 48, 1996.
50 Promulgated on September 10, 1996, in *Official Gazette* No. 77, 1996.
51 See part D.
52 Promulgated on May 28, 1996, in *Official Gazette* No. 45, 1996.
53 Promulgated on December 6, 1996, in *Official Gazette* No. 104, 1996.
54 Promulgated on November 22, 1996, in *Official Gazette* No. 100.
55 Article 4.
56 Article 7.
57 Article 149(1) of the Constitution.
58 Decision No. 13, 1996, on constitutional case No. 11, 1996.
59 Decision No. 14, 1995.
60 Decision No. 7, 1996, on constitutional case No. 1, 1996.
61 Decision No. 21, 1996, on constitutional case No. 19, 1996.
62 Decision No. 21, 1995.

CHAPTER TWO
CROATIA

I. GENERAL DESCRIPTION OF THE ADMINISTRATIVE LAW SYSTEM

1. ESTABLISHMENT AND GENERAL FEATURES OF THE MAJOR ADMINISTRATIVE INSTITUTIONS AND PROCEDURES

The basic administrative institutions of the Republic of Croatia were established with the adoption of the 1990 Constitution (published in the *Narodne novine*, the official gazette of the Republic,[1] No. 56/90 from December 22, 1990). Articles 107-113 of the Constitution regulate the formation and operation of the Cabinet of the Republic, which is defined as the major holder of executive power. Members of the Cabinet are its president, vice-presidents, ministers and other junior members. Article 114 of the Constitution proclaims that the "organisation of the state administration is regulated by law".

The operation of the Cabinet is further regulated by special laws and its rules, while the inner organisation of the ministries represented in the Cabinet[2] is regulated by decrees. The Cabinet issues decrees, which have to be in accordance with the Constitution and the laws; it also proposes draft laws and the state budget to Parliament (Sabor) and implements laws and other regulations passed by Parliament. The Cabinet is accountable to the President of the Republic and to the Chamber of Representatives (the lower, representative house of the bicameral Parliament). According to Article 98 of the Constitution, the President of the Republic nominates and dismisses the president of the Cabinet (the Prime Minister). He also nominates and dismisses the vice-presidents and members of the Cabinet upon a proposal of the president of the Cabinet.

In Croatia only one judicial body deals with administrative law issues—the Administrative Court. The structure and the competence of this court are determined by the Law on Courts.[3] Article 21 of this Law rules that the Administrative Court "decides on actions challenging final administrative acts and performs other functions conferred to it by the law".

The procedure before the Administrative Court is called "administrative dispute (resolution)". It is regulated by the Law on Administrative Disputes.[4] This law has been incorporated into the legal system of the independent Republic of Croatia by the Law on the Adoption of the Law on Administrative Disputes.[5]

Another major law regulating administrative procedure is the Law on the General Administrative Procedure.[6] It sets out the general rules applied to all administrative procedures except for judicial administrative dispute resolution. It regulates all lower levels of administrative decision-making in all branches of the local and central administration.

2. STRUCTURE OF THE EXECUTIVE

2.1 The highest executive body in Croatia

The supreme executive body in the Republic is the Cabinet. In accordance with Article 107 of the Constitution, the Cabinet "performs executive powers according to the Constitution and the law". According to Article 98 of the Croatian Constitution, the President appoints and dismisses all members of the Cabinet without consulting the Parliament or any other organ of the state. However, according to Article 113 of the Constitution, Parliament is vested with the right to vote no confidence in the Cabinet.

This right may be exercised upon the proposal of at least one-tenth of the MPs in the Lower (legislative) House for a vote of no confidence in the president of the Cabinet, in any of the Cabinet's members or in the entire Cabinet. A vote of confidence in the Cabinet may be demanded by its president as well. The vote cannot be carried out until three days after the initial proposal has been made. The vote of no confidence must be supported by a majority of the MPs in the Lower House. If the proposal is rejected by the Lower House, the MPs who have proposed the vote are precluded from putting forward another motion of no confidence within the following three months. If no confidence is voted in the president of the Cabinet or in the entire Cabinet, the president of the Cabinet must offer his resignation to the President of the Republic, who dissolves the Cabinet. If no confidence is voted in a member of the Cabinet, the president of the Cabinet can either offer his resignation to the President of the Republic or can propose to the President of the Republic to discharge that member of the Cabinet.

2.2 The role of the President of the Republic

Article 111, paragraph 1 of the Constitution establishes the procedures of political accountability of the Cabinet to Parliament, and Article 112, paragraph 2, proclaims that the Cabinet is to be approved by the majority of the MPs in the Lower House. Even so, for the first seven years of Croatian independence, Parliament has never voted no confidence in a member of the Cabinet or in the whole Cabinet. Nor has Parliament ever challenged the choice of the President of the Republic, of a member of the Cabinet, or the PM. The reason for this is that the ruling party, the Croatian Democratic Union, has had a stable majority in the Parliament since 1990. Furthermore, this party has demonstrated considerable internal discipline and loyalty to the President of the Republic. It may be safely concluded that through his constitutional powers and the support of the majority in Parliament, the President of the Republic has totally controlled the activities of the Cabinet since 1990.

3. RELATIONS BETWEEN THE CENTRAL AND THE LOCAL ADMINISTRATION

The relations between the central and the local administration are regulated by the Constitution and a number of other laws. Article 128 of the basic law provides for the establishment of local government; Article 130, paragraph 3 states that "some functions of the central administration can be transferred by a law to the local administration..." The right to local government consists in authorisation to decide on issues of local importance, particularly concerning urban development, urban planning, common utilities, childcare, social work, cultural and sports activities, technical and technological education as well as environmental protection.

The Law on Local Government and Administration[7] (Article 1) states that "...the municipalities and the cities are units of local government, while the counties are units both of the local administration and the central administration." Furthermore, the Law on the System of the State [central] Administration[8] (Article 3) provides that the bodies of the central administration are "the ministries, state administrative organisations, county offices and the City Office of the City of Zagreb." The central government has the power to interfere with the activity of the local government in cases defined by law. According to Article 62 of the Law on the System of the State Administration, the Cabinet can annul the regulations of the units of local administration acting in the field of competence of the central administration. The local administration is responsible to the central government for the execution of policies and special tasks falling within the competence of the central administration but conferred to the local authorities by laws or other acts.

Pursuant to Article 81 of the Law on Local Government and Administration, the Cabinet can dissolve the representative body of the unit of local administration in a number of cases:

1. If it repeatedly passes general acts that are unconstitutional, unlawful or contrary to other regulations, or if it repeatedly and gravely violates the law or other regulations;
2. When the municipal chairman, city mayor or head of county is not elected within 90 days from the convocation of the representative body of the local government;
3. If one-half or more members of the representative body of the government unit resign;
4. If the budget of the local government unit has not been approved within the legally prescribed time;
5. If the representative body of the government unit passes decisions threatening the sovereignty and territorial integrity of the Republic.

A further form of intervention by the central administration in the activities of the local government is provided for by Article 83 of the Law on Government and Administration. Pursuant to it, the Ministry of Justice and Administration may discharge a municipal chairperson or city mayor if he or the body he presides over repeatedly violate the Constitution and the laws or ignore the orders of the central administration regarding the exercise of powers delegated to the local government by the central administration.

Furthermore, the central administration has important checking powers over the local government in the appointment of the heads of counties and the Mayor of Zagreb.[9] According to Article 31 of the Law on Local Government and Administration, the heads of counties, as the highest level of the local administrative hierarchy, as well as the Mayor of Zagreb, have to be confirmed by the President of the Republic after they are elected by the local representative bodies. Article 33 of the same law rules that: "Within 14 days after receiving a negative decision on the request for confirmation of the head of county, the county representative body has to elect another one. If it fails to do so or if the President of the Republic rejects its second proposal, the President of the Republic shall nominate within 14 days a new head of the county". The same procedure applies to the election of the Mayor of Zagreb.[10]

4. NORMATIVE ACTS OF THE ADMINISTRATION

4.1 Normative acts of the President of the Republic

The President of the Republic passes two kinds of normative acts: ordinances and legislative decrees or "decrees with legal power". The former require no parliamentary approval, while the latter, as an exercise of delegated legislative prerogative, are subject to approval by the Parliament (according to Article 101 of the Constitution). The decrees with legal power are passed, according to the same article, "in a state of war or in a state of imminent peril concerning the independence and unity of the Republic or when the bodies of the state government are unable to perform their constitutional duties". If the Parliament is dissolved, it has to approve the decree as soon as it is reconvened.

4.2 Normative acts of the Cabinet

The Cabinet does not enjoy the right to delegated legislation according to the Constitution. However, according to the Law on the Prerogatives of the Cabinet to Regulate by Decrees Issues within the Competence of the Lower House,[11] the Cabinet can regulate mostly specific economic issues within the original constitutional competence of the Lower (legislative) House. The exercise of these prerogatives is subject to approval of the Lower House under the same conditions as the legislative decrees of the President of the Republic.

The government can pass secondary legislation in the form of decrees, ordinances and other regulations, none of which is subject to subsequent legislative approval. The ministries pass regulations, orders and instructions within their competence, all without further legislative approval.

5. SYSTEM OF COURTS DEALING WITH ADMINISTRATIVE LAW ISSUES

5.1 The administrative court of Croatia and its basic procedures

The system of courts was established in its present form by the Law on the Courts.[12] According to this law there is only one administrative court in Croatia, the Administrative Court of Croatia. The jurisdiction of this body is twofold: it decides on petitions against final administrative acts for which there are no remedies within the internal administrative procedure; and it performs other functions as prescribed by the laws.

Articles 6–8 of the Law on Administrative Disputes[13] prescribes that an administrative dispute can be initiated only against an ***administrative act***. An administrative act is, according to Article 6 of the same Law, "an act with which an organ of the state or a legal person with public authority, when exercising their public powers, decide about rights and obligations of individuals or legal persons in administrative matters". Article 7 of the Law rules that an administrative dispute procedure can be initiated against administrative acts passed at the second (appellate) level of administrative decision-making (in regular administrative procedure) or against an administrative act passed at the first level of administrative decision-making, against which no internal administrative appeal is allowed.

6. SPECIAL ADJUDICATIVE BODIES

The Ordinance on Establishment of Courts for Officials[14] ordained the creation of seven specialised courts for officials, as well as of one second-level (appellate) Higher Court for Officials. Article 2 of this Law rules that these courts decide on instances of "grave violations of official duties by public officials".

The Regulation on the Commission on Civil Service of the Second Level[15] set up a body authorised to consider complaints against decisions of the Commission for Civil Service of the First Level. These commissions act in cases of conscientious objections to military service, regulated by Article 70 of the Law on Defence.[16]

7. GENERAL PROCEDURAL CODES AND LAWS

There are two major laws on administrative procedure in Croatia. The first one is the Law on the General Administrative Procedure.[17] This is the general law to be followed by all state administrative bodies, administrative organisations and legal persons with public authority when they exercise their public authority in deciding about administrative matters. This law regulates the procedures of administrative decision-making and the right to internal appeal within the administrative hierarchy.

The Law on Administrative Disputes[18] is the law regulating judicial dispute resolution in administrative matters. Unlawful administrative acts passed in the second (appellate) level of administrative decision-making or in the first level, if an internal administrative complaint is not allowed by the law, can be challenged before the Court.

7.1 Levels of administrative decision-making

Croatian administrative law doctrine divides the administrative process into different levels or stages of decision-making. The first level of administrative processes represents the initial decision-making by an administrative agency, which normally results in the issuance of or the refusal to issue an administrative act. The party concerning which the act has been issued has the right to file a complaint within the administrative hierarchy in accordance with Article 223 of the Law on the General Administrative Procedure. Internal complaints cannot be filed against decisions passed by the representative body of a local government unit (municipality, city or county) or the Parliament. The complaint should be filed within 15 days after the decision is received by the complaining party. The filing of the complaint marks the beginning of the second level of administrative decision-making, which consists in administrative consideration of appeals.

The process before the Administrative Court of Croatia represents the third level of administrative decision-making: the level of judicial review of administrative action. It is initiated by filing an action with that court. There is a fourth level of administrative processes. If a public prosecutor finds that the law has been violated contrary to the public interest, he can file "a demand for the protection of lawfulness" before the Supreme Court of Croatia. In cases of violation of constitutional rights of citizens or legal persons, a procedure can be initiated before the Constitutional Court, but only after all the other remedies have been exhausted. The constitutional review represents the fifth and last level of administrative process. Not every administrative act must go through all five stages of decision-making. For instance, some acts are excluded from the scope of the internal administrative appeal; others are not subject to judicial review.

7.2 Judicial review of administrative action

An action challenging an administrative act is to be filed with the Administrative Court of the Republic of Croatia within 30 days after the administrative act has been received by the party who files the action. As already mentioned, this procedure is called administrative dispute (Article 24, paragraph 1 of the Law on Administrative Disputes). The action can be filed directly, by handing it in to the Court, or by mail. The action can also be dictated to a Court official or to an official of some other regular court. Administrative dispute is the only (ordinary) form of judicial review of administrative acts.

7.3 Acts excluded from the scope of judicial review or the scope of internal administrative appeal

According to Article 9 of the Law on Administrative Disputes, an administrative dispute (judicial review) cannot be initiated against:

1. Administrative acts passed in matters in which judicial protection is ensured outside the procedures of administrative dispute resolution (in some other form of judicial protection, for instance, through quasi-judicial specialised bodies);
2. Administrative acts passed in matters for which special laws do not allow for administrative judicial review;
3. Administrative decisions of the Parliament or the President of the Republic.

Administrative acts exempted from judicial review by special laws are relatively rare. For instance, the Law on the Election of Representatives to the Parliament of the Republic of Croatia[19] provides that "objections to irregularities in the process of nomination of candidates and in the process of election of representatives are filed with the Electoral Commission of the Republic within 48 hours, not counting the day on which the disputed act or activity has been performed". According to Article 57, paragraph 1 of the same Law, "a complaint against a decision of the Electoral Commission can be filed with the Constitutional Court".

Some acts are excluded from the scope of internal administrative appeal. For example, according to Article 34 of the Law on Administrative Inspection,[20] objections (internal appeal) against decisions of the head of an administrative inspectorate are not allowed. Also, pursuant to Article 230, paragraph 2 of the Law on Marriage and Family,[21] "the custodial organs follow their own professional methods and code of ethics" when they decide on the modalities of custodial protection. This is an exception from the general clause of Article 230, paragraph 1, ordering the custodial organs to implement the Law on the General Administrative Procedure.

7.4 Legal grounds for judicial review of administrative action

The legal grounds for the initiation of judicial review are given in Articles 7 and 8 of the Law on Administrative Disputes. Article 7 rules that: "An administrative dispute proceeding can be initiated against administrative acts passed in the second level of administrative decision-making. An administrative dispute proceeding can be initiated against administrative acts passed in the first level of administrative decision-making, if internal (second level) is not allowed in the particular case." Article 8 states: "An administrative dispute can be initiated when an authorised administrative organ fails to pass an administrative act, under the conditions given by this law."

7.5 Judicial remedies

Article 42, paragraphs 1-3 of the Law on Administrative Disputes rule that the Court decides by a verdict whether an action can be accepted or rejected as ungrounded. If accepted, the Court annuls the challenged administrative act. When the Court finds that the challenged administrative act has to be annulled, it can, if the circumstances and the facts allow, decide by a verdict on the merits of the case. In this case, the verdict replaces the annulled act.

8. OMBUDSMAN

The Law on the Ombudsman,[22] adopted in 1992, laid the legal grounds for establishing the position of ombudsman in Croatia. Article 3, paragraph 1 of this law reads states "The ombudsman examines individual cases of the violation of rights of citizens caused by organs of the state administration, bodies with public authority or employees in these organs and bodies". According to Article 6, "the ombudsman does not interfere in pending judicial cases". He warns, informs, proposes and gives recommendation to the relevant bodies and organs. These bodies and organs have to respond to the ombudsman within 30 days, informing him about the measures they have undertaken concerning his recommendations. The ombudsman can investigate cases upon citizens' demand, as well as on his own initiative. One of his prerogatives is control over penitentiaries and similar institutions.

The law, adopted five years ago, obliged the ombudsman to enact the Rules on Inner Organisation of the ombudsman institution. Nevertheless, such rules have not been yet published. Moreover, the ombudsman has failed to appoint his three deputies as required by the law, and he did not begin work until January 1, 1994. His only report, on his activities in 1994, was submitted to Parliament in March 1996. The report was rejected by Parliament. In that report the ombudsman almost completely failed to address human-rights problems, but instead engaged in "political evaluations and defamation".[23] After the rejection of the report, the ombudsman resigned. A new one has been appointed, but he had not submitted a report of his activities in 1996 at the time of writing.

9. OTHER FORMS OF CONTROL OVER THE ADMINISTRATION

9.1 State Audit Office

The Law on Public Audit[24] established the Budget Audit Office in 1993. According to Article 2, paragraph 1 of this law, the state auditors have the duty to "examine financial transactions related to public spending". According to Article 2, "the audit procedures consist of the evaluation of the efficiency and economic rationality of public spending". Article 3 states that the audit has to be carried out whenever necessary and at least once a year. To date the State Audit Office has published a number of critical reports. For instance, in its report on government spending in 1994, the State Audit claimed that 10 percent of the state budget had been mis-spent.

9.2 Inspectorates

Articles 23–32 of the Law on the System of State Administration[25] established the institution of inspectorates within the organs of the central administration and local government. The basic task of the inspectorates is to control whether the administrative organs are passing general and individual acts in accordance with the law and other regulations. The Law on Administrative Inspection Office[26] defined the competencies of the inspectorates (Article 16). Pursuant to this law, the inspectorates examine the fulfilment of the obligations of the administrative organs in the realisation of the rights and duties of the citizens. They also control the procedures of accountability of the administrative organs to the representative bodies of the local administrative units. The inspectorates supervise the administration of the regulations relating to the organisation and work of the administrative organs, the legality of the regulations passed by the local administrative units, the publicity of the administrative organs' activities, and the administration of the regulations relating to employment contracts.

9.3 Public prosecutors

According to Article 52 of the Law on the General Administrative Procedure, the public prosecutor is authorised to "protect public interests in administrative proceedings by having the procedural status of a party in them". Article 250 of the same law authorises the public prosecutor to initiate "the renewal of the proceedings". Furthermore, Article 262 grants the prosecutor a right to file "a demand for the protection of lawfulness". These "demands" fall in the category "extraordinary legal remedies" (aimed at the reconsideration of final administrative acts).

Finally, the public prosecutor may, pursuant to Article 2, paragraph 4 of the Law on Administrative Disputes, initiate administrative dispute proceedings "if the law has been violated by an administrative act in favour of an individual or legal person". According to Article 21 of the same law, the public prosecutor may initiate administrative dispute proceedings against a final administrative act.

10. PARLIAMENTARY COMMITTEES SUPERVISING THE ADMINISTRATION

The Croatian Parliament (Sabor), as a two-chamber representative body, has two committees competent to deal with administrative issues. The Upper House (Zupanijski dom) has no legislative prerogatives. The Committee for Internal Policy and Local Government, as a consultative body of the Upper House, is, according to Article 57 of the Rules of Procedure of the Upper House,[27] authorised to "discuss and propose preliminary opinions... on the internal organisation and competence of the state bodies and local administration units, on the establishment, dissolution and integration of local administration units, as well as to examine the functioning of the representative and other bodies of the local administration units".

The Upper House delivers opinions and preliminary opinions on laws passed by the Lower House regulating the central state administration and the local administration. In doing so, the Upper House in the majority of cases bases its opinion on the findings of the relevant Committee. When that opinion or preliminary opinion reaches the Lower (legislative) House, its Committee for Internal Policy and National Security must discuss the issue and elaborate a position on it; the recommendations of the Upper House have no binding effect on the Lower House. Neither committee exercises direct control or supervision over the administration.

Special ad hoc committees, regulated by the Law on Investigative Panels,[28] were never established during the first seven years of Croatian independence. Although the opposition in Parliament has demanded their formation on many occasions, especially concerning the processes of granting concessions, privatisation, and financial pyramid schemes, the ruling majority has always blocked the formation of such investigative bodies.

II. DEVELOPMENTS IN ADMINISTRATIVE LAW DURING 1996-1997

A. THE CONSTITUTION AND CONSTITUTIONAL LAWS

There were no constitutional amendments during the period under discussion, except for the adoption of a constitutional law authorising the International Tribunal in the Hague to try Croatian citizens indicted for war crimes committed in the war in the former Yugoslavia. Article 9, paragraph 1 of the Constitutional Law on the Co-operation of the Republic of Croatia with the International Tribunal[29] states that the Republic will "transfer its jurisdiction over criminal offences for which a trial is pending in the Republic of Croatia, if these offences are under the International Tribunal's jurisdiction."

Under Article 25, paragraph 1 of the same Law, the International Tribunal may initiate criminal proceedings in the Republic of Croatia, by demanding that the authorised state bodies of the Republic of Croatia start an investigation and collect evidence and other data on certain criminal offences. The tribunal can also order the collection of data on other important facts, the issuance of warrants, and the deliverance of summonses and writs sent by the International Court to citizens of Croatia, as well as the performance of other activities. The administration is obliged to comply with these orders. The Law further provided for a complicated procedure for extradition of indicted persons. It involves three different levels of decision-making: county courts, the Supreme Court and the Constitutional Court (Articles 20–24).

B. LEGISLATION AND OTHER NORMATIVE ACTS

1. PROCEDURAL AND ORGANISATIONAL LAWS

1.1 Laws on the structure and the prerogatives of the administration

One of the major acts adopted in this area was the Law on Authorisation of the Cabinet of the Republic of Croatia to Regulate Certain Questions under the Competence of the Parliament.[30] The law authorised the government to regulate issues originally under the constitutional competence of the Lower House. The authorisation concerns mainly macro-economic issues.

As some parts of Croatian territory were still under the control of the Serbian paramilitary forces, the Cabinet passed the Decree on the Office of Temporary Administration for the Establishment of Croatian Rule on the Territory of Eastern Slavonia, Baranja and West Srijem.[31] Article 2, paragraph 1 of this Decree determines that "the Office shall act within the jurisdiction of the Cabinet, providing expertise and other support for the establishment of Croatian authority over Eastern Slavonia, Baranja and West Srijem, according to the Erdut and Dayton agreements".

In October 1996 the Parliament adopted the Law on Modifications and Amendments on the Law on the Competence of the Ministries and the State Organisations.[32] The law introduced some minor changes and redefined some of the prerogatives of the major administrative agencies.

1.2 Direct democracy and local government

The Parliament adopted in 1996 the Law on Referendum and Other Forms of Direct Involvement of the Citizens in the Activities of the Central and Local Administration.[33] Article 2, paragraph 1 of the Law establishes that "the referendum is a form of direct involvement of the electorate in decision-making on issues with constitutional significance (general referendum) or on issues concerning the local administration of the counties, cities and municipalities, as regulated by their statutes and the law (local referendum)". Paragraph 2 of the same Article establishes that "other forms of direct decision-making and expression of the political will of the citizens are advisory referenda, local meetings of the citizens and common petitions".

The Law on the Territories of the Counties, Cities and Municipalities of the Republic of Croatia[34] provided new rules for the organisation of the local and central administration units. The law established that the counties are simultaneously organs of the central and the local administration: their double character has been determined by Article 131, paragraph 1 of the Constitution of the Republic of Croatia as well.[35]

2. SUBSTANTIVE LEGISLATION AND REGULATION

2.1 Laws on the management of the economy: privatisation

The 1996 Law on Privatisation[36] regulated the status and the role of the Croatian Privatisation Fund. The earlier Law on the Croatian Fund for Privatisation[37] rules that the Fund gives professional and administrative support in the process of privatisation of state enterprises (which, in the former Yugoslavia, were called "socially owned enterprises"). The Fund is also responsible for the privatisation and management of state-owned enterprises (upon authorisation by a law or a decision of the Cabinet). It is further entrusted with the management of the enterprises in which it is itself an owner, and for their restructuring and sale as well as for the purchase and establishment of new enterprises. It may also have other prerogatives established by a law. Article 6 of the Law on the Croatian Fund for Privatisation sets up the executive body of the Fund: an Executive Committee of nine members, nominated by the Parliament. The Fund is managed and represented by its president.

In keeping with Article 6, paragraph 4 of the Law on Privatisation, the Minister of Privatisation enacted the Rules on Trade of Shares, Property and Property Rights through Public Auctions.[38] Those rules state that the announcement of a public auction "must be published in domestic and/or international mass-circulation periodicals" (Article 2, paragraph 2 of the Rules). It is further established that the information on the auction should be communicated to "all interested persons who are, according to valid regulations, entitled to submit their offer or application for participation". The interested parties should be informed about all substantive elements of the government offer: these elements must be set out and exhaustively enumerated in the relevant auction documents. Article 5, paragraph 3 of the Rules provides that "persons who have submitted their offer or their representatives may be present at the opening of offers". A considerable shortcoming of the Rules, however, is the lack of provisions regarding possible conflicts of interest or bias in the administering of the auctions. This is especially disturbing in view of the numerous allegations that high-ranking public officials have benefited unlawfully from the process of privatisation.

2.2 Restitution

The Law on Compensation for Property Seized by the Yugoslav Communist Authorities regulates the conditions and procedures of compensation for private property seized by the Yugoslav communist authorities and subsequently turned into "socially owned property" by confiscation, nationalisation, agrarian reform and other acts. Under the Law the former owners may initiate a procedure at the county office where their property is located. There have been eight county offices in every county established by the Decree on the Establishment of County Offices.[39] They are administrative bodies covering various areas of activity. Article 78 regulates that the criteria for evaluation of real estate property covered by the Law on Compensation (including agricultural land, woods, woodland, apartments, ships and enterprises) will be passed by "the competent ministers within a one-year period" without specifying what ministers are referred to. Regulations to that effect have not been passed to date. Since the procedure of decision-making by the county offices has not yet been regulated, the Law on General Administrative Procedure should apply as a general norm.

Although Article 49 of the Law on Compensation declares that the principle of restitution is a basic principle of that piece of legislation, an important proviso introduced by Article 52, paragraph 1 weakens it. According to this proviso, "property will not be returned to the ex-owners if third persons have obtained that property in ownership or if they have obtained it in their possession based on a valid legal grounds for acquiring ownership, unless provided otherwise by this law". As a result, a relatively small part of the properties once seized by the communist regime will be returned to their ex-owners. The Union of the Former Owners took this as a betrayal of the Croatian Democratic Union's promise, in 1990, of total restitution. In addition, the compensation prescribed by the Law on Compensation is payable mostly in state bonds, rather than in money, and seems to be set far below the market prices of real estate property. Moreover, by the time this piece of legislation was enacted a great deal of the property regulated by it had already been privatised–of course, not in favour of the original owners. Unlike in some other countries, in Croatia the process of privatisation preceded the process of restitution. In addition, since the very process of privatisation has been marred by allegations of corruption and governmental favouritism, it is not likely that the limited restitution will be viewed by the public as a restoration of social and historical justice, as it was undoubtedly intended.

2.3 Financial management

Three major laws were passed in this area during the period under discussion. First, the Law on Credit Relations with the Foreign Countries[40] regulates "the modes and conditions of concluding, registering and executing credit deals with foreign countries" (Article 1). Article 14, paragraph 1 of the same Law rules that credit deals with foreign countries must be registered with the National Bank of Croatia. The Bank establishes: "1) the extent and purpose of loans and financial credits; 2) the obligation to report deposits in kuna (the national currency) comparable to the credits taken." Under the Law, the Republic of Croatia and the National Bank of Croatia do not guarantee the obligations of domestic individuals or legal persons who have concluded credit deals with individual or legal persons from abroad. In the Law there are no criteria for the approval of credits involving foreign legal persons or individuals; nor are there provisions about the procedure of approval of the credits by the National Bank. The Law further rules that "citizens of the Republic of Croatia who do not run their own business may not approve credits to a foreign person. Citizens of Croatia may receive credits from abroad for personal needs only."

Second, the Law on the Modes and Conditions of Payment of the Credit and Other Obligations Based on Agreements with the Member States of the Club of Paris[41] the Republic of Croatia accepted "28.49 per cent of the debts previously accumulated or guaranteed by the former Socialist Federal Republic of Yugoslavia, based on bilateral agreements with the member states of the Club of Paris".

Finally, the Law on Custom-Free Zones[42] regulates the establishment of those zones, their organisation, management and the performance of the activities in them, the payment of taxes in zones, supervision of the execution of laws in zones and punitive norms.

2.4 Laws on transport

The Law on Contracts in Railroad Traffic[43] regulates "the relationships established by contracts on transportation of passengers and goods in domestic railroad traffic and international railroad traffic..." (Article 1). The Law regulates the following matters: contracts on transportation of passengers, responsibility of carriers, contracts on transportation of luggage, personal luggage, contracts on transportation of goods, haulage papers, transportation costs and receiving, checking and determination of weight and content of transported goods, customary and other procedures, changes in contracts on transportation, and others.

The Law on Safety of Road Traffic[44] contains norms on roads, traffic regulations, traffic signs, duties in case of traffic accidents, limitations on traffic, drivers, vehicles, and special safety measures. It also regulates road traffic safety, sport and other programs and activities on roads, punitive norms and authorisations to pass regulations for the execution of this law.

The Law on Public Roads[45] regulates the building and maintaining of public roads, measures for the protection of public roads and traffic, concessions on public roads, management of public roads, financing of public roads, supervision and inspection of public roads as well as sanctions in case of violation of its provisions.

2.5 Laws on media and information

Article 18 of the Law on Public Information,[46] adopted by Parliament in 1996, provides that a publisher, before publishing a periodical, has a duty to inform the state body competent to deal with public information. That body is required to issue a certification if all the information required by this law is included in the report. The certification has to be delivered to the publisher within three days, and if this time limit is not observed, the publisher is allowed to distribute its periodical to the public, as if the certification has been issued.

The Law on the Protection of Secrecy of Data[47] regulates the kinds of state secret and their degrees. The kinds of secrets are military secrets, official secrets, business secrets and professional secrets. The degrees are state secrets, secrets, and confidential secrets (Article 3). Article 13 of the Law regulates that "the heads of public bodies and authorised officials of the Republic of Croatia may, under special regulations, within their competencies and according to the law or other regulations, determine kinds and degrees of secrets, measures for protecting them, as well as the persons familiar with the content of those secrets".

2.6 Laws on education

The Law on Recognition of Foreign Schools' Certificates and University Diplomas[48] establishes that the recognition of foreign elementary and secondary school certificates and university diplomas is to be performed by the Ministry of Education and Sport, while the higher levels of education (masters, doctoral and post-doctoral) are recognised by the public professional councils for particular studies. Those professional councils have to decide about the recognition within three months after the request is filed with them. The procedure of recognition is not regulated, nor are concrete criteria set.

2.7 Laws on health care

Considerable legislative activity took place in the area of health care during 1996 and the first months of 1997. The Law on Sanitary Fitness and Control of Food and Goods of General Usage[49] sets out the criteria of sanitary fitness as well as the rules of sanitary control and transport and distribution of food, including drinking water available through the public water supply. The law sets sanitary standards for goods of general usage as well as equipment for production of food, toys for children, cosmetics, detergents, tobacco and its derivatives and other goods coming into direct contact with human skin. The law prohibits the advertising of goods, if such advertising could lead to false conclusions about the goods' ingredients and characteristics. The advertising of tobacco and alcohol is prohibited.

The sanitary control over the production and traffic of goods and objects of general usage is performed by sanitary inspectors, while goods of animal origin are subject to inspection by veterinary inspectors. The Ministry of Health Care enacts regulations on the inspection on the state borders. The veterinary and sanitary inspectors may, according to Article 38 of the law, temporarily ban the production and traffic of goods of general usage, if they doubt the goods are sanitary, until laboratory tests prove that they are sanitary. The inspectors can ban the traffic and usage of unsanitary goods and objects of general usage, order the confiscation and destruction of unsanitary goods, ban the import of goods, and ban the usage of objects, premises and devices for the production of such goods.

The Law on Protection at Work,[50] adopted in July 1996, defines restrictive measures regarding the protection of non-smokers and the ban on usage of alcohol and other addictive substances. The Law obliges employers to impose strict restrictions on the usage of those substances on working premises.

The process of licensing medical establishments was regulated by Articles 33–48 of the Law on Health Protection,[51] which, together with the Law on Health Insurance,[52] formed the basic legal framework of Croatian health care legislation. Under these laws, the institutions of health protection are organised within the Network of Health Insurance, regulated and governed by the Ministry of Health Care. Within the Network there are health institutions owned by the state or the county, as well as private establishments. The Network is organised in accordance with the Plan of Health Protection of the Republic of Croatia, enacted by the Cabinet. The health institutions outside the Network may also offer health care, but without reimbursement for their services from the Ministry of Health Care. The Ministry of Health Care is authorised to give its consent to the establishment of health institutions, regardless of their involvement in the Network. The Minister may also authorise the opening of the institution to the public after the evaluation of its premises, staff and other conditions. There are no further norms regulating the process of evaluation.

C. REGULATION

1. REGULATIONS ON PROCEDURAL ISSUES AND STATE ORGANISATION

In 1996, the Cabinet passed the Decree on the Office for Establishment of Croatian Rule on the Territory of Eastern Slavonia, Baranja and West Srijem.[53] It set up a body whose purpose is to give professional and other support to the establishment of Croatian rule on the territories occupied by the Serbian paramilitary units. The introduction of this body and its activities are to be in accordance with the agreements from Erdut and Dayton signed by the parties in the conflict under the supervision of the international community. The Office is under the Cabinet's supervision.

Based on Article 2, paragraph 2 of the Constitutional Law on the Co-operation of the Republic of Croatia with the International Court in The Hague, the Cabinet enacted the Decree on the Office for Co-operation with the International Court.[54] The Office co-ordinates the work of the state bodies and legal persons in the Republic, which co-operate with the International Court. It is under the supervision of the Cabinet.

2. SUBSTANTIVE REGULATIONS

2.1 Privatisation

Under the mandate given in Article 6, paragraph 4 of the Law on Privatisation the Minister of Privatisation enacted three regulations:

1. The Regulation on Sale of Shares, Stakes, Property and Property Rights by Public Auctions;
2. The Regulation on the Conditions and Modes of Exchange of Shares or Stakes;
3. The Regulation on Free Delivery of Shares.

All three regulations elaborate in detail particular issues of the process of privatisation.

Based on Article 39, paragraph 4 of the Law on Agricultural Land,[55] the Cabinet passed the Decree on the Criteria and Procedure for the Institution of Usufructs.[56] The decree regulates the priorities and procedures for the institution of a special type of usufructs, offered for free for 30 years on land owned by the Republic, in favour of needy veterans of the 1991–1995 war, families of those killed in that war, and refugees.

2.2 Environment

The Decree on the Standards of the Quality of Sea Water and the Sea Beaches[57] sets standards concerning the resort areas during the tourist season. The Decree is passed by the Cabinet and is based on Article 23, paragraph 3 of the Law on Protection of the Environment.[58] The central part of that Decree consists of tables defining the levels of sea pollution and the methods of analysis of pollution. Further, Article 11 of the Decree regulates that the legal persons authorised to examine the quality of sea water and the sea beaches have to send their reports to the county offices competent to deal with those problems. The county offices have to hand the reports over to the State Administration on the Protection of Environment.

The Regulation on the Types of Waste[59] classifies the wastes depending on their chemical and physical characteristics as well as their source. It also provides rules for the management of wastes, as well as the disclosure of information on that matter. The Regulation sets out procedures for the chemical and physical testing of different wastes and determines sanctions in cases of violation of the rules. The implementation of the Regulation is within the jurisdiction of the Head of the State Administration on Protection of the Environment, as defined in the Law on Waste.[60]

Based on the same Law, the Head of the State Administration on Protection of the Environment enacted the Regulation on the Management of Waste Used for the Packing of Industrial Products.[61] It regulates the modes and conditions of collection of this kind of waste, its registration (depending on its substance), recycling, disposal and sanctions for the violations.

One of the major acts in this area passed by the Cabinet was the Decree on Environmental Impact Assessment[62] enacted by the Cabinet on the basis of the Law on Protection of the Environment.[63] The Decree enumerates the procedures of environmental impact assessment, the content of the assessment reports, the bodies considering the reports, the rules of public participation, the criteria of decision-making, and other issues. Article 11 of the Decree describes the establishment of the Commission for Assessment of Impacts on the Environment. Its members are appointed by the Government depending on the character of the particular project or potential impact that has to be assessed. The rules on public participation are set out in Article 19 of the Decree, which prescribes that the entire documentation on the environmental impact assessment report has to be disclosed and made available to the public for a period of between 15 and 60 days before the final decision of the Commission. The announcement about how the public can access the information must be published in at least one mass-circulation periodical, as well as in the official gazette of the local administration unit.

2.3 Traffic and transport

In the Decree on the Conditions for Granting Concessions for Harbour Traffic[64] the Cabinet prescribed what technical and technological requirements an establishment has to meet in order to get concessions. The Decree further set out professional requirements for the employees, rules of competition, procedures, criteria and terms for issuance of the certificate of granted concession. It also determined the prices of concessions, the guarantees for and supervision over the performance of contractual obligations. Article 8 of the Decree establishes a commission authorised to decide on the applications for concessions. It must publicly open all offers within 24 hours after the contest has been closed and decide on the best offer using eight criteria: impact on the growth of the traffic in the harbour; bank guarantees; environmental protection; utilisation of harbour capacity, price, conditions of payment, references, and other advantages. The procedure before the Commission is not exhaustively regulated by this Decree, nor are any procedural guarantees given, except for the right to file a complaint on the decision of the Commission before the Board of Managers.

The Decree on the Conditions and Procedure for Granting Concessions on Waters and Public Water Utilities[65] was enacted by the Cabinet in November 1996. This Decree enumerates situations in which there is no need to ask concession for using waters, regulates the periods for granting concessions, the basis for determination of the amount paid for concession, and the procedure for granting concessions. The public auctions for concessions have to be announced in the official gazette "Narodne novine". The Decree enumerates five criteria for deciding on the offers, but, like the Decree on Concessions in Harbours, it does not determine the priorities among them.

2.4 Education

There were two major administrative acts in this area during the discussed period, which set standards for the teachers and other experts involved in the educational process in primary and secondary schools. The first was the Regulation on the Professional Requirements and Pedagogical and Psychological Education of Teachers and Specialists in Elementary Schools.[66] The second was a similar regulation passed concerning secondary education: Regulation on the Professional Requirements and Pedagogical and Psychological Education of Teachers and Specialists in Secondary Schools.[67]

2.5 Health Care

The Regulation on the Content, Terms and Procedure of Professional Advancement and Tests of Professional Skills of Dentists[68] establishes a commission at the Administrative Council of the Chamber of Dentists, which is designed, among other things, to periodically check the skills of dentists.

The Regulation on the Composition, Authority and Modes of Activity of the Controllers and Medical Commissions of the Croatian Health System[69] authorised special administrative bodies (medical commissions) and their officials (controllers) to supervise the compliance of the medical institutions with their contractual obligations toward the system of health care as well as the Ministry of Health Care. The regulation rules that the medical commissions of the system are professional and medical bodies, which perform expert assessments and submit reports, evaluations and opinions in cases when required by the law or other regulations.

2.6 Refugees

By the Decree on Rights of Returnees[70] the government determined the procedures under which the refugee status of certain groups of refugees was to be with held. The reason for the act was the fact that some territories of Croatia had been liberated by government forces from Serbian paramilitaries. Therefore, after basic infrastructural and housing preparation of the areas, some refugees were in a position to return to their homes. Under the Decree those refugees are given deadlines to return to their homes. By doing so they either become "returnees" and enjoy specific rights and privileges, or lose both the status of "refugees" and "returnees".

2.7 Others

The Program of the Croatian State Support Agency for Stimulating Economic Activities in the Territory of Special Importance[71] was enacted by the Cabinet of Croatia in February 1996. The aim of the program is to support the development of the parts of Croatia liberated from the Serbian paramilitary forces (almost one-third of the territory of Croatia) as well as to facilitate the self-employment of the victims of the war. The program was enacted according to Article 4, paragraph 3 of the Law on the Croatian State Support Agency.[72] The Agency itself has been established in order to transfer financial funds to the former refugees in order to facilitate their return to their homes.

2.8 Informal rules

The concept of "informal rules" is not familiar to Croatian administrative law doctrine. However, the present practices of the administration do reveal certain tendencies to rely on informal rules, especially in the area of public official recruitment. The most important informal rule in this context seems to be the "ban" on employing citizens of non-Croat ethnicity. The victims of this rule are Muslims and, especially, Serbs. The ban covers the recruitment policies of state ministries, state organisations and other institutions.[73] According to the most recent data available (1991), the population of Croatia is composed of 78 per cent ethnic Croats, 15 per cent Serbs, and small minorities of other nationalities (Muslims, Italians, Hungarians, and others). Official statistics on the ethnic breakdown of employees in Croatia do not exist for the state administration or any industrial sector.

D. JUDICIAL DECISIONS

The Constitutional Court of Croatia is the only court in the country whose decisions are published regularly and in their entirety in "Narodne novine", the official gazette of the Republic. In its decisions the Constitutional Court rules about the conformity of laws with the Constitution as well as the conformity of regulations with the laws and the Constitution. The Constitutional Court may annul unlawful and/or unconstitutional regulations and suspend unconstitutional laws.

The Supreme Court is the highest judicial institution dealing with criminal and civil adjudication, while the Administrative Court of Croatia is the only administrative court and the highest level of administrative decision-making. They both decide only on individual cases and individual acts. They announce their decisions only to the parties involved in the concrete proceedings. Their decisions are not published systematically nor *in intero*. Selected holdings of those courts have been published in certain academic journals and books. Usually parts of the "reasoning" are published together with the holdings of individual cases. Both the Supreme Court and the Administrative Court focus strictly on concrete cases of litigation and are reluctant to offer general interpretations that would guide the lower courts and administrative bodies. Their decisions are important for the lower-level courts mostly through their argumentative power and the professional respectability of their members. However, they do not have a legally recognised or constitutionally established character of precedents. All juridical decisions of all courts within the system of regular jurisprudence have an identical structure. First, there is an "introduction" with the name of the court, parties, representatives and a description of the issue in question as well as the legal ground for litigation. Second, there is a holding (verdict) and then "explanation" or reasoning.

The most important decision of the Constitutional Court in terms of judicial review of administrative action was the Decision of November 13, 1996.[74] It obliged all administrative organs to publicise and include in their decision full reasoning. The publicising of the decision and the inclusion of adequate reasons is a sine qua non for a valid administrative decision: the violation of these requirements is a ground for the invalidation of the decision by the courts. The Decision further prohibits referring to the "public interest" as a justification for not providing adequate substantive reasons for a particular individual decision.

E. THE WORKINGS OF OMBUDSMAN, PROSECUTORS, AND OTHER ADMINISTRATIVE INSTITUTIONS

In general, statistical information is lacking on the operation of the administrative law system in Croatia. The Programme of Statistical Research of the Republic of Croatia, under which yearly statistical analyses are carried out, does not cover the operation of administrative appeal and judicial review of administrative action processes.

1. THE OPERATION OF OMBUDSMAN

The (in)activity of the first ombudsman (1994–1996) has already been discussed above. His report for 1994, presented to Parliament in 1996, was rejected, leading to the ombudsman's resignation. His successor has not yet reported on his activities in 1996. In April 1997 he reported gross violations of human rights of Serbs in some parts of Croatia. This caused a wide range of reactions, from the approval of a few independent newspapers, through the silence of the opposition, to the condemnation of the government and the parliamentary majority.

Some unofficial statistics were given in the 1994 report of the first ombudsman.[75] According to them, from June 2, 1993, when the Lower House elected the first ombudsman, until the end of 1994, 505 complaints had been filed with the Office of the Ombudsman. Forty per cent of them were rejected by the ombudsman as unfit for the initiation of proceedings. Most of those accepted involved violations of the rights of residence, errors in civil and criminal proceedings, and violations of the right to work. Other significant groups of violations were recorded in the spheres of denationalisation and restitution of ownership rights and social protection for families, Croatian soldiers, and pensioners. There were also cases related to the processes of privatisation, environmental protection, building rights, and others. Oddly, no complaint was filed concerning the mass exodus of Serbs from Croatia.

2. THE OPERATION OF THE STATE AUDIT OFFICE

The State Audit Office submitted its report on the public financial activities in 1994/95 on the session of the Lower House of the Parliament held between January 17 and 20, 1996.[76] This was the first official public audit report. The report establishes a number of violations of financial rules by the administration. For instance, according to the report, it was impossible to carry out an audit in the Ministry of Agriculture, because the entire book-keeping records for a few months were missing. Furthermore, during 1994 the same ministry spent some 410 million kuna (1 DM = 3.6 kuna) and only 6.6 million kuna was properly accounted for. By the end of the year, significant funds for the development of agriculture remained unutilised, although the need for this money was admittedly great.

In the same period, the Employment Division spent only 420 million kuna, although 625 million kuna was apportioned for its activities (unemployment in Croatia is between 15-30 per cent, depending on the sources). It was further established in the report that many local administration units had not determined their budgets or had done so improperly. In half of the local administration units, incomes and expenditures were not balanced. A variety of different non-budget sources of income to which those units were entitled remained unutilised, while they still received financial support from the state budget. The decision to impose local taxes was not made by the local representative bodies (as constitutionally required) but by the local administration. Almost 90 per cent of the local administration units had no records of their real estate properties.

As stated in the report of the State Audit Office, the Parliamentary Committee for Financing and State Budget has established that in some cases during the privatisation process, persons involved in the administering of public auctions appeared to end up as successful buyers. Furthermore, in some cases users of state budget funds did not return their financial surpluses in the state budget after the closing of the budget year, but instead lent that money to commercial banks. One of the most interesting findings of the report was that no public audits had been performed in two ministries, the Ministry of Defence and the Ministry of Police, which spend around 20 per cent of the GNP. Furthermore, no audits were performed in public enterprises, public funds and banks operating with public money. It was also established that around 10 per cent of the whole state budget had been misspent in 1994.

Despite these findings, the Parliament fully accepted the State Audit Office's report. The Parliament also decided that:[77] "a) The Ministry of Internal Affairs, the Public Prosecutor, the Financial Police and the Tax Revenue Division must submit reports within three months to the Lower House of the Parliament, informing the Parliament about the steps taken in relation to the findings of the Public Audit Report for 1994; b) The Cabinet must within three months submit to the Lower House a report on the responsibility of individuals employed in the bodies supervised by the Cabinet in relation to the findings of the Report... The Ministry of Administration must do the same regarding the units of local administration..."

Based on this decision of the Parliament, the Cabinet, after five months, reported before the Lower House of the Parliament that: "...the Financial Police initiated six criminal proceedings, the Ministry of Internal Affairs 13 criminal proceedings...The Tax Revenue Division initiated procedures against misdemeanants and the same is done by the Financial Police [the number of procedures was not mentioned]..."[78] The report listed the names of dismissed and disciplined senior public officials.

The opposition in the Parliament concluded that the report hid more than it revealed and that almost all the answers to concrete parliamentary questions were missing. The Parliament ordered the Government to rework and supplement its report, which was never done. The other public bodies, which were to submit reports to the Parliament on the findings of the State Audit Office, did not do this either.

All this raises serious doubts about the responsibility of the Croatian administration to the Parliament and the other democratically elected bodies. The general disregard of the procedures of administrative accountability has been further demonstrated by the failure of the Administrative Inspection Office to submit periodical reports to the Parliament as required by the Law on the Administrative Inspection Office.[79]

The Chapter has been prepared on the basis of information provided by Alexander Dordević

NOTES

1 Hereinafter the official gazette will be referred to as "NN".

2 Not all ministries are represented in the collective organ, the Cabinet of Ministers.

3 *NN*, No. 3/94 of January 21, 1994

4 *Slujbeni list SFR Jugoslavije* , the official gazette of the former Yugoslavia (hereafter referred to as "*Sl.l.*") No. 4/77 of January 14, 1977.

5 *NN*, No. 53/91 of October 8, 1991.

6 Sl.l. of the former Yugoslavia, 47/86 of August 15, 1986, incorporated in the Croatian legal system by the Law on Adoption of the Law on the General Administrative Procedure, *NN* 53/91 of October 8, 1991.

7 *NN*, No. 90/92 of December 30, 1992.

8 *NN*, No. 75/93 of August 13, 1993.

9 Zagreb is the capital of Croatia; it accounts for one-third of the population and 50 per cent of GNP.

10 Articles 20–21 of the Law on the City of Zagreb, *NN*, No. 90/92 of December 30, 1992.

11 *NN*, No. 90/96 of October 25, 1996.

12 *NN*, No. 3/94 of January 14, 1994.

13 *Sl.l.*, No. 4/77 of January 14, 1977, adopted as a law of the Republic of Croatia by the Law on Adoption of the Law on Administrative Dispute, *NN*, No. 53/91 of October 8, 1991.

14 *NN*, No. 45/95 of July 5, 1995.

15 *NN*, No. 24/92 of April 25, 1992.

16 *NN*, No. 74/93 of August 6, 1993.

17 *Sl.l.* of the former Yugoslavia No. 47/86 of August 15, 1986 adopted as a Law of the Republic of Croatia by the Law on Adoption of the Law on the General Administrative Procedure, *NN* 53/91 of October 8, 1991.

18 *Sl.l.* No. 4/77 of January 14, 1977, adopted as a law of the Republic of Croatia by the Law on Adoption of the Law on Administrative Disputes, *NN* No. 53/91 of October 8, 1991.

19 *NN*, No. 30/93 of April 15, 1993.

20 *NN*, No. 17/86 of April 29, 1986.

21 *NN*, No. 11/78 of March 3, 1978.

22 *NN*, No. 60/92 of October 1, 1992.

23 *Izvješća Hrvatskog Sabora* No. 166/1996, p. 37, of April 19, 1996.

24 *NN*, No. 70/93 of March 20, 1993.

25 *NN*, No. 75/93 of August 13, 1993.

26 *NN*, No. 17/86 of April 29, 1986.

27 *NN*, No. 55/95 of August 4, 1995.

28 *NN*, No. 24/96 of April 3, 1996.
29 *NN*, No. 32/96 of April 26, 1996.
30 *NN*, No. 90/96.
31 *NN*, No. 1/96 of January 5, 1996.
32 *NN*, No. 92/96 of October 30, 1996.
33 *NN*, No. 33/96 of April 30, 1996.
34 *NN*, No. 10/97 of January 30, 1997.
35 *NN*, No. 56/90 of December 22, 1990.
36 *NN*, No. 21/96 of March 14, 1996.
37 *NN*, No. 84/92 of December 4, 1992.
38 *NN*, No. 44/96 of June 5, 1996.
39 *NN*, No. 116/93 of December 30, 1993.
40 *NN*, No. 43/96 of May 31, 1996.
41 *NN*, No. 34/96 of May 3, 1996.
42 *NN*, No. 44/96 of June 5, 1996.
43 *NN*, No. 87/96 of October 16, 1996.
44 *NN*, No. 59/96 of July 17, 1996.
45 *NN*, No. 100/96 of November 28, 1996.
46 *NN*, No. 83/96 of October 8, 1996.
47 *NN*, No. 108/96 of December 23, 1996.
48 *NN*, No. 57/96 of July 12, 1996.
49 *NN*, No. 1/97 of January 3, 1997.
50 *NN*, No. 59/96 of July 17, 1996.
51 *NN*, No. 1/97 of January 3, 1997.
52 *NN*, No. 1/97 of January 3, 1997.
53 *NN*, 1/96 of January 3, 1996.
54 *NN*, No. 61/96 of July 19, 1996.
55 *NN*, No. 54/94 of July 13, 1994.
56 *NN*, No. 61/96 of July 19, 1996.
57 *NN*, No. 33/96 of April 30, 1996.
58 *NN*, No. 82/94 of November 11, 1994.
59 *NN*, No. 27/96 of April 10, 1996.
60 *NN*, No. 34/95 of May 24, 1995.
61 *NN*, No. 53/96 of July 3, 1996.
62 *NN*, No. 34/97 of April 2, 1997.
63 *NN*, No. 82/94 of November 11, 1994.
64 *NN*, No. 52/96 of June 28, 1996.
65 *NN*, No. 99/96 of November 26, 1996.
66 *NN*, No. 47/96 of June 14, 1996.
67 *NN*, No. 1/96 of January 5, 1996.
68 *NN*, No. 22/96 of March 20, 1996.
69 *NN*, No. 95/96 of November 13, 1996.
70 *NN*, No. 33/97 of March 28, 1997.
71 *NN*, No. 10/96 of February, 6, 1996.
72 *NN*, no. 29/94 of April 11, 1994.
73 This information is based on a number of informal interviews carried out by our Croatian contributor with senior public officials from the Ministry of Urban Development.
74 *NN*, No. 103/96 of December 6, 1996.
75 *Izvješća Hrvatskog Sabora*, No. 166, pp. 37–38.
76 *Izvješća Hrvatskog Sabora*, No. 159/96 of February 22, 1996.
77 *Izvješća Hrvatskog Sabora*, No. 159/96, p. 19, of February 22, 1996.
78 *Izvješća Hrvatskog Sabora*, No. 180/96 p. 44, of October 10, 1996.
79 *NN*, No. 17/86 of April 29, 1986.

CHAPTER THREE
THE CZECH REPUBLIC

I. GENERAL DESCRIPTION OF THE ADMINISTRATIVE LEGAL SYSTEM

1. HISTORY OF THE ADMINISTRATIVE LEGAL SYSTEM

1.1 The Austro-Hungarian heritage

The origins of the major institutions of government and the courts, as well as of the administrative procedures, date back to the second half of the 19th century, when the Czech lands constituted a part of the Austro-Hungarian Empire. It was during this period that the "police state", in which the administration was not bound by law, was replaced by the "liberal state" in which the sovereign and the whole executive were subject to the rule of laws adopted by Parliament.[1]

The Supreme Administrative Court, established in 1875,[2] played an important role in the development of administrative law.[3] The Court was authorised to find "modes of administrative proceedings" and evaluate the "adequacy" of their implementation by the administrative authorities.[4] Various basic principles of administrative proceedings were brought into existence by the jurisprudence of the Supreme Administrative Court.[5] The institution of the Supreme Administrative Court carried over into the First Czechoslovak Republic, created in 1918.[6]

1.2 Major administrative rules and codes

The first comprehensive regulation of administrative proceedings,[7] which reflected the Supreme Administrative Court's jurisprudence, was adopted in 1928. New government orders regulating administrative procedures were applied after World War II in communist Czechoslovakia (1955 and 1960). Finally, they were replaced by the 1967 Code of Administrative Procedures, [8] which is still in force.[9]

2. THE STRUCTURE OF THE EXECUTIVE

2.1 Central government

The supreme body of the executive branch, consisting of a Prime Minister, deputy prime ministers, and ministers,[10] is the Government. It takes decisions collectively by a vote of the majority of its members.[11] Although the Czech Republic has a bicameral Parliament, composed of the Chamber of Deputies and the Senate, the Government is accountable only to the former.[12]

The Government may ask the Chamber of Deputies for a vote of confidence, and the Chamber of Deputies may express non-confidence in the Government. The Deputies are entitled to demand information and explanations from members of the Government as well as from other heads of administrative agencies. Members of the Government and the heads of agencies have a duty to provide any requested explanation within 30 days, unless they are prevented from doing so by legislation which governs secrecy or prohibits the publicising of information.[13] Furthermore, a Deputy has the right to pose written and oral parliamentary questions to the Government or to its members. Oral questions are answered on Thursdays from 4 to 5 p.m. A written question has to be answered within 30 days of its submission.[14]

2.2 Administrative division and local government

The Czech Republic is a centralised state (due to the failure to establish regions with elected assemblies, i.e. "higher territorial self-governing entities", which the Constitution envisages[15]). The existence of a bipartite administration, rooted in mid-19th-century Austria, consisting of state administration and local government, has deeply influenced relations between the central and local administration.[16]

Local administration consists of both state organs (i.e. State District Offices—local branches of the central administration) and bodies of the local government (i. e. municipalities, independently administered via an assembly involved with local government issues in a restricted territorial context). Self-government of the municipalities is guaranteed by the Constitution.[17] They may be endowed with "secondary"/"commissioned" jurisdiction (i.e. when they are allocated tasks usually performed by the state administration) and also have the power to issue generally binding ordinances within their jurisdictional ambit. If such ordinances exceed their jurisdiction in breach of law, they may be repealed by the Constitutional Court on a proposal by the head of the State District Office.[18]

Apart from the State District Offices, there are also numerous specialised bodies of local state administration (e.g. police, military, financial or customs administration). All of them are local branches of the central administration and are bound by orders issued by the superior state authorities.

Finally, the professional self-governing bodies constitute a separate category. These bodies (e.g. the Chamber of Architects or the Chamber of Lawyers) enjoy relative autonomy, although the state authorities and the courts supervise them in a manner prescribed by the law.

2.3 Acts of the government

The Government has the power to issue decrees for the implementation of and within the scope of the acts of Parliament.[19] The ministries, other administrative agencies, and territorial self-governing bodies may issue such by-laws, unlike the Government, only if they are explicitly authorised to do so by a particular act of Parliament.[20] In contrast, the President of the Republic is not authorised to issue normative regulations: he can issue orders to the army only in his capacity as commander-in-chief.

Government decrees and the ordinances of ministries do not require the approval of Parliament. However, if an implementing regulation is to be issued for a bill that is discussed by the Chamber of Deputies, the Organising Committee of the Chamber may ask the submitting party to provide a draft of it. The submitting parties must always submit the draft of such a regulation if it is to enter into force simultaneously with the concerned bill.[21]

Except for the above-mentioned secondary legislation implementing acts of Parliament, the Parliament may not delegate its legislative power to either the Government or the President. If the Chamber of Deputies is dissolved, the Senate adopts legal measures on a proposal by the Government regarding matters which cannot be delayed and which would otherwise require the enactment of an act of Parliament. However, the Senate may not adopt legal measures regarding the Constitution, the state budget, the final State Budgetary Account Report, the Electoral Law, and international treaties on human rights.[22]

The Government cannot delegate its power to issue decrees to other administrative authorities. Nor can it empower the ministries or other administrative authorities to issue regulations for the implementation of these decrees.[23]

3. SYSTEM OF COURTS DEALING WITH ADMINISTRATIVE LAW ISSUES

3.1 The structure of the judicial system

At present, there is no separate system of administrative courts. Since the early 1990s, when judicial review of the administrative acts was reintroduced after 40 years, the administrative law cases have been decided by the courts of general jurisdiction and partly by the Constitutional Court.[24] The concept of a "single system of courts" was challenged by the 1993 Constitution,[25] which provides for the establishment of a Supreme Administrative Court.[26] However, the Supreme Administrative Court has not been established yet.

Currently, the judicial hierarchy has four tiers. There are district or municipal courts, circuit courts, high courts, and the Supreme Court. The first three instances are mostly involved in the judicial review of administrative acts, whereas the Supreme Court operates as an appellate body in relation to specific categories of administrative decisions such as the decisions of the Central Electoral Committee.

3.2 Jurisdiction of the courts

The jurisdiction of the courts, when a) exercising judicial review of administrative action or b) deciding on the "remedies against decisions of public authorities", is regulated by Title 5 of the Code of Civil Procedures (C.C.P.).[27] The main difference between the two modes of review proceedings is that in the former case the administrative decision remains effective after the beginning of the proceedings, whereas in the latter it is not.[28]

District courts review decisions on administrative offences. The major courts of general jurisdiction exercising judicial review of administrative action, however, are the circuit courts. The high courts review decisions of the central bodies of state administration (i.e. ministries) with the exception of the decisions related to pensions, employment and sickness insurance, which are examined by the circuit courts.

Courts are called to review the *legality* of the decisions taken by: a) the bodies of the state administration; b) the organs of local government; c) the bodies of the professional self-government, and d) other legal entities, if the law entrusts them with deciding on rights and obligations of physical and legal persons in the sphere of public administration. The reference to "legality" seems to indicate that the courts can only decide on matters of law and cannot deal with matters of fact or merits. The issue of the court's jurisdiction in judicial review cases has not, however, been clarified in any single opinion. The Constitutional Court has pointed out[29] that there is no settled doctrine on this issue. On the one hand, the High Court in Prague has held that the establishment of facts and the submission of evidence relative to facts are excluded from the scope of judicial review. Academic scholars, on the other hand, have argued against this viewpoint. In any case, it is generally agreed that the courts do not have full jurisdiction to review administrative law cases on their merits.

3.3 Special quasi-judicial bodies

Special quasi-judicial bodies or tribunals operate in the sphere of professional self-government (e.g. Disciplinary Commission of the Chamber of Architects). These tribunals usually act as first-instance adjudicators, whereas the courts are given the jurisdiction to decide on the remedies against the decisions of these tribunals.

4. GENERAL PROCEDURAL LAWS, CODES OF ADMINISTRATIVE LAW

4.1 Major laws of administrative procedure

The general administrative procedural law is the Administrative Procedures (Code of Administrative Procedures, C.A.P.) Act.[30] Despite the fact that the C.A.P. was adopted 30 years ago, it has never been directly amended. The C.A.P. governs proceedings according to which state authorities decide on the rights, interests and duties of the citizens in the sphere of state administration unless a specific law provides otherwise.[31]

4.2 Basic procedures of appeal within the administrative hierarchy

The C.A.P. stipulates, in Section 53, that a party to administrative proceedings has the right to appeal, unless a law provides otherwise. The administrative authority deciding on appeal is the "closest superior administrative body to which the body that issued the contested decision is subordinated". An appeal may also be launched against the decision of a central body of the state administration (i.e. where there is no superior body). In this situation the authority deciding on remonstrance is the head of the central body of the state administration concerned (e.g. a minister heading the ministry that issued the contested decision). It is by virtue of these provisions that the general principle of two-instance administrative proceedings has been established.[32]

The appeal has to be submitted to the authority that has issued the judgement within 15 days of the delivery of the decision. The first-instance authority may reconsider its decision and grant the application, provided that nobody except the applicant is affected. If the first-instance authority does not correct its own decision, it shall submit the appeal with all the documents attached to the superior authority within 30 days. The appeal has a suspensive effect.

The majority of administrative decisions can be appealed within the framework of the administrative hierarchy (internal appeal). Exceptions to this rule fall into two categories: a) those cases where a special law provides for the appeal to a court, and b) those cases where the C.A.P. does not apply and the specific law does not guarantee the right to appeal. Such cases are numerous, especially in administrative proceedings carried out in the jurisdiction of the local administration (i.e. municipalities).

4.3 Basic procedures of judicial review of administrative action

The right to seek judicial review of administrative action is provided for in the Charter of Fundamental Rights and Liberties (hereinafter the Charter). Article 36, paragraph 2 of the Charter stipulates that "anybody who claims that his rights have been violated by a decision of public administration may turn to a Court for a review of the legality of such a decision, unless a law provides differently". The review of decisions affecting the fundamental rights and freedoms listed in the Charter may not be excluded from the jurisdiction of the courts.

The application for judicial review is to be submitted within two months of the delivery of the final administrative decision. The application for judicial review has to specify what (in the applicant's view) constitutes the "illegality" of the disputed decision and what his proposed remedy is. Unless the claimant has a law degree, he or she should be represented by a lawyer. The procedures are slightly different in cases when the claimant has the right to seek remedies from the court (for example, representation by a lawyer is not mandatory). In such cases, the application to the court to grant remedies against a decision of an administrative authority has to be submitted within 30 days of the delivery of the decision but, again, the only ground for invoking judicial review is the "illegality" of the administrative decision.

4.4 Administrative acts exempted from judicial review

The exceptions to the right to seek judicial review are specified in Section 248 of the Code of Civil Procedures (C.C.P.) There are four broad categories of such exceptions:

- Decisions that by their nature do not concern the rights and duties of individual physical or legal persons, such as the generally binding normative acts or decisions relating to the organisation of the administration;
- Ten specified categories of decisions, such as the decision where the appellate body is a court, commands by army officials, or decisions by the administrative authorities which are of preliminary, procedural or disciplinary nature or decisions to grant benefits, where there is no legal right to such benefits;
- Specific decisions by administrative bodies listed in Annex A to the C.C.P. This lists decisions in the specific spheres of state administration and has more than 50 items. In some of the listed cases it is obvious that the review of a decision would be impractical (e.g. the review of a physician's decision that an employee is temporarily unable to work). In other cases, the rationale for exclusion is the discretionary nature of the decision;
- Decisions where judicial review is excluded by specific laws.

The negative enumeration of exceptions to the generally applicable principle of judicial review of administrative action is very broad and raises numerous problems.[33]

4.5 Judicial remedies

When a court exercising judicial review finds that the administrative decision is not correct in terms of legality, or that the facts of the case have not been established sufficiently, it quashes the decision and (depending on the case) the previous decision of the first-instance authority. Then the court returns the case to the administrative agency responsible for making the decision on its merits. The administrative authorities are bound by the legal opinion of the court.[34] The application for judicial review does not have a suspensive effect on the execution of the administrative decision. The court may, however, postpone the execution upon a proposal of the submitting party. By contrast, the application for remedies against administrative decisions suspends implementation of the original decision.

4.6 Exceptions from the provisions of the administrative procedure code

As indicated above[35] there are many exceptions to the applicability of the C.A.P. Two observations are essential: a) if the particular law establishes specific administrative procedures in the sphere of state administration, it takes priority; b) in general, the C.A.P. does not govern administrative procedures in the field of territorial and professional self-government.

The specific administrative procedures referred to under a) are applied, for instance, in the sphere of construction or administrative criminal law. In b), the sphere of local self-government the C.A.P. is applicable only if the law specifically provides so. The non-applicability of the C.A.P. is determined historically: in 1967 when the C.A.P. was adopted, local self-government did not exist. This situation creates certain difficulties, for instance, with regard to the right to appeal.[36]

The C.A.P. also applies in the field of financial administration covered by the Administration of Taxes and Fees Act.[37] It does not, however, cover the handling of petitions and complaints by citizens.

4.7 The procedures related to administrative offences

There is a distinction, both in Czech legal theory and practice, between individual administrative acts granting rights and creating duties and administrative acts imposing sanctions. The liability for administrative offences is regulated by the "penal administrative law," which forms a specific part of administrative law. This penal administrative law theory distinguishes two principal categories of administrative offences: a) misdemeanours perpetuated by individuals and b) "other administrative offences" committed either by individuals or by legal persons.[38]

The first category of administrative offences is regulated by Act No. 200/1990 Coll., on Misdemeanours. The law defines various types of misdemeanours and establishes procedures for imposing sanctions. The Administrative Procedure Code applies as subsidiary legislation in these proceedings. The municipalities, the State District Offices, and the police are the competent administrative authorities to deal with misdemeanours. The accused person has a right to appeal. An appeal always has a suspensive effect. An important principle derived from the criminal law is expressed in Section 82: the appeal authority may not impose a more severe sanction than the one imposed by the first-instance decision-maker. Decisions on misdemeanours are subject to judicial review carried out by the district courts under the Civil Procedure Code. In certain cases, however, judicial review is excluded, for instance if the highest possible fine does not exceed 2000 crowns (USD 65).

The "other administrative offences" (as well as some misdemeanours) are not exhaustively described in a single piece of legislation, but definitions do exist in discrete sections of specific administrative laws. Imposing sanctions, mainly fines, for these types of administrative offences is governed procedurally by the Administrative Procedure Code.

5. THE INSTITUTION OF OMBUDSMAN

(See Part II - Introduction)

6. OTHER FORMS OF SUPERVISION OVER THE ADMINISTRATION

In addition to the supervision of the administration by the legislature and the judiciary, there are also other specific systems of supervision, such as the supervision carried out by the Supreme Audit Office. This is an independent body established under Article 97 of the Constitution. It is charged with the supervision of the management of state property and public finances and the implementation of the state budget. The jurisdiction of the Office is defined by Act No. 166/1993 Coll., as amended. It may carry out supervision over the ministries and the other administrative bodies as well as physical and legal persons (with the exception of the Czech National Bank and the Security Intelligence Service). The Office publishes its findings in the Official Bulletin and submits them to the Chamber of Deputies, the Senate, the Government and also to ministries, if they request so. It also publishes annual reports which are submitted to the Chamber of Deputies, the Senate, and the Government.

The other specific systems of supervision consist of the general hierarchical supervision carried out by superior bodies of state administration and supervision by specialised administrative agencies, often called inspectorates (e.g. the Environmental Inspectorate).[39]

7. PARLIAMENTARY COMMITTEES

Both chambers of Parliament may establish as their bodies investigative committees and commissions. It is not permissible for a Deputy or a Senator who is a member of the Government to be part of a parliamentary committee, investigative committee or commission.[40] A commission to investigate "matters in the public interest" may be established on the basis of a proposal from at least one-fifth of all deputies.[41] The resolution of the Chamber of Deputies whereby an investigative commission is established must contain an exact specification of the matter to be investigated and a deadline by which the commission shall submit its findings. The commission may interrogate witnesses and hear experts.[42]

II. DEVELOPMENTS IN ADMINISTRATIVE LAW DURING 1996-1997

INTRODUCTION

Judging by the quantity of the legal regulations issued, administrative law is one of the rapidly expanding branches of law in the Czech Republic. However, this extensive growth has not been countered with complementary reform of the administrative law proceedings and institutions.[43] 1996 and the first quarter of 1997 have not brought any significant changes in this respect.

One of the underlying factors in this unsatisfactory situation is that no agreement was reached among the major political actors on two constitutional issues: the establishment of regions and the setting up of the Supreme Administrative Court. Both of these changes are prescribed by the 1993 Constitution. Although the bill on regional administration (so called eight-plus-one version, i.e., eight regions plus the capital, Prague) was introduced in the spring of 1996 by a junior ruling coalition party–the liberal Civic Democratic Alliance–it failed to win the prescribed three-fifths majority of votes.

Nor has the necessary political consensus between the government and the opposition been achieved with regard to establishing the Office of Ombudsman. The idea has been widely discussed by legal scholars[44] and received considerable support primarily from the left-wing opposition, some NGOs, and the President. In 1996, the Bill on the Public Defender of Rights was introduced by the group of opposition Social Democrats.[45] According to the bill, an ombudsman, elected by the Chamber of Deputies, would be charged with powers to exercise extra-judicial protection of citizens and private actors against the incorrect decisions or lack of decisions of the administrative authorities. The Bill was strongly opposed by Prime Minister Vaclav Klaus's Civic Democratic Party.

Opponents of the ombudsman issue raised two major arguments. First, they claimed that the powers of the ombudsman would be excessive and infringe upon the existing constitutional division of powers. Second, they argued that the existing system of judicial review of administrative action guarantees adequate protection. Although the Bill initially found support among some members of the smaller governmental coalition parties, it failed to gain the necessary majority in the chamber on March 25, 1997.

A critical observer of the legal developments, the Czech Helsinki Committee, suggested that administrative law reform may be also hampered by the fact that no single state body is charged with the drafting and adoption of legislation on administrative procedure.[46] In any case, this role had not been fulfilled satisfactorily by the Office for Legislation and Public Administration abolished after the 1996 parliamentary election.

The lack of political will to launch a comprehensive reform of the public administration, and the justified critique of inflexible functioning of the state administration by citizens, led Prime Minister Klaus to seek to fight the bureaucratisation of the administration in informal ways. The Commission to Fight Bureaucratisation, composed of 26 volunteer politicians and experts, was established in early November 1996.[47] It deals with citizens' complaints of state bureaucracy's excesses in various areas, identifies backlogs of public administrations, and suggests solutions directly to the ministries and agencies. Executive powers have not been conferred on the Commission, nor has it been equipped with a sufficient permanent staff. Unsurprisingly, it was soon overwhelmed by complaints from citizens. The solutions to the problems suggested by the Commission were not taken seriously by the authorities or officials concerned. Even in the cases in which they were examined they were ultimately rejected as generally incompetent. Consequently, after seven months in existence, the commission announced that it would dissolve itself.

Against this background, the most important impetus for the reform of administrative proceedings, and particularly in judicial review of administrative acts, has been brought about by the Constitutional Court. The Court shaped judicial review proceedings by insisting on and creating the right of a party to a public hearing. After reversing a number of earlier judicial review decisions on the bases of inadequate application of Section 250f of the C.C.P. (which allowed for courts to decide "in simple cases" of judicial review without public hearing), the Constitutional Court abolished the very provision as unconstitutional.

In addition, the Constitutional Court expressed (in subsequent rulings in judicial review cases) a very critical opinion of the current system of judicial review as a whole. The justices expressed scepticism that the existing system of judicial review was compatible with Article 6 of the European Convention on Human Rights (ECHR) and the relevant provisions of the domestic Charter. The Constitutional Court also urged the establishment of a Supreme Administrative Court. According to the Constitutional Court, the issue is vital, since at present it is compelled to act as a supreme administrative tribunal. (See also D.1.)

In view of the necessity of a comprehensive reform of administrative law, the changes in the powers of the central bodies of state administration that 1996 brought about seem of minor importance. Perhaps the only exception is the decision to create an Office for the State Information System. Pursuant to the government proposal, the Office shall also be charged with the protection of personal data held in all existing information databases.[48]

Finally, a summary of the current scholarly discussions of administrative law theory and practice may help shed light on administrative law developments during the year.[49] An interesting academic debate on the legal nature of municipal ordinances issued in exercise of the autonomous competence of the municipalities was initiated by certain controversial Constitutional Court rulings.[50] Several academic articles appeared on electoral issues related to the 1996 parliamentary and

Senate elections.[51] The academic discussion on the role of the ombudsman continued[52] and the leading legal journal, *The Lawyer*, published major administrative law contributions on the changes in the state administration of waters,[53] on the access to environmental information,[54] on the historical development of the taxation of income[55] and the publication of legal regulations.[56] The specialised *Journal of Administrative Law* published theoretical articles dealing with the status of legal persons under public law, and delegated legislation. Other important issues addressed in 1996 by administrative law scholars included the need to regulate the status of civil servants and the nature of administrative procedures in the sphere of environmental protection.

A. THE CONSTITUTION

Except for Constitutional Act No. 75/1997 Coll., fixing some minor changes of the border between the Czech Republic and Slovakia, no constitutional amendments have been adopted.

B. LEGISLATION

1. PROCEDURAL AND GENERAL ORGANISATIONAL LAWS

1.1 Establishment of a second high court

On January 1, 1996, in addition to the High Court in Prague, a second High Court was established in Olomouc. On the same date certain changes in the organisation of the judicial system under the amendment to Act No. 335/1991 Coll. on Courts and Judges came into effect.[57] The changes mainly affected the division of jurisdiction between the high courts and the Supreme Court. From the point of view of administrative law, the abolition of Section 17 of Act No. 335/91 Coll. is important. It provided for the establishment of criminal, civil, commercial and administrative panels ("boards") of judges at the high courts. The boards can "express opinions" (make interpretations) on the interpretation of laws and legal regulation. At present the competence to issue "opinions" rests exclusively with the Supreme Court. However, the Supreme Court has no separate administrative law panel.

1.2 Changes in the structure of government

The first significant change in the structure of the central bodies of the state administration was the abolition of the Ministry of Privatisation in spring 1996.[58] The powers and the functions of the Ministry of Privatisation were subsequently transferred to the Ministry of Finance.

Further, major changes in the structure of the ministries and the other central bodies of the state administration were enacted after the 1996 parliamentary election in November 1996.[59] The main reforms involved the abolition of the Ministries of Economics, Economic Competition and Transportation as well as the Czech Commission for Scientific Degrees. The Office for Legislation and Public Administration, a special advisory organ to the Government, was also abolished. Its legal co-ordination function has been transferred to the Ministry of Justice. In their place, the Ministry of Local Development, the Ministry of Transport and Communication, the Office for the Economic Competition and the Office for the State Information System have been established.

The new Ministry of Local Development took over many of the competencies previously exercised by the Ministry of Economics. It is responsible for regional development policies, including support for local crafts and industries, housing, territorial planning and construction legislation, investment policies and tourism.

The competencies of the Ministry of Transport and Communication cover transport, postal and telecommunications services, except for certain matters relating to radio and television broadcasting. (These are supervised by a special Radio and Television Broadcasting Board.)

The competencies of the newly created Office for Economic Competition, which replaced the Ministry for Economic Competition, are defined by a separate law.[60] The main tasks of the Office are to create favourable conditions for the promotion and protection of economic competition, to take measures against monopolies and to supervise public tenders. The seat of the Office is in Brno.[61]

The competencies of the Office for the State Information System are also to be defined by a separate law. They shall include both the keeping of the State Information System and the protection of the personal data held in all information databases.[62]

2. SUBSTANCE

2.1 Privatisation and restitution

2.1.1 PRIVATISATION

As already mentioned, the Ministry of Privatisation has been abolished, since no further mass privatisation is foreseen.

2.1.2 RESTITUTION

In order to better understand the developments in the restitution of property to former owners, a brief account of the major restitution laws is necessary. The Remedying of the Consequences of Certain Injustices Relating to Property Act,[63] the Extrajudicial Rehabilitation Act,[64] and the Adjustment of Property Rights in Land and other Agricultural Assets Act[65] are the three most important laws regulating the restitution of property. According to these acts, adopted in 1990 and 1991, the restitution of expropriated property applies only to confiscations that occurred between February 25, 1948, and January 1, 1990. The restitution is for Czech citizens only.

The defined time period for compensatable confiscation excludes the Sudeten Germans who were dispossessed of their property at the end of the war (and in most cases also expelled from the territory of the State). In principle, only individuals (physical persons), the original owners and their descendants, can regain the property. There is, however, a certain exception to the rule embodied in Act No. 403/1990 Coll., which also provides for the restitution by "private legal persons" of certain properties confiscated in the late 1950s. In general, restitution is possible if the property is held by the state or a legal person. If the property is held by an individual, a financial compensation calculated according to the criteria laid down by the law is paid by the state.

Plots of lands are restituted in real boundaries, if such restitution is feasible. If the restitution in real boundaries is not possible (e.g., the land is legally used by other person or a building has been built on it, etc.[66]), the owners are compensated with other plots of land. Financial compensation is possible if the owner has not been compensated with other lands.

Houses and apartments are given back to the former owners if they are either in possession of the state or legal persons or if they were acquired by physical persons illegally. Otherwise a limited financial compensation is paid to the original owner. The new owners of the houses are bound by the existing lease contracts. (The restitution of individual apartments is rare as it was uncommon in the past to own single flats.)

In general, industrial property was not given back, but privatised either through "coupon privatisation" or in other ways. There are two main underlying factors of this development. First, the industrial property was, in the overwhelming majority of cases, held by legal persons (e.g. commercial companies) which were excluded from restitution. Second, it is important to note that the main wave of nationalisation took place before February 25, 1948, i.e. before the period covered by the restitution acts.

Against this backdrop, significant changes were introduced in 1996. The Amendment[67] to the Adjustment of the Property Rights in Land and Other Agricultural Assets Act[68] provided new opportunities for Czech citizens who had previously been denied the right to claim back agricultural property because they did not meet the permanent residence requirement prescribed by law (i.e. primarily Czech emigrants living abroad). Since the residence condition was abolished by the Constitutional Court, the Act merely instituted a new six-month period in which emigrants can claim their former property. The restitution is, in principle, an administrative procedure. This is illustrated, for example, by the fact that the competent authorities to decide on claims are state land authorities. Appeals against their decisions may be lodged with the Court.

2.2 Environment

The aforementioned changes in the system of the Central Bodies of Administration[69] led to a transfer of functions from the Ministry of Environment to the Ministry of Agriculture in the field of water protection. The central body supervising activities related to waters is the Ministry of Agriculture. The Ministry of the Environment is competent only for the protection of the natural water resources and the protection of the quality of waters.

Another new piece of legislation important for the protection of the environment is the Peaceful Use of the Nuclear Energy Act.[70] It regulates the use of nuclear energy and the conditions for carrying out activities related to the use of nuclear energy, the system of the protection of persons and the environment, the civil law liability for nuclear damages, the conditions for the storage of nuclear wastes and related issues. The administration and supervision of the use of nuclear energy is carried out by the State Office for Nuclear Safety. The Ministry of Industry and Commerce is a founder of the organisation called the "Administration of the Nuclear Waste Disposal Sites". The Organisation carries out activities connected with storage of nuclear waste. In proceedings under this Act, the C.A.P. applies as subsidiary legislation.

Act. No. 16/1996, Coll. on the Conditions of the Import and Export of the Endangered Species of Wild Animals and Plants and on Measures on Their Protection determines the state administrative authorities competent in this field. They are the Ministry of the Environment, the Inspectorate of the Environment, the district offices and the Administration of the National Parks and the Administration of the Protected Land Areas. The Ministry of the Environment is empowered to issue lists of endangered species. The export or import of endangered plants or animals is allowed only with the special permission of the Ministry. The permission to import endangered species issued by the Ministry presupposes a prior permission by the state of origin of the endangered plant or animal. The law also regulates the compulsory registration of certain animals and plants: the individual animal or plant is to be registered with the district authority. The C.A.P. applies as subsidiary legislation.

2.3 Traffic and transport

Act No. 12/1997 Coll. on the Safety and Smooth Operation of Land Traffic determines the hierarchy and the competencies of the responsible authorities in this field, i.e. the Ministry of the Interior and the police. Within the framework of the police, specific tasks are carried out by the District and Circuit Traffic Inspectorates and the Directorate of the Traffic Police Service at the Police Presidium as a central body.

Another law regulating transport is Act No. 49/1997 Coll. on Civil Aviation. It regulates the conditions for construction and operation of aeroplanes and airports, the conditions for the use of air transport, and the conditions for providing air transport services and related issues. Further, it establishes a new administrative authority: the Office of Civil Aviation. The Office, which is subordinated to the Ministry of Transport and Communications, will replace the existing State Air Supervision Office. The Minister appoints the head of the Office and also approves the Statute of the Office. The Office keeps the register of the aeroplanes operated by Czech domestic legal persons or Czech citizens and issues certificates to authorise the use of aeroplanes or their components.

2.4 Administration and management of socio-cultural processes

The growing complexity of socio-cultural processes is reflected in the increasingly detailed legal regulation governing fields like media regulation, health care, and social security. An exhaustive account of the development in this field would go beyond the scope of this article. The following notes cover only the most important developments.

2.4.1 REGULATION OF THE MEDIA

There are two principal laws regulating the press: Act No. 81/1966 Coll. on the Periodical Press and other Mass Media (amended in 1990 and 1992) and Act No. 37/1995 Coll. on Non-Periodical Publications (i.e. books etc.). To publish either periodical or non-periodical printed matter requires merely a registration. The law on the periodical press is often criticised for failing to provide adequate guarantees for journalists' access to administrative documents. The Ministry of Culture's response is that a new press law is under preparation.

The audiovisual sector is governed by Act No. 468/1991 Coll. on Radio and Television Broadcasting. The law distinguishes two types of broadcasters: a) those who are entitled to broadcasting on the basis of law and b) those who were issued a special licence or permission.

The first category, the public broadcasters, is represented by Czech Radio[71] and Czech Television.[72] The broadcasting done by both these institutions is financed by radio and television fees respectively. Currently there are two private and two public television channels and several dozen private radio stations in the Czech Republic. The underlying purpose of Czech Radio and Czech Television is to serve the public and provide objective information. Such aims are promulgated by various stipulations–e.g., the broadcasting of advertisements by Czech Television is strictly limited to 1 per cent of the daily broadcasting time.

Licences and registrations for private radio and television broadcasting are issued by the Board for Radio and Television Broadcasting. The status of the Board is regulated by Act No. 103/1992 Coll. It is composed of nine members, elected by the Chamber of Deputies for a period of six years, and is accountable to the Chamber of Deputies. The members of the Board may not hold office in political parties and may not have any financial interest in broadcasting.

2.4.2 HEALTH CARE AND SOCIAL INSURANCE

Act No. 48/1997 Coll. on Public Health Insurance, accompanied by a series of implementing by-laws, was initiated by a ruling of the Constitutional Court.[73] This explains why the Act does not incorporate many new arrangements: most of the provisions of the governmental regulation were incorporated into the new law. According to it public health insurance covers all permanent residents and employees whose employer is headquartered in the Czech Republic. The duty to pay insurance fees is shared between employers and employees, while the state pays for certain categories of persons (e.g. children, pensioners, the handicapped, soldiers, and prisoners) from the state budget. The law identifies which categories of medical treatment are covered, partially covered or not covered by the public insurance.

Another piece of legislation relevant to health care is Act No. 79/1997 Coll. on Medicaments. It regulates: a) the development, production, preparation, distribution, control, and destruction of medicaments; b) the medicaments' registration, prescription, and handover to users. The main state authorities with administrative competence in human medicaments are the Ministry of Health Care and the State Office for Supervision of Medicaments. The administration in the sphere of veterinary medicaments is carried out by the Ministry of Agriculture, the State Veterinary Administration, the Office for State Control of Veterinary Medicaments and the district and municipal veterinary authorities. The State Office for Supervision of Medicaments decides on the registration of medicaments. Further, it keeps the records of registered medicaments, issues permissions for clinical tests of medicaments, and decides on the withdrawal of certain types of medicaments from circulation. It is also responsible for supervision of producers and distributors of the medicaments. The Office for State Control of Veterinary Medicaments decides on the registration of veterinary medicaments and keeps the register of veterinary medicaments.

The Act establishes special administrative procedures for registration of both human and veterinary medicaments. Physical or legal persons whose domicile or seat is not in the territory of the Czech Republic must be represented in these proceedings by a person who is a permanent resident. The responsible state authorities have to arrive at a decision within 18 months from the delivery of the application. If all the legal conditions are met, the registration cannot be denied.

2.5 Administration and Management of Political Processes

With the exception of the law regulating the access to the former state police files, the new legislation in the area of the management of administrative and political processes is represented by various amendments to laws adopted in the early 1990s.

The amendment to Act No. 423/1991 Coll. on the Association in the Political Parties and Political Movements[74] regulates the financing and the commercial activities of political parties and movements. It introduces a general ban on the involvement of political parties in commercial activities. Political parties can only establish a company or have shares in companies operating in very specific areas such as publishing or cultural activities. The Act provides an exhaustive list of the legally acceptable financial sources of the political parties. The parties have the duty to submit to the House of Deputies annual financial reports which are available to the public. If a report is incomplete or not submitted at all, the Ministry of Finance is authorized to freeze the subsidies to the party from the State.

The above-mentioned Act No. 140/1996, Coll. on the Access to the Files of the Former State Police opens to the general public the previously secret records of investigation conducted by the state police under communist rule. The Law requires the Ministry of the Interior to inform citizens about the existence of their personal file (i.e. a specific set of documents kept by the state police about an individual) or a file containing personal data concerning them. The Ministry is obliged to provide access to the file to the person concerned if the file still exists physically. The requests for access to the files must be submitted to the Ministry in writing. The Ministry must answer the request concerning the personal file within 90 days, whereas the request concerning a file containing personal data is to be answered without unnecessary delay. The Law also provides for the protection of personal data of third persons by requiring that all information concerning the private and family life of such persons be blacked out before access to the file is provided. The Law will enter into effect on December 1, 1997.

The powers of the Ministry of the Interior (the central state authority responsible for citizenship issues) were extended by the amendment to Act No. 40/1993 Coll. on the Acquisition and Loss of Citizenship of the Czech Republic.[75] This amendment permits the Ministry to waive, at its discretion, the condition of "clean criminal record in the last five years" with regard to naturalisation requests by citizens, or former citizens, of the Slovak Republic who have had continuous permanent residence on the territory of the Czech Republic since December 31, 1992. The amendment also introduces very strict conditions for the revocation of Czech citizenship, which should eliminate the risks of statelessness. The amendment to the Citizenship Act is a reaction to criticism of the restrictive 1993 Citizenship Act adopted after the dissolution of Czechoslovakia.

Amendments to the 1992 Aliens Act and to the 1990 Refugee Act were introduced by Act No. 150/1996 Coll. The amendment introduces stricter conditions for residence of foreigners regarding, for instance, the availability of financial means and housing. The Ministry of the Interior, which is the responsible central authority for aliens, has the right to take fingerprints of foreigners who are to be deported or who are banned from the Czech Republic. With regard to the 1990 Refugee Act, the amendment introduces changes reflecting a humanitarian spirit. The provision that allowed only persecuted aliens to maintain refugee status for five years has been lifted. The amendment also facilitates the naturalisation of refugees by reducing the waiting period from 10 to five years.

C. REGULATION

1. ACTS OF THE HEAD OF STATE

As mentioned, the President does not have the power to issue normative acts.

2. GOVERNMENTAL REGULATION

The legal regulations issued by the ministries are numerous, often very detailed and of a very specialised nature, such as the health care regulation mentioned above (e.g. the list of medicaments covered by the General Health Care Insurance). Two sets of regulations can be viewed as illustrative, albeit non-exhaustive, examples in this area.

First, Government Decree No. 324/1996 Coll. on the Conditions of Providing Subsidies to Private Schools, Pre-school and School Facilities regulates the state subsidies provided by the school authorities to private primary and secondary schools as well as kindergartens and similar educational facilities. The subsidy is provided upon application and on the basis of a contract between the educational facility and the school authority. The amount of the subsidy depends on the number of pupils and amounts to 60 per cent of the sum provided by the government for public elementary schools and 50 per cent for a secondary school. Under specific circumstances, the subsidies may be increased up to 90 per cent for elementary schools and secondary schools and up to 100 per cent for special schools, such as schools for mentally or physically handicapped children.

Second, Order No. 88/1996 Coll., issued by the Ministry of the Interior implements Act No. 553/1991 Coll. on the Municipality Police. It regulates the professional attestations of the members of the Municipality Police Forces. The assessment of the required knowledge of legislation is to be tested by the examining board set up by the Ministry of the Interior.

D. JUDICIAL DECISIONS

INTRODUCTION

The procedural as well as substantive conditions for final judgement by a court resolving a civil law dispute and determining rights and obligations of the parties as well as other forms of decisions in civil proceedings are regulated in detail in Sections 152–175 of the C.C.P. These general rules also apply to judgements and decisions issued within the framework of judicial review of administrative acts.

All judgements have to be declared publicly. A judgement contains a decision on the merits of the case (holding), the reasoning of the court (i.e. substantiation of the decision), information on the right to appeal, and information on the execution of the judgement. Important judicial decisions serving as precedents are published in the *Collection of Judicial Decisions and Opinions* edited by the Supreme Court. The *Collection* is rightly criticised for being a subjective "selection"[76] rather than a "collection". Since the *Collection* does not include all relevant judgements, an important role in making the existing jurisprudence publicly known is played by specialised legal periodicals.[77] Significant judicial decisions relating to administrative law issues are published, usually in an abridged and abbreviated form, in the *Journal of Administrative Law*.[78] Most of the 1996 issues of the journal consisted of coverage of the relevant decisions in 1994 and 1995. A more timely, though not very systematic, source of information is provided by some commercial Czech legal information databases, such as ASPI (Automatic System of Legal Information) or LEGSYS.

A distinct category of judgements represents the findings (i.e. decisions on the merits of a case) and resolutions of the Constitutional Court. The form and structure of the Constitutional Court's decisions, as well as their publication, are regulated by Act No. 182/1993 Coll. on the Constitutional Court. All findings of the Constitutional Court are published annually in the *Collection of the Findings and Resolutions of the Constitutional Court*.[79] Findings on proposals to abolish law or other legal regulations are also published in the *Collection of Laws* (also known as the *Official Gazette*). In both cases the decisions and the relevant part of the substantiation that shows the legal opinion of the Court and the underlying arguments are published. Furthermore, the Constitutional Court may decide to publish, in the *Collection of Laws*, any of its decisions it believes to be of general importance.

1. THE CONSTITUTIONAL COURT

Numerous Constitutional Court rulings deal with judicial review cases. This is best explained by the Constitutional Court in its finding of September 12, 1996:[80]

"The resolution of controversial legal issues, the expression of opinions, and the harmonisation of jurisprudence in the sphere of judicial review of administrative acts should belong to the court that represents the top of the system of administrative courts, most likely to the Supreme Administrative Court envisaged by the Constitution. Since such a court does not exist, the Constitutional Court has no other option than in some cases...to substitute such a tribunal".

The following annotations include only the most important Constitutional Court judgements relating to administrative law.

In July 1996 the Constitutional Court issued a finding relating to the free medical care provision (Article 31) of the Charter of the Fundamental Rights and Liberties. The Court examined and set the limits of the powers of the ministries to legislate.

Article 31 of the Charter provides that "citizens have the right to free medical care on the basis of public insurance and under conditions established by law". The Court held that regulations issued by the executive are not laws (i.e. acts of Parliament) foreseen by the Charter. It argued that if health care providing for full or partial payments to patients was defined in by-laws the fundamental right and liberties would fall into the purview of the executive. The Court therefore abolished a whole package of health care regulations as of April 1, 1997.

The Chamber of Deputies and the Minister of Health Care defended the regulations. They argued on legal grounds that the right to free medical care does not belong to the fundamental rights and liberties. (The Charter lists the right to medical care under Title IV, "Social, Economic and Cultural Rights".) Therefore, the regulation via by-law is permissible. The underlying practical argument was that ministries are better equipped to elaborate and issue specific regulations requiring expert knowledge.

The finding of the Constitutional Court of November 5, 1996,[81] addressed the issue of fairness of administrative decision-making in the absence of any applicable procedural rules prescribed by law. The Court ruled that applicability of the C.A.P. may not be excluded if the law does not provide for any alternative procedures.

The case was submitted to the Constitutional Court by the High Court in Prague, which was acting under the provisions of the C.C.P. on judicial review of administrative decisions.[82] An applicant to the High Court contested a letter by the Ministry of the Environment of dubious content allegedly denying the approval of the export of certain protected animals. The issue was not the content of the letter but the applicable administrative procedures under which the decision of the Ministry on the export has to be issued. The Act exempted this kind of decision-making from procedures prescribed by the C.A.P., but failed to introduce any specific procedural provisions.

In the opinion of the High Court, this was contrary to Article 2, paragraph 3 of the Constitution and Article 2, paragraph 2 of the Charter. Both articles state that the state power serves all citizens and may be executed only in cases, within limits and in a manner established by law. The High Court argued that the exclusion of the applicability of the procedures prescribed by the C.A.P. created a situation in which the Ministry can arbitrarily refuse to issue an approval of export or even refuse to issue any decision at all. It further argued that the non-existence of any procedural arrangement has further severe consequences; for example, the authority is not bound to protect the rights and interests of citizens.

In their letter to the Constitutional Court, the Chamber of Deputies asserted that the contested provision excludes from procedures prescribed by the C.A.P. activities that constitute the "expression of state sovereignty". The failure to provide for alternative specific procedures means that the authority has to follow the "general principles of administrative proceedings".

The Constitutional Court agreed with the High Court's arguments. In addition, the Constitutional Court declared that this amounts to infringement of Article 36 of the Charter, which provides for a fair hearing.

The Finding of the Constitutional Court of November 27, 1996,[83] upholding the constitutionality of certain provisions of Act No. 110/1964 Coll. on Telecommunications addressed the issue of whether and under what conditions the administrative authorities may decide on civil law obligations.

The case was submitted to the Constitutional Court by the High Court in Prague, which had exercised judicial review of administrative action. The High Court argued that Section 21 (paragraphs 1 and 2) of the Telecommunications Act is incompatible with Article 6. 1 of the ECHR–i.e. with the right to an independent, impartial tribunal in determining of civil rights and obligations–since the law extended the jurisdiction of administrative authorities (the Ministry of Economics and the Czech Telecommunications Office) to all decision-making in the sphere of telecommunications, including the determination of civil obligations, such as the obligation of the user to pay the provider for the services (phone bills).

The Ministry argued that Section 36 (paragraphs 1 and 2) of the Charter prescribes that some civil rights, with the exception of fundamental human rights and civil liberties, are determined by institutions other than courts. It further pointed to the non-legal aspects of the arrangements, namely the high number of disputes concerning the payment for services.

The Constitutional Court examined the problem in a broader context (referring, e.g., to the EC Directive 95/62) and concluded that Article 6.1 of the ECHR does not require the contracting parties to entirely exclude administrative authorities from determining rights and obligations of physical and legal persons. In the Court's opinion, the essence of the problem is not in the incompatibility of the challenged provision with Article 6.1 of the ECHR. Rather, the Court suggested, the problem is the absence of a legal provision that would guarantee the right to full review of administrative decisions issued in administrative proceedings by an independent and impartial tribunal satisfying the condition of Article 6.1 of the ECHR. Hence, the real problem is the existing system of judicial review of administrative acts which limits the review to the legality of the decisions and apparently excludes the possibility of the Court's examining the facts of the cases.

2. SUPREME ADMINISTRATIVE COURT

As indicated earlier, there is no Supreme Administrative Court in the Czech Republic. The function of the Court is partially carried out by the Constitutional Court.

3. ORDINARY ADMINISTRATIVE COURTS AND ADMINISTRATIVE AGENCIES

In the following section a brief survey of the most notable Supreme Court, Circuit Court and District Court decisions is provided. A brief note is also made on three interesting decisions issued by the heads of central administrative bodies.

In its decision of March 13, 1996,[84] the Supreme Court specified the contents of the rule against bias in relation to the members of the Supreme Audit Office:

"Bias...is in fact a subjective relation (attitude) of the controlling subject to the subject under control or to the controlled persons. The bias may not be evaluated by the controlling subject itself; however, it shall be obliged to report to entities stipulated in Section 20, paragraph 2 of the above act any facts which may indicate bias...[A]pplications of the controlling subject for initiation of civil proceedings against the controlled person constitute a fact which may indicate bias on behalf of the controlling subject against the controlled person. The category of 'controlled person' shall also include, in a case of a controlled legal entity, the statutory body of the legal entity (i.e. the Minister, should the control performed by the ministry headed by the same Minister be in issue)."

The decision was issued on appeal by a member of the Supreme Audit Office against the decision of the Disciplinary Chamber of the Office.

The Decision of the High Court in Prague of June 25, 1996,[85] relates to the problem of null and void administrative decisions. The Court dealt with the procedures to be followed by the competent state authorities pursuant to Section 11, paragraph 7 of the Act No. 229/1991 Coll. on the Adjustment of the Property Rights in Land and Other Agricultural Assets (one of the restitution laws). The Court ruled that where a decision of the Land Office is appealed to its superior administrative authority (i.e. the Central Land Authority), that appealed decision is null and void if the law provides for an appeal procedure before a court. If there is no legal provision for the authoritative declaration that such void decisions are nonexistent, then it is the responsibility of the courts in judicial review proceedings to formally abolish such a decision for illegality.

The Circuit Court in Ceske Budejovice determined in its decision of May 7, 1996,[86] that the abolition on procedural grounds of the payment order issued by the Finance Office did not imply a decision on the termination of the tax procedures. The reason was that, in this case, the tax had not been settled in the proceedings in which the tax declaration had been submitted. A new decision by the Financial Office could be issued in the form of a new payment order.

The resolution by the same court of November 31, 1996,[87] relates to the scope of judicial review in cases relating to tax proceedings. The Court dealt with whether it could review a decision of the Financial Directorate to allow (or to deny) the review of the decision of the Financial Office under Section 55 of Act No. 337/1992 Coll. on the Administration of Taxes and Payments. The Court held that the administrative procedure under Section 55 has two phases: the first phase, when the decision to grant judicial review is taken by the Financial Directorate, and the second phase, when the decision on the merits of the case is taken by the Financial Office. It held that the court is not competent to review a decision issued in the first phase of the procedure, since it is of procedural nature and, as such, is excluded from the judicial review of administrative acts.

The decision by the Minister of the Environment of May 16, 1996,[88] issued on the proposal of the Commission on Remonstrances, held that the administrative interlocutory injunction under Section 43 of the C.A.P. may be issued by the administrative authority during the concrete administrative proceedings. An independent administrative proceeding aimed exclusively at the administrative interlocutory injunction is not permissible.

In another decision on remonstrance issued on September 16, 1996,[89] the Minister of the Environment dealt with one particular aspect of the division of jurisdictions between the courts and the administrative authorities. The issue was whether the ongoing judicial litigation concerning property rights constitutes a "decision on a preliminary question" in the administrative proceedings under Section 88 of the Construction Act, concerning the removal of a construction, and thus constitutes a reason for the interruption of the proceeding pursuant to Section 29 of the C.A.P. The Minister decided that this is not so: the judicial proceeding deals with the relationships under civil law, while the administrative proceeding deals with public law relationships.

An interesting decision by the Ministry of Interior–Section for Civil Administration of June 24, 1996,[90] concerns the "abuse" of administrative proceedings to register a civil association and the possibility of a "bypass" of the law by the petitioner.

In this case a group of persons, whose participation in the proceedings is prescribed by the law, started administrative proceedings to register an organisation of foreign nationals "A" under Act No. 116/1985 Coll. on the Establishment of Organisations with an International Element. The Ministry of Interior rejected the application as the prior consent (prescribed by the law) of the Ministry of Foreign Affairs on the registration had not been obtained. The applicant did not appeal against the decision. Instead, he submitted an application to the Ministry of the Interior to register a civil association "B" under the Civil Association Act. The Ministry of the Interior rejected the application, arguing that "the situation in which the applicant has not made use of the right to appeal against the decision, but has submitted another application identical in content under another legal regulation, is viewed by the Ministry as an attempt to bypass the law. Such a step is...contrary to the protection of public order". Furthermore, the Ministry invoked Article 20, paragraph 3 of the Charter, which allows for the limitation of the freedom of association if it is necessary for the protection of public order.

E. INVESTIGATION PARLIAMENTARY COMMITTEES

During the analysed period, some serious problems in the banking sector were manifested in the collapse of several smaller banks. On the proposal of the opposition Social Democrats, the Chamber of Deputies voted on October 1, 1996, to set up a special 12-member committee to investigate the collapse of one of them–the Kreditni Banka. On December 31, 1996, the chairman of the committee issued a preliminary report[91] that was discussed by the Chamber on April 1, 1997. The one-page report analysed the collapse from two perspectives: the provision of suspect credits in the years from 1991 to 1993 (a matter that is also being investigated in criminal proceedings against certain members of the management of the bank), and in the broader framework of the developments in the banking sector. The final report of the committee was discussed in May 1997.

Another commission was created in early November 1996 to investigate the privatisation and functioning of one of the largest steel producing companies in the Czech Republic, the POLDI Kladno.[92] POLDI had faced serious economic problems for more than a year. The commission was set up after the government accused the principal owner of POLDI, Mr. Stehlik, of mismanagement. As the task of the committee proved more complex than expected, the original term for submission of findings (the end of February 1997) was extended to December 31, 1997. On March 6, 1997, a court ordered that bankruptcy proceedings be started against POLDI. Mr. Stehlik and his son, a former director of POLDI, are currently under criminal investigation for dubious business deals. The commission intends to analyse the audit reports and bookkeeping of the 18 daughter companies of POLDI.

The Chapter has been prepared on the basis of information provided by Andrea Baršova

NOTES

1 Madar, Z (ed.), *The Dictionary of Czech Law*, Part II, Linde, 1995, p. 1072 (in Czech).

2 Act No. 36/1876 Coll. of the Laws of Empire.

3 It must, however, be noted that already seven years earlier, in 1867, the Court of the Empire ("Reichsgericht") was established by a Fundamental State Law (Act No. 144/ 1867 Coll. of the Laws of the Empire). The Court of the Empire was conferred jurisdiction to review decisions of administrative authorities if the applicant claimed that an administrative act violated his basic civil and political rights guaranteed by the 1867 Bill of Civil and Political Rights. The Court existed until 1918, when in the newly created Czechoslovakia, the powers of the Court were taken over by the Supreme Administrative Court (Act No. 3/1918).

4 Hendrych, D., *The Administrative Law–General Part*, C. H. Beck/SEVT, Prague 1994, p. 139-140.

5 Jiri Hoetzel, a distinguished Czech legal scholar, made the following observation in 1934: "The administrative procedure as a whole is, in fact, built up on the jurisprudence of the Supreme Administrative Court..." (*The Dictionary of Public Law*, Volume III, Brno, 1934, p. 921, in Czech).

[6] The Supreme Administrative Court and the unique system of administrative law review it carried out was abolished in 1952. Judicial review of administrative acts was reintroduced after 40 years, in 1991, in the form of judicial review carried out by the system of ordinary courts.

[7] Government Order No. 8/1928 Coll.

[8] C.A.P., Act. No. 71/1960 Coll.

[9] The main heritage of the communist regime, also mirrored in the 1967 Code of Administrative Procedure, is the centralised hierarchical structure of administrative authorities.

[10] Article 67, Constitution.

[11] Article 76, Constitution.

[12] Article 68, paragraph 1, Constitution.

[13] Section 11, Rules of Procedure of the Chamber of Deputies.

[14] Section 110–112, Rules of Procedure of the Chamber of Deputies

[15] This fact is often explained as a reaction to the split of Czechoslovakia. "Above all, many Czechs blame the division of Czechoslovakia on federalism. As a result, politicians a priori considered such a system as being unsuitable for the Czech Republic.' This superstitious rejection of federalism might explain the rigid centralism of the present Czech state. Rychetsky, P., *The Czech Constitution in Its Fifth Year*, The New Presence, April 1997, p. 8. (in English). Mr. Rychetsky is the Chairman of the Senate Constitutional and Legal Committee.

[16] A simple and practical definition of self-government is provided by O. Vidlakova in the *Journal of Administrative Law*: "The self-government is a part of the public administration carried out by an entity, different from the state, in most cases a public law entity, that is, in the case of the territorial self-government the self-governing entity (municipality or the higher territorial self-governing unit) or, in the case of professional self-government, the chamber". (Vidlakova, O., *Public Administration or Management*?, Journal of Administrative Law, 1/1996, p. 16, in Czech).

[17] Article 99.

[18] Section 64, paragraph 3 of the Act No. 112/1993 Coll. See also: Grospic, J., "Generally Binding Ordinances Issued in the Autonomous Competence of Communities in the Light of Constitutional Court Jurisdiction", *The Lawyer* 1/1997, pp. 23–52, at p. 29 (in Czech with an English summary).

[19] Article 78, Constitution.

[20] Article 79, paragraph 3, Constitution.

[21] Rules of Procedure for the Chamber of Deputies, Article 86, paragraph 4.

[22] Article 33, Constitution.

[23] Pavlicek, V.–Hrejbek, J., *The Constitution and the Constitutional System of the Czech Republic*, Volume I, Linde, Prague, 1994, p. 183 (in Czech).

[24] See Part II, D, 1. In the period 1952–1991 the system of judicial review of administrative acts was virtually non-existent. The appeal to court was permissible only in a very narrowly tailored category of cases relating to the social security benefits.

[25] Article 91.

[26] Bicovsky, J., "The Problems of Judicial Review", *Administrative Law*, 3/1996, pp. 156–163, at p. 157 (in Czech).

[27] Section 244 to 250.

[28] The former presents a generally applicable rule while the latter covers a group of cases established by specific laws. With regard to the definition of the latter group the situation is "chaotic and not transparent, there is no official list of such decisions...." In: Bures, J.– Drapal, L., *The Civil Procedure Code—Commentaries*, first edition C. H. Beck/SEVT, Prague, 1994, p. 538 (in Czech).

[29] E.g. in its Finding No. 1/1997 Coll. (See Part II. D. 1).

[30] No. 71/1967 Coll.

[31] See below, 4f.

[32] Matrasova, E. et el., *Administrative Procedure Code—Commentary*, Linde, Prague, 1993, second edition, p. 83 (in Czech).

[33] Bures, J.–Drapal, L, *The Civil Procedure Code—Commentary*, C. H. Beck/SEVT, first edition, 1994, Prague, p. 505 (in Czech).

[34] Section 250 j, C.C.P.

[35] 4, a.

[36] Hendrych, D., *Administrative Law—General Part*, first edition, Prague, C. H. Beck/SEVT, 1994, p. 141 (in Czech).

[37] No. 337/1992 Coll.

[38] Cerveny, Z.-Slauf, V.: Law of Misdemeanours, Linde, Prague, 1995, p. 15

[39] Prucha, P., *Administrative Law—General Part*, Masaryk University Brno, 1996, pp. 209–219 (in Czech).

[40] Article 31 and 32, Constitution.

[41] The Senate, composed of 81 Senators elected in single districts on the basis of majority rule, was only created after the Senate election in November 1996. The Senate has not set up any investigatory committee to date. A special Commission has been set up to draft the rules of procedures. Until these are adopted, the Rules of Procedure of the Chamber of Deputies apply. (Senate Print No. 1.)

[42] The detailed rules of procedure including, for instance, the duty to testify, are set out in the Appendix to the Rules of Procedure of the Chamber of Deputies.

[43] Zarecky, P.-Vidlakova, O., "The General Questions of the Reform of Public Administration", *Journal of Administrative Law*, 6/1993, p. 321 ff. (in Czech).

[44] See, for instance, the articles by J. Skala in *The Lawyer* 2/1994 and in *Legal Horizon* 3/1994 and V. Sladecek in *Journal Administrative Law* 2/1993, 3/1993, 4/1995, and *The Lawyer* 4/1995.

[45] House Print No. 25.

[46] *1996 Czech Helsinki Committee Report on Human Rights*, p. 61, in Czech.

[47] No official report on the activities of the Commission has been published as of May 1, 1996. The information on its activities can be found in newspaper articles. See, for instance, *Dnes*, May 22, 1997 and May 24, 1997.

[48] See B.1. 1.2.

[49] The survey is based on the following periodicals: *The Lawyer (Pravnik)*, published by the Academy of Sciences, *The Journal for Legal Science and Practice (Casopis pro Pravni Vedu a Praxi)*, published by the Masaryk University in Brno, *The Journal of Administrative Law (Spravni Pravo)*, published by the Ministry of the Interior and *The Legal Practice (Pravni Praxe)*, published by the Ministry of Justice.

[50] Articles by J. Spacil in *State Administration and Self-Government* 10/1996, P. Zarecky and V. Vopalka in *Journal of Administrative Law* (2/1996 and 3/1996) and J. Grospic in *The Lawyer* 1/1997.

[51] An article by J. Simicek in *The Lawyer* 12/1996 and articles by J. Filip in the *Journal for Legal Science and Practice* 1/1996, 2/1996 and 3/1996.

[52] An article by V. Sladecek and S. Skulova in the *Journal for Legal Science and Practice* 2/1996 and 4/1996.

[53] An article by M. Kondl, *The Lawyer* 5/1997.

[54] An article by E. Kruzikova, *The Lawyer* 1/1996.

[55] An article by J. Barta, *The Lawyer* 4/1996.

[56] An article by F. Cvrcek, *The Lawyer* 7/1996.

[57] Act No. 239/1995 Coll.

[58] Act No. 135/1996 Coll.

[59] Act No. 272/1996 Coll., on Certain Changes in the System of the Central Bodies of State Administration amending Act No. 2/1969 Coll., on the establishment of Ministries and Other Central Bodies of State Administration.

[60] Act No. 273/1996 Coll.

[61] Brno is also a seat of the Constitutional Court and the Supreme Court.

[62] The bill defining in detail the competencies of the Office for State Information System (Print No. 14) was submitted by the Government to the Chamber of Deputies in the autumn of 1996 and approved in March 1997. It was, however, vetoed by the Senate. The Senators opposed the idea that the Office, which is an executive body administering the State Information System, would also supervise the protection of personal data gathered by governmental entities (e.g. the police). The Office finds itself at present in a "legal vacuum". The Bill as amended by the Senate shall be discussed in the Chamber of Deputies again in the summer 1997. See also: Vesely, J., "The Protection of Personal Data and the Bill on the Competencies of the Office for the State Information System", *Legal Practice* 2/1997, pp. 131–135 (in Czech).

63 Act No. 403/1990 Coll.
64 Act No. 87/1991 Coll.
65 Act No. 229/1991 Coll.
66 See Article 11 of the Act. No. 229/1991 Coll.
67 Act. No. 30/1996, Coll.
68 Act No. 229/1991 Coll.
69 Act. No. 272/1996 Coll., see B. 1. b.
70 Act No. 18/1997 Coll.
71 Established by Act No. 484/1991 Coll.
72 Established by Act No. 483/1991 Coll.
73 The Court determined that the providing of health care cannot be regulated by Ministerial Ordinances–see D.1.
74 Act No. 322/1996 Coll.
75 Act No. 139/1996, Coll.
76 1996 *Helsinki Committee Report on Human Rights*, p. 62, in Czech. The Collection is published in Czech with a brief English annotation.
77 Recently, *The Administrative Practice–Journal*, published by the Ministry of Justice,–started to publish a list of all decisions published by various specialised legal periodicals.
78 *Administrative Law Journal*, a specialised journal for the sphere of state administration and administrative law, is issued six times in a year. It is published by the Ministry of the Interior.
79 The Collection is published by the Constitutional Court.
80 The IV. Senate of the Constitutional Court, Decision No. 35/1996.
81 Published in the Official Gazette under No. 3/1997 on Eluding Reference to Section 5 paragraph 6 in Section 90 paragraph 1 from the Act No. 114/1992, on the Protection of the Nature and the Countryside.
82 Under Article 95, paragraph 2 of Constitution the Court that concludes that the law which it has to apply is unconstitutional, shall refer the case to the Constitutional Court.
83 Published as No. 1/1997 Coll.
84 File No. Nkn 1/95, Collection of the Judicial Decisions and Opinions 4/96.
85 File No. 6 A 152/94.
86 File No. 10 Ca 45/96.
87 File No. 10 Ca 230/96.
88 File No. M/1751/96, SRK/230/P-407/96 published in *Bulletin of the Environment* 3/1996.
89 File No. M/3106/96, SRK/385/R-470/96.
90 File No. II/s-OS/1-1294/1245/96r.
91 House Print 115/97.
92 *The Parliament Herald (Parlamentni Zpravodaj)* No. 7, 1996-97, p. 321 (in Czech).

CHAPTER FOUR
ESTONIA

I. GENERAL DESCRIPTION OF THE ADMINISTRATIVE LEGAL SYSTEM

1. A BRIEF ACCOUNT OF THE HISTORY OF THE ADMINISTRATIVE LEGAL SYSTEM IN ESTONIA

1.1 Establishment of the major governmental institutions: legal framework

The Government of the Republic (hereinafter Government) was established by the Government of the Republic Act in 1992 in accordance with the Constitution of the Republic of Estonia[1] (hereinafter Constitution). Three years later this law was replaced by a new Government of the Republic Act[2] (hereinafter Government Act). The new Act declares that the Government of the Republic holds executive power pursuant to the Constitution and the laws and exercises its prerogatives directly or through government agencies.[3] Under this law, the agencies of the executive branch are divided into two categories: *Government* agencies and *state* agencies, administered and governed by the Government agencies.[4] The main function of the state-financed Government agencies is to exercise governmental power. Specifically, these agencies are the ministries, the State Chancellery, the county governments, executive agencies and inspectorates, as well as the regional offices (local branches) of the latter two categories.[5] They are all accountable to the Government or to the corresponding minister, who directs and co-ordinates their activities and supervises them. The new Act reorganised the executive to consist of 26 agencies and 13 inspectorates (instead of the former 36 agencies and 10 inspectorates).

The second category–state agencies administered by the Government agencies–is also financed from the state budget. However, the principal function of these agencies is not to exercise executive governmental power but to provide services to the Government agencies or perform other state functions in the cultural, educational, social, and other areas.[6]

The Government Act also provides that the Government may not consist of more than 15 members and lists those members (ministers).[7] The members of the Government are prohibited from holding any other state or local government office or belonging to the management board or supervisory board of a commercial enterprise. Their position is also incompatible with operating as a trader or working in any other remunerative office, except for research and teaching.[8]

1.2 Establishment of administrative courts

The administrative courts were established in 1991 by the Courts Act.[9]

1.3 Major procedural laws and codes

The major procedural codes in Estonia are the Administrative Procedure Code[10] (hereinafter APC); the Civil Procedure Code [11](hereinafter CiPC); the Criminal Procedure[12] (hereinafter CrPC); the Constitutional Review Procedure Act[13] (hereinafter CRPA); the Criminal Appeal and Cassation Procedure Code,[14] and the Administrative Offences Code.[15]

In addition, in accordance with Article 46 of the Constitution, the Response to Petitions Act was adopted in 1994.[16] It provides state agencies, local governments and their officials with the appropriate procedural format for response to memoranda and petitions filed with them by citizens.

2. THE STRUCTURE OF THE EXECUTIVE

2.1 The highest executive body in Estonia

Estonian legal theorists debate whether the President of the Republic or the Government of the Republic is the highest executive body.[17] While the President of the Republic (hereinafter President) does have certain executive powers, the bulk of these are, in reality, exercised by the Government, which is headed by the Prime Minister.

2.1.1 FORMATION OF THE GOVERNMENT

The Government is accountable to the *Riigikogu* (Parliament). First, in order to obtain its mandate, the Government has to receive a vote of confidence from Parliament.[18] As outlined in the Constitution, the President designates a candidate for Prime Minister who, within two weeks, presents the list and the structure of the Government to the *Riigikogu*. Without a debate and by an open, absolute majority vote, the *Riigikogu* decides whether to authorise the designated candidate to form a government. If the designated candidate is not so authorised, this process is repeated. The right to nominate a candidate will transfer to the *Riigikogu* if a second candidate is not appointed by the Parliament within seven days, if the Parliament declines to appoint a candidate or if the second candidate does not get authorisation from the *Riigikogu*. If the candidate nominated by the *Riigikogu* fails to present a list of the Government to the President within 14 days, the President declares extraordinary elections to the *Riigikogu*. Thus the *Riigikogu* plays the decisive role in the formation of the Government.

2.1.2 CONFIDENCE PROCEDURES

The *Riigikogu* may express no confidence in the Government, the Prime Minister or a minister by an absolute majority vote.[19] Such a motion is initiated by at least one-fifth of the members of the *Riigikogu* and cannot be decided before the second day after the motion, unless the Government decides so. If no confidence is expressed in the Government or the Prime Minister, the President may, on the proposal of the Government and within three days of the vote, declare extraordinary elections to the *Riigikogu*. If no confidence is expressed in a minister, the Chair of the *Riigikogu* notifies the President, who in turn releases the minister from office.

2.1.3 QUESTIONS AND INTERPELLATIONS

The Constitution gives the members of the *Riigikogu* the right to address interpellations to the Government of the Republic and its members. The inquiries must be answered not later than on the 20th sitting of the *Riigikogu* from the date on which the inquiry is filed.[20] The *Riigikogu* Procedure Act[21] provides that replies to interpellations must not be longer than seven minutes and that up to three questions may be posed by the interpellator. The replies must not be longer than one minute. No debate may be opened on the replies of the government.

2.2 Relations between the central and the local administration

2.2.1 COUNTY GOVERNORS

Administratively, Estonia is divided into 15 counties, each of which is directed by a county governor. He is appointed to the office, for a term of five years, by the Government on the proposal of the Prime Minister. Local government representatives must approve the appointment by a majority vote. If the local government representatives fail to approve two successive candidates, the Government may appoint a person who has not previously been a candidate, without requesting approval from the local government representatives.[22]

2.2.2 MUNICIPALITIES

A local government is either a city or a rural municipality. Altogether, there are 254 local governments in Estonia. Each local government has a local government council, from which its executive body is formed.[23]

The county governors are the link between the Government and local governments, and are responsible for both the regional policy and other issues concerning the relations between central administration and local governments.[24] They also supervise the legality of secondary legislation of specific application passed by the local government councils and their executive bodies in the county.[25] If, upon the proposal of the county governor, a local government council or its executive body does not bring a particular piece of legislation of specific application into conformity with the Constitution, an act or other legislation, the county governor can file a protest with the administrative court pursuant to the procedure prescribed in the APC.[26] A county governor may also file a petition with the Legal Chancellor[27] for a review of the lawfulness of the secondary legislation of a local government body.

3. NORMATIVE ACTS OF THE ADMINISTRATIVE AUTHORITIES

3.1 The acts of the President

According to Article 109 of the Constitution, the President issues decrees that carry the same legal weight as the acts of the *Riigikogu*. Such decrees must bear the counter-signatures of the Chairman of the *Riigikogu* and the Prime Minister. Pursuant to Article 110 of the Constitution, however, the President may not enact, amend or repeal by decree the Constitution, the acts set out in Article 104 of the Constitution (acts concerning state and Government functioning, among others) or acts establishing state taxes or the state budget. The President may issue decrees only when the *Riigikogu* is unable to convene,[28] and such decrees must be either ratified or repealed by the *Riigikogu* upon its convention.

Although not constituting legislation in the proper sense, the President also has the power to promulgate the acts of the *Riigikogu* by way of resolution. According to Article 107 of the Constitution, if the President refuses to promulgate an act, he or she must return the act together with a reasoned resolution to the *Riigikogu* for a new debate and decision. If the *Riigikogu* returns the act to the President for proclamation, he or she must proclaim it in force or ask the Supreme Court to declare the law unconstitutional. The President must promulgate the law if the Supreme Court declares it constitutional.

3.2 The acts of the Government

The Government and its ministers issue *regulations* and *orders* on the basis of and for the implementation of legislative acts.[29] Regulations are of general application[30] and are issued for the management of Government agencies, and for the exercise of supervisory control over Government agencies.[31] An order issued by the Government is of specific application. Both regulations and orders must be published in the *Riigi Teataja* (the state gazette).

Ministers may also issue *regulations* and *directives*, and certain officials may issue directives with respect to the organisation of the work of their agencies.[32]

3.3 Normative acts of departments and the local administration

The directors general and the officials of the executive agencies or inspectorates may issue *precepts* and *decisions* concerning specific cases in their exercise of state supervision.[33] The procedure for the issuance of such precepts and decisions is yet to be specified by a separate act.

Local government councils may issue *regulations* and *resolutions,* [34] and the executive bodies of the local government councils may issue *regulations* and *orders.*[35]

The *Riigikogu* is not required to approve any secondary legislation other than its own non-legislative acts (i.e. resolutions, statements, declarations, addresses). Furthermore, the legislative powers of Parliament cannot be delegated to the Government.

4. DESCRIPTION OF THE SYSTEM OF COURTS DEALING WITH ADMINISTRATIVE LAW ISSUES

4.1 The administrative law courts separate from the criminal and civil law courts

Generally, administrative judges form administrative courts (panels) within the *county and city courts,* which are the courts of first instance for civil and criminal law matters. If necessary, separate administrative law courts are formed.[36]

The *circuit courts* are courts of appeal and are divided into three panels: civil, criminal, and administrative. If an administrative panel is not formed in a given circuit court, administrative appeals are heard by the civil panel.

In the *Supreme Court,* civil, criminal, and administrative panels review court judgements by way of cassation. The Constitutional Review Panel of the Supreme Court hears applications from the President, the Legal Chancellor and lower courts regarding the constitutionality of legislation.

4.2 Jurisdiction of the courts

The administrative courts hear administrative cases which are within their jurisdiction[37] as provided by the Administrative Offences Code[38] and APC. The civil law courts have jurisdiction over civil law cases as specified by the General Principles of the Civil Code Act[39] and the Civil Code[40] in accordance with the CiPC. Similarly, criminal law courts have jurisdiction over criminal law matters regulated by the Criminal Code[41] and the CrPC.

4.3 Quasi-judicial institutions

Courts are the sole administrators of justice according to Article 146 of the Constitution. Section 1 of the Courts Act has a similar provision and states that justice is administered only by courts in Estonia. They must be independent in their activities and must administer justice in accordance with the Constitution and the laws.

Notwithstanding these legal requirements, there are quasi-judicial bodies for adjudicating cases requiring professional expertise. Two examples of quasi-judicial bodies will suffice to illustrate the point:

1. The by-laws of the Auditors Association[42] provide that the Association may impose disciplinary punishment and deprive auditors of their license;
2. Subsection 4(5) of the Estonian Bar Association Act[43] provides that its Professional Conduct Committee is competent to consider matters arising from breaches of professional ethics and disciplinary requirements.

Furthermore, the Labour Disputes Committee, acting pursuant to the Resolution of Individual Labour Disputes Act,[44] represents an optional quasi-judicial body. Both employees and employers may seek a resolution of disputes by a court pursuant to the CiPC or by the Labour Disputes Committee. However, if one of the parties has submitted a request to the Committee, a court may not hear the case.

5. GENERAL PROCEDURAL LAWS OR CODES OF ADMINISTRATIVE LAW

5.1 Administrative Procedures

There is no single, exhaustive code of administrative procedure in Estonia. Instead, the administrative procedures of appeal and judicial review are elaborated in the Administrative Procedure Code, the Civil Procedure Code, the Response to Petitions Act, and the Administrative Offences Code.

5.1.1 INTERNAL APPEAL PROCEDURES

i) Challenging of Administrative Acts and Legislation of Specific Application

According to Article 46 of the Constitution, everyone has a right of recourse to state agencies, local governments and their officials. An internal administrative appeal, i.e. disputing certain acts and legislation of administrative bodies, may be instituted by submitting a memorandum or petition to the appropriate agency. The general procedure for review of and response to memoranda and petitions, the review and response to which is not provided for in other acts, is described in the Response to Petitions Act.

Under this law state agencies, local governments, and their officials are required to register the memoranda and petitions addressed to them and respond to them in writing not later than within one month after the receipt of the petition or memorandum. If further investigation is needed, the deadline may be extended for up to two months. The complainant must be informed of the extension in writing.[45]

It is prohibited for the recipient of a memorandum containing complaints to forward it to the bodies or officials whose activities are the subject of the complaint.[46] If a complainant does not agree with a decision made on the basis of a memorandum or petition, the complainant has the right to appeal to a higher state body or court. Where the decision was made by the executive body of a local government council, the appeal must be addressed either to the corresponding council or to a court.[47] Where no response is given to the memoranda and petitions, or the response is inadequate, the official is held responsible by way of a disciplinary or court procedure.[48]

Pre-trial (internal review) procedures for settling certain types of disputes may be prescribed in special acts.[49] This is a voluntary alternative, however, because a person always has the right to recourse to the courts based on Article 15 of the Constitution. This states that everyone whose rights and freedoms are violated has a right to recourse in the courts.

ii) Application by a person regarding legislation of general application

Pursuant to the Legal Chancellor Activities Organisation Act,[50] every person has the right to file a petition with the Legal Chancellor to review the conformity of an act or other legislation of general application with the Constitution or the law.[51]

5.1.2 PROCEDURE FOR SEEKING JUDICIAL REVIEW BEFORE A COURT

The procedure for recourse to an administrative court is provided for in Chapter II of the APC.

i) Application by individuals regarding legislation of specific application or administrative acts

Protests against a piece of legislation or an act of a body, agency or official referred to in Section 4 of the APC may be filed with an administrative court by a body which, by law, has been assigned a supervisory function over the activities of the bodies, agencies, and officials referred to in Section 4 of the APC. *Complaints* are filed by all other persons or bodies. If the law requires a pre-trial procedure for the resolution of certain complaints or protests, recourse to an administrative court may be taken only after the complaint or protest concerning a violation of rights or restriction of freedoms has been denied in full or in part in the pre-trial procedure.[52]

The territorial jurisdiction of the administrative courts is stipulated in Section 6 of the APC. Unless otherwise provided by law, the above-mentioned complaints and protests are filed with an administrative court according to the location of the body or agency or the place of employment of the official whose legislation or act is complained of or protested against.

Section 7 of the APC provides a time limit for filing a complaint or protest. The filing with an administrative court must take place by the deadline stated in the specific law regulating the case. Where such a deadline is not provided by a specific law, the application must be filed within one month after the complainant became or should have become aware of the violation of his or her rights or freedoms. If the law requires a pre-trial procedure for resolution of a complaint or protest, the limitation period for recourse to an administrative court begins to run on the date the complainant learned of the result of the pre-trial procedure.

Section 8 of the APC specifies the content of the complaint or protest. They must be filed in writing, be signed by the complainant or protester and must set out the character of the alleged violation. The decision of the court of first instance may be appealed in accordance with the APC.

ii) Application by a court or the Legal Chancellor to the Constitutional Review Panel of the Supreme Court concerning legislation of general application

The courts and the Legal Chancellor may file an application directly with the Supreme Court in order to verify the conformity of legislation of general application to the Constitution or law. If, in the course of a trial, a court concludes that the applicable legislation is in conflict with the Constitution, the court will declare the legislation unconstitutional and refuse to apply it. The court will notify the Supreme Court and the Legal Chancellor of its decision and initiate constitutional review proceedings in the Supreme Court.[53] The application must set out the particulars of the legislation contested and the reasons of the applicant.

If the Legal Chancellor, in reviewing legislation, a complaint or protest, finds that a legislative act of general application is, fully or in part, in conflict with the Constitution or the law, he or she can require the legislative body to bring it into conformity with the Constitution and the law within 20 days. If the body which has passed the disputed act of general application does not comply, the Legal Chancellor applies to the Constitutional Review Panel of the Supreme Court to declare the legislative act or some of its provisions invalid.[54]

5.1.3 SCOPE OF AND GROUNDS FOR JUDICIAL REVIEW

No administrative acts are exempt from judicial review in Estonia. Section 15 of the Constitution states that everyone whose rights and freedoms are violated has the right of recourse to the courts. Everyone has the right, while his or her case is before a court, to petition for any relevant law, other legislation or procedure to be declared unconstitutional. The courts must observe the Constitution and declare unconstitutional any law, other legislation or procedure, which violates the rights and freedoms provided by the Constitution or which is otherwise in conflict with the Constitution.

Legislation of general application is subject to review by the Constitutional Review Panel of the Supreme Court according to Section 4 of the CRPA. Resolutions passed by the *Riigikogu* are also subject to review by the Constitutional Review Panel of the Supreme Court, even though such resolutions are considered to be legislation of specific application.[55]

According to Section 5 of the APC, anyone who finds that his or her rights have been violated or freedoms restricted by legislation or an act of a body, agency or official referred to in Section 4 of the APC may file a complaint with an administrative court. An association of persons, including an association which is not a legal person, also has the right of recourse to an administrative court in the interests of its members or other persons if its founding document, articles of association or relevant law grants it this right. This right also extends to a local government or a national minority cultural autonomy agency.

According to Section 3 of the APC, an administrative court has within its competence the resolution of complaints about and protests against the acts of the bodies of executive power, local governments, national minority cultural autonomy agencies or officials referred to in Section 4 of the Code. The courts can also decide on complaints of and protests against decisions of electoral committees in the cases prescribed by the law and disputes arising from administrative contracts. Finally, the jurisdiction of the administrative courts covers the review of administrative offences decisions pursuant to procedures provided for in the Administrative Offences Code, as well as the resolution of other matters which are placed within the competence of an administrative court by specific laws.

The competence of the administrative courts does not cover complaints and protests referred to in subsection 3(1) of the APC if their resolution is related to a civil law dispute belonging within the competence of a county or city court. Requests and complaints about legislation of general application which are subject to resolution pursuant to the procedure provided for in the CRPA are also excluded, as well as the requests and complaints to be resolved pursuant to the procedure provided for in the CiPC or CrPC.

Section 4 of the APC lists the bodies, agencies, and officials whose acts can be complained about or protested against in administrative review proceedings. A complaint or protest may be filed pursuant to clause 3 (1) 1) with an administrative court with respect to:

1. Legislation or an act of the Government of the Republic, a ministry, executive agency, inspectorate, another body of executive power or their officials;
2. Legislation or an act of a county governor, individual members of a county government, a body performing the administrative functions of a county or their officials;
3. Legislation or an act of the representative body of a national minority cultural autonomy agency, its executive body or an official of the latter;
4. Legislation or an act of a local government council, its executive body or an official of the latter;

5. Legislation or an act of another autonomous agency or its official;
6. Legislation or an act of a police chief, police inspector, notary person or an official of the Vital Statistics Registry Office;
7. Legislation or an act of a non-profit association or the directing body of a union of these associations or their officials;
8. Legislation or an act of an electoral commission.

For the purposes of the APC, "official" means an official of a body or agency referred to in clauses 4 (1) 1)–5) of the APC who, by law or other legislation, has been assigned administrative, managerial, operative or organisational functions or functions of authoritative representation.

The secondary legislative acts concerning which a complaint or protest may be filed with an administrative court are resolutions, orders, directives or other acts of a body, agency or official referred to in clause 4 of the APC, the content of which is not of general application, as well as administration contracts.

5.1.4 JUDICIAL REMEDIES

Subsection 20 (1) of the APC specifies the orders that an administrative judge may issue:

1. He or she may declare the legislation or the act complained about or protested against unlawful in full or in part;
2. He or she may deny the request for judicial review; or
3. He or she may terminate or suspend the activities of, or fine, a non-profit association or a union of these associations for a violation of the law.

A court order or ruling which is made on the basis of a complaint or protest and concerning which an appeal or special complaint is not filed enters into force after 10 days from its announcement. If an appeal or special complaint has been filed, the court order or ruling enters into force after its announcement by a circuit court. A copy of the court order or ruling which has entered into force is to be promptly sent to the body of executive power, local government, national minority cultural autonomy agency or their officials with respect to whom the court decision has been made.[56]

The Constitutional Review Panel of the Supreme Court may, pursuant to subsection 19 (1) of the CRPA, issue an order to:

1. deny an application;
2. satisfy an application and declare the legislation of general application invalid in full or in part.

The order enters into force on the day of pronouncement; it is final and cannot be appealed.[57] The implementation of orders of the Supreme Court are mandatory for all state authorities, local governments, courts, officials, and legal and natural persons.[58]

6. OMBUDSMAN

There is no formal office of the ombudsman in Estonia. The formal supervision of the constitutionality of legislation and acts is threefold. Thus, in addition to the preventive supervision over the laws by the President, in the form of a suspensive veto, and the supervision for legality and constitutionality by the Constitutional Review Panel of the Supreme Court, the Legal Chancellor has the power to exercise supervision over all levels of legislation.[59]

The Legal Chancellor is appointed to office, for a term of seven years, by the *Riigikogu* upon a proposal of the President and is independent. He is removable from office only by a court order. Every person has the right to file a petition with the Legal Chancellor to control the conformity of a law or other legislation of general application with the Constitution or the law. Copies of all legislation must be sent to the Legal Chancellor.

The Legal Chancellor reviews legislation of general application of the legislative and executive power as well as the acts of the local government.[60] If a conflict between these acts and the Constitution or other laws is found, the Legal Chancellor requests that the issuing body amend the act to ensure legal conformity.[61] If the act conflicts with a treaty of a specified duration, the Legal Chancellor will request suspension of the legal instrument for that time. In exceptional cases, if he or she finds that the legislation of general application endangers the life or health of natural persons or violates a treaty in force, he or she proposes that the issuing body suspend the force of the legislation until it is brought into conformity with the Constitution and the laws. The Legal Chancellor can ask the Supreme Court to declare legislation unconstitutional if the issuing body fails to comply within 20 days after receipt of the Chancellor's proposal.[62]

7. OTHER FORMS OF SUPERVISION OVER THE ADMINISTRATION

7.1 Budget Audit Office

The State Audit Office (hereinafter SAO) is an independent state body. It exercises economic control in order to contribute to the preservation of, and to ensure the prudent use of, state assets via auditing, pursuant to the State Audit Office Act.[63] The SAO audits the financial activities of the agencies of the executive, legislative, and judicial power, as well as state enterprises and local governments, with respect to state assets and recipients of state funds or property. It also supervises the compliance of public procurement with legislation and contracts.[64] In order to perform these duties, the chief auditors have the right to enter upon the premises of, demand and remove documents from, and carry out tests and measurements on, the entity under audit.[65] The Auditor General may issue regulations and directives for the organisation of the work of the SAO.[66]

7.2 Inspectorates

The inspectorates are government agencies which operate within a ministry. They are responsible for state supervision and apply enforcement powers of the state according to law.[67]

7.3 Public prosecutors

Among other duties, the Public Prosecutor exercises state supervision over the legality of police activities and the legality of surveillance agency activities with the Surveillance Act. The Public Prosecutor also initiates the contestation of oaths of officials and prosecutions thereof.[68]

8. PARLIAMENTARY COMMITTEES

Although the parliamentary standing committees do not exercise direct supervisory control over the administration, they do monitor the way in which the Government administers those laws.[69] There are 10 standing committees representing the following areas: finance, economics, constitutional issues, law, foreign affairs, national defence, cultural affairs, social affairs, rural life, and environment. Each of these committees is responsible for the bills in its area until the act is passed by the *Riigikogu* in the final reading. They also have the right to initiate acts.

According to Section 17 of the *Riigikogu* Procedure Act, the *Riigikogu* may form ad hoc and select committees in order to perform either specific or temporary tasks. The *Riigikogu* may also determine their membership, scope and terms of authority. Once the activities of the ad hoc and select committees has been terminated they must present a report to the *Riigikogu*. As of 30 April 1997, there were four ad hoc and select committees.

II. DEVELOPMENTS IN ADMINISTRATIVE LAW DURING 1996-1997

INTRODUCTION

During 1996, several important changes took place in the Estonian administrative law system. First, the court system was restructured to accommodate the institution of judge's assistant. This restructuring occurred due to provisions of the Commercial Code, the Land Register Act and the Marital Property Contract Act, which prescribe various forms of registration and administrative paperwork. These prescriptions added to the workload of the courts because, although somewhat removed from the more essential functions of the court, they are still within the court's jurisdiction. The introduction of the judge's assistant was intended to alleviate some of the work pressures on the courts.

Second, local government elections were held in Estonia in 1996. The *Riigikogu* passed a new Local Government Election Act just in time for the elections. The most significant change resulting from this Act concerned the status of aliens since, under certain conditions, they were permitted to vote.

A considerable part of the second half of this chapter is devoted to the changes in land reform. Problems arising from land reform accounted for a huge part of administrative decisions during 1996 in Estonia. Indeed, more than half of the matters heard by the administrative courts in the first instance concerned ownership reform.[70] Estonia has tried to finalise its land reform for several years now, since economic growth and development are believed to depend in part on a stable resolution of land ownership uncertainties. In addition to the Land Reform Act, several other acts such as the Land Utilisation Planning Act, the Planning and Construction Act and the Land Assessment Act were amended.

Another important change in the Estonian legislative landscape was the ratification of the Convention on the Status of Refugees and Protocol (January 31, 1967) on the Status of Refugees and the Refugees Act. According to Mart Nutt, a member of the Constitutional Committee of the *Riigikogu*, many states have identified the ratification of this Convention as a precondition for the abolition of their visa requirements. The ratification of the Convention in turn requires the institution of a domestic act governing refugees. Mr. Nutt also suggested that the existence of a Refugees Act is critical to Estonia's aspirations for EU membership.

Another important change was the invalidation of the USSR domestic passport. This passport was declared invalid as a means of identification as of the middle of May 1997. This amendment has been on the books for some time, but its prescribed entry into force had been postponed many times. A. Kollist, the head of the Citizenship and Migration Agency, stated that in order to declare this identification invalid, all stateless persons had to be issued with alien's passports and a residence permit, and foreign nationals had to be provided with residence permits.

A. THE CONSTITUTION

There were no constitutional amendments during the last year.

B. LEGISLATION (ACTS)

1. PROCEDURAL AND GENERAL ORGANISATIONAL LAWS

1.1 The organisation of the judicial system

The Status of Judges Act, the Courts Act, the Land Register Act, Commercial Code, and the Marital Property Register Amendment Act[71] brought about considerable change in the manner in which the more routine court orders are issued. Specifically, they created the position of "judge's assistant" (*kohtunikuabi*). There was a debate among the drafters whether the term should be "judge's assistant" (*kohtunikuabi*) or "assistant judge" (*abikohtunik*). The term "judge's assistant" was finally chosen, as the qualifications and the requirements of the oath of office are less than those for a judge.[72] Similarly the terms of their accountability are different. Whereas judges and lay judges are independent and exercise their powers only in accordance with the law, judge's assistants, in issuing orders, should follow the instructions of a judge.[73]

The position of judge's assistant was created to alleviate some of the pressures on the court system with respect to issuing orders concerning the Land Register, Commercial Register and Marital Property Register. Prior to the entry into force of this amending act, judges appointed by the chief judge of a county or town court issued register entry orders and imposed fines.[74] After the amendment, such orders and fines of, for example, up to 400 days' wages are issued or imposed by judge's assistants. Furthermore, in the Commercial Code, an appeal from such an order or fine is made to the same judge's assistant, who must review the appeal within 15 days. If the appeal is denied or allowed only in part, the appellant may submit the appeal to a judge for review. The provisions for the judge's review of the matter are the same as prior to the amendment: the application must be filed within 15 days from the decision of the judge's assistant, unless extraordinary circumstances justify the disregard of the limitation.

A judge's assistant must have a higher legal education and be at least 21 years of age. He or she must have passed the judge's assistant examination, in all but exceptional circumstances, and is appointed to the office by the Minister of Justice. The competition committee for such positions consists of two judges of a court of first instance appointed by the Chief Justice of the Supreme Court, one judge's assistant, and two representatives of the Ministry of Justice appointed by the Minister of Justice.

Pursuant to this amending act, the Minister of Justice issued a regulation approving the Court Register Department Administration Rules.[75] The regulation prescribes that the register departments of the courts must include a department head, who is a judge appointed by the chief judge of the county or town court; judge's assistants; and clerks. Non-profit associations and foundations continue to have their registers maintained under the previous system with the direct involvement of judges.

1.2 Laws concerning the structure and the prerogatives of the administration

A new Local Government Council Election Act[76] was passed in time for the local government elections held on October 20, 1996. Its most important feature was that it allowed aliens to vote in local government elections for the first time.[77] In order to be eligible to vote, the aliens had to satisfy the following requirements: a) to have attained 18 years of age by election day; b) to have resided permanently in the territory of the local government since January 1, 1996, and c) to have submitted an application for a residence permit and have a decision on the application. Additional provisions were also made for Paldiski, a region formerly accessible only to the Soviet (later Russian) army. Local government elections in that area were held for the first time, and provisions for their administration had to be organised separately.[78]

2. SUBSTANCE - LEGISLATION

2.1 Management of the Economy: Privatisation

The Use of Money Received from Privatisation Act[79] requires that the revenue from privatisation should be deposited in specified proportions into special-purpose bank accounts. The law regulated the revenue received pursuant to the Privatisation Act,[80] or from the privatisation of municipal property by local governments, the privatisation of state-owned residential and non-residential real estate property, and the privatisation of state land based on the Land Reform Act. The special-purpose bank accounts in practice directly earmark the money for compensation of former owners, environmental protection, land reform, establishment of reserve funds and other purposes. Local governments, for example, must use the local government relocation funds for subsidising or reimbursing occupants of residential real estate property in the purchase of the property upon its return to its former owners.

The county governor supervises local governments in relation to the administration of the funds received from privatisation. The Minister of Economic Affairs supervises the re-privatisation of state residential real estate property and state-owned apartments, while the Minister of Finance supervises the administration in relation to all other issues specified in the act.

The law gives a number of enforcement mechanisms to the supervising authorities. For example, if funds are not deposited within 12 business days, the Minister of Finance has the right to issue a directive demanding remittance of a fine for the delay of 0.5 per cent per day of the amount due.

2.2 Ownership and management of (agricultural) lands

2.2.1 RESTITUTION OF LAND

The Act on Amendments to Legislation Concerning the Land Reform[81] brought about serious changes in this area of economic reform. The purpose of the Act is to resolve the problems related to land reform as a whole. It provides more precise rules of land reform and reduces the amount of secondary legislation. At the same time, however, no changes have been made in the basic principles of land reform concerning, for example, successors or the rights of the owners of buildings.[82]

The philosophy behind this Act is based on the principle that it was only the *possession* and not the *right to ownership* of the former owners that had been disrupted and violated during the time of Soviet rule. Registered immovable (real estate) property had been in the bad faith possession of the USSR. The Act remedies this situation and restores the property to the Republic of Estonia. According to this philosophy, Estonia is not a possessor in bad faith, since it has not expropriated the property unlawfully. Therefore, the property is to be duly returned.

Under the law, restitution is to be conducted as an extra-judicial procedure.[83] If property is not returned in the course of carrying out the reform procedures by the administration, it could be claimed by its owners before a court.

Section 1 of the Land Reform Act has been significantly amended. According to the amendment, the purpose of the Land Reform Act is the restructuring of entire relations concerning land ownership. Prior to the amendment, the purpose was to directly regulate the relations concerning land ownership.

Prior to the amendment, contractual use of agricultural land was regulated by the Land Reform Act. Since then, only building leases established for the benefit of the owner of buildings as movables, leases of state-owned agricultural lands to current users, and the establishment of usufruct for the benefit of persons who use land on the basis of the Estonian SSR Farm Act,[84] are regulated by the Land Reform Act. Contractual use of state-owned land in any other manner is covered by the State Assets Act.[85] Private owners of land must observe the provisions of the Law of Property Act[86] and the Civil Code in lease contracts.[87]

Significant changes were introduced concerning the exact procedure of restitution.[88] Subsection 6 (1) provides that land is to be returned to the owners as determined only on maps and plans. Previously this option was available by virtue of subsection 20 (5) of the Land Cadastre Act[89] and a regulation of the Government issued on its basis. Under the new arrangement, on-site determination of a plot of land takes place later and at the request and expense of the owner of the land.

Section 8 of the Amendments to Legislation Concerning Land Reform Act introduced some changes in the Land Use Planning Act.[90] According to the amendment, local governments are responsible for land use planning. This is an activity which was largely in the domain of the county governments. County governors still exercise supervision over the legality of land use planning effected by local governments. According to the amendment, the change of the plan for land use in the course of the land reform is carried out at the expense of the parties and not at the expense of the state. If the land is owned by the state, it is considered to be a party.

The other significant amendment to Section 6 of the Land Reform Act was the addition of subsection (4): now, the partial return of land is permitted only if sufficient reasons exist. The partial return of land was formerly permitted but is now considered economically inefficient. Previously, registered immovable property in the cities was not returned if buildings belonging to other persons were situated on the plot and if it was impossible to divide the registered immovable property in accordance with the law. Section 7 of the Land Reform Act has been amended in such a way as to allow the return of land irrespective of whether the property is capable of being divided. However, land that is adjacent to the buildings or structures of another person and is necessary for the servicing and use of the buildings will not be returned.

Further amendments concerned the definition of "lands necessary for the servicing and use of a building". This has now been established on the basis of the procedure prescribed in the Planning and Construction Act.[91] Under the former situation this was done pursuant to a procedure established by the Government of the Republic. The Planning and Construction Act includes public process and more effectively protects the rights of persons entitled to restitution. Basically, the procedure was greatly simplified.

Section 21 was added to the Planning and Construction Act. According to the amendment, public discussion and presentations are not mandatory, as they generally are, in relation to the preparation of a local plan with not more than three single-family dwellings, cottages or garden houses. They may be substituted with the written consent of the owners of the registered immovable property and the holders of a right to use land in the planning area. According to the amendment of Section 22 of the same act, a local plan need not be approved by a county government if it is prepared in accordance with a general plan and there are no unresolved planning disputes. Such local plans are also excluded from supervision.

According to the amendment to Section 7 of the Land Reform Act, an owner of a plot of land no longer has the right of pre-emption upon disposition of a building situated on his or her land.

Section 11 has now been repealed and, hence, the Land Reform Act ceases to provide for substitution of land. This was formerly effected on the basis of a local government order, while privatisation was done by entering into a contract with the state. According to subsection 16 (5) of the Act on Amendments to Legislation

Concerning Land Reform, applications for substitution of land are deemed to be equal to applications for privatisation by right of pre-emption.

Section 12 of the Land Reform Act, which provides for the return of land to joint owners, has also been amended. The amendment affects the restitution of lands under buildings beyond the city limits. Land under buildings and land necessary for servicing buildings is now returned according to the share of common ownership in the building. The rest of the land is returned as separate registered immovable property in accordance with the shares recognised in the accepted claim for restitution. In registering immovable property the entitled subjects may also agree to different proportions.

Amendments have been also made to the Land Assessment Act[92] with respect to the basis for determining compensation. Previously, the basis for determining compensation was the value of land as of 1940, which was later amended to be the current assessed value of land. Assessment of the value of land for which compensation is sought is now required to be carried out pursuant to the accepted customs and the internationally recognised principles of land assessment.

A significant amendment to Section 14 of the Land Reform Act concerns the situation in which several entitled persons have applied for the restitution of a plot of land. In such cases the land is not to be divided among them but will, instead, be returned into their common ownership and may be subdivided later at the request and expense of the owners.

According to the amendment to Section 15 of the Land Reform Act, return of or compensation for land is decided by the local government pursuant to a procedure established by the Government of the Republic. Before the amendment the authority authorised to return or compensate for land was not specified by law. The county governors exercise supervision over the return of land and have the right to apply measures provided in the Government Act.

Section 17 of the Land Reform Act, which provided for restrictions on the minimum size of a lot upon division of land, has been repealed. According to the Land Cadastre Act the smallest cadastral unit may be 30 square metres.

New provisions in Sections 19 (1) and 19 (2) of the Land Reform Act have expanded the categories of persons entitled to a right to restitution. The succession of the right of restitution is now effected via the Law of Succession Act,[93] which entered into force on January 1, 1997.

The chapter on privatisation of land has been significantly amended. According to the amendments to subsection 20 (2) of the Land Reform Act, privatisation of a building in state or municipal ownership, together with the land, is now regulated on the basis of and pursuant to the procedure provided for in the Privatisation Act. The Privatisation Agency had thus far privatised buildings as movables. The competence of the Privatisation Agency Council has been expanded, since before it was the Government of the Republic which decided on the sale of land to legal persons. Land is sold by the state upon the privatisation of a building or upon the transfer of shares of a state-owned commercial enterprise. For the latter option, the land must be transferred to the balance sheet of the enterprise before the transfer of stocks.

The assessment of land under buildings is done by the Privatisation Agency. The local governments are responsible for the determination of the purpose and assessable value of the lot and of the lot itself.

According to the amendments to Section 21 of the Land Reform Act, anyone may acquire land in the course of the reforms, unless otherwise provided by law. The most significant amendment here is that aliens may purchase land under buildings and necessary for the servicing of buildings, as well as land used on the basis of the Farm Act, without permission. Previously, they could only purchase land necessary for the servicing of a dwelling and could privatise land under other buildings only by permission of the Government of the Republic and the local government. Under the new arrangement, the government may prescribe areas where aliens or Estonian legal persons in private law need permission from a county governor in order to privatise land. In so doing, the opinion of the relevant local government must also be considered.

Amendments to Section 22 of the Land Reform Act introduced the mechanism of restricted auction for the privatisation of land, in addition to the already existing public auction, and the right of pre-emption. The purpose of the restricted auction is to promote the purchase of land by certain types of persons who, from a social perspective, have some preferential rights. These are persons to whom land was not returned due to the physical impossibility of doing so, young families, tenants living in restituted houses, and natural persons engaged in agricultural production. The county governor, after taking the relevant local government's opinion into account, decides which lots are to be privatised and who will be invited to participate in an auction.[94]

Privatisation can be competently authorised by the county governor according to the new Section 22 of the Land Reform Act. Local governments continue to carry out the preliminary activities necessary for privatisation. According to subsection (2), a county governor or the Privatisation Agency may, in agreement with a local government council, authorise the local government to organise the privatisation of land by a right of pre-emption on behalf of the state. Where there are buildings on land which must be privatised by the Privatisation Agency, the land on which they stand must also be privatised by the Agency. The same applies if there are buildings owned by a legal person whose shares or stocks were sold by the Privatisation Agency.

A new Section 22 of the Land Reform Act regulates the payment for land. The selling price of land to be privatised by a right of pre-emption is the assessed value of the land. This is also the starting price of land to be privatised by auction. Detailed procedures and conditions regulate payment in different cases.

Fundamental amendments have been made to Section 23 of the Land Reform Act, which sets out the privatisation procedure. Privatisation by a right of pre-emption may be effected on the basis of plans and maps and may be initiated before a decision on the return of land is made, hence speeding up the procedure. A decision concerning an application for privatisation by a right of pre-emption is made within three months after the submission of the application.[95] Land is privatised at the expense of the purchaser. An important simplification of the process is that upon privatisation of land, contracts of sale and other types of contracts may be entered into in unattested written form.[96]

Subsection (7) was added to clause 28 of the Land Reform Act, requiring land which was in the ownership of a local government on June 16, 1940, to be transferred into the ownership of the local government.

Section 30 of the Land Reform Act has been repealed. Now, the problems concerning the administration of state lands are resolved pursuant to the State Assets Act. Only the retention of land in state ownership is carried out on the basis of the Land Reform Act.

Finally, the new Section 36 of the Land Reform Act prescribes that the current rights of use of land terminate upon the restitution or privatisation of the land.

The Act on Amendments to Legislation Concerning Land Reform has facilitated a far-reaching land reform and has resolved many of the problems that arose in the process of land restitution.

2.2.2 REAL ESTATE PROPERTY RIGHTS OF ALIENS

The Restrictions on Transfer of Immovable Property Ownership to Aliens, Foreign States, and Legal Persons Act[97] deals with the transfer of immovable property to an alien or a foreign legal person, the transfer of possession of immovables to an alien or foreign legal person, and the transfer of ownership and possession of immovables to a foreign state. For the purposes of the Act, an alien is a person who is not an Estonian citizen.

The power to grant permission for the sale of land to an alien rests with county governors. Permission for the sale of land to a foreign state may be granted by the Minister of Foreign Affairs or by the Government of the Republic. Subsection 2(3) of the Act specifies the districts in which the acquisition of land by an alien is prohibited, although the Government of the Republic has the right to make exceptions in certain cases.

The Act does not apply to:

1. the transfer of an apartment ownership and to the ownership or the possession of an apartment building lease;
2. the transfer of immovable property ownership or possession of a property held by the state or a local government unit;
3. succession;
4. the transfer of an immovable to the joint ownership of spouses, if at least one of the spouses is an Estonian citizen; and
5. if otherwise provided for in a foreign treaty ratified by the *Riigikogu*.

2.3 Environment

The Vienna Convention for the Protection of the Ozone Layer, concluded at Vienna on March 22, 1985, was ratified[98] and entered into force on January 15, 1997. Together with it, the Montreal Protocol on Substances Damaging the Ozone Layer, concluded at Montreal on September 16, 1987, was also ratified.

2.4 Customs

The International Convention on Harmonisation of Border Control of Goods, concluded in Geneva on October 21, 1982, was ratified[99] and entered into force on June 4, 1996. The Convention aims to facilitate the movement of goods by reducing the number and level of controls over the sea, air, or land transportation of goods for import, export or transit.

2.5 Health care

The Psychiatric Care Act[100] regulates the procedure and conditions for providing psychiatric care to a person, the relationships between the person and the psychiatric medical institutions, the obligations of the local governments and the state in providing psychiatric care as well as the rights of the person under psychiatric care.[101] Psychiatric care may be obtained by individuals on their own decision. Persons without full and active legal capacity may receive psychiatric care on the recommendation, or with the consent, of their legal representative.[102] The Act also provides for cases in which psychiatric care may be prescribed without the person's consent.[103] The Act amends Section 17.2 of the APC and allows for the granting, extension or revocation by an administrative court judge of the permits for mandatory psychiatric care regardless of the consent of the person. An application for a judicial decision is filed by the chief physician of a hospital and is heard promptly by a judge without a court session. Permissions are granted for 30 days and may be extended for up to 90 days. Psychiatric care without consent of the person may be terminated prematurely upon the decision of two psychiatrists on the conditions specified in the Act: the court must be notified of this by the chief physician. An administrative court judge may terminate a permission as well, based on the application of a spouse, legal representative or close relative of the person or on the protest of an official exercising supervision; the judge is also obliged to hear the opinion of the chief physician of the hospital or its representative. Regardless of the consent of the person, decisions concerning psychiatric care must be justified and in writing, with a copy sent to the applicant or the protester of the decision.[104]

2.6 Historical heritage

The Museum Act[105] regulates the activities and organisation of museums and museum collections.[106] There are three different types of museums: state, municipal, and private museums. The by-laws of state museums are approved by a minister or county governor, while those of the municipal museums are approved by the local government councils.[107] The Act also provides for central museums designated by the Government of the Republic, and county museums specified by the Minister of Culture.[108]

Supervision over museum collections is exercised by the Ministry of Culture.[109] The Council of Museums is an advisory body in the area of government of the Ministry of Culture, and advises the Minister of Culture on matters arising from the Act. It consists of the representatives and founders of museums, and its membership and by-laws are approved by the Minister of Culture.[110]

2.7. Administration of Political Processes

2.7.1 NATIONAL SECURITY

The Emergency Situation Act[111] provides the bases, conditions, and procedures for the declaration of an emergency situation as well as the measures that may be implemented and the rights, duties, and liability of persons in such a situation.[112] Pursuant to Section 87 of the Constitution, an emergency situation may be declared in the event of natural disaster or catastrophe or to prevent the spread of an infectious disease. The Government of the Republic declares an emergency situation in the entire state or part of it. He will also appoint as director of the emergency situation the minister in whose area of government the events justifying the emergency situation have occurred.[113] For violations of certain requirements of the Act, health protection agency officials, the policc, fire brigade, and the rescue commands have the right to impose fines.[114]

The State of Emergency Act[115] provides the bases, conditions and procedure for the declaration of a state of emergency and the competence of agencies in such a state. It also provides the measures that may be implemented during a state of emergency and the rights, obligations and liability of the persons therein.[116] During a state of emergency, the following groups of rights and freedoms are suspended:

a. rights to self-realisation, freedom of movement, inviolability of the person, choice of occupation, freedom of association;

b. rights to possession, use, and disposal of owned property;

c. rights to inviolability of the home, movement and choice of residence, immigration to and emigration from Estonia, confidentiality of mail, telegraph, telephone and other commonly used means of communication;

d. rights to access to information intended for public use, access to information in the state agencies, local governments and their archives, free dissemination of ideas, opinions, beliefs and other information in print, picture or other means, and peaceful assembly and meeting without prior permission.[117]

Section 17 specifies what measures the Government of the Republic is permitted to take in a state of emergency; the Government is also authorised to repeal orders of the commander of the state of emergency and of the Chief of Interior Defence. The Legal Chancellor exercises supervision over the legislation concerning a state of emergency, and issued during the state of emergency, for its conformity with the Constitution and other acts.[118]

The Act Amending the Gathering, Recording, Preservation and Use of Materials from Foreign Security and Intelligence Agencies Formerly Active in Estonia Organisation Act[119] transferred the responsibility for maintaining and ensuring access to this information from the State Archive to the State Chancellery.

The State Secrets Amendment Act[120] amended the State Secrets Act[121] by determining the categories of persons who have the right of access to and use of state secrets. There are three categories of authorised persons: a) officials who have the right ex officio; b) officials who hold a permit for employment in an office related to the use and protection of state secrets; c) persons who hold a permit to use state secrets. The officials who have the right to use state secrets ex officio are the President, *Riigikogu* and Government members, the Chief Justice and the justices of the Supreme Court, the Commander and the Commander-in-Chief of the Defence Forces, the Legal Chancellor, the Auditor General, the President and the Chairman of the Bank of Estonia, the State Secretary, and the Public Prosecutor. As of the entry into force of the amendment, all others must hold permits in order to use state secrets. The procedure for granting, refusal to grant, and revocation of permits is provided for in the amendment.

The European Convention on the Suppression of Terrorism Ratification Act[122] entered into force with reservations to part of Article 1 of the Convention as permitted by Article 13 of the Convention.

2.7.2 MEETINGS, MANIFESTATIONS AND STRIKES

The Public Meetings Act[123] provides the requirements which must be observed in organising a public meeting. The Act is based on Article 47 of the Constitution,[124] and its purpose is to ensure the right of persons to assemble peacefully and to conduct meetings in accordance with the fundamental rights, freedoms, and obligations of the individuals.[125] The Act does, however, prescribe restrictions on the organisation and conduct of public meetings. These are considered necessary in order to ensure public order and the safety of participants at public meetings.[126]

At least seven days prior to a public meeting, the organiser must notify the following authorities of the meeting:

1. the rural municipality or city government on the territory where the meeting is to be held,

2. the county government, if the meeting will be held on the territories of several local governments, and

3. the Government of the Republic, if the meeting will be held on the territories of several counties.[127]

Officials of the above-mentioned authorities must deliver a notice regarding the registration of the public meeting notification to the organiser immediately after the receipt of the notification.[128]

2.8 Citizenship and administrative status

2.8.1 RESIDENCE OF FOREIGN NATIONALS; REFUGEES

The Convention on the Status of Refugees and the Protocol (January 31, 1967) on the Status of Refugees Accession Act[129] were ratified by the *Riigikogu* unanimously. The ratification of this Convention is a precondition for Estonia to join the European Union. Mart Nutt, a member of the Constitutional Committee of the *Riigikogu*, stated that this ratification was one of the most important events of the year.[130] The Accession Act provides for reservations to the Convention with respect to Articles 23, 24, 25 and 28 (1) as permitted by Article 42 (2) of the Convention.

The Convention imposes obligations on the signatory states. Certain obligations aim at providing guarantees for the Western countries against refugees who may use Estonia as a transit destination to them. The ratification of the Convention was also a precondition for the abolition of the visa requirements for Estonians travelling to Norway and Sweden.

The importance of the entry into force of the Refugees Act[131] (upon the entry into force of the above-mentioned Convention) cannot be overstated. The concepts and terminology of the Convention and the Protocol have, by virtue of this Act, been adopted into the domestic legislative framework of Estonia. The Act provides for the rights and obligations of refugees in accordance with the Convention.

In general, the Government may grant asylum to a refugee if he or she is persecuted in his or her country of citizenship or permanent residence for reasons of race, religion or political opinion. Asylum may also be granted to the spouse or a minor of a refugee on the basis of the refugee's application. The Government may not grant asylum to economic refugees, persons who have committed crimes against peace or humanity or those who may pose a threat to the security or public order of Estonia.

The Act provides that applicants and refugees have the right of recourse to the courts if their rights and freedoms are violated,[132] and provides for the bases for termination of refugee status.[133]

2.9. Other legislation

The Personal Data Protection Act[134] provides for the protection of the fundamental rights and freedoms of the individuals with regard to processing of personal data. This right must be balanced against the right of persons to freely obtain information and disseminate it for public use. Personal data is divided into sensitive and non-sensitive data. Data is not classified as personal if a concrete person cannot be identified on its basis.[135] Sensitive personal data revealing the religious, political or other beliefs of an Estonian citizen, or an alien residing in Estonia on the basis of a permanent residence permit, may only be processed (this includes disclosure to a third person) with the consent of the person. In other cases, processing or disclosure to a third person of such data is permitted without the consent of the person if the processing is carried out to fulfil obligations prescribed by the law or with the consent of the person unless the processing is contrary to a law or other legislation. Similar restrictions apply to the processing of sensitive personal data revealing ethnic or racial origin, state of health, sexual life, criminal convictions, court-imposed punishments or a criminal proceeding.[136] The Data Protection Supervision Authority is responsible for the monitoring of the compliance with the Act by issuing mandatory precepts to processors of personal data. Disciplinary, administrative, and criminal liability may be sought from persons for violation of the Act.

C. REGULATION

1. OWNERSHIP AND MANAGEMENT OF (AGRICULTURAL) LANDS

The Government of the Republic Regulation Procedure for Exercising Supervision over the Land Reform[137] has been adopted in compliance with clause 30 of the Agricultural Reform Act.[138]

The Minister of Agriculture and the county governors exercise supervision over agricultural reform under conditions provided for in this procedure. Supervision is exercised on the basis of an application by an agricultural reform committee, local government, entitled subject, or on the initiative of the supervisor.[139]

Depending on the results of the inspection, the Minister of Agriculture has the right, under clause 4, to:

1. appoint a trustee on the proposal of a county governor or local government council;
2. make binding proposals to the agricultural reform committees, representatives of the state, a trustee or a liquidator, and other persons involved in the process, to remedy discovered deficiencies and violations; and
3. require a county governor to commence compulsory liquidation of an agricultural co-operative.

Under the regulation, the county governors have the right to:[140]

1. make a proposal to the Minister of Agriculture concerning the appointment of a trustee;
2. make binding proposals to the agricultural reform committee, representatives of the state, a trustee or a liquidator, to remedy discovered deficiencies.

2. ENVIRONMENT

In a effort to harmonise the Estonian legislation with treaties and the European Union legislation, many environmental regulations were passed by the Minister of the Environment. For example, the Regulation on the Levels of Toxic Substances in the Motor Vehicle Fumes and the Levels of Noise of Vehicles[141] brought some of the Estonian standards into conformity with European standards.[142] One of the results of the amendment is that the mandatory annual safety checks of motor vehicles for technical compliance are now more stringent.

3. FINANCE

The Government of the Republic Regulation Procedure for Regular Assessment of Land[143] was adopted in compliance with subsection 5 (4) of the Land Assessment Act. The procedure prescribes the bases for determination of the assessed value of land. The regulation provides the procedures for obtaining necessary information for the regular assessment of land, and for settling disputes in administrative procedure arising from the regular assessment of land.[144]

The State Land Board organises, according to the provisions of clause 8, the assessment in co-operation with the county governments. The county governor designates a person who participates in the assessment in co-operation with an assessor designated by the Land Board, and a representative of the county cadastre department.[145] Public hearings of relevant documentation take place after assessment. Amendment proposals may be made during the public hearings.[146] If an objection is submitted after the specified deadline, a deposit must be paid to the county cadastre department in the amount of the sum that the claimant seeks to have deducted from the land tax. Expenses incurred in the course of resolving an unjustified objection are met out of this deposit. The remainder of the deposit is returned to the person who has submitted the objection, and the entire deposit is to be returned if the objection is accepted.[147]

4. TRANSPORTATION

The Government of the Republic Regulation Accession to the European Agreement on International Road Transport of Dangerous Shipments (ADR)[148] was adopted as prescribed by clause 7(1) 5) of the Foreign Relations Act.[149]

Accession to the above-mentioned agreement, concluded in Geneva on September 30, 1957, its appendices and also the Protocol of October 28, 1957, amending clause *a* of Article 1, and clause *b* of subsections 14 (1) and (3), was ordered by the Government. The Ministry of Foreign Affairs was made responsible for communicating the corresponding notice of accession to the Secretary General of the United Nations. Responsibility for the performance of the obligations arising from the agreement now rests with the Ministry of Transport and Communications. Following the requirements of the international agreement, this Minister approved the Regulation Procedure for Transportation of Dangerous Shipments.[150]

5. EDUCATION

The Government of the Republic approved the regulation "Higher Education Standards"[151] and adopted it via clause 5(2) 7) of the Education Act.[152] According to clause 4 the Ministry of Education supervises the implementation of the Standards. The Standards specify the general requirements for higher education and form one of the bases on which education licences and accreditation of university programmes are issued.[153] They also provide for the general requirements for school, degree, diploma and medical degree programmes. The regulation specifies the necessary qualification of teachers and professors.

6. HEALTH CARE

The Minister of Social Affairs approved the regulation "Advertising of Medical Products"[154] pursuant to the Medical Products Act.[155] This secondary legislative act regulates the advertising of medical products to the public and to the pharmaceuticals industry, as well as the use of samples. The Agency of Medicines is the body which monitors the compliance with the regulation.

7. CITIZENSHIP AND ADMINISTRATIVE STATUS

The Government of the Republic regulation "Declaration of the Invalidity of the Domestic Passport of the Former USSR as a Means of Official Identification in the Republic of Estonia"[156] was passed pursuant to clause 66 of the Identification and Citizenship Documents of Estonian Citizens Act.[157] Before this regulation took effect, Andres Kollist, head of the Citizenship and Migration Agency, stated that in order to declare this identification invalid, all stateless persons had to be issued alien's passports and residence permits, while the foreign nationals had to be provided with residence permits. He estimated the number of persons who had not applied for a residence permit, and were therefore illegally in Estonia, to be approximately 20, 000.[158]

8. RESIDENCE OF FOREIGN NATIONALS AND REFUGEES

The Government of the Republic passed the regulation "Conditions and Procedure for Issuing Alien's Passport.[159] The regulation is based on Section 8 of the Aliens Act.[160]

An alien's passport is issued, extended, renewed, exchanged, held in deposit and declared invalid by the Citizenship and Migration Agency under clause 1. The procedure provides for the format of and the information to be entered in the passport. The conditions of issuance are also prescribed.

9. MINORITIES

The Government of the Republic passed the regulation "Procedure for Maintenance and Use of Lists of National Minorities".[161] The regulation is based on subsection 7(2) of the Cultural Autonomy of National Minorities Act.[162]

For a national minority to claim cultural autonomy, it is necessary to produce a list of persons constituting the minority. Such lists may be prepared, according to clause 1, by cultural associations or their unions. The application is submitted to the Minister of Culture, who must arrange for the publication of a notice in an Estonian- and a Russian-language daily newspaper. In order to review the application, the Minister of Culture forms a committee consisting of representatives of the associations of the cultural minority, the Ministry of Culture, and the Ministry of Internal Affairs. The proposals submitted by the committee to the Minister of Culture are not binding. These lists are also the basis for the preparation of polling lists in order to elect the members of the cultural councils and the other institutions of the cultural autonomy.

A note on informal rules: There is no such jurisprudential concept in Estonia, and it is very difficult to discover the existence and use of such rules.

D. JUDICIAL DECISIONS

INTRODUCTION: STRUCTURE OF JUDGEMENTS AND PUBLISHING REQUIREMENTS

The official reporter of judicial decisions, legislation, and treaties is the *Riigi Teataja*, the state gazette. It is regulated by the *Riigi Teataja* Act.[163] In accordance with this act the *Riigi Teataja* is divided into four parts which are composed of divisions.

The entire rulings of the Constitutional Review Panel of the Supreme Court are published in Part I, Division 3.[164] In Part III of the *Riigi Teataja*, judgements of the Supreme Court, the entire rulings of the Supreme Court *en banc* are published in Division 1. The decisions of the Criminal Panel of the Supreme Court are published in Division 2, of the Administrative Chamber of the Supreme Court in Division 3, of the Civil Chamber of the Supreme Court in Division 4, and of the Special Panel of the Supreme Court in Division 5.[165] The names of persons mentioned in a ruling, except for the names of the judges, may be changed or initials may be used instead.[166]

The rulings themselves are published in the form required of the court procedure laws. The CiPC requires that judgements be in writing and signed by all judges who heard the matter. If the decision was made by a vote, the dissenting opinion(s) are summarised and appended to the decision.[167]

Judgements in the courts of first instance enter into force on the day the 10-day period for appeal expires; in the courts of appeal and in the Supreme Court, judgements enter into force on the day they are pronounced. Apart from those issued by the Supreme Court, there is no requirement for judgements to be published, but copies are sent to the parties not in attendance within five days of the pronouncement of the judgement. The parties in attendance may obtain copies after that time.[168]

The APC requires that judgements be written by the judge himself or under dictation by a court secretary. After making a decision the administrative judge publicly pronounces the judgement not later than within three days after the closing of the court session. The date of pronouncement of the judgement is communicated to the parties to the proceeding. If, in the course of deliberation, it becomes evident that the resolution of the filed complaint or protest is related to a civil law dispute belonging to the competence of a county or city court, the administrative court terminates the proceedings and proposes to the filer of the complaint to file an action pursuant to the CiPC.[169]

A copy of the court decision or ruling must be sent promptly to the body of executive power, the local government, the national minority cultural autonomy agency or the official whose legislation or act is complained about, as well as to the filer of the protest. The complainant must be sent a copy of the court decision or ruling, even if the complainant or his or her representative have not participated in the review of the complaint, or at the request of the complainant.[170]

Court judgements enter into force 10 days after their pronouncement. If an appeal or special complaint is filed, the judgement enters into force with the pronouncement of the judgement by the circuit court.[171]

1. CONSTITUTIONAL COURT

1.1 Judicial review of administrative action

The ruling of November 22, 1996 of the Administrative Panel of the Supreme Court on the Cassation complaint by the representative of A.V. in applying subsections 5 (1) and (4) of the Administrative Procedure Code[172] had important administrative law consequences. The facts of the case were as follows. Article 28 (2) 2) and subsection (3) of the Agriculture Reform Act provide for the opportunity to settle disputes extrajudicially. An entitled subject has the right to appeal a decision of a reform committee to the local government council. If the entitled subject does not agree with the council decision, then it may appeal to a court. The issue was whether the appellant, who had not waited for the council decision, had the right to appeal directly from the reform committee decision to a court. The panel held that the Agriculture Reform Act did not provide for a mandatory pre-trial procedure. The Court found that the provisions do not require that the appellant appeal to the local government council at all. He or she may appeal directly to a court, which is required to hear the matter.

While precedent is not binding on lower courts, it is nevertheless taken into account by those courts. A lower court would be unlikely to ignore such a ruling, since it could be certain that its decision would be appealed and subsequently quashed.

2. SUPREME ADMINISTRATIVE COURT

As already discussed, the highest administrative court is the Supreme Court. Both the Constitutional Review Panel of the Supreme Court and the Administrative Law Panel of the Supreme Court preside over administrative and constitutional matters.

3. ORDINARY ADMINISTRATIVE COURTS - STATISTICS

The following section provides an overview of the administrative cases heard by courts in 1996.[173] (Table 1)

Table 1 (Estonia) Cases before the Estonian administrative courts of first instance in 1996

Cases relating to	Number of cases	Percentage of total
Public service	68	6 per cent
Education and culture	2	0.1766 per cent
Defence forces	17	2 per cent
Citizenship and migration	54	5 per cent
Economic activities (excluding ownership reform), including licences	28	2 per cent
Taxation	54	5 per cent
Ownership reform		
a) restitution to persons	520	46 per cent
b) restitution to local governments	2	0.1766 per cent
c) privatisation	114	10 per cent
Social welfare (excluding health insurance)	34	3 per cent
Health insurance claims	0	0 per cent
Other	239	21 per cent
Total	**1132**	**100 per cent**

E. WORKINGS OF OMBUDSMEN, INVESTIGATORY PARLIAMENTARY COMMITTEES, PUBLIC PROSECUTORS, ETC.

1. PUBLIC PROSECUTOR

Supervision over police administrative and investigatory activities is conducted by the Public Prosecutor's Office. According to the Public Prosecutor's Office Annual Report, in 1996 there were 111 violations of law discovered in the administrative activities of the police, and 377 in their investigation activities. The Public Prosecutor's Office issued 164 precepts with respect to unlawful activities of the police, 62 disciplinary procedures were initiated and seven protests were filed with the administrative courts.

No applications, complaints or other information regarding violations of oaths or oath requirements by officials were received by the Public Prosecutor's Office in 1996.

2. AD HOC AND SELECT PARLIAMENTARY COMMITTEES

As of April 30, 1997, there were four ad hoc and select committees.

2.1 The *Riigikogu* Ad Hoc Committee on the Supervision of the Lawfulness of the Activities and Investigation Operations of the National Security Police Board

The committee was founded by a resolution of the *Riigikogu* on June 1, 1995. The authority of the committee will end with the termination of the term of the present *Riigikogu*.

2.2 The *Riigikogu* Ad Hoc Committee on the Application of the Anti-Corruption Act

The committee was founded by resolution of the *Riigikogu* on August 2, 1995. The powers of the committee will end with the dissolution of the present *Riigikogu*.

2.3 The *Riigikogu* Ad Hoc Committee on Ascertaining the Circumstances of Transactions with Property Transferred to Local Governments in the Course of the Ownership Reform

The committee was founded by a resolution of the *Riigikogu* on September 18, 1996. The committee will terminate its activities on December 15, 1997.[174]

2.4 The *Riigikogu* Select Committee on European Affairs

The committee was founded by a resolution of the *Riigikogu* on January 23, 1997.

Two committees terminated their activities for the period of January 1, 1996, to April 30, 1997, on April 1, 1997:

2.5 The *Riigikogu* Select Committee on Ascertaining the Facts Discovered during the Search in the SIA Private Detective Agency[175]

2.6 The *Riigikogu* Select Committee on Ascertaining the Circumstances relating to the Sale of Roubles[176]

3. STATE AUDIT OFFICE

According to the 1996 SAO Annual Report (1995 figures in brackets), the SAO carried out 161 (187) audits in 196 (232) bodies. A total of 533 (555) violations of legislation were found.

Where audits related to property reform were done, the SAO noted that the impact of the reform on the economy was not immediate. The main emphasis, therefore, was not on the evaluation of economic efficiency but on the activities of state bodies responsible for reform management and the existence of and adherence to relevant rules and procedures. In relation to the preservation and use of state assets, the 1996 audits emphasized the comprehensiveness of the register of state assets and its effectiveness.

The audits of 1996 reached the following conclusions:

a. Expenses have been paid contrary to the purposes for which funds have been granted (e.g. excessive administrative costs, inadequate salaries, unreasonable foreign travel expenses, etc.);
b. Many state agencies have excess office space which they rent out to private businesses;
c. Foreign aid is not always fully registered;
d. Internal accounting procedures are not efficient;
e. Internal control systems are inefficient; and
f. Open tenders are not used when undertaking major renovations.

The State Audit Office made recommendations for the correction of the deficiencies and errors. The conclusions and recommendations of the Office have been disclosed and reported to the audited entities and in the media. Improvement of economic management was also recommended, especially in the following areas:

a. Regulating the use of state assets appearing on privatisation lists;
b. The practice of introducing instructions for registering and evaluating of confiscated goods by the National Customs Office;
c. The practices of introducing accounting instructions;
d. The salary system of public servants;
e. The setting and establishing of the price of land and the taxes;
f. Administrative law procedures related to the management of the economy;
g. Procedures regulating the process of transferring state assets to persons in private law.

The Chapter has been prepared on the basis of information provided by Piret Lappert and Ellen Valter

NOTES

1 28.06.1992; RT I 1992, 26, 349; 03.07.1992
2 13.12.1995; RT I 1995, 94, 1628; 1.01.1996 as amended (hereinafter as am.).
3 Section 1.
4 Section 38.
5 Section 39.
6 Section 43. Two examples will help illustrate the difference between the two types of agencies. First, the Marine Traffic Control Centre (a state agency) was established (29.11.1996; RTL 1996, 146, 718; 01.01.1997) at the Maritime Administration (a government agency) which is subordinate to the Ministry of Transport and Communications (a government agency), pursuant to clause 68 of the Government Act. While both the Maritime Administration and the Ministry of Transport and Communica-

tions set policy goals, the Marine Traffic Control Centre directs marine traffic as its primary function by implementing the policies set by the government agencies.

Second, certain schools, research centres, museums and land irrigation agencies (state agencies) are under the administration of the Ministry of Agriculture (a government agency). Pursuant to clause 49 (1) 19) of the Government Act the Minister of Agriculture determines their structure, operations, and administration (14.04.1997; RTL 1997, 61, 339; 30.04.1997). The above-mentioned institutions are not policy-setting or regulatory institutions. They merely implement governmental policies.

[7] Section 3.

[8] Section 4, Constitution Section 99.

[9] 23.10.1991; RT 1991, 38, 472; 01.01.1993 as am.

[10] 21.06.1993; RT I 1993, 50, 694; 15.09.1993 as am.

[11] 19.05.1993; RT I 1993, 31, 538; 15.09.1993 as am.

[12] Code 06.01.1961; consolidation RT I 1995, 6, 69; 01.04.1961 as am.

[13] 05.05.1993; RT I 1993, 25, 435; 24.05.1993.

[14] 21.06.1993; RT I 1993, 50, 695; 15.09.1993 as am.

[15] RT 1992, 29, 396 as am.

[16] 27.06.1994; RT I 1994, 51, 857; 25.07.1994 as am.

[17] K. Merusk, ***Haldusõiguse õpik***, Tallinn: AS Juura, 1995 (hereinafter Merusk), p. 94.

[18] Constitution Section 79.

[19] Constitution Section 97.

[20] Constitution Section 74.

[21] RT I 1994, 90, 1517 as am., Art. 165.

[22] Government Act Section 83.

[23] Local Government Administration Act RT I 1993, 37, 558 as am. (hereinafter Local Government Act) Section 4.

[24] Government Act Section 84.

[25] Government Act Section 85.

[26] Government Act Section 85 (4).

[27] see part I.5, *infra*.

[28] Constitution Section 109.

[29] Government Act Section 26, Constitution Section 86.

[30] This terminology was arrived at by the Estonian Translation and Legislative Support Centre to cope with the inordinate amount of Estonian terminology describing various types of acts and secondary legislation. All of these refer to legislation, primary or secondary. Decisions issued by administrative bodies are referred to as small "a" acts and are not considered to be legislation in any form.

"Legislation of general application" is binding upon all. Forms of legislation of general application are the Acts of the ***Riigikogu***, decrees of the President, and regulations of the Government of the Republic, ministers, the President of the Bank of Estonia, rural municipality or city council, rural municipality or city government (the executive of the council) and corporations in public law.

"Legislation of specific application" is binding upon subjects specified within the item of legislation itself. Forms of legislation of specific application are the resolutions of the ***Riigikogu***, the Prime Minister, county governors, rural municipality or city governments (the executive of the rural municipality or city council), and rural municipality district or city district managers.

It may be argued that one or the other is more general or specific than another form of legislation: still the distinction is valid in Estonian legal theory. We have tried to convey the English equivalents of the delineation in descriptive terminology.

[31] Government Act Section 27.

[32] Government Act Section 50,54 and the Constitution Section 94.

[33] Government Act Section 75.

[34] Local Government Act Section 23.

[35] Local Government Act Section 31.

[36] Constitution Section 148, Courts Act Section 1(2) and Section 18(1).

[37] Courts Act Section 19.

[38] RT 1992, 29, 396 as am.

39 RT I 1994, 53, 889 as am.
40 Eesti NSV ÜNT 1964, 25, 115 as am.
41 RT 1992, 20, 287 as am.
42 RTL 1994, 5 as am.
43 RT 1991, 45, 546 as am.
44 RT I 1996, 3, 57.
45 Subsection 3.
46 Section 5.
47 Section 9.
48 Section 10.
49 This does not include the general provisions of the Response to the Petitions Act.
50 RT I 1993, 25, 436; 24.05.1993 as am. (hereinafter LCAOA).
51 LCAOA Section 12.
52 APC & 5(4).
53 CRPA Section 5.
54 Constitution Section 142.
55 Ibid., p. 124.
56 APC Section 22.
57 CRPA Section 20.
58 CRPA Section 23.
59 LCAOA Section12.
60 Constitution Sections 139 and 140.
61 LCAOA Section 15.
62 LCAOA Section 17.
63 RT I 1995, 11, 115 as am. (hereinafter SAO Act).
64 SAO Act Section 6.
65 SAO Act Section 24.
66 SAO Act Section 12.
67 Government Act Section 72.
68 Public Prosecutor Act RT I 1993,11,184 as am. Section 2.
69 Estonian Ministry of Foreign Affairs Information Bulletin 22, 5/1994.
70 Part II.D.3.
71 26.06.1996; RT I 1996, 51, 967; 29.07.1996.
72 Status of Judges Act, RT I 1991, 38, 473 as am., Section 3 (6.1), 8.
73 Status of Judges Act Section 17 (1.1).
74 E.g. Commercial Code RT I 1995, 26-28, 355 as am., Section 24.
75 4.09.1996; RTL 1996, 102, 574; 1.10.1996.
76 16.05.1996; RT I 1996, 37, 739; 8.06.1996 as am.
77 Section 43.
78 Section 44.
79 3.04.1996; RT I 1996, 26, 529; 3.05.1996 as am.
80 RT I 1993, 45, 639 as am.
81 30. 04. 1996; RT I 1996, 36, 738; 7. 06. 1996 as am.
82 P.Pärna, "Maareformi seaduse muudatused" *(1996) Juridica* (hereinafter Pärna), p. 221.
83 Law of Property Act Implementation Act, RT I 1993, 72/73, 1021 as am..
84 ÜVT 1989, 39, 611 as am.
85 RT I 1995, 22, 327 as am.
86 RT I 1993, 39, 590 as am.
87 Ibid., p. 222.
88 Section 6.
89 RT I 1994, 74, 1324 as am.
90 RT I 1995, 14, 169 as am.
91 RT I 1995, 59, 1006 as am.
92 RT I 1994, 13, 231 as am.

93 RT I 1996, 38, 752 as am.
94 Land Reform Act Section 23.
95 Subsection (3).
96 Subsection (5).
97 29.05.1996; RT I 1996, 39, 766; 7.06.1996.
98 11.09.1996; RT II 1996, 33, 119; 12.10.1996.
99 6.02.1996; RT II 1996, 7, 24; 4.03.1996.
100 12.02.1997; RT I 1997, 16, 260; 16.03.1990.
101 Section 1.
102 Section 3.
103 Section 11.
104 Section 20.
105 13.11. 1996; RT I 1996, 83, 1487; 14. 12.1996.
106 Section 1.
107 Section 6.
108 Section 8.
109 Section 12.
110 Section 7.
111 10.01.1996, RT I 1996, 8, 164; 16.02.1996.
112 Section 1.
113 Section 18.
114 Section 32.
115 10.01.1996; RT I 1996, 8, 165; 16.02.1996.
116 Section 1.
117 Section 4.
118 Section 40.
119 12.06.1996; RT I 1996, 48, 940; 19.07.1996.
120 5.06.1996; RT I 1996, 42, 809; 30.06.1996.
121 RT I 1994, 45, 720.
122 29.01.1997; RT II 1997, 5, 20; 01.03.1997.
123 26.03.1997; RT I 1997, 30, 472; 2.05.1997.
124 Section 1.
125 Clause 11.
126 Clause 12.
127 Subsection 7 (1).
128 Subsection 8 (5).
129 19.02.1997, RT II 1997, 6, 26.
130 K. Malmberg, "Pagulased said seaduse" *Eesti Päevaleht*,19.02.1997.
131 18.02.1997; RT I 1997, 19, 306.
132 Subsection 7 (7).
133 Section 19.
134 12.06.1996; RT I 1996, 48, 944; 19.07.1996.
135 Section 4.
136 Section 9.
137 14.01.1997; RT I 1997, 8, 56; 23.01.1997.
138 RT 1992, 10, 143 as am.
139 Clause 2.
140 Clause 5.
141 24.07.1996; RTL 1996, 144, 698; 1.01.1997.
142 In particular, with the *Agreement Concerning the Adoption of Uniform Condition of Approval and Mutual Recognition of Approval for Motor Vehicle Equipment and Parts* concluded in Geneva on March 20, 1958, and the following EU directives: 70/156/EEC, 70/157/EEC, 72/306/EEC, 84/424/EEC, 92/53/EEC, 92/55/EEC and 92/97/EEC.
143 15.04.1996; RT I 1996, 26, 535; 14.04.1996.

[144] Clause 1.
[145] Clause 10.
[146] Clauses 14–15.
[147] Clause 20.
[148] 28.05.1996; RT II 1996, 8, 72; 21.06.1996.
[149] RT I 1993, 72/73, 1020 as am.
[150] 15.01.1996; RTL 1996, 43–45, 292, 1.06.1996 as am.
[151] 26.11.1996; RT I 1996, 84, 1508; 10.12.1996.
[152] RT 1992, 12, 192 as am.
[153] Clause 1.
[154] 29.03.1996; RTL 1996, 50, 314; 1.04.1996.
[155] RT I 1996, 3, 56.
[156] 11.02.1997; RT I 1997, 14, 241; 15.05.1997.
[157] RT I 1993, 43, 618.
[158] A. Parmas, "Mullu sai kodakondsuse üle 20 000 inimese", *Eesti Päevaleht* (January 9, 1997).
[159] 16.01.1996; RT I 1996, 5, 100; 23.01.1996.
[160] RT I 1993, 44, 637 as am.
[161] 1.10.1996; RT I 1996, 72, 1272; 9.10.1996.
[162] RT I 1993, 71, 1001.
[163] RT I 1993, 20, 352.
[164] Legislation of the *Riigikogu*, the President of the Republic, and the Government of the Republic.
[165] Section 6 (3).
[166] Section 10 (4).
[167] Section 231.
[168] Section 246.
[169] Section 20.
[170] Section 21.
[171] Section 22.
[172] RT III 1996, 2, 16.
[173] The data is cited from information provided by the Court Statistics Department at the Ministry of Justice.
[174] RT I 1997, 11, 102.
[175] RT I 1997, 11, 102.
[176] RT I 1997, 11, 102.

CHAPTER FIVE
HUNGARY

I. GENERAL DESCRIPTION OF THE ADMINISTRATIVE LEGAL SYSTEM

1. HISTORY OF THE ADMINISTRATIVE LEGAL SYSTEM IN HUNGARY

1.1 Establishment of the main institutions

The executive institutions were established in their present form at the beginning of the political transition period in 1990. These executive organs were created by the amendment of the Constitution in 1990.[1] The main executive organs are as follows: 1) the Government, which consists of the Prime Minister and the ministers, and 2) local governments, which are regulated both by the Constitution and Act LXV of 1990 on local governments. The old system of the local governments was transformed by this act. The main feature of this change is decentralisation: local governments are entitled to exercise wider functions and have become fairly independent from the central administrative organs.

There are also a number of organs regulated by the Constitution that supervise the administrative system. Theoretically, these organs do not form part of public administration. First, there is the state Prosecution Office. The scope of the Prosecution's competence was radically curtailed by an amendment to the Constitution. While the Prosecution had the authority to supervise the public administrative system, according to the new regulation the Prosecution's main task is to assure the legality of the criminal procedure.[2] The reason is that the former right of the Prosecution to supervise the administration served the interests of the Communist Party. For this reason this right was abolished during the first year of the political transition.

Secondly, the Constitutional Court is a new organ established by the amendment of the Constitution;[3] it has proven to be a major check on the administration and the governing majority in Parliament. Thirdly, the institution of the Ombudsman was established in 1990.[4] Finally, the Audit Office is a new supervisory body established by the amendment of the Constitution.[5] The activity of these supervisory authorities is regulated by separate legislative acts.

The Administrative Court was established in 1990. This court is not mentioned in the Constitution, as only the civil law courts have the right to proceed when administrative decisions are contested. The amendment to the Constitution declares that the courts supervise the legality of the administrative decisions.[6] The detailed conditions of this appeal are regulated in Act IV of 1957 on the Administrative Procedural Law.[7] The relevance of the new regulation is that earlier the right of appeal to the court was an exception, but according to the new regulation it is a main rule. The supervision of administrative decisions by the civil courts was generally accepted by this amendment.[8]

1.2 Adoption of the major procedural laws

The major procedural rules were enacted by Act IV of 1957 on Administrative Procedural Rules. The basic rules of this act have not changed since then, with one exception. This is the aforementioned act on the appeal of the administrative decisions by the civil courts in 1991. The main feature of the Act on Administrative Procedural Law is that it establishes the main administrative procedural rules that must be applied if other administrative procedural rules do not contain rules for the given case.[9] Numerous legal acts contain administrative procedural rules concerning special fields of administrative law. These administrative rules, such as competition law, foreign trade law, and licensing, determine other administrative procedural rules to the field they regulate, as well as substantial legal rules.

2. THE STRUCTURE OF THE EXECUTIVE

2.1 The Government

The Government is the highest executive body. The Prime Minister is elected by the Parliament on the basis of nomination by the President of the Hungarian Republic. Ministers are appointed by the President of the Hungarian Republic on the basis of nomination by the Prime Minister.[10] The list of the ministries is regulated by Act LXVIII of 1990 on the List of the Ministries. This act changed several times during seven years that followed.

The main tasks of the Government are:

- to implement the acts of the Parliament and control the work of the ministries;
- to control the other administrative bodies under the Government's control;
- to shape the policy of economic development, foreign affairs, culture, health care, welfare, etc.;
- to pass government decrees and resolutions;
- to ensure legality by reversing resolutions and actions that are against any act passed by Parliament.[11]

Ministers are accountable to the Government and Parliament. This means that they are obliged to report their activities to these bodies. The Prime Minister is accountable to Parliament and must report his activity to it. If 20 per cent of the Members of Parliament initiate a motion of no confidence against the Prime Minister, the Parliament will vote on this matter. If the majority of Members of Parliament express their non-confidence, the Government has to resign.[12]

2.2 Local government

The Audit Office supervises the economic activities of local governments from a financial point of view.[13] Parliament has the right to dissolve the representative body of the local government if its activity goes against the Constitution. The mayor of the local government must be invited to the meeting of Parliament to present the opinion of the representative body relating to the matter.[14]

The Government supervises the local governments through the Minister of the Interior and the leader of the Administrative Office.[15] The leader of the Administrative Office is appointed by the President of the Hungarian Republic on the basis of the Prime Minister's proposal.[16] The Minister of the Interior has the right to supervise the activities of local governments in terms of their legality, and also supervises the activities of the leaders of the Administrative Offices.[17]

The leader of the Administrative Office supervises the local governments in the given region and the capital in terms of legality: he or she calls the attention of the representative body to the violation of law and obliges it to eliminate any violation.[18]

If the representative body does not implement this action, the leader of the representative body can open a legal procedure against the decree at the Constitutional Court or against a resolution at civil court. The leader of the Administrative Office can decide in administrative cases, or has the right to decide if the administrative decisions are appealed.[19]

2.3 Acts of the administration

The President of the Hungarian Republic does not have the right to pass legal norms. The Government can pass governmental decrees and resolutions. These legal norms cannot be in contradiction with acts. The Prime Minister and ministers have the right to pass decrees.[20]

Act XI of 1987 on Legislation contains more detailed rules about these legal norms. Parliament does not approve these legal norms. Parliament cannot delegate legislative powers to the Prime Minister or the Government. The Government or the ministries have to implement the act if the act entitles the Government or the minister to do so. But this governmental or ministerial decree cannot be contradictory to the provisions of the act nor regulate an issue other than that defined by the act.[21]

3. SYSTEM OF COURTS DEALING WITH ADMINISTRATIVE LAW ISSUES

3.1 Structure of the judicial system

There are two types of court dealing with administrative issues: the Constitutional Court and the civil courts. The members of the Constitutional Court are elected by Parliament on the basis of representing political parties having seats in the legislature (Parliament). The Constitutional Court has the right to supervise the decrees of the local government to determine whether they are in accordance with the Constitution. If the Constitutional Court finds that a decree is in contradiction with the Constitution, the Court can reverse it. Any individual or legal person can open a legal procedure before the Constitutional Court and ask it to revise the decree of the local government.[22]

Courts which deal with disputes over the administrative decisions are the common civil courts. The procedural rules of these courts are based on Act III of 1952 on Civil Law Procedural Rules. An administrative decision can be contested at the civil court if it violates a legal rule. This means that the administrative decision cannot be contested if it was made in the scope of its discretion. (One example would be if the administrative authority did not award social assistance to the party because it found that the party was not in real need.[23]) The right of the party to contest the administrative decision in a case of violation of law is a general rule with only a few exceptions. These exceptions are enumerated in the Act on Administrative Procedural Rules. The sentence of the civil court can be appealed at the county or capital civil court. The civil law court repeals the administrative decision if it violates the law and obliges the administrative authority to resume the case.[24]

3.2 Quasi-judicial bodies

There are no special quasi-judicial bodies for adjudicating cases requiring professional expertise.

4. GENERAL PROCEDURES OF APPEAL AND JUDICIAL REVIEW CODES OF ADMINISTRATIVE LAW

The code of administrative procedure is Act IV of 1957 on the Administrative Procedural Rules.

4.1 Internal appeal

Procedures for appeal before an administrative authority that has made a decision: the appeal must, in every case, be submitted to the administrative authority that made the decision. If the administrative authority admits that its decision violates the law, it can modify or withdraw it, or if it does not agree with the appeal, it forwards it to its superior authority. (The superior authority is generally the head of the Administrative Office.[25])

Procedures for appeal before a superior administrative organ: this is the most common form of appeal of an administrative decision. The right of the party to the appeal is basically unlimited. This means that every decision can be appealed when it is a decision of the case on its merits. In exceptional cases the administrative decision cannot be appealed before the superior administrative authority. In these cases the decision can be contested directly before the civil law court.[26]

The party does not need to explain the reason for the appeal or submit arguments. This is because the superior authority has to examine the decision and the entire procedure regardless by whom and why it is appealed; hence the superior authority is not limited by the appeal. After the superior authority has examined the decision and the procedure, it can affirm, alter or repeal the decision (paragraph 63).

If the superior authority alters the decision, it can be both *reformatio in peius* and *reformatio in melius*: the decision of the superior authority can withdraw the right that was awarded by the decision of the authority of first instance. If further evidence is needed for the decision, the superior authority repeals the original decision and obliges the authority of the first instance to proceed again in the case. The superior authority gives directions to the authority of the first instance concerning the procedure, the evidence, and so on. However, the superior authority cannot determine or refer to the decision on its merits.[27]

Supervisory action of the superior authority: this authority is generally not the head of the Administrative Office, but the chief administrator of the local government of the county or capital. This kind of action can be initiated only by the chief administrator and can only occur if the original decision violated the law.

The chief administrator can alter or repeal the original decision. This right is limited in several instances: for example, if the decision has been judged by a civil court or has gone into effect and would mean the withdrawal of the right of the party given by the original decision.[28]

4.2 Judicial review

As mentioned, supervision of administrative decisions by civil courts became general practice in 1991. Thus, with few exceptions, every administrative decision can be contested before a court if it violates legal rules.[29]

The party who intends to contest the administrative decision can open a civil law procedure at the civil court. The party will be the plaintiff, and the administrative authority that made the administrative decision will be the defendant. The plaintiff has to show in his or her statement of claim that the administrative decision violates a legal rule and has to submit the reasons for it. The party has an important obligation to give reasons in the statement of claim. The other condition for contesting an administrative decision before a civil court is that either the administrative appeal has been concluded or there is no administrative appeal provided by law.[30]

This legal procedure before a civil court is called an administrative procedure, which means that civil procedural rules must be applied. These general rules are supplemented with special procedural rules regulated by the Act on Civil Procedural Rules in a separate chapter of the act.[31] The court has the right to suspend the execution of the administrative decision; it must be executed if the administrative authority obligated the parties do so with reference to the public interest or an important interest of one of the parties.[32]

4.3 Administrative acts excluded from judicial review

The Act on Supervision of an Administrative Decision by a Civil Court enumerates exceptions that are excluded from judicial review. These exceptions fall into two categories. One is determined as a general rule: administrative decisions cannot be contested before a civil court if they are made in the scope of discretion. An interpretation of legal rules, in order to decide whether the decision was made in the scope of discretion, is needed in every case.

The other group of exceptions includes the following cases:

- If another act excludes judicial review. Although any act is entitled to do so, there is no example of this.
- If the administrative decision aims at the execution of a judicial sentence. An example would be an administrative decision that obligates a mother to let the father see the child, which is otherwise ordered by the judicial sentence of divorce.
- If the administrative decision is a licence or foreign trade matter.
- If the subject of the administrative decision is related to weapons, drugs and the production of radioactive materials.
- If the administrative decision is connected with military issues.[33]

4.4 Judicial remedies

The main rule of the Act on Civil Law Procedure provides that if a court finds a violation of law, it must reverse the administrative decision and obligate the administrative authority to proceed again. In exceptional cases, the court can alter the administrative decision. The order and the reasons for it obligate the administrative authority in the subsequent administrative procedure.

Although judicial review occurs under civil law procedural rules, this does not mean that the remedies of civil law can be applied. For example, claims for damages cannot be submitted in this procedure. Thus remedies of judicial decision must maintain the framework of administrative substantial law. In most cases the final decision is made by the administrative authority under the direction of the judicial sentence.[34]

5. OMBUDSMAN

The institution of the ombudsman is regulated by Act LIX of 1993 on the Ombudsman. The main task of the ombudsman is to investigate actions violating constitutional rights and to remedy them.[35] Parliament elects a general ombudsman and has the right to elect a special ombudsman if the defence of an important constitutional right requires it.[36] At the moment, there are two special ombudsmen in Hungary: the ombudsman of data rights protection and the ombudsman of minority rights.

Any individual can initiate the action of the ombudsman if the action or decision of the public authority has caused any injury by violation of a constitutional right. A precondition of the action of the ombudsman is that all rights of appeal have been used in the administrative and juridical proceedings. The ombudsman can undertake actions without the initiative of the individual, if he or she knows of any abuse.

During his investigation the ombudsman has broad authority to clarify the facts: he or she can enter any office, ask for any information and examine any document. If the ombudsman detects the abuse of any constitutional rights, he or she can make a proposal to the administrative authority to eliminate the abuse. If the administrative authority does not agree with or is unwilling to implement the proposal, the ombudsman may report this to Parliament. The Act does not contain any regulation about the action of Parliament on the report.

If the ombudsman states that the abuse of the administrative authority is also a crime or other violation of the law, he or she can initiate legal proceedings. The ombudsman of data rights protection can publish the fact of the abuse in the media. However, the ombudsman does not have the right to take an action that involves sanctions.[37]

6. THE AUDIT OFFICE AND THE PUBLIC PROSECUTOR

The Audit Office is the financial-economic control authority of Parliament and is regulated by Act XXXVIII of 1989. The Audit Office has the right to supervise the state budget and its operation in terms of legality and effectiveness. The Audit Office reports the results of its investigations to Parliament. This report must be published in every case.[38] The Audit Office has the right to investigate every organisation holding state property. The Audit Office can supervise the economic activity of the political parties, too, but only from the point of view of legality (paragraph 25).

As mentioned before, the right of the public prosecutors to an investigation of legality was narrowed down to criminal procedures. However, the Prosecution still has the right to supervise administrative legal procedures from the point of view of legality. The prosecutor can lodge a protest if an administrative decision violates the law.

The protest does not withdraw the right of the party entitled by the administrative decision. If the administrative authority does not agree with the protest, the dispute between the prosecutor and the administrative authority will be decided by the superior administrative authority.

7. PARLIAMENTARY COMMITTEES

The committees of Parliament have an important role in the supervision of the administration. In their scope, the committees can initiate an investigation in any case. Legal persons and individuals are obligated to be present before the committees and to give them required information. If the invited person does not do so, he or she is in direct violation of the Constitution. Otherwise the Constitution does not contain any regulation of the consequences of such an act.

The committees can make a proposal to the administrative authorities, who are obligated to deal with it on its merits. However, the proposal of the committee cannot limit the scope of the administrative authority. Parliament can establish ad hoc committees if needed in a special case.[39] In 1996 an ad hoc committee investigated the biggest privatisation corruption scandal since the start of the 1989 reforms.

II. DEVELOPMENTS IN ADMINISTRATIVE LAW DURING 1996-1997

A. THE CONSTITUTION

Amending the Constitution is the most problematic question of legislation. The draft of the new Constitution was ready for over two years, but members of the opposition parties did not vote for it in Parliament. Several drafts have been made since then. In the last of these, there are no amendments that would have significant effects on the administrative system.

For example, although there is a new chapter in the draft Constitution that deals with public administration, it is no more than the regulation of some administrative law principles on the constitutional level. Yet one new rule in the Constitution is that if there is a dispute between the Government in its supervision of legality, the Audit Office in its supervision of economic and budgetary activities, and the local governments, the civil court will have the right to decide the case.

The new draft chapter of the Constitution about public finance affairs determines the basic rules of the state budget, but these provisions have already been regulated by other acts. A new provision to be enacted in the Constitution is the right of Parliament to decide about further state debts, a decision which must be based on the majority of votes. Finally, a probable constitutional amendment will require public property to be regulated by an act.

B. LEGISLATION

1. PROCEDURAL AND GENERAL ORGANISATIONAL LAWS

As mentioned, the most important procedural and organisational laws were enacted at the beginning of the 1990s.[40] There have been no major changes in this area during the period reviewed.

2. SUBSTANCE

2.1 The management of economy

2.1.1 PRIVATISATION

Act IV of 1997 amended Act XXXIX of 1995 on Privatisation. This latter Act established fundamentally new institutions for the privatisation process. The amendment of this regulation has two aims: to promote the urgency and legality of privatisation. These aims were inspired by the privatisation scandal that occurred in 1996.

Act XL of 1995 on Public Procuring was amended by Act XIII of 1997. This new regulation extends the force of the Act on Public Procuring to the State Privatisation and Holding Company (ÁPV Rt.) This declaration intends to promote legality in the operation of the ÁPV Rt.

The 155/1996 (X.16.) Government Decree amended the title of the Minister for Privatisation, a position established by Government Decree 17/1995 (III.1.). According to this new regulation the Minister for Privatisation went from being a minister without portfolio to a minister who is a member of the Government. This amendment tries to strengthen the power of the administrative organ directly responsible for privatisation.

The Hungarian privatisation process, which remains an unresolved issue, occurred differently than in other post-communist countries. The reason was historical: from the 1960s a special economic administration system had developed in Hungary as a result of incremental economic reforms. The main characteristic of this so-called "market socialism" was that legal regulations aimed to create market institutions, albeit with a high level of state intervention. Most of the resulting market mechanisms and institutions served as a basis for the new administrative system.

One of the experimental institutions of the former regime was the so-called "self-governing enterprises". In this arrangement, most property rights belonged to the administrative organs before being handed over to the state-owned enterprises and came to be exercised by self-governing bodies within these. The administrative authority that had established the state-owned enterprises supervised their operation only from the point of view of legality and could not intervene in economic decisions.

This kind of independence made "spontaneous privatisation" possible during the last communist government at the end of the 1980s. In 1989 legal regulations were passed that gave the enterprises an opportunity to become commercial companies in which property rights were exercised by the former self-governing bodies.

In order to obtain capital investment and reduce the companies' debts, the self-governing bodies sold some shares to foreign investors and banks. In most cases, the managers themselves also bought shares. One of the advantages of this form of privatisation was that, by being based on the company's decision, it could adapt fairly well to the new economic circumstances, increase capital, reduce debts and generate income for development.

The first democratic government exerted strong administrative control on each step of the privatisation process in 1991. As a result, a total "re-nationalisation" of the state-owned enterprises took place. The State Property Agency, which until then had merely been an advisory body, became an administrative organ under the government's direct control. The State Property Agency put state enterprises under its administrative control and exercised property rights without censure or publicity. This organisation was not in fact based on executive powers but on ownership. Its decisions could not be contested either by administrative or judicial means.

According to some critics, this kind of government attitude echoed the old administrative culture, which tried to strengthen its power by widening its managerial functions. For example, the government tended to appoint its own supporters to the most important economic positions, and the bids invited by the State Property Agency were awarded to members of the political elite by giving them loans on advantageous terms.

This kind of privatisation is often called an "unrestricted political privatisation". Public opinion increasingly expressed the need for decentralisation and the democratisation of privatisation. In other words, it was necessary to base the entire process on clear legal regulations and more differentiated forms. This new regulation would ensure that other claimants of privatisation, such as the employees, claimants of re-privatisation, public foundations and public bodies, were also able to take part in privatisation.

This new concept of privatisation came into being only after the socialist-liberal government came to power in 1995.[41] The main aim of the reforms was to implement privatisation as soon as possible, because the state-owned companies were being run by the State Property Agency in a way that generated serious losses. Although Act XXXIX of 1995 regulates the opportunity for other groups to share in the privatisation, that privilege is given mainly to foreign investors.

The model of privatisation in Hungary considers that the main function of privatisation is not merely the transformation of state ownership from public to private, but also the acquisition of capital and management skills in order to develop enterprises. Since domestic capital investment was lacking in Hungary, privatisation to foreign companies seemed to be the only solution. International monetary organisations (like the IMF and the World Bank) also urged this: in other words, they demanded income from privatisation so that the state could pay its debts.

Act XXXIX of 1995 aimed to establish an administrative system based on legality. For this reason, special importance was given to the various kinds of control over the ÁPV Rt. While the legal form of the State Property Agency was previously a public authority, the ÁPV Rt. was established as a joint-stock company. The relevance of the transformation of the legal form is that the joint-stock company can be controlled through its boards in a more effective way, as the accountability for its decision is precisely regulated. The ÁPV Rt. is a special joint-stock company: it is not under the force of the Act on Commercial Companies, but under that of the Act on Privatisation.

Parliament and the Audit Office have the right to supervise the activity of the ÁPV Rt., and Parliament's approval is needed for the Government's most important privatisation decisions. However, the right of the Parliament and the Audit Office to supervise the ÁPV Rt. does not mean a continuous supervisory activity. The ÁPV Rt. has to report its activities to Parliament and the Audit Office every year, or earlier, if required. The members of the Board of Directors and the Board of Supervision are appointed by the Government, and they have their own legal responsibility for their decisions. The accountant of the ÁPV Rt. is appointed by the Minister for Privatisation. Appointment to these positions is always based on the proposal of the chairman of the Audit Office. The Minister for Privatisation appointed by the Government has the right to exercise the state property rights in the ÁPV Rt.

The Act also declared that the privatisation process must always be well publicised and transparent which means that tenders must be openly published and the reasons for the decision must be written in a memorandum. The principles of privatisation that must be followed during the decision-making are also regulated in the Act.

A year after this new Act on Privatisation was passed, a massive corruption scandal was exposed in Parliament by a member of the Free Democrats (the liberal party). The background of the scandal involved legal disputes between the ÁPV Rt. and the local governments of the capital; the leaders of the ÁPV Rt. made contracts with a private attorney for consulting activity. According to the contract made between them, the private attorney was entitled to negotiate with the local governments. On the surface the payment was meant for negotiation with the local governments; however, this was done for a suspiciously large sum of money.

An ad hoc parliamentary committee and the Central Police began to investigate the case. It soon emerged that the money from the bank account of the private attorney was transferred directly to the bank account of the Socialist Party. It turned out later that the Free Democrats, their coalition partner in the government, also shared this money. Both of these ruling political parties were involved in the scandal, so the investigation was suppressed. The chiefs of police were fired and replaced by new supporters of the Government. The parliamentary committee continued to investigate the case, because its members were mostly from the opposition parties of the Parliament. Naturally, this committee had less effective means than the police would have had during the investigation. Thus the parliamentary committee closed its investigation without any substantive result.

The criminal procedure initiated by the Prosecutor's Office has not been finished. The private attorney and the managers of the ÁPV Rt. are the accused in the criminal procedure. (These aforementioned facts are based on media accounts: the scandal was extensively covered at the time.) The Prime Minister denied in interviews that the political parties had anything to do with this scandal instead blaming the managers of the ÁPV Rt. Yet the Minister for Privatisation had to resign.

Public opinion did not find the Prime Minister's explanation convincing. Many believed the political elite had stolen state property and used the managers of the ÁPV Rt. and the private attorney as a means to this end. Furthermore, when the scandal broke out, the political elite denied responsibility for the corruption scandal. Several respected leaders of the Free Democrats resigned after the scandal was exposed, saying they wished to distance themselves from what had happened. The Socialist Party continued to stand behind the statements of the Prime Minister.

The new legal regulations passed in 1997 aimed to refine further the rules of the Act on Privatisation in order to avoid further abuses. For this reason the position of Minister for Privatisation was strengthened. The ÁPV Rt. was put under the control of the Act on Public Procurement. The Act on Public Procurement contains detailed regulations and tries to give guarantees of legality when public authorities administering state property make business contracts with private firms. The aim of this Act is evidently to avoid corruption. After this amendment to the Act has been enacted, the economic activity of the ÁPV Rt. will be subject to these legal rules.

The last amendment to the Act on Privatisation also aimed to eliminate the opportunity for corruption. The first paragraph obligates the ÁPV Rt. to create an internal controlling system in the form of a by-law that can assure the continuous supervision of privatisation transactions. This by-law of the ÁPV Rt. must be made under the direction of the Audit Office and is approved by the Government. According to paragraph 6 of the memorandum, the business transactions of the ÁPV Rt. must be published and deposited in the National Archives.

The amendment to the Act on Privatisation also contains technical business rules which can promote an even quicker implementation of privatisation. This regulation reflects on Hungarian economic policy, which considers the most reasonable course of action if privatisation is implemented in almost every area of the economy, and for foreign investors.

It may be argued that, in spite of the refined regulations designed to control the privatisation process in a more effective way, the activity of the ÁPV Rt. is under the control of the Government rather than of other public authorities. That is, while the Parliament and the Audit Office have neither sufficient scope nor means to supervise the privatisation process, the Government has wide latitude to control the ÁPV Rt. by appointing its leaders. The other consequence is that even the most refined legal regulation cannot hinder corruption in a social environment where respect for the rule of law, as well as a proper political culture, is lacking.

2.1.2 COMPETITION LAW

Act LVII of 1996 on Competition repealed the former Act LXXXVI of 1990 on Competition. While the new Act amended only some details of the substantive competition law, procedural rules were regulated on a new basis. Both acts regulate all the areas of competition law. The question was raised as to a unified procedure unitied suiting all the subject matter regulated by the acts. This problem has been reflected in the legal practice of the Office of Competition, which advocated the modification of the former legal procedural rules.

The question of procedural rules applied in competition law is a vague area even in the developed Western European countries. Historically, the law of unfair competition dates back to the origins of capitalism. This area deals with legal disputes of competitors among equal parties of the market. For this reason these legal disputes are judged in a civil law procedure. Both acts follow this traditional solution and declare that a legal procedure for the unfair activities can be opened before civil court under civil law procedural rules.

The law of competition (law of cartel, law of fusion and abuse of monopoly situation) developed later, during monopoly capitalism, and protected competition as the institution serving the public interest. This area of competition law is based on a hierarchical connection between the competitor and the public authority. This is because the administrative organisation representing public interest–the assurance of competition in the market–is allowed to intervene in a legal way if competition is jeopardised.

As a consequence, public law must be applied in the field of competition law. In the United States, where the dichotomy of public/private law has not developed, competition law is applied by civil courts. Two models have evolved in Continental Europe regarding the civil law (the public law character of its legal systems).

In one model, the procedural rules of competition law have an administrative law character and administrative organ processes. Substantive legal rules are determined in a general way so that the administrative authority has wide discretionary powers in decision-making. This kind of regulation allows the administrative authority to interpret the law when it is applied and gives the Government the opportunity to implement its economic policy through the legal practice of the administrative authority in a very direct way.

The other model of competition regulation principles contains precisely defined substantive rules, and specified (in the law) courts have the right to proceed. Procedural rules that are applied have a judicial rather than administrative character. In this model, the aim of the legislator is to keep the practice of competition law independent from the day-to-day changes of economic policy. Judicial features of procedural rules and refined substantive law can evidently serve this aim.

In the Acts on Competition, procedural issues are also regulated, although in a separate chapter from the law of unfair competition. As mentioned in the first part of the study, the Act on Administrative Procedural Law is subsidiary, which means that the rules of the Act must be applied only if the special administrative procedural rules do not contain regulations applicable to the case.

The former Act LXXXVI of 1990 on Competition contained procedural rules on competition law. Both administrative and judicial elements were regulated by the former act in these procedural rules. Although Act LVII of 1996 amended most of the procedural rules, the organisational system and legal regulation of competition law is still a vague area in Hungary.

This vagueness is partly because there are other administrative organisations that have the right to decide cases of competition. The Office of Competition has the right to decide legal disputes of abuse monopoly in a situation in licensing or rejection of cartels and mergers, in approval of a price increase, and in customer complaints. According to the former Act on Competition, the customers had the choice to open legal procedures before either the civil court or the Office of Competition.

The legal regulation that allows the customer to sue the competitor before the civil court and the Office of Competition at the same time is unreasonable, incoherent and ineffective. Furthermore, customers can open an administrative procedure before another administrative authority–the Customer's Supervisory Body. The organisational system of these authorities is independent from both the civil court and the Office of Competition and is under the supervision of the Minister of Commercial Affairs.

Government Decree 199/1996 (XII. 22.) amended Decree 95/1991 (VII. 23.) on the Customer's Supervisory Body. The customers' supervisory bodies under the supervision of the central Customers' Supervisory Body were transferred by this amendment into the organisation of the Administrative Offices of the County/Capital Local Governments. The main function of these administrative offices is the supervision of the local governments from the point of view of legality. Naturally, the activity of the supervisory bodies of customers represents the interests of the customers. So this organisational reform is not in accordance with the character of these public authorities.

If many customers are involved in a case, the representative organisation of customers has the right to sue the competitor before a civil court. This special type of legal procedure is initiated by the so-called "public interest" action, and the court has the right to impose a special sanction in the sentence. This legal procedure is regulated by the Act on Competition. The fact that most legal disputes submitted to the Office of Competition have been complaints by customers about the quality of goods shows the special importance of this field and indicates the effectiveness of the new regulation.

The Office of Competition also has the right to supervise prices in a limited scope. In other words, some private firms were obliged by a Government decree to report if they were going to increase their prices. It was within the jurisdiction of the Office of Competition to examine whether the increased price was reasonable.

Apart from this prerogative, the Office of Competition did not have the right to determine the prices of utilities; these are determined by ministers and local governments through their decrees. If the utility is under a price regulation determined by ministries or local governments, the private company operating the utility is obligated to apply this price. If the decree which determines the price is violated, the Office of Competition will decide the case as an appeal authority.

However, if the price is unregulated, the Office of Competition supervises the price only if a private firm abuses its monopoly position and increases the price. In practice, the Office of Competition has initiated an investigation of the price only if it has been a "typical" violation of competition law.

Nevertheless, the Office of Competition has not yet elaborated a clear practice that could serve as a uniform basis for its acting as a regulatory body. This may have been unavoidable because an increasing number of legal procedures have been opened by customers against the private utility companies before the Office of Competition. In the absence of exact regulations, the Office of Competition has discretion to decide whether to proceed in these cases. Naturally, this kind of practice promotes the development of vague rules of application of the prerogatives of the Office, which is becoming a quasi-regulatory body.

From the point of view of legality it would be better if the power of regulation over the utilities was exercised by only one public authority, whether by the Office of Competition or by another public authority. The ministries and the local governments that determine the prices of the utility services in their decrees are not capable of implementing this goal. It is generally accepted that regulatory bodies must be independent from government authorities and must have professional skills. Furthermore, if prices are determined in decrees, it is very difficult to challenge them. (Theoretically, decrees can be contested before the Constitutional Court, but this is not a typical instance of control for constitutionality.)

The practice of the developed Western countries shows that the "regulated sector" (utilities) is treated as a separate part of the economy. This is because the regulated sector has features that distinguish it from the sphere of competition. For example, in monopoly situations the continuity of and general access to the service require a more intensive administrative regulation. This problem was not solved in the field of competition law until quite recently in Hungary. The problem is closely related to the privatisation of utilities in Hungary, which has been implemented rapidly during the last few years. The stipulation of fees for the services after privatisation is a sensitive question. The private company operating the utility naturally insists on a reasonable profit. On the other hand, increasing fees is against the customers' interest. During the communist era, when the utilities were operated by state-owned enterprises, low utility fees served social policy. Nowadays, citizens do not earn enough to pay the market-based fees for the utilities; therefore privatisation of this field has led to certain social tensions.

The Government has passed decrees that obligate it not to alter the price stipulated in the contract made between a foreign company and the ministry. These contracts are generally not open to the public and evidently are a compromise between the interest of the foreign investor and the interests of the public: the profitability of the business must be assured. For this purpose, legal procedures initiated by the customers in order to contest increasing prices of utilities were suppressed. The Office of Competition stated in its decision "a lack of jurisdiction" as a ground for the inadmissibility of the complaints. This kind of legal regulation and practice serves the foreign-investment-oriented economic policy rather than the interest of the customers.

The amendment of the new Act on Competition did not reflect these problems. As mentioned, the new Act modified the substantive competition law in some detail, reflecting the difficulties of applicability in legal practice. The procedural rules of competition law have been amended, although the organisational system remains unchanged.

At present, the chairman and the vice-chairmen of the Office of Competition are appointed by the President of the Hungarian Republic on thc basis of the reference of the Prime Minister. However, though Parliament has the right to listen to candidates, the reference of the Prime Minister prevails in the appointment. The chairman of the Office is obligated to report on the annual activity of the Office to Parliament.

This supervision cannot balance the prevailing power of the Government over the determination of policy that the Office has to follow in its legal practice (paragraphs 33–35). The legal practice of the Office shows that the Government can control the Office by the appointment of its leaders. The vague substantive law of the regulated sector can directly promote Government intervention in the policy of the Office in this matter. The new regulation of procedural rules, which aims to establish a more refined procedural framework, cannot eliminate the influence of the Government over the practice of the Office if the clear regulation of substantive law is lacking.

The new Act declared that many of the provisions of the Act on Administrative Legal Procedure cannot be applied in the procedure of competition law before the Office. The competition law procedure had a more judicial character even before this amendment. The new Act extended the investigation period, which evidently emphasises the criminal law procedure character of the first period of investigation.

The wide rights of investigators and judges during the procedure also show a criminal law character. For example, these officials have the right to enter every office of the parties concerned, request any information, look at any documents, and even sequester any document.

The second period, the trial held by the Council of the Office, also contains very specific elements dictated by the characteristics of competition law. For example, questions of parties' business secrets need special regulation. Also, the costs of the procedure paid by the parties and the deadlines differ from the rules of administrative procedure. The sanctions applied in the competition law procedure are also distinctive. However, the most important sanction, the fine, is a typical administrative law sanction. Licensing is also an administrative procedure. Cases of abuse through monopoly and the complaints of customers have a judicial character where the parties represent divergent interests.

The new regulations established a procedure in order to enforce the decision of the Council of the Office more effectively. It is the duty of the investigator to examine whether the decision of the Council of the Office has been implemented by the obligated party. If the decision of the Council has not been implemented voluntarily, the investigator will order its enforcement. The decision of the Council can be appealed before the civil court on the basis of the Act on Administrative Procedural Law.

In conclusion, the regulation of the new Act on Competition established a more refined procedure and extended the jurisdiction of the Office to investigate cases and enforce its decisions in a more effective way. The new regulation achieved this mainly through judicialisation of the procedure.

2.1.3 ADMINISTRATIVE SUPERVISION OVER MONEY AND CAPITAL MARKET

A new regulation altered the supervision system over the money and capital market in 1996. Before the reform, a number of public authorities supervised the areas of money and the capital market, such as the banking system, the security market and the stock exchange. Act CXIV of 1996 on the State Supervisory Authority of the Money and Capital Market established one administrative authority to supervise this area.

Act CXI of 1996 on the Security Market and the Stock Exchange regulates the operation of private companies dealing with selling securities and the Stock Exchange, although it also contains procedural rules applied by the State Supervisory Authority of the Money and Capital Market. Act CXII of 1996 on the Commercial Banks and Act CXIII of 1996 on the Housing Banks follow the same principles of regulation as the Act on Security Market and Stock Exchange.

Act CXXIX of 1996 amended Act LX of 1991 with respect to the Hungarian Central Bank. While the security market has been improved since the transition, there were previously inefficiencies in the operation of the banking system. The most problematic issues were the privatisation of the state-owned banks and the connection between the Central Bank and the Government. Privatisation of most state-owned commercial banks was scheduled to be implemented by the end of 1997. However, Act CXXIX of 1996 re-regulated the jurisdiction of the Central Bank.

In Hungary reforms to achieve economic liberalisation began in the 1960s: the banking system had to be adjusted to the changed circumstances. Previously, all banks performed the same functions and came under the state budget control. The lack of jurisdiction of the Central Bank meant that the banks' functions were limited to execution of the central state plan and financing of state investments. The indirect economic administrative system that took shape after the 1960s needed a banking system that could promote the development of a capital-based market. In this case, the role of the banking system would have been to influence market processes by economic regulators on the basis of the central economic policy.

For this reason, the functions of the central and credit banks were divided in the late 1980s. The Central Bank, as part of the administrative organisation system, performed only monetary regulatory functions, but five state-owned commercial banks were separated from the Central Bank. Although the Central Bank was empowered with monetary regulatory rights, its close dependence on the Government was maintained.

The Government appointed the president of the Central Bank, and it was empowered to set credit and monetary policy. Furthermore, legal rules set by the government and the Ministry of Finance were obligatory for the activities of the Central Bank. But budget policy had the greatest influence on the Central Bank's operations: the budget deficit was financed by the central bank's credits, and the amount was not limited by any legal rule.

The legal regulations of the transition stated the independence of the central bank from the Government in 1991: Act LX of 1991 on the Central Bank declared that the Government could not control the activities of the Central Bank. The role of the Government relating to monetary policy was narrowed down to an advisory capacity and representation by a minister in the Bank's meetings. The Minister of Finance only had the right to reconcile monetary policy and the financing of the budget deficit with the Central Bank. Moreover, the president and vice-president of the Central Bank were appointed by the President of the Hungarian Republic. The directors of the Board of Supervision were appointed by Parliament.

The Central Bank is a joint-stock company under state ownership, but it is also a quasi-public authority endowed with executive power. Thus the Central Bank has the right to pass decrees which are obligatory for commercial banks and which provide monetary regulations. The other executive task of the Central Bank is the supervision of commercial banks to determine whether they are operating according to the provisions of its decrees.

However, the intervention of public administration began to prevail once more, with an adverse effect on the operation of the capital market. Although the Act on the Central Bank limited the amount of credit to be given to the budget by the Central Bank, the budget could pressure the Central Bank to issue government securities. So the budget's financial demands still affected the capital market and squeezed credit out of the commercial banks, increasing inflation in the economy.

Gradually, the state monopoly of banking activity was dissolved, and, consequently, new banks have been established, primarily by foreign investors, since 1990. The Office of Banking Supervision was established in 1991 under the Government's direction. The main function of the Office was to guarantee the interests of investors. The Office gave the licences needed for the establishment of banks. Besides the technical, financial and personnel requirements, the Office had to investigate whether the bank's business plan served the interests of the investors. The supervision of the Office was extended to the commercial bank's activity from the aspects of legality and safety of investment. The Office had the right to apply several sanctions in cases of abuse, such as to oblige the bank to take necessary measures, impose fines, withdraw licenses and relieve managers from their office.

Obligatory privatisation was also legislated in order to decrease the scope of public administration in this sphere. But in reality the opposite trend occurred until 1996. The state-owned credit banks suffered heavy losses partly because they had many unrepayable debt claims in state-owned enterprises and partly because of the old management. Therefore, the state saved them from bankruptcy with an increase of capital subsidy and consolidation of credit. As a consequence, the proportion of state ownership in the banking sphere has increased by 70 per cent. The property rights were exercised by the State Property Agency and later by the Ministry of Finance. Obviously, these administrative organisations are not designed to have business interests in the banks' activities, which led, among other things, to banking scandals in many cases.

It became more and more evident by 1995 that public administration cannot assume many divergent functions (supervisory, monetary and managerial) at the same time. The Central Bank saved the state-owned credit banks from bankruptcy with refinancing credits, and the Office of Banking Supervision performed a lenient supervisory activity over them. Furthermore, the Central Bank determined high reserve rates for the credit banks in order to balance the budget. Consequently, saving state enterprises from bankruptcy hindered the managerial state's monetary and supervisory functions. The state thus found itself in a contradictory position.

The economic policy of the socialist-liberal Government sought to hasten privatisation in the banking sphere. Most state-owned banks have been privatised by foreign investors in recent years. Capital investment and managerial skills were generated in the banks as a result of privatisation. Also, the elimination of the state's ownership interest also promoted a more market-oriented operation in the banking sphere. New regulation legislated in 1996 aimed to reform the supervisory and monetary functions of the state over the banking system.

Act CXXIX of 1996 restricts the power of the Government to obligate the Central Bank to finance the state budget.[42] The Central Bank can have financial connections only with the state budget in the state financial system and is responsible for this activity directly to Parliament. The Act declares that the Central Bank cannot give credit to the state budget, with one exception. If the state budget has temporary liquidity difficulties, the Central Bank can provide liquidity credit to the Government, but the amount of this credit cannot be more than 2 per cent of the annual income of the state budget.

The Central Bank cannot buy government securities directly from the Government. If the Central Bank does so, it must be based on market conditions. Both of the regulations aim to limit the extent to which the Central Bank finances the deficit of the state budget and thus causes inflation. No doubt the new regulation has reduced the government's opportunity to pressure the Central Bank to finance the deficit of the state budget. But the question remains whether the exception still entitles the government to apply such pressure, or whether the regulation can serve as an effective limitation, especially since the prime minister retained the right to appoint the chairman of the Central Bank after the amendment to the Act on the Central Bank.

Paragraph 24 of the Act modified the status of the Central Bank when it takes loans in currency from international monetary organisations. According to this regulation the Central Bank is the representative of the state as opposed to the trusted party of the Government, as it is in the former regulation. However, the question arises whether this new status supposes that Parliament passes laws for every new loan. The distinction between the usage of "Government" and "State" is consistent with such an interpretation, although the legal sources are ambiguous on the issue.

Act CXI of 1996 on the Security Market and Stock Exchange regulates the conditions of all activities in the security market. It is within the powers of the State Supervisory Authority of Money and the Security Market to give licences to private companies for activities relating to securities. This public authority's task is to supervise the activity of the private company and the Stock Exchange both from the point of view of legality and business efficiency. The State Supervisory Authority has wide latitude in the investigation of these companies and can apply sanctions regulated by the Act. The procedure of the State Supervisory Authority is based on administrative principles and subsidiary to the Act on Administrative Procedural Law. Sanctions, such as the withdrawal of a license, the imposition of a fine, etc., show the administrative character of the process. While the former regulations contain detailed rules concerning the activities of securities, the amendment of the former act establishes even more refined rules. This more refined regulation will enable a more effective supervisory activity of the State Supervisory Authority based on legality.

Act CXII of 1996 on Commercial Banks follows the principles of the aforementioned Act on the Security Market and Stock Exchange in the regulation of the procedure of the State Supervisory Authority. The establishment of the Insurance Foundation is probably a reaction to the banking scandals of recent years. It is obligatory for commercial banks to join the Insurance Foundation. If a commercial bank goes into bankruptcy, the Foundation will pay compensation for the investors.

Act CXIII of 1996 on Housing Banks established special banks for giving citizens loans on special terms so that they can buy houses on the open market. The Government's new housing policy has been implemented by the establishment of these banks. Local governments have not implemented the obligatory provision of public housing. This new housing policy, which aims to promote the acquisition of houses by citizens by offering them loans on special terms from the state budget, is an admission of the fact that the local governments lack the financial resources to solve this social problem.

As mentioned before, Act CXIV of 1996 on the State Supervisory Authority of Money and Security Market established one public authority to replace the many existing before, for the supervision of the money and security market. The State Supervisory Authority is controlled by the Government much more than are other supervisory public authorities. Neither Parliament nor the President of the Hungarian Republic has the right to supervise the activity of the State Supervisory Authority or to appoint its heads.

In conclusion, privatisation and competition are under tight Government control, and the amendments of legislation during the last two years have only slightly changed this (especially in the field of money and security markets).

2.2. Management of Socio-Cultural Processes:

2.2.1 WELFARE SYSTEM AND SOCIAL SERVICES

Besides the privatisation scandals, amendments to the laws regulating welfare have attracted significant public attention. The decrease of social welfare services has been more and more obvious since the transition, but the amendment of these acts based on the new economic policy has radically cut basic social allowances. These acts were contested before the Constitutional Court.

Social policy since the transition has been elaborated on the basis of the "premature welfare state" theory. The political elite asserts that the former communist regime shouldered far more welfare services than it could implement. Thus state withdrawal from the field of welfare is deemed necessary. This kind of approach of social policy tends to refer to the neo-liberal economic policy of developed Western countries which shifted social services from the public sector to the private sphere.

However, the social policy proclaimed by the new political elite since the transition differs significantly from Western neo-liberal economic policy. For privatisation of welfare services in the West does not mean any decrease of services, but rather their provision by private firms, presumably resulting in better quality. State withdrawal from welfare in Hungary is closely connected to the problem of the limited state budget. Since the political elite is able to ensure its income from other sources, it has no interest in enacting an effective tax system that could serve the development of a solid state budget.

The private sector is not sufficiently developed to allow the state to withdraw from the provision of welfare services. Market conditions have been created, but there are relatively few private initiatives in the field of welfare, as most individuals do not earn enough to pay for private services. In the wake of the political transition, this kind of social policy does not appear to be an attractive proposition.

The uncertainty of the legal regulation concerning welfare reflects the above-mentioned social policy in a very indicative way. Constitutional law aspects of administrative law regulating welfare services are a vague area even in the continental Western countries. Continental European legal systems traditionally regulate the general principles of public administration in their constitutions. The concepts of the "social state of the rule of law" and "welfare state" express that it is the responsibility of public administration to assure welfare for its citizens.

The relevance of the constitutional regulation of social rights is that the right to welfare can be enforced under the law by the Constitutional Court. Theoretically, social rights are considered equal to civil rights, but legal practice also shows the inefficiency of constitutional regulation. Social rights could probably be regulated as efficiently as civil rights, but the political elite has little interest in doing so.

As a result, social rights, as opposed to civil rights, are not regulated as substantive rights. However, international treaties, such as the European Social Charter, require that social rights should be enforced both in legislation and legal practice. Still, the provisions of the Charter do not oblige its member states to implement such legislation. One consequence of this kind of constitutional regulation is that it is at the legislator's discretion to establish a framework for administrative regulation in the area.

One of the previous drafts for a new Hungarian Constitution contained no reference to any social rights. The liberal party (the Free Democrats) stated that it was not reasonable to regulate any constitutional right which could not be implemented. Public opinion was generally against such ideas of limited state responsibility in the area of social security. After this draft was rejected by Parliament, a new draft was accepted, which once more provided for social rights. This was because of the increasing demand to join European international treaties which have extensive social-rights provisions.

The latter draft of the Constitution recognises the right of the citizens to health care and social security. However, the next provision declares that the state is obligated to implement this goal gradually, in accordance with its economic abilities. One version of the draft intends to ensure the right only to basic health-care services. This regulation shows a compromise between international legal requirements and an avoidance of any concrete commitment for the state.

The practice of the Constitutional Court, similarly to the new economic policy, shows a "liberal" tendency. Social rights are less and less substantive in constitutional interpretations. They amount to handouts for the poorest people. Social security does not mean that social allowances must keep pace with inflation. Apart from the value of the allowances, measure and form (substantive or discretionary) cannot be interpreted on the basis of constitutional provisions; they always depend on the economic potential of the state.

Interpretations by the Constitutional Court state that it is within the powers of the legislature to determine social services and aids. This kind of interpretation implicitly allows the government free rein to reduce social services through legislation, since there is no minimum level for social services and allowances.

Act III of 1993 on Social Services has been amended several times, most importantly by Act XXII of 1996, Act CXXVIII of 1996, and Act XVIII of 1997. Most social services and aid regulated by the Act on Social Services are based on discretionary governmental decisions. The public authority providing social aid has the right to decide whether to give the aid, which in practice means a lack of a substantive right to social aid.

One of the amendments establishes an exception from this general rule of discretionary decision-making. Paragraphs 4 and 7 of the Act on Social Services oblige local governments to provide aid, food and shelter for those persons whose life and health are jeopardised by the lack of them. Usually it is residency that obliges the local government to provide social services for the party. But the Act declares that homeless people must also receive these allowances. The amendment to the Act on Social Services also established a new form of regular social aid in 1996. Regular social aid can be provided for the disabled, the elderly, and those who no longer have the right to unemployment benefits, provided they have no other income or property.[43]

Although some of these provisions of the new regulation try to widen social services, the rest of them clearly narrow down the conditions for eligibility. This means that fewer and fewer people have the right to social aid under this regulation. And, as indicated, the administrative authority has the right of discretion in almost every case. These circumstances have led to radical cuts in the provision of social allowances by local governments, for instance, in unemployment benefits. Act CVII of 1996 amended Act IV of 1991 on Unemployment Benefits. The amendment established new support for unemployed people who start entrepreneurial activities; it also offered support for education for young people to help them find a job more easily.[44] Although these forms of support introduced new forms of benefits for the unemployed, the absolute amount of other benefits, such as aid for the unemployed, has been reduced.[45]

Other social services and allowances provided by social insurance, such as pensions, health care services, maternity benefits and sick leaves and pay, generally have substantive right character. These allowances are regulated by Act II of 1975 on Social Insurance and Act XXV of 1990 on Family Support Aids. Act XXII of 1996 and Act of XVIII of 1997 amended these acts. The most important maternity benefits have been eliminated by the amendments. This act was contested before the Constitutional Court. Regarding health care, an increasing number of services which were previously free of charge must now be paid for under the regulations of 1996–97.

There is only one exception from the aforementioned tendency of decreasing social allowances. It is the sphere of pensions, where there was an increase by Government Decree 23/1996 (II. 9.). The increase of allowances did not keep pace with the inflation rate. Nevertheless, the exeption made for pensions shows that the government considers the pensioners' vote important.

The Chapter has been prepared on the basis of information provided by Maria Bordás

NOTES

1 Act LXIII of 1990 on the Amendment to the Constitution.
2 Paragraphs 51-53.
3 Paragraph 32/A.
4 Paragraph 32/B.
5 Paragraph 32/C, D.
6 Paragraph 50.
7 This Act was modified by Act XXVI of 1991, which established supervision by the civil court of the administrative decisions.
8 Paragraph 72.
9 Paragraph 3.
10 Paragraphs 33-34. of the Constitution.
11 Paragraph 35. of the Constitution.
12 Paragraph 39/A of the Constitution.
13 Act LXV of 1990 on Local Governments, paragraph 92.
14 Paragraph 93.
15 Paragraph 95.
16 Paragraph 100.
17 Paragraph 96.
18 Paragraph 98.
19 Paragraph 99.
20 Paragraph 35 (2) of the Constitution.
21 Paragraph 15.
22 Paragraph 32/A of the Constitution and paragraphs 37-43. of Act XXXII, of 1989 on the Constitutional Court.
23 Paragraph 105. of Act IV of 1957 on the Administrative Procedural Law.
24 Paragraph 106.
25 Paragraph 61.
26 Paragraph 62.
27 Paragraph 64.
28 Paragraph 71.
29 Paragraph 72.
30 Paragraph 72.
31 Chapter XI.
32 Paragraph 73.
33 Paragraph 87/2.
34 Chapter XI. of the Act on Civil Procedural Law.
35 Paragraph 1.
36 Paragraph 2.
37 Paragraphs 7-10.
38 Paragraphs 5-10.
39 Paragraph 21. of the Constitution.
40 See Sections 1.2 and 4.
41 Act XXXIX of 1995 on Privatisation.
42 Paragraph 19. (1-4).
43 Paragraph 37/A.
44 Paragraph 17. and paragraph 19/A of the Act and (III.5.) of Government Decree 39/1977.
45 Paragraphs 24-38.

CHAPTER SIX
LATVIA

I. GENERAL DESCRIPTION OF THE ADMINISTRATIVE LEGAL SYSTEM

1. LEGAL STATUS OF THE REPUBLIC OF LATVIA AFTER THE COLLAPSE OF THE SOVIET UNION

1.1 The re-establishment of the state of Latvia

On May 4, 1990, the Supreme Soviet of the Latvian Soviet Socialist Republic adopted a Declaration "On the Renewal of the Independence of the Republic of Latvia".[1] In conformity with this constitutional act, the power of the Satversme (Constitution) of the Republic of Latvia of February 15, 1922, was re-established on the territory of the Republic of Latvia. The official name of the State, "The Republic of Latvia", was re-established as well. It was determined simultaneously that until the time of adoption of a revised Satversme only four articles of the old document, those which could be altered by a referendum in compliance with Article 77 of the Satversme, would remain in force. These articles were: a) Article 1, stating that Latvia shall be an independent democratic republic; b) Article 2, proclaiming that the sovereign power of the Latvian State belongs to the people of Latvia; c) Article 3, determining that the territory of the Latvian State consists of Livonia, Latgale, Courland and Zemgale, within the boundaries stipulated by international treaties; d) Article 6, according to which the Saeima (Parliament) is to be elected by universal, equal, direct and secret vote on the basis of proportional representation.

The Declaration provided for the possibility of provisional implementation of those constitutional and legislative acts of the Latvian SSR that were in force in Latvia when the Declaration was adopted, insofar as they did not contradict Articles 1, 2, 3 and 6 of the Constitution of the Republic of Latvia. The supremacy of the fundamental principles of international law over national law was recognised.

Another significant legislative bill, the "Declaration on the Accession of the Republic of Latvia to International Instruments Relating to Human Rights", was also adopted on May 4, 1990.[2] The Republic of Latvia acceded to the basic international instruments: the Universal Declaration of Human Rights; the International Covenant on Economic, Social and Cultural Rights; the International Covenant on Civil and Political Rights; the Convention on the Elimination of All Forms of Discrimination against Women; the Declaration on the Elimination of All Forms of Intolerance and Discrimination Based on Religion or Belief; and the Convention on the Rights of the Child.

Accession to these instruments conforms to the Declaration, which acknowledges the special significance in guaranteeing human rights of the international instruments adopted by the UN, its specialised agencies and those adopted by the Conference on Security and Co-operation in Europe (at their Helsinki, Madrid and Vienna meetings).

1.2 Major legal acts

On August 21, 1991, the Supreme Council of the Republic of Latvia adopted the Constitutional Law "On the Republic of Latvia's Status as a State".[3] In conformity with this Law the Supreme Council resolved:

"1. To declare Latvia as an independent, democratic republic, in which the sovereign power of the Latvian State belongs to the people of Latvia and its sovereign state status is determined by the Satversme of February 15, 1922;

2. To repeal Article 5 of the Declaration "On the Renewal of the Independence of the Republic of Latvia" defining the transition period for the de facto restoration of the Republic of Latvia's state power;

3. Until the time when the occupation and annexation of Latvia is finally liquidated and the Saeima (Parliament) of the Republic of Latvia is convened, supreme power is to be executed exclusively by the Supreme Council of the Republic of Latvia. Only the laws and resolutions of this supreme state power are legally in effect on the territory of the Republic of Latvia;

4. This constitutional law is in effect upon its adoption."

The importance of the Constitutional Law "The Rights and Obligations of a Citizen and a Person", passed by the Supreme Council on December 10, 1991,[4] has been maintained from the period of renewal of independence until today. Unfortunately, the Satversme has not regulated this issue. The Law states that "all persons in Latvia are equal under the law regardless of race, nationality, sex, language, party affiliation, political and religious persuasion, social, material and occupational standing and origin".

1.3 First general elections and the re-enforcement of the Satversme

In the autumn of 1992 the Supreme Council passed the Law "On Elections" and, in conformity with it, the Saeima was elected in June 1993. The elections were free and democratic.

In its first session on July 6, 1993, the Saeima re-established in full the authority of the Satversme of the Republic of Latvia adopted on February 15, 1922. On July 15, 1993 the Law of April 1, 1925, "The Structure of the Cabinet of Ministers", was renewed and, in accordance with it, the structure of the executive system of the Republic was formed.

The Law "On Judicial Power" was passed by the Supreme Council on December

15, 1992, before the elections for the Saeima. This established the principles and guarantees of the independence of the judiciary, its structure, the status of judges, and other significant issues.

1.4 Major procedural laws and codes

The codes of the former Soviet Republic of Latvia remained in force until adequate amendments could be made and adopted in the form of new codes. These old codes consisted of the Civil Procedure Code (adopted on December 27, 1965), the Criminal Procedure Code (adopted on January 6, 1991) and the Code of Administrative Offence (adopted on December 7, 1984). Although work on drafting the new codes has begun, it has been a protracted process. Similarly, even though the procedural codes have been drafted, they have not yet been passed. It became evident that an additional procedural code, the Administrative Procedural Code, was necessary, but not much action was taken. It was only on June 13, 1995, that a kind of temporary solution to the problem was effected via the adoption, by the Cabinet of Ministers, of Regulations No. 154 "Regulations on Administrative Process". This came into force on September 1, 1995, but is not wholly satisfactory, as the Regulations only partly refer to administrative processes. It is, therefore, still necessary to introduce a codified law on administrative procedure.

2. STRUCTURE OF THE EXECUTIVE

2.1 The highest executive body in the country

In conformity with the Satversme and the Law "On the Structure of the Cabinet of Ministers", the Cabinet of Ministers is the highest executive body of the Republic of Latvia, and the state administrative institutions are subordinated to it. The Cabinet of Ministers consists of the Prime Minister and the ministers nominated by him or her: the Ministers of Environmental Protection and Regional Development, of Defence, of Foreign Affairs, of Economics, of the Interior, of Education and Science, of Agriculture, of Transportation, of Welfare, of Justice, of Finance, of Culture and the Minister of Special Assignment for the Affairs of the European Community.

2.2 Structure of the Cabinet

The Prime Minister may nominate one Deputy Prime Minister and one or several ministers for special assignments: they act as full-fledged members of the Cabinet. The Prime Minister may also appoint a state minister who supervises a specific department under the jurisdiction of the relevant ministry. The state minister shall independently supervise his or her department within the ministry, albeit acting in co-ordination with the relevant minister. The state minister may participate in the meetings of the Cabinet in the capacity of an advisor. He or she only has the right to vote on issues which concern his or her department. In accordance with a suggestion of the ministers, the Prime Minister may appoint parliamentary secretaries. The parliamentary secretary assists the minister in maintaining contact between the ministry and the Saeima and its committees.

2.3 Formation of the Cabinet

In conformity with Article 56 of the Satversme, the President of State shall entrust an individual with forming the Cabinet. This person shall report on the composition of the Cabinet to the President and the Chairman of the Saeima, who should present this report before the Saeima at its sitting. The Cabinet takes office after the Saeima and, having heard both the report of the Prime Minister on the composition of the Cabinet of Ministers (including state ministers) and the declaration on the planned activities of the Cabinet of Ministers, gives the Cabinet its vote of confidence by the adoption of a special resolution. Individual ministers and state ministers who are subsequently appointed by the Prime Minister need a special resolution by the Saeima on a vote of confidence. The Saeima expresses a vote of confidence in the Cabinet of Ministers either by adopting a resolution to that effect or by rejecting the draft of the annual state budget submitted by the Cabinet of Ministers. The Saeima expresses a vote of no confidence in an individual minister or state minister by resolution. The vote of no confidence expressed to an individual minister also applies to the state ministers and parliamentary secretaries of the respective ministry. If the minister resigns from office on his/her own accord or on the request of the Prime Minister, then the state ministers and parliamentary secretaries of the respective ministry also lose their positions.

In accordance with Article 27 of the Satversme, the Saeima has the right to address to the Prime Minister, or to any other minister, interpellations or questions to which they, or officials empowered by them, shall reply. At the request of either the Saeima or its committees, the Prime Minister, or any other minister, is obliged to place relevant papers and documents at their disposal.

2.4 Prerogatives of the Cabinet

In conformity with Article 13 of the Law "The Structure of the Cabinet of Ministers", the Cabinet of Ministers discusses or resolves all issues which, in compliance with the Satversme and the laws, are within its competence. The Cabinet of Ministers executes the following functions: it 1) initiates laws,[5] 2) issues normative acts,[6] 3) nominates or confirms officials, 4) drafts the budget and submits it to the Saeima and 5) proclaims the state of mandatory defence if the State is threatened by foreign invasion. The extremely important regulative function of the Cabinet of Ministers, which reflects the state policy, is established by Article 61 of the Satversme. It manifests itself in the co-ordinating activities of various ministries and ensures the planned character of the performance of the executive institutions in different spheres.

Of vital significance are the "Regulations of the Internal Order and Procedure of the Cabinet of Ministers",[7] which were passed on April 30, 1996. They were passed to regulate the internal order and procedure of the Cabinet of Ministers and determine the order according to which the Cabinet of Ministers and its committees should discuss the draft legislative acts submitted by a proponent, items relating to the procedure of the several ministries and other items proposed for consideration.

2.5 The President of the Republic

The President of the State is to be elected, in compliance with Article 35 of the Satversme, by the Saeima for a period of three years. Election occurs by secret ballot with a majority of not less than 51 votes. Presidential duties and obligations are defined by the Satversme and include the right of legislative initiative,[8] the right to ask for a revision of a law,[9] the right to promulgate laws,[10] the right to submit a draft elaborated by the electors to the Saeima and announce a referendum,[11] the duty to be the chief of the armed forces of the State,[12] the right to declare war,[13] the right to take steps indispensable to the military defence of the country,[14] the right to represent the state, to receive accredited representatives of foreign states as well as to carry out the decisions of the Saeima concerning the ratification of international treaties,[15] the right to appoint commanders-in-chief[16] and Latvian representatives abroad,[17] the right to propose the dissolution of the Saeima,[18] the right to pardon criminals,[19] the right to convoke extraordinary meetings of the Cabinet,[20] and others.

The President makes decisions and passes declarations and orders. Under Article 53 of the Satversme, all the decrees of the President of the State are to be countersigned by the Prime Minister or by the minister concerned, who thereby assumes full responsibility for the decrees (except in cases of dissolution of the Saeima and when choosing and appointing the person entrusted to form the Cabinet). The laws promulgated by the President of the State are published in the newspaper *Latvijas Vestnesis*, in the native language of the State. The President of the State is not responsible to any other person or body for his political activities.

3. THE RELATIONS BETWEEN CENTRAL AND LOCAL ADMINISTRATION

The status of local administration of the state is determined by the "Law on Local Government", adopted on May 19, 1994.[21] Each year, before the beginning of the economic year, the Cabinet of Ministers makes an agreement with local governments about the issues to be co-ordinated and the procedure of their review. According to Articles 86–90 the Cabinet of Ministers and local governments work together on issues such as: 1) the drafting of laws and regulations of the Cabinet of Ministers concerning local governments, 2) the size of grants and special-purpose subsidies allocated to local governments in the current budgetary year, 3) the order of fair distribution of local government financial resources, 4) the maximum size of salaries of local government officials and employees, 5) the sources of financing the administration of matters provided by Article 8 of this law, 6) other issues of local government, the regulation of which is within the competence of the Cabinet of Ministers.

In this process of co-ordination, local governments are represented by the public organisation of local governments, established in accordance with the provisions of Article 96 of the "Law on Local Governments". Local governments are represented by an authorised agent or the chairman of the local government of the respective region on issues concerning a separate local government. The results of negotiations on such issues must be recorded in the protocol of the agreement. The protocol of the negotiations about the agreement or disagreement concerning the draft laws prepared by the Cabinet of Ministers must be enclosed in the corresponding draft law and sent to the Saeima. The protocol of negotiations about disagreement on issues in the competence of the Cabinet of Ministers must be reviewed by the government. Local governments or their non-governmental organisations also have the right to submit proposals on legislative amendments to the Cabinet of Ministers.

4. CATEGORIES OF NORMATIVE ACTS OF THE ADMINISTRATION

4.1 Normative acts of the Cabinet of Ministers

Article 14 of the Law on the Structure of the Cabinet of Ministers states that the Cabinet of Ministers may only issue normative acts or regulations in the following cases: 1) in accordance with the procedure prescribed in Article 81 of the Satversme; 2) if the law specifically authorises the Cabinet of Ministers to do so: the authorisation should include directions for the content of the regulation; and 3) if the respective issue is not regulated by law. The regulations cannot contradict the Satversme and the laws and, furthermore, they should indicate the legal basis (laws) upon which they have been issued.

Article 81 of the Satversme states that in cases of urgent necessity between parliamentary sessions the Cabinet should have the right to issue regulations carrying the force of law. These regulations should not modify: a) the law of elections for the Saeima; b) the laws bearing on the administration of justice; c) the budget; and d) the laws passed by the Saeima then in power. They must not refer to amnesty, the issue of treasury notes (bonds), state taxes, customs duties, railway tariffs or loans. Moreover, they will be annulled if not presented to the Saeima within three days of the opening of the following session.

In conformity with Article 83 of the "Rules of Procedure of the Saeima", any regulations issued by the Cabinet under Article 81 of the Satversme which have been submitted to the Saeima not later than three days after the opening of the current session of the Saeima are reviewed by the Presidium of the Saeima to reach a conclusion concerning the further procedure of the review. If any regulations issued by the Cabinet under Article 81 of the Satversme have been submitted to the Saeima later than three days after the opening of the current session of the Saeima, they are considered null and void. If the Saeima fails to make a decision to forward to its committees the regulations issued by the Cabinet under Article 81 of the Satversme, the regulations will be considered rejected. They shall become null and void as of the day of their rejection. If the regulations issued by the Cabinet under Article 81 of the Satversme have not been adopted in the legislative procedure within six months from the day when the decision to forward the regulations to the committees was made, they shall become null and void. The regulations issued by the Cabinet under Article 81 of the Satversme shall also become null and void if they have not been adopted in the legislative procedure within the term of office of the Saeima which has forwarded them to the committees.

Directives (regulations, instructions and recommendations) passed by the Cabinet of Ministers are published in the official newspaper *Latvijas Vestnesis,* in the native language of the State. Regulations, instructions or recommendations of the Cabinet of Ministers take effect from the next day after publication in *Latvijas Vestnesis,* if no other date has been specified. Regulations, instructions or recommendations of the Cabinet of Ministers may be proclaimed secret under a special law. In such cases, they should not be published and shall become effective from the date of their adoption, unless otherwise provided by a special decision of the Cabinet of Ministers. Regulations of the Cabinet of Ministers are effective in the entire territory of Latvia, and no person has the right to plead ignorance of them.

4.2 Normative acts of ministers, internal normative acts, and informal normative acts

The Cabinet of Ministers has the right to pass internal normative acts, instructions and recommendations.[22] They, or a minister, may only issue instructions binding on the institutions subordinate to them in the following cases: 1) if the law or regulations specifically authorise the Cabinet of Ministers or an individual to do so; or 2) if the respective issue has not been regulated by regulations or by a law.

Furthermore, the Cabinet of Ministers or an individual minister may issue recommendations to their subordinate institutions where the law or regulations prescribe that this institution has the right to discretionary decision-making in a particular area.[23]

In practice, in the exercise of the prerogative to adopt recommendations, the ministers and some other high officials of the ministries issue regulations that could be regarded as normative acts.[24] There are cases when different institutions (like boards, departments, services, foundations and other offices) that are subordinate to a ministry pass orders and letters with a compulsory or normative nature, even though the Law "The Structure of the Cabinet of Ministers", passed on February 6, 1997,[25] as well as other laws do not envisage it. Not all of the legal documents are published in official publications. For example, a letter (brief) of the State Revenue Service of April 11, 1997, "On the Application of the Excise Tax",[26] and a letter (brief) of March 12, 1996, of the State Revenue Service "On Business Income Tax" have not been published. The compulsory nature of these two documents to all legal and physical persons is determined by Regulations of the Cabinet of Ministers.

4.3 Normative acts of the local administration

The status of local administration is determined by the "Law on Local Government" adopted on May 19, 1997.[27] The Dome (Council) can pass binding regulations, statutes, instructions or recommendations.[28] The Decisions of the Dome should comply with the Satversme, the "Law on Local Government" and other laws and regulations of the Cabinet of Ministers. The regulations are binding on all the physical and legal persons in the respective administrative territory. Those issued by the city Domes must be published in the official newspaper not later than two weeks after their adoption, except when they become effective on the day when they are announced. The binding regulations issued by the *pagasts* (small town) local administration must be placed in a visible position in or outside the Council building not later than two weeks after their adoption. They become effective on the day after placement.

5. SYSTEM OF COURTS DEALING WITH ADMINISTRATIVE LAW ISSUES

There are no separate administrative courts in Latvia. Administrative law cases are reviewed in accordance with the ordinary procedure set by law. The Law "On Judicial Power" states that in the Republic of Latvia, an independent judicial power exists alongside the legislative and the executive power. The judicial power belongs to the district (city) courts, the regional courts, and the Supreme Court.[29] Judgements and sentences are to be passed solely and exclusively by the courts.

The principles and procedure for adjudication of cases are provided by the Satversme, the law "On Judicial Power" and by the Laws of Civil Procedure, Criminal Procedure and the Code of Administrative Offences.

5.1. Structure of the judicial system and the scope of jurisdiction of the different courts

The Constitutional Court of Latvia was founded in December 1996. Its activity is established by the "Constitutional Court Law", passed on June 14, 1996.[30] It is an independent institution of judicial power, which, within the jurisdiction set forth in the Constitution of the Republic of Latvia and in this Law, decides on cases concerning the compliance of laws and other legal norms with the Constitution, as well as other cases placed under its jurisdiction by this Law. It reviews cases regarding: 1) compliance of laws with the Constitution; 2) compliance with the Constitution of international agreements signed or entered into by Latvia; 3) compliance of resolutions of the Saeima with the Constitution and other laws; 4) compliance with the Constitution and other laws of regulations and other normative acts of the Cabinet of Ministers as well as of normative acts issued by institutions or officials subordinated to the Cabinet of Ministers; 5) compliance of acts of the President of State, Chairperson of the Saeima, and the Prime Minister with the Constitution and other laws; 6) compliance with the Constitution and other laws of other normative acts issued by institutions or officials confirmed, appointed or elected by the Saeima; 7) compliance with the Constitution, other laws and regulations of the Cabinet of Ministers, of binding regulations and other normative acts issued by the Dome (Council) of municipalities; 8) compliance with the law of an order by which a minister duly authorised by a law to do so has rescinded binding regulations issued by the Dome of a municipality and 9) compliance of the national legal norms of Latvia with the international agreements entered into by Latvia, which are not contrary to the Constitution.

There are administrative judges in the district (city) court who individually review cases that result from administrative legal relations, as well as other cases assigned for their review in accordance with a law. The regional court is a court of first instance regarding civil law cases, criminal cases and administrative cases. The regional court also acts as a court of appeals regarding civil law cases, criminal cases and administrative cases which have been reviewed individually by a district (city) court judge. There are five regional courts in the country: the Riga Regional Court, the Kurzeme Regional Court, the Latgale Regional Court, the Vidzeme Regional Court, and the Zemgale Regional Court.

The Supreme Court consists of a Senate and two court panels: the Civil Court Panel and the Criminal Court Panel. The Court Panel is a court of appeal for cases which have been reviewed by the regional courts acting as a court of first instance. The Supreme Court Senate acts as a Supreme Court of Appeals for all cases which have been reviewed by the district (city) courts and the regional courts. The Senate of the Supreme Court is a court of first instance for cases on the decisions of the Council of State Control adopted according to Article 21 of the Law "On State Control". The Senate consists of the Chief Justice of the Supreme Court and senators (justices of the Senate). It is composed of three departments: the Civil Department, the Criminal Department, and the Administrative Department. The latter has not yet been formed.

All Supreme Court justices form the Plenum (general meeting of justices). The Plenum is, therefore, a general meeting of court panel justices of the Supreme Court and Senate justices. It adopts binding interpretations for the courts on the application of laws and forms the court panels and the departments of the Senate.

6. SPECIAL QUASI-JUDICIAL BODIES FOR ADJUDICATING CASES REQUIRING PROFESSIONAL EXPERTISE

There are no such bodies in Latvia.

7. AN ACCOUNT OF THE GENERAL PROCEDURAL LAWS OR CODES OF ADMINISTRATIVE LAW

There is no special Administrative Procedure Code in Latvia. Procedural rules can be found in different normative acts: the Code of Administrative Offences, the Civil Procedure Code, the Procedure Rules of Administrative Acts and other legal documents.

7.1 The procedures for appeal before administrative agencies (internal appeal)

Although the Code of Administrative Offences was passed in 1984, several amendments have been introduced to it since the re-assertion of Latvia's independence. The Code defines an administrative offence and penalty, different kinds of sanctions and fines, the procedure of passing a decision and the institutions authorised to review administrative offences. A special chapter deals with administrative responsibility for specified offences. The fourth part of the Code regulates record-keeping. Considerable attention is paid to norms regulating legal relations, the procedure of reviewing cases, the right to judicial review (appeal), and the submission of a protest.

Thus, Article 271 regulates the procedure of reviewing administrative cases and verifying evidence if the case is being reviewed by an individual judge. In compliance with paragraph 2 of Article 279, the judgement of the judge of the district (city) court is final and may not be appealed. Only the prosecutor, according to Article 282 of the Code of Administrative Offences, may submit a protest. The case will be reviewed at a higher instance.

7.2 Procedures of judicial review (external review)

Chapter 24 of the Civil Procedure Code provides a procedure of reviewing complaints brought by individuals concerning the actions of state institutions or their officials on the imposition of administrative penalties. Article 241 provides a procedure for reviewing complaints about unlawful activities of government and local administration institutions or their officials.

Chapter 24 of the Civil Procedure Code states that any physical person has the right to submit a complaint to the court if he or she believes that his or her rights have been violated by the activity (decision, ruling) of the government or the local administration. A complaint is to be submitted no later than a month after receiving a refusal (in the framework of the internal appeal procedures) to satisfy the claim or if no resolution has been received. The above cases should be reviewed in the presence of a public prosecutor. The court reviews the case within 10 days from the day of the receipt of the complaint.

7.3 Categories of administrative acts excluded from judicial review

Some acts of officials or the government and the local administration in Latvia may not be subject to judicial review if so determined by specific laws. There are a number of such laws; for instance, the Law "On Privatisation of State and Local Government Property" was passed on February 17, 1994.[31] In compliance with this, the Cabinet of Ministers authorised a Council (consisting of representatives delegated by the factions of the Saeima) to supervise the process of privatisation. The law excluded the possibility of trying the case in court.

Further, in conformity with the "Law on Citizenship", passed on July 22, 1994,[32] the Cabinet of Ministers passed Regulations No. 29 of February 7, 1995 "On Testing the Knowledge of the Persons who Want to Obtain Latvian Citizenship through Naturalisation".[33] The Regulations determine the procedures for testing the persons who want to obtain Latvian citizenship through naturalisation to determine their command of the Latvian language, their knowledge of the basic principles of the Satversme, the Law "On the Rights and Obligations of a Citizen and a Person", the text of the national anthem and the history of Latvia. Under Article 32 the applicants for Latvian citizenship have the right to appeal the decision of the examining commission of the Department of Naturalisation within 10 days from the test. The Department of Naturalisation reviews the complaint of the applicant within two weeks after receiving the complaint, and, after a repeated examination of the test papers, adopts a decision. The final decision of the Department of Naturalisation may not be appealed.

Following the provisions of the Law "On State Defence", passed on November 24, 1994,[34] the Cabinet of Ministers passed Regulations No. 91 "Regulations of Military Service".[35] Article 10 of the Regulations determines a procedure of reviewing complaints. In cases of dispute the soldiers have the right to appeal decisions of their immediate superiors to more senior commanders as well as to the Minister of Defence, whose judgement is final. The normative act does not provide for organisation of an independent (external) institution to review the dispute.

On August 30, 1994, the Cabinet of Ministers, under Article 81 of the Satversme, passed Regulations No. 177 "On Medical Treatment" and Regulations "On Certification of Doctors Authorised to Practice"[36] defining the procedure of reviewing complaints. If the person to be certified is dissatisfied with the decisions of the Commission of Certification of the Latvian Doctors' Union, he or she may submit a written complaint to the Latvian Doctors' Union. A special commission reviews the complaint within 30 days and sends a written reply to the claimant. If the reply does not satisfy the claimant, he may appeal to the Ministry of Welfare, whose decision is final.

7.4 Judicial Remedies

A court may, while reviewing a complaint filed by individuals against the acts (decisions) of the administration denying rights of physical or legal persons, consider the acts unlawful. It may then make a judgement about the validity of the complaint and point out the obligation of the official, government or local government institution to eliminate the violation of the law. If the court establishes that the acts (decisions, rulings, or lack of action) appealed against are within the framework set by law, it will refuse to redress the complaint.

While reviewing complaints about taxes, debts, and other kinds of payment the court either dismisses the appeal or invalidates the act (resolution) and orders the authority to return the sum collected illegally.

To prevent violations of the law, the court forwards the judgement to the authority appealed against or to a higher institution or official. The government institution, certain officials or the local government institution whose activities (decisions) have been appealed against must inform the Court and the physical and legal person, no later than a month after the day when the judgement becomes effective, what measures have been taken.

8. OMBUDSMAN

There is no ombudsman (in the exact sense of the word) in Latvia. Similar functions are, however, exercised by the National Human Rights Office. Following the Law "On the Latvian Human Rights Office" passed on December 5, 1996,[37] the Latvian Human Rights Office (hereinafter the Office) is an independent State institution that guarantees the observance of the fundamental rights and freedoms of the individuals and citizens of the Republic of Latvia in accordance with the Satversme, the ratified international human rights treaties and the Constitutional Law "On the Rights and Obligations of the Individual and Citizen". One of the responsibilities of the Office is to inquire into any complaint related to the abuse of human rights. The procedure of reviewing complaints is regulated by this law and the Law "Procedure of Reviewing Complaints, Recommendations and Applications by State and Local Government institutions", passed on December 27, 1994.[38]

The Office does not investigate a complaint if a court verdict has already come into force in a civil, criminal or administrative case concerning the violation of human rights indicated therein and reached against the same person and for the same violation. In compliance with Article 8 of the Law, when investigating a complaint of a violation of human rights, the Office is entitled to resolve the conflict by a procedure aiming at conciliation. If successful, a conciliation protocol is signed by the parties and approved by the Director of the Office. The Director of the Office does not approve the conciliation of the parties if it is not in accordance with the law, or if it violates the rights of someone or his or her legally protected interests. If conciliation cannot be achieved, the Office advises the parties, in writing, of its opinion and proposals in the form of recommendations. Article 9 points out that the Office presents its suggestions and recommendations for the prevention of violations of human rights and forwards them to the relevant institution or official. The official to whom the proposal is forwarded is obliged to reply to the Office in writing within one month.

9. OTHER FORMS OF SUPERVISION OVER THE ADMINISTRATION

9.1 The State Control (Audit) Office

Article 87 of the Satversme states that the State Control Office shall be an independent collegiate institution. The State Controllers are appointed in the same manner as the magistrates (the judges) but for a definite term during which they cannot be dismissed except by a court decision. The organisation of the State Control Office and its competency are fixed by the Law "On the State Audit Office", passed on October 28, 1993.[39]

Under Article 1 of the Law the State Control Office is an independent collegiate institution that audits the authorities and agencies managing state property and assets. Only the Saeima cannot be audited by the State Audit Office. The law defines the procedure of appointing the members of the State Audit Office, its structure and competence as well as the financing of the State Audit Office and the responsibility of its employees.

On September 7, 1995 the Law "Regulations on Audit by the State Control" was adopted.[40] It determines the procedure of auditing and defines different kinds of audits. Under the law, extra charges (fines) are imposed if an institution, its officials or a physical person with their financial activities or transactions have incurred losses to the State or to the local government.[41]

9.2 Public Prosecutors

On May 19, 1994, the Saeima adopted the Law "On the Public Prosecutors".[42] The law defines the purpose, functions, activities, authority, and structure of the institution of public prosecutor and its status. One of the functions of the prosecutors is to protect the rights and lawful interests of individuals and the State in accordance with the law.

Upon learning of a violation of a law and in accordance with the procedures provided by the law, the prosecutors are obliged to examine whether: 1) the information contains any evidence of a crime, 2) the lawful interests and rights of incapacitated persons, those with limited capability, the handicapped, minors, those imprisoned or those unable to defend their rights have been violated.

In addition, it is the responsibility of the prosecutors to take all measures required for the protection of the rights and lawful interests of the persons and the State when: 1) the necessity of such an examination is confirmed by the prosecutor general or a senior prosecutor, 2) the President of the Republic of Latvia, the Saeima or the Cabinet of Ministers orders that the facts be examined concerning a violation of the law, 3) it is provided so by a specific law.

The prosecutors also examine cases upon petitions by individuals. The petitions must allege a violation of an individual's rights or lawful interests. Also, the petition must have already been reviewed by a competent public authority and denied or not answered within the deadline set by the law. Such petitions shall be submitted to the prosecutor's office. According to Article 17 of the Law, while examining petitions in accordance with the procedures set by law, the prosecutors shall be entitled: 1) to require and receive any normative acts, documents and other information from the public offices of the executive branch, the banks, the State Audit Office, local governments, enterprises, authorities and organisations as well as to enter the premises of such institution without any restriction, 2) to require an interrogation, examination, audit or expert assessment to be performed by the directors of any office, enterprise, organisation, or other institution as well as to have specialists and assistants during the interrogation and 3) to invite any person and to require explanations on violations of law (in the event of a failure to appear before the prosecutors upon invitation, the prosecutors may order the summoning of persons by the police.)

Upon discovering a violation of law the prosecutors may, depending on its character: 1) warn about the impermissibility of such a violation, 2) submit a protest or petition for its elimination, 3) submit a claim or petition to a court, 4) initiate criminal proceedings, or 5) initiate procedures for administrative or disciplinary liability.

If the behaviour of a person indicates that a violation of law or a possible unlawful action has been committed, the prosecutor must warn the person about the impermissibility of such a violation of law in writing.

In compliance with Article 19 with the Law on Public Prosecutors, the prosecutor has the right to submit a "protest" (a special form of prosecutor's appeal). Protests may be submitted on any illegal enactments passed by the Cabinet of Ministers, ministries, departments or any other public institution of the executive branch, the banks, the State Audit Office, local government and others. The protests are considered and the prosecutors notified of the decisions made within 10 days from the date such a protest is received. If such a protest is submitted to a collective institution, the prosecutor may set a longer term for review. In the event of an unreasonable rejection of a protest or a failure to submit a reply, the prosecutors are entitled (within one month from the expiration of the period for consideration) to ask a court to change or revoke the unlawful enactment and to bring the responsible person to justice. The claim of the prosecutor to a court has a suspensive effect on the challenged administrative act.

If it is necessary to stop an unlawful action, to eliminate the consequences of such an action or to prevent a violation of law, the prosecutor may submit a petition in writing to the respective authority, enterprise, organisation, official or person. The prosecutor sets the time for replying and the character of the necessary action, after considering the type of violation and the time period needed for its elimination. If the requirements set in a petition are not complied with, the prosecutor is entitled to bring an action to a court.

10. PARLIAMENTARY COMMITTEES

Article 25 of the Satversme states that the Saeima shall elect committees and determine the number of their members and their duties. The committees are entitled to ask the respective ministers and local government to supply any information necessary for their work and to invite responsible representatives of the ministries and the local government to their meetings for the purpose of obtaining explanations. The committees may continue their work between sessions of Parliament.

In compliance with Article 173 of the Rules of Procedure of the Saeima, a parliamentary investigation committee has the right to invite and question private persons and, if necessary, in co-operation with experts, to interrogate and audit the Government and the local governments. The committees may also investigate private establishments and enterprises, provided that they directly or indirectly receive state grants, subsidies, credits or state-placed orders or participate in the privatisation of government or local Government property. If the persons, establishments or enterprises referred to in this article do not fulfil the requirements of the parliamentary investigation committee with regard to the questioning or audit, the police, upon the request of the committee, must carry out coercive measures to ensure the enforcement of the above requirements.

Since the beginning of the changes in 1989 and the reinstatement of the Satversme in 1993, about a dozen parliamentary investigation committees have been established. For instance, a committee investigating an attempt to organise a coup d'état was established on August 22, 1991. On October 27, 1994, a parliamentary investigation committee to appraise the legality of granting and record keeping of as well as the utilisation of credits guaranteed by the State was established. Another parliamentary investigation committee was established on January 24, 1996, to investigate the bankruptcy of the Baltija Bank and to appraise the submitted projects for its rehabilitation. Another committee, investigating the legality and conformity with the interests of the State and the Community of the National Council of Radio and Television, was established on November 14, 1996. On March 20, 1997, a committee was set up to determine the legality of granting G-24 credits, the possibilities of repayment of the credit, and the terms of personal liability for embezzlement. March 24, 1997, was the date of establishing the parliamentary investigation committee that had to appraise the legality and conformity with the interests of the State and the community of the privatisation of the joint-stock company Unibank of Latvia and the State joint-stock company Latvian Savings Bank.

The committees are established on the basis of the principle of proportional representation of the parliamentary factions. They complete their work with a report to the Saeima. The Saeima adopts a decision, appraising the performance of the committee, and charges the Cabinet of Ministers or some other state institutions with the task of reviewing the conclusions and recommendations of the parliamentary investigation committees. The Cabinet of Ministers, or another state institution, submits its conclusions to the Saeima and, if necessary, undertakes the relevant measures.

II. DEVELOPMENTS IN ADMINISTRATIVE LAW DURING 1996–1997

INTRODUCTION

One of the most important events in administrative law during the 1996–1997 period in Latvia was the establishment of the Constitutional Court. The legal framework for setting up the Court was provided by an amendment to the Satversme and the adoption of the Law "On the Constitutional Court". Thus, in December 1996 a completely new institution, the Constitutional Court of the Republic of Latvia, was established. It reviews cases concerning the compliance of laws and other legal norms with the Constitution as well as the compliance of regulations and other legal norms adopted by the Cabinet of Ministers, or by institutions (and officials) subordinated to it, with the Constitution, other laws or directives of the Cabinet of Ministers.

In February 1997 fresh legislation was introduced as a new government was formed. First, the number of ministers was reduced and a Law "On The Structure of the Cabinet of Ministers" was adopted. Second, at the beginning of 1997 a Law "On Meetings, Demonstrations, and Pickets" was passed by Parliament.

Furthermore, significant changes are expected in the local government system since enforced legislative amendments envisage the liquidation of the district local governments as of December 31, 1997. Other significant amendments changed the subordination of the Border Guard Forces at the end of 1996. At present the forces are responsible to the Ministry of the Interior (previously they were under the command of the Ministry of Defence). At the beginning of 1997 the Regulation "On Passports of Non-Citizens of Latvia" was passed. The Regulation concerns a very sensitive political issue: the status of the non-Latvian minorities. Hence the Regulation is crucial for the implementation of international standards in the sphere of human rights.

A. THE CONSTITUTION

In 1996 only one amendment to the Satversme was passed: on July 5, 1996, the Saeima passed the Law "Amendment to the Satversme of the Republic of Latvia".[43] The Amendment introduced a new Article 85 of the Satversme, which states that "[t]here is a Constitutional Court in Latvia that shall review cases concerning the compliance of laws and other legal norms with the Constitution, as well as other cases placed under its jurisdiction. The Constitutional Court has the right to declare laws and acts or parts of them null and void. The judges of the Court are appointed by the Saeima (for a period determined by law) by secret ballot and majority vote (not less than 51 deputies)".

Before the adoption of this Amendment, Article 85 stated that the institution of jury existed in Latvia, pursuant to a special law. However, after the reinstatement of the Satversme, no special laws to that effect have been passed, and no jury has been established.

B. LEGISLATION

1. PROCEDURAL AND GENERAL ORGANISATIONAL LAWS

1.1 Laws on the Judicial System

On June 15, 1994, the Law "On Judicial Power" was amended.[44] In conformity with the amendment, Article 9 of the Law (which stated that on issues of constitutional review, judgements were given by the Supreme Court) was deleted. This function of the Supreme Court had never been exercised. "On Judicial Power" was supplemented with amendments via norms which established the Constitutional Court that, together with the district (city), regional, and Supreme Court, exercise judicial power in the Republic of Latvia. The "Constitutional Court Law" regulates the activity of the Constitutional Court. This important law was only passed on June 5, 1996, and in December of that year the new independent institution, the Constitutional Court of the Republic of Latvia, was established.

On September 28, 1995, the Saeima passed the Law "Amendments to the Law On Judicial Power,[45] and, in conformity with it, Article 8 of the Law "On Judicial Power" was deleted. Article 8 determined the rules on passing judgement on disputes arising within administrative procedures. From the effective date of the law, all the cases connected with administrative action are in the competence of the district (city), regional, and the Supreme Court in accordance with the norms of the Code of Civil Procedure. The cases pending before the Commercial Court could still be reviewed by the Commercial Court, but only until December 15, 1995. Thus, in 1996 the Commercial Court ceased to exist in Latvia.

On January 29, 1997, the Saeima adopted amendments to the Law "On Judicial

Power".[46] It determined that new departments, namely departments of land registration, shall be established at the regional courts. The departments are judicial institutions and are engaged in the management of land registration (and the process of restitution). Their activity is regulated by the Law "On Judicial Power", the law "On the Restoration of Validity of the Land Registration Law of December 22, 1937, and the Procedures of Enforcement" adopted on March 30, 1993,[47] and other laws determining the registration of immovable property and their confirmation in the Land Register. The judges of the newly established departments have the status of a judge of a district (city) court.

On September 21, 1995, the Law "On Corruption Prevention" was passed.[48] It states that judges are to be considered public officials. Therefore, on May 23, 1996, the law "On Judicial Power" was amended.[49] Article 14 of the Law was supplemented with new legal norms stating that the judge and lay judges shall abstain from taking part in court sessions under the law.

1.2 Laws on the structure and the prerogatives of the administration

At the end of 1996 the Government resigned and, in compliance with the Satversme, the President of the State nominated Andris Đónle to form a government. On February 13, 1997, the Saeima gave a vote of confidence to the Cabinet of Ministers. The Cabinet of Ministers consisted of the Prime Minister, two deputy prime ministers, one of whom, simultaneously, is the Minister of Environmental Protection and Regional Development, and the Ministers of Defence, of Foreign Affairs, of Economics, of the Interior, of Education and Science, of Agriculture, of Transportation, of Welfare, of Justice, of Culture and the Minister of Special Assignment for the Affairs of the European Community.

On February 27, 1997, a vote of confidence was given to the Minister of Finance. Simultaneously, an announcement of four state minister posts was made: that of the State Minister of Revenue at the Ministry of Finance, the State Minister of Health Protection at the Ministry of Welfare, the State Minister of Local Governments, and the State Minister of Environment–both at the Ministry of Environmental Protection and Regional Development. In compliance with the Regulations of the Saeima, the Prime Minister issued Regulations No. 35 on February 17, 1997[50] and Regulations No. 60 on February 27, 1997 on the Composition of the Cabinet of Ministers.[51]

In compliance with the Law "On the Structure of the Cabinet of Ministers" on April 30, 1996, a new Regulation No. 160 "Of the Internal Order and Procedure of the Cabinet of Ministers" was issued by the Cabinet of Ministers. The present regulation determines the internal order and procedure of the Cabinet of Ministers and the order according to which the Cabinet of Ministers and its committees discuss draft legislative and other issues.

According to this act, first, the *regulations* of the Cabinet of Ministers are normative legislative acts containing norms binding on all natural and legal persons.

The regulations of the Cabinet of Ministers, which are issued under Article 81 of the Satversme, must comply with the provisions of laws in form and content. Second, the *instructions* of the Cabinet of Ministers are internal normative legislative acts addressed only to exhaustively enumerated public institutions: the State Chancellery, the ministries and the institutions under their subordination or the whole public administration as defined by Article 58 of the Satversme.

The structure of the Regulation is as follows (chapter by chapter): I) Terms used in the Present Regulations, II) General Provisions and Classification of Draft Legislative Acts, III) Submission of Draft Legislative Acts to the State Chancellery, IV) Preparation of Conceptual Issues, V) Meeting of State Secretaries and the Inter-ministerial Meeting, VI) Progress of the Draft Legislative Acts Submitted to the State Chancellery, VII) Cabinet Committees, VIII) Progress of a Draft Legislative Act after the Cabinet Committee Sitting, IX) Cabinet Sittings, Their Preparation, and Procedure, X) Formation and Entry into Force of the Legislative Acts Issued by the Cabinet of Ministers, XI) Functions of the Prime Minister, XII) Ranks of the Cabinet Members, XIII) Procedure of Sending the Cabinet Members on Official Business Trips, XIV) Procedure of Appointment and Dismissal of the Officials and Attribution of Special Service Designations and Work Titles, XV) Procedure of Viewing and Registration of International Agreements, XVI) Ensuring the Implementation of the Saeima Resolutions, XVII) Ensuring the Implementation of the Legislative Acts and Other Documents Issued by the Cabinet of Ministers, XVIII) Viewing of the Resident's Applications, Proposals and Complaints, and XIX) Final Provisions.

Under Article 40 of the Regulations to co-ordinate the opinions and to prepare the draft legislative acts for deliberation at the sitting of the Cabinet of Ministers, the draft legislative acts are initally deliberated in the committees of the Cabinet of Ministers. The Prime Minister determines the membership of the committees and the time and place of the sittings.

On January 7, 1997, the Cabinet of Ministers adopted "Amendments to the 'Regulation on the Internal Order and Procedure of the Cabinet of Ministers'."[52] Under the new arrangement, the number of committees is to be set by the Prime Minister. Therefore, on January 21, 1997, Order No. 13 of the Prime Minister "On Membership of the Committees and the Time and Place of the Sittings"[53] was passed, and only one committee was established instead of the previous three committees. The second item of the Order stated that members of the committee were the members of the Cabinet.

The Law the Structure of the Ministries[54] was adopted on February 6, 1997, and, when it became effective, Regulation No. 5 of the Cabinet of Ministers, adopted under Article 91 of the Satversme on January 14, 1994, was declared null and void. The new law states that a ministry is a centralised administrative body that helps the Cabinet of Ministers to execute the duties and obligations determined by the law and the Satversme. The Law enumerates the ministries of the Republic of Latvia. (As mentioned above, at the moment there are 12 ministries). Each ministry acts independently, in compliance with the law, and within the jurisdiction determined by the Cabinet of Ministers. The Cabinet of Ministers confirms the regulations of every ministry. The Regulation points out the functions of the ministries and their basic obligations, the areas of responsibility of the minister (and the state minister if there is one), the institutions subordinated to the ministry, the state companies subordinated to the ministry and the structure of the ministry.

The Law "On the State Audit Office"[55] was amended on November 6, 1996. Under the amended Law, the State Audit Office has the right to monitor the collecting and spending of the budget as well as to control the legality and efficiency of the action of local authorities. Up to that time the State Audit Office had only monitored the state budget and the management of state property. Therefore on March 13, 1997, the Law "On Local Government"[56] was amended. Article 5 of this Law was supplemented with a legal norm determining the right of the State Audit Office to monitor financial activities of local governments in compliance with its competencies.

1.3 Electoral laws

In March 1997, local government elections took place. Procedure for the elections was established by the Law "On the Elections of City, District or Pagasts Council" adopted on January 13, 1994. The Law was amended before the elections on November 6, 1996. One of the most essential amendments was an increase in the number of restrictions concerning the right to become a candidate. For instance, the Law was supplemented with legal regulations stating that individuals who had been engaged in the activities of the Communist Party of the Soviet Union or Latvia after January 13, 1991, should not be registered as candidates for the elections of the Dome (Council). Unfortunately, the procedure for establishing membership in the Communist Party was not prescribed, and this omission caused difficulties in the judicial review of some cases.

Further amendments to the Law "On Elections of City, District and Pagasts Council" were approved on December 6, 1996. They envisage the liquidation of the local authorities of the districts. The Law states that the local councils of the districts, elected on May 29, 1994, will continue to carry out their obligations and responsibilities guided by the laws and the regulations of the Cabinet of Ministers. From 1998, there will be only two levels of local government: the city and the pagasts councils. The Cabinet of Ministers was commissioned with the task of submitting drafts on the reorganisation of the district local authorities to the Saeima.

1.4 Laws on the general procedures of appeal and judicial review of administrative action

On September 13, 1995, "Amendments to the Code of Civil Procedure of the Republic of Latvia"[57] were adopted. In accordance with the Amendments, the Supervisory Authority, whose function was to review effective judgements, was liquidated. It was decided that cases reviewed in the first instance, or rulings adopted before October 15, 1995, should be reviewed by the Supervisory Authority only until January 13, 1996. The new law prescribes that judgements in civil cases (of the court of first instance) and in administrative law cases should be reviewed by the Appellate Instance or Cassation Instance. Thus the scope of judicial review was extended and a form of extra-judicial supervision was abolished.

Furthermore, the procedure for reviewing civil cases, as well as administrative law cases, underwent essential changes on October 3, 1996.[58] In conformity with the Amendments to the Code of Civil Procedure, the judge of the district (city) court reviews cases individually. Before the Amendments became effective, civil cases at the court of first instance were reviewed collectively by the judge and two lay judges, with the exception of the cases which the judge of the court of first instance could review individually (e.g. petitions for levy of provisions, cases connected with violation of labour law, etc.). At the same time the Code of Civil Procedure was supplemented with Chapter 33F entitled "Cases on Insolvency of Companies". The Amendments to the Code were passed in compliance with the Law "On Insolvency of Companies and Enterprises" passed on September 11, 1996.[59] The Amendments to the Code of Civil Procedure determine that cases concerning the insolvency of companies and enterprises should be reviewed by the judge of the court of the district in which the company or enterprise is located. It is stated that the court reviews complaints of the activities of the receiver. According to the Law "On Insolvency of Companies and Enterprises", a "receiver" is an official, authorised by a court, who administers the process of establishing insolvency, performs duties determined by the law and is responsible for his activities (in accordance with the procedure set by the law). Such complaints were not previously reviewed by the courts. To retry a complaint from the meeting of creditors about the activity of the receiver at court, the complaint must be filed with the receiver, who either reviews it or rejects it within two weeks. The court retries a complaint from the committee of creditors about the activity of the receiver, if the complaint has been approved by the meeting of creditors. The court retries the complaint of any creditor or debtor if: 1) the complaint has been filed with the receiver and he has neither rejected nor responded to it; 2) the meeting of creditors has refused to appeal to court. If the court establishes that some action of the receiver is unlawful, it satisfies the claim and orders the receiver to comply with the law.

2. SUBSTANTIVE LAWS

2.1 Management of the Economy: Privatisation

The procedure of privatisation of state or local government property is elaborated in the Law "On Privatisation of the Objects of the State and Local Government Property", passed on February 17, 1994.[60] It defines the principles of foundation and performance of the Privatisation Agency, set up on March 29, 1994, in compliance with Regulation No. 149-R of the Cabinet of Ministers. The Privatisation Agency, subordinated to the Ministry of Economics, is a non-profit organisation. It draws up drafts of the Cabinet of Ministers on the privatisation of state property, organises and carries out evaluation of the enterprises and concludes agreements on the sale of enterprises on behalf of the State, etc.

Amendments to the Law "On Privatisation of the Objects of the State and Local Government Property" (passed on December 24, 1996) supplement the Law with a legal norm, envisaging the establishment of a Court of Arbitration obliged to enforce the regulations of the Government. The Court of Arbitration reviews disputes among privatised enterprises and enterprises to be privatised on problems of civil liability, legal relations, and conflict of interest as well as any other disputes, if the parties have agreed on it.

Regulations confirmed by the Cabinet of Ministers regulate the activity of the Privatisation Agency. Thus, Directive No. 110 "Regulations of the Non-profit Organisation State Joint-Stock Company 'Privatisation Agency' " was adopted on March 25, 1997.[61] In accordance with the Regulations the governing bodies of the Agency are the shareholders' meeting, the Council, and the Board of the Agency. The Council of the Agency supervises the activity of the Agency and, in compliance with Article 10 of the Regulations reviews complaints about decisions about state enterprises to be privatised. If a decision adopted by the Board does not meet the requirements of the legislation and resolution, the Council, pointing out the norm of legislation that has been violated, asks the Board to correct its action.

On June 21, 1995, the Saeima passed the Law "On Privatisation of State and Local Government Apartment Houses"[62] which established the procedure of privatisation of state and local government apartment houses. One of the objects of the Law was to develop the market of immovable (real estate) property. Privatisation of apartment houses is organised by the privatisation commissions of cities and pagasts. Their activity is regulated by the law "On Privatisation of State and Local Government Apartment Houses" and the respective Regulation of the Dome worked out in conformity with the standard regulations confirmed by the Cabinet of Ministers. The Central Privatisation Commission supervises the process of privatisation. Its functions are stated in Article 59 of the Law "On Privatisation of State and Local Government Apartment Houses." For example, it has the right to inspect the legality of the performance of the Privatisation Commission of the city or the pagasts, to suspend unlawful decisions of the Privatisation Commission until they are reviewed at a Dome session and to give accounts on the process of privatisation to the Cabinet of Ministers, etc. On November 28, 1996, the Amendments to the Law "On Privatisation of State and Local Government Apartment Houses" were passed,[63] and the scope of authority of the Central Commission of Apartment Houses was thereby increased. Thus, for instance, the Central Commission of Apartment Houses was granted ownership rights over the apartments of state apartment houses until their privatisation as well as powers to co-ordinate the transfer of state-owned apartment houses to the local governments.

One of the most essential amendments to the Law "On Privatisation of State and

Local Government Apartment Houses" was passed on November 28, 1996. It is supplemented with Chapter 16, "Ownership Rights over State Apartments until Their Privatisation". The rules of this chapter are to be applied when a local government has not started privatising an apartment house and the tenants of the apartment house wish to obtain the ownership rights until the time of its privatisation.

2.2 Privatisation of land

The procedure of privatisation of land is established by the Law "On Privatisation of Land in the Countryside" of September 9, 1992.[64] The 1995 law stated that the land should be in the possession of the citizens of the Republic of Latvia, the local government, legal persons registered in Latvia (including enterprises whose share capital is owned more than 50 per cent by the citizens of Latvia), and foreign enterprises registered in Latvia, from the countries which have signed international agreements with Latvia on promoting defence and investment, effective and ratified by the Saeima. The Amendments to the Law "On Privatisation of Land in the Countryside" passed on December 5, 1996, increased the number of the non-citizens of the Republic of Latvia authorised to obtain the right to ownership of agricultural land by inheritance. The above-mentioned persons should receive the written consent of the chairman of the Council of the Pagasts to retain the right to ownership of land. A physical person who is not a citizen of the Republic of Latvia does not have the right to own land in border areas, in the territories of reserves, in the defence zones of the Baltic Sea and the Riga Bay dunes, and the land useful for the agricultural and forestry needs of the community (in accordance with the master plan of the pagasts).

On October 24, 1996, the Saeima passed the Law "On Agriculture".[65] The objective of the Law was to ensure the development of one of the basic branches of the national economy, agriculture, and to establish sustainable policy in this area. One of the tasks of the Law is to create preconditions for elaborating efficient agricultural policies during the transition period until Latvia is admitted into the European Union. The Law's provisions include those connected with the agricultural policy, the procedure of its implementation, the promotion of the market of produce, the financial support of the state, the protection of producers, and the utilisation and preservation of land. Article 19 of the Law determines the responsibilities of the institutions of the State for the execution of state administration functions: 1) the Cabinet of Ministers must elaborate the conception of agricultural policy, 2) the function of the Ministry of Agriculture is to implement the agricultural policy, 3) the responsibilities of the Ministry of Foreign Affairs include the preparation of documents and agreements in the sphere of agriculture upon the accession to international organisations or treaties and agreements.

2.3 Environmental protection

The protection of natural resources in Latvia is regulated by the Law "On Environmental Protection" adopted on August 6, 1991,[66] and other normative acts. Natural resource ownership rights in the Republic are regulated by the basic laws of the Republic of Latvia and other normative acts. The Law states the area of responsibility of the Cabinet of Ministers, the Ministry of Environmental Protection and Regional Development and the institutions of local governments.

The Ministry of Environmental Protection and Regional Development is the main executive institution engaged in elaborating and implementing the State policy in the spheres of environmental protection and regional development of the State, tourism, construction, and geology. On October 16, 1996, the Cabinet of Ministers passed Regulation No. 409 "On the Procedures of the Board of Local Government Matters at the Ministry of Environmental Protection and Regional Development".[67] The Board of Local Government Matters was declared to be under the jurisdiction of the Ministry of Environmental Protection and Regional Development.

The major responsibilities of the Board are to implement the local government reform; to elaborate the principles of administrative territorial reform; to check the compliance of the decisions adopted by the local governments with the laws and other normative acts and to elaborate draft laws and drafts of other normative acts in conformity with the normative acts and the requirements of the European Union and the "White Book". The "Regulations of the Board of Local Government Matters" were confirmed on January 14, 1997.[68]

On September 9, 1996, the Cabinet of Ministers passed "Regulations of the Latvian Foundation of Environmental Protection".[69] It determines the establishment of the Foundation of Environmental Protection in Latvia and the procedure of saving, management, and spending of funds. The Foundation is a state institution subordinated to the Ministry of Environmental Protection and Regional Development. It was established to manage the special budget of the State Environmental Protection. This function is performed by a special Council of the Foundation, appointed by the Minister of Environmental Protection and Regional Development. It includes representatives of the Ministries of Economics, Finance, Environmental Protection and Regional Development as well as other state institutions. The Council of the Foundation forms the Consultative Board, inviting representatives and experts of local governments, trade unions, and non-governmental environmental-protection organisations to take part in its work. The members of the Consultative Board are given the opportunity to learn about the projects to be discussed. The decisions of the Board are not binding but have the status of recommendations.

The law "On Forest Management and Exploitation" was passed on December 1, 1994.[70] In conformity with Article 60 of the Law, the management of this sector is exercised by the State Forestry Department (and the institutions subordinated to it), the local government, and the environmental-protection institutions. Amendments to the law were passed on April 2, 1997, and in accordance with them the

State Forestry Department was subordinated to the Ministry of Agriculture. Earlier it was subordinated to the State Minister of Forestry, but when the post of the State Minister of Forestry was liquidated, the legal status of the institution changed.

On April 22, 1997, the Cabinet of Ministers adopted Regulation No. 154, confirming the "Status of the State Forestry Department". The document determined the responsibilities of the Department, its structure, subordination and also the institutions subordinated to it. On May 2, 1996, the Saeima passed the Law "On the Entrails (Core) of the Earth".[71] The Law establishes the procedure as well as the requirements of rational, complex and environmentally harmless exploitation of the entrails of the earth. Article 4 of the Law names the institutions supervising the exploitation of the entrails of the earth, including the Ministry of Environmental Protection and Regional Development, the State Geological Service, and the local governments of cities and pagasts, and states their functions.

The Law "On Hazardous Wastes" was adopted on March 30, 1993.[72] It established a procedure for the management of hazardous wastes in the territory of Latvia in accordance with the following principles: to protect the environment, people's health, the property and interests of physical and legal persons from the consequences of hazardous wastes. Essential amendments to the Law were made on December 17, 1996.[73] The Amendments establish that in certain individual cases the Cabinet of Ministers can approve the import of hazardous wastes for recycling or processing from Lithuania and Estonia if there are international agreements to that effect (before the Amendments were passed, it was forbidden to import wastes into the Republic of Latvia.) It is, however, still prohibited to import hazardous wastes from Third World countries through Lithuania and Estonia. In compliance with Article 2 of the Amendments, the Ministry of Environmental Protection and Regional Development, in co-operation with the Ministry of Welfare, must work out substantive norms and criteria to determine what wastes should be regarded as harmful and hazardous. The Cabinet of Ministers confirms these norms. The Amendments to the Law increase the scope of competence of the Ministry of Environmental Protection and Regional Development with regard to management of the harmful wastes. The Ministry determines the disposal, collection, storage, and recycling sites for the processing of harmful wastes. Article 10 of the Law establishes the obligations of the physical and legal persons engaged in the management of such wastes. The Amendments to the Law prescribe that any violation of the Law will result in the termination of the activity and the revocation of the permits issued by the Ministry.

The new Article 12 of the Law determines the functions of the non-governmental Environmental Protection Service, namely, to verify that environmental-protection normative acts are observed by physical and legal persons concerning the management of harmful waste. The new Article 13 regulates the exchange of information, to ensure that any information on activities with harmful wastes is accessible to state and local government institutions and the non-governmental Environmental Protection Service.

In conformity with "The Fishing Law" passed on April 12, 1995,[74] the Cabinet of

Ministers adopted Regulation No. 1 of January 16, 1996 "On the Lease of Waters, Water Reservoirs and Fishing Rights, and the Procedure for Using Fishing Rights".[75] They regulate the lease, in part or in full, of lakes, rivers, water reservoirs, the Latvian territorial waters of the Baltic Sea and Riga Bay and determine the procedures of concluding industrial fishing rent agreements and sales, as well as the procedure of usage of fishing rights and fish resources under the management of the local governments. Renting of private water resources is not subject to these Regulations. In conformity with the Regulation, state-owned water reservoirs and rivers may be rented for fishing to physical and legal persons for a period from five to 30 years. The procedure is performed by the Department of Fish Farming in co-ordination with the Regional Environmental Boards and pagasts or city governments.

Amendments to the Law "On Natural Resources Tax" were adopted on December 19, 1996.[76] The Amendments supplemented Article 15 of the Law with a new clause 3. It states that exploitation permits concerning exploitation of the entrails of the earth issued in compliance with the procedure established by the Law "On the Entrails of the Earth," cannot be sold. In accordance with the Law, exploitation permits for several kinds of natural resources and permits for the discharge of polluting substances, in strictly determined regions and industrial enterprises, shall be introduced. Licensing shall be introduced for the import or sale of products harmful to the environment. The issues of licensing, the procedures of payment and different performances concerning the permits, are regulated by Regulations No. 434 of the Cabinet of Ministers of November 19, 1996 (Regulations on Licensing Individual Categories of Entrepreneurs).

In conformity with the Law "On Natural Resources Tax", the Cabinet of Ministers adopted Regulation No. 155 "On Water Usage Permits,"[77] which established the procedure of applying for and receiving water usage permits, as well as the responsibilities and rights of the officials issuing permits and the persons using water. Consequently, these permits are issued by the Regional Environmental Board after receiving an application (certified by the local city or pagasts government) from the applicant.

2.4 Financial laws

The Law "On Land Tax"[78] was amended on December 27, 1996. Article 4 of the Law "Areas of Tax-Exempt Land" was supplemented with legal norms envisaging that the lands under the jurisdiction of the Ministry of Defence and the lands assigned to religious organisations shall not be exempt from taxation.

The status, performance and supervision of crediting institutions are regulated by the "Law on Crediting Institutions" adopted on October 5, 1995.[79] In the Republic of Latvia a crediting institution functions as a bank, a savings-and-loan bank or a foreign branch bank. In Latvia the crediting institutions can operate only after having been granted a license by the Bank of Latvia. On March 29, 1996, the Ministry of Finance adopted Directive No. 166 "On the Regulations of the State Treasury" (not published). The State Treasury is an institution subordinated to the Minister of Finance that assigns and performs payments for definite purposes from the State Budget, manages and supervises inspections of the state budget, and carries out other functions pertaining to the management of the financial system. Previously the State Treasury Department of the Ministry of Finance was entrusted with these functions.

On May 30, 1996, amendments were made to the "Law on Crediting Institutions"[80] and, in compliance with them, the Law was supplemented with a provision stating the obligation of any crediting institution (on the request of the State Treasury) to inform it about the accounts and banking operations of the State budget institutions.

Relevant amendments were made to the Law "On State Revenue Service" on January 16.[81] The Law On State Revenue Service" was passed on October 28, 1993.[82] The State Revenue Service is an administrative institution subordinated to the Minister of Finance. It ensures the registration of taxpayers, the collection of taxes, duties, and other obligatory payments established by the State in the territory of the Republic of Latvia, and in the free customs zone. Apart from this, it also implements customs policies and regulates customs-related matters.

The Customs Board and the Department of the Financial Police form the apparatus of the State Revenue Service. The latest amendments prescribe that the Law "On the State Civil Service" should not be applied on the State Revenue Service (including Customs), its officials and employees. Their legal relations are regulated by ordinary labour legislation.

2.5 Regulation of mass media

Control of the formation, registration and supervision of mass media and the press is regulated by the Law "On Press and Other Mass Media" of December 20, 1990[83] and "The Law on Radio and Television" of August 24, 1995.[84]

On October 10, 1996[85] and April 17, 1997,[86] Amendments were made to "The Law on Radio and Television" that redefined some of the functions of the National Board of Radio and Television. In compliance with the Law, the National Board of Radio and Television is an independent institution, which represents the interests of the community in the sphere of electronic communication and controls their performance to ensure the observance of the Satversme, "The Law on Radio and Television", and other laws, as well as to ensure the freedom of speech and information.

The Board is appointed by the Saeima, which elects its nine members to four-year terms of office. "The Law on Radio and Television" contains a statement of the Board's functions, for example, to issue broadcast and re-transmission permits as well as cable television and cable radio registration cards. Radio permits are issued for five years, television permits for seven years and cable television permits for 10 years. In compliance with the amendments on broadcast and cable radio and television registration cards, the National Board of Radio and Television informs the Enterprise Register within two weeks about the issuance of permits and registration cards, or the termination of the activity of the applying broadcasting organisation. Previously the Board had to inform the Enterprise Register about any changes in the company management as well.

On April 17, 1997, Amendments to the Law "On Press and Mass Media" were adopted.[87] These Amendments were made in accordance with the Amendments to the law of April 17, 1997, "On the Enterprise Register of the Republic of Latvia".[88] In compliance with the Amendments, the scope of the functions of the Enterprise Register of the Republic of Latvia has been increased. At present, it registers enterprises, companies and also mass media (previously this function was performed by the Ministry of Justice). The Register also controls the compliance of the documents of foundation and performance of mass media with the laws and other legal acts.

Article 12 of the Law "On Press and Mass Media" was amended simultaneously. It prescribes that the Prosecutor General, the Minister of Finance, and the Chief State Notary of the Register (previously the Minister of Justice) have the right to submit an application to initiate a case concerning the termination of the activities of an institution or a form of mass communication. The court can decide to terminate activities if: 1) the institution has advocated violence or unlawful activities, 2) it has propagated the idea of disobedience to the laws of the Republic of Latvia, 3) it has not paid taxes established by the laws of the Republic of Latvia and has not provided information required by the laws to the State Financial Inspectorates, 4) it publishes information that has been declared slanderous and insulting by a court judgement or has revealed a state secret, stirred up racial or ethnic discord, or spread military propaganda, and, finally 5) within a period of one year it has repeatedly violated the law.

2.6 Management of socio-cultural processes

In accordance with "The Law on Higher Educational Establishments" of November 2, 1995,[89] the Cabinet of Ministers adopted Regulation No. 370 "On Accreditation of Higher Educational Establishments".[90] The Regulation establishes the procedure of accreditation of state or private (i.e. founded by a legal person) higher educational establishments. Special accreditation certificates are to be issued to authorise the higher educational establishments. On July 2, 1996, Amendments to the Regulations[91] were adopted, establishing that a new non-profit institution, a limited liability company called the Higher Education Quality Assessment Centre, is to be formed. This examines the required educational programmes and the student assessment (evaluation) process of the higher educational establishments. The Centre provides expert advice and summarises information essential for the accreditation of a specific educational programme or whole universities. In conformity with Article 28 of the Law, the Centre establishes the Assessment Committee after taking into consideration the recommendations of the Board of Rectors, the Department of Higher Education, the Latvian Science Council, and the Latvian Academy of Sciences, as well as observing the requirements of the European Union. The Assessment Committee is comprised of Latvian and foreign experts. Further, the Amendments prescribe that the Department of Higher Education will adopt the decision on accreditation while the State Minister of Higher Education and Science (previously, the Minister of Education and Science) confirms it.

On February 12, 1996, Directive No. 58 of the Ministry of Education and Science "On the Procedure of Issuing Licenses to Open Comprehensive, Vocational, and Special Educational Establishments, and Start Their Operation" was adopted (not published). The Regulation establishes, in accordance with the Directive of the Ministry of Education and Science, the formation of the Licensing Commission, which is authorised to license the performance of comprehensive educational establishments. The Commission, consisting of not less than five members, decides whether to issue a license or deny the application, as well as whether to revoke an existing license or to renew it.

On July 2, 1996, the Cabinet of Ministers adopted Regulation No. 238 "On Licensing Higher Educational Establishments".[92] The Regulation establishes the procedure of issuing licenses to a legal person who is the founder of a higher educational establishment. The Licensing Commission decides whether to issue, refuse or revoke a license. The licenses are issued for three years.

The Cabinet of Ministers passed Regulation No. 117 "On Medical Treatment" on August 30, 1994.[93] It regulates legal relations in the sphere of medical treatment with the task to ensure quality prevention, diagnostics, and treatment of illnesses as well as the rehabilitation of patients. The Amendments to the Regulation of January 10, 1997,[94] establish that the Cabinet of Ministers determines: a) the procedure of financing the health care system, b) the kinds and scope of medical treatment that are financed from the state budget, the special health care budget and the patient himself (stating the procedure of payment of the latter). Previously the Cabinet of Ministers established the scope of medical treatment to be financed from the budget of the local governments as well, whereas presently local governments themselves decide on the relevant procedures.

On April 2, 1996, the Riga Dome adopted Regulations No. 30/63 "On Issuing Licenses to Doctors". A special Licensing Commission of the Dome Health Care Department, consisting of seven members, was appointed. The Regulation establishes the activities of the Licensing Commission and states which individuals (persons) have the right to receive a license. It also establishes the procedure of licensing, revocation or suspension of licenses. In accordance with Paragraph 2.5 of the Regulation, the decision of the Commission on refusing an application for a license, revocation or suspension of a license can be appealed in court.

In compliance with the Regulation "On Medical Treatment", the Cabinet of Ministers adopted Regulation No. 373 "On the Quality Control Inspectorate of Medical Care and Evaluation of Work Ability".[95] The Inspectorate is a new administrative institution formed by the Cabinet of Ministers and subordinated to the

Ministry of Welfare. It has control over all medical institutions and companies, regardless of their administrative subordination and form of ownership, and is engaged in determining the quality of medical care and evaluation of work ability. The chief executive of the Inspectorate reviews the conclusions of the experts of the Inspectorate where cases are disputed. His or her decision can be appealed in court.

On July 4, 1995, the Cabinet of Ministers adopted Regulation No. 187 "On Certification of Practising Doctors".[96] In compliance with the Regulation, the Ministry of Welfare adopted Order No. 68 "On the Commission Examining Conflicts Concerning the State Sickness Benefits (Payments) Foundation" (unpublished). In accordance with the Order, the Commission examines various kinds of conflicts, for example, between the sickness foundation of a local government and a state medical institution, or between sickness foundations of different local governments. Applications should be submitted to the Commission if the conflicts have not been resolved by the parties themselves. The decision of the Commission is binding on all parties involved in the dispute. If one of the parties is not satisfied with the decision of the Commission, it can appeal the decision in court.

2.7 Management of cultural heritage

The Cabinet of Ministers adopted Regulation No. 232 "On the Inspectorate of State Monuments of Culture and Their Protection" on June 25, 1996.[97] It was passed in accordance with the Law of February 12, 1996, "On Protection of Monuments of Culture". The Inspectorate is a state civil service subordinated to the Ministry of Culture. Article 4 of the Regulation establishes the most important responsibilities of the Inspectorate, such as the regular inspection of the monuments of culture to ensure their protection, as well as the collection of information on the owners of the monuments and the persons responsible for the utilisation and preservation of the monuments of culture. Additionally, the Inspectorate, in co-operation with the Ministry of Interior, examines objects of art and issues permits for their export to foreign countries. The powers of the Inspectorate for Protection of the State Monuments of Culture are set out in the Law "On Protection of Monuments of Culture".

2.8 Administration of political processes

The Law "On the State Border," which was passed on October 27, 1994,[98] was amended by the Saiema on December 12, 1996.[99] In accordance with these Amendments the Border Guard forces and their personnel are presently subordinated to the Ministry of the Interior. Previously the Border Guard forces were subordinated to the Ministry of Defence. To administer the process, a special commission was formed in compliance with the Regulation "On the Commission Providing Transfer of Border Guard Forces into Subordination of the Ministry of the Interior"[100] of January 16, 1997, passed by the Cabinet of Ministers.

Also on January 16, 1997, the Saeima passed the Law "On Meetings, Demonstrations, and Strikes".[101] It determines the procedure of organising meetings, demonstrations, and strikes. According to Article 12 of the Law, a special permit from the local government or state institutions is not needed to organise a meeting, a demonstration or a strike if they are in conformity with the law. The organisers must submit an application to the local government of the city or the pagasts of the administrative territory where the respective activity is to be held.

The Law states the requirements for the contents of the application and establishes the procedure of reviewing the application by the local government. The application must be reviewed within three days, but not later than 48 hours before the beginning of the activity. The official of the local government will immediately issue a reasoned written refusal if the organiser has not taken into consideration the requirements of the Law or if the activity can endanger the security of the state or the community, or the health and morality of the community, as well as the rights and freedoms of the people. Further, the activity may be banned if it may provoke violence or the perpetration of a crime. The refusal can be appealed in court. The court must review the case within three days in compliance with the procedure set by the Civil Procedure Code.

On December 18, 1996, Amendments were made to the Law "On the Entry and Temporary Residence of Foreigners and Stateless Persons in the Republic of Latvia".[102] In some cases foreign citizens and stateless persons are allowed to stay in the Republic of Latvia without a residence permit for more than three months but less than a year. This is possible only in cases when the person has received a visa through a procedure established by a regulation of the Cabinet of Ministers and when his or her stay in Latvia is connected with scientific research, educational assignments, commercial activities, assistance to public institutions or the local governments of the Republic of Latvia or implementation of international projects and international contracts.

The Amendments have extended the time limit for submitting a new application for a residence permit, after refusal, from 10 days to one month. The Law envisages that the Minister of the Interior can cancel the decision of the Department of Citizenship and Immigration, or its head, to issue a residence permit or refuse it, if the decision was unlawful. In contrast with the previous arrangement, the decision can be appealed in court. The following persons have the right to appeal the decision: a) the interested person who is temporarily residing in the Republic of Latvia, and b) the resident of Latvia who has invited the foreign citizen or the stateless person if the application to receive a residence permit has been refused and if the invitation is connected with family reunion. Before the adoption of the Amendments only the resident of the Republic of Latvia could submit a claim. At the same time restrictions have been added to the Amendments stating that the residence permit will be refused if the person does not possess a health insurance policy guaranteeing payment for medical care during the period of stay in the Republic of Latvia.

The procedure of annulment of residence permits has been also amended. For instance, residence permits were previously annulled if the holders were registered at the narcotics health centre; at present the law does not envisage this. Furthermore, the chiefs of the Police Department and their superiors are obliged to submit an application to the Department of Citizenship and Immigration demanding the revocation of a residence permit if the holder has been found guilty by a court of committing a crime. The same follows if he has no legal means of subsistence, or if the authorised state institutions suspect him of endangering the public order and the security of the State. Recently, in a number of cases the head of the Department of Citizenship and Immigration has ordered individuals to leave the territory of Latvia. Contrary to the previous situation the decision of the head of the Department of Citizenship and Immigration can now be appealed in court within seven days after receiving the order.

Further amendments have been enacted to the effect that the Department of Citizenship and Immigration, which is responsible to the Ministry of the Interior, in co-operation with state and local government institutions, may check if the person who has received a departure order has voluntarily left the country. The Law is supplemented with a new chapter, "Banishment of a Person from the Country". In compliance with the chapter, the Border Guard forces and the State Police carry out the task of banishing the person from the country. If the person has unlawfully entered the country, the Chief Battalion Commander of the Border Guard forces or his deputy has the right to demand his or her banishment from the country. The supplement establishes the procedure of banishment and the rights of the person who has been banished from the country.

On January 21, 1997, the Cabinet of Ministers adopted Regulation No. 49 "On Non-Citizen Passports".[103] The Regulation establishes the rights of citizens of the former USSR who are residing in Latvia but are not citizens of the Republic of Latvia or any other country. It grants the right of receiving identification and travel documents compatible with international standards, and determines the procedure for issuing non-citizen passports. It also states that the inland passports of the former USSR shall be invalid as of January 1, 2000.

C. A NOTE ON INFORMAL RULES

There were no cases in which informal rules used by administration have been publicly debated. These rules may be viewed as a problem in our system, but there is no jurisprudential concept referring to the phenomenon of "informal rules" because in the transitional period this theory of administrative law has been poorly developed in Latvia.

D. JUDICIAL DECISIONS

INTRODUCTION

According to the procedural norms set up in the Civil Procedure Code and the Criminal Procedure Code, the structure of a judicial decision consists of an introduction, justification (reasoning), and conclusion (holding). Judgements are not usually published. Lately, a number of judgements on interesting cases tried by the regional courts and the Supreme Court have been published in the official newspaper of the Republic of Latvia, *Latvijas Vestnesis*. This work is done mostly on the initiative of the journalists of this newspaper. According to Article 33 of the "Constitutional Court Law" the verdict of the Constitutional Court is to be published in the newspaper *Latvijas Vestnesis* within five days after being announced. The holding of the verdict must also be published in the gazette *Zinotajs*. Once a year the Constitutional Court must publish a collection of its verdicts, including all verdicts in full and the individual opinions of the judges in all of the cases.

1. THE CONSTITUTIONAL COURT

On April 28, 1997, the Constitutional Court of Latvia reviewed its first case involving judicial review of administrative action.[104] The regulation involved had been passed in compliance with the procedure set by Article 81 of the Satversme of the Republic of Latvia and in conformity with Regulation No. 54 of the Cabinet of Ministers of March 14, 1995, "On Purchase Prices of Electrical Energy Generated in the Republic of Latvia". The case was related to a determination of the scope of the prerogatives of the government.

The Constitutional Court decided that Regulation No. 23 of January 10, 1997, "Amendments to the Law 'On Regulating Business Activity in the Energy Sector'" was not in conformity with Article 81 of the Satversme of the Republic of Latvia and, therefore, was null and void as of the announcement of the verdict. It also ruled that Regulation of the Cabinet of Ministers No. 54 of March 14, 1995, "On Purchase Prices of Electrical Energy Produced in the Republic of Latvia" was not in conformity with Article 14 of the Law "On the Structure of the Cabinet of Ministers" and was thus null and void as of October 11, 1995.

The facts of the case were as follows. On September 6, 1995 the Saeima passed the Law "On Regulating Business Activity in the Energy Sector" and on December 21, 1995, the Cabinet of Ministers submitted a draft law to the Saeima "Amendments to the Law 'On Regulating Business Activity in the Energy Sector' ", intended to delete clauses 5 to 10 of Article 27 of that Law. On November 25, 1996, the Saeima passed the Law "Amendments to the Law 'On Regulating Business Activity in the Energy Sector'". By virtue of Article 8 of this Law, clauses 5, 6, 7 and 8 of Article 27 of the Law "On Regulating Business Activity in the Energy Sector" were deleted, but the Saeima rejected the motion of the Cabinet of Ministers to delete clauses 9 and 10 of Article 27.[105]

Then, on January 10, 1997, the Cabinet of Ministers, in compliance with the procedure set by Article 81 of the Satversme of the Republic of Latvia, passed Regulations No. 23 "Amendments to the Law 'On Regulating Business Activity in the Energy Sector'", which formulated clause 9 of Article 27 in a new wording, while clause 10 of Article 27 was deleted. On March 7, 1997, 35 deputies of the Saeima submitted an application to the Constitutional Court petitioning to annul Regulations No. 23 and pointing out that the Cabinet of Ministers had violated the restriction of Article 81 of the Satversme that regulations may not change laws passed by the Saeima then in power. The Court agreed that the Saeima had completed its legislative function at its meeting on November 25, 1996, by rejecting the motion of the Cabinet of Ministers and deciding to leave the legal norms passed by the previous Saeima as valid. The principle behind the decision was that the "laws passed by the Saeima then in power", as used in Article 81 of the Satversme, should be interpreted as referring to *any* legislative act of the Saeima (including the rejection of a motion or a draft of the government). Furthermore, the Latvian legislative traditions concerning the publication of a law introducing amendments to an existing law do not require special indication or reference to either the debate on an article that has taken place in Parliament or the fact that the wording of the article has remained unchanged.[106]

2. THE SUPREME COURT

As stated above, according to the Law "On Judicial Power", all Supreme Court justices form the Plenum (general meeting of justices). The Plenum adopts compulsory explanations for the courts on the application of laws. However, there have not been interpretations of generalising types of cases related to administrative relations or administrative law doctrines binding for the lower courts in the decisions of the Plenum.

3. ORDINARY COURTS: STATISTICS ABOUT THE CASES ARISING FROM ADMINISTRATIVE RELATIONS

The number of cases arising from administrative law relations reviewed in the district courts is as follows: in 1995 - 2121 cases (in Riga - 1504), in 1996 - 1414 (in Riga - 684). These statistics have been provided by the Ministry of Justice of the Republic of Latvia.

E. WORKINGS OF OMBUDSMEN, INVESTIGATORY PARLIAMENTARY COMMITTEES, PUBLIC PROSECUTORS, ETC.

There are no annual reports published by the Parliamentary Committees or the Public Prosecutors, except for the State Audit Office reports. Unfortunately, the 1996 report of the State Audit Office of the Republic of Latvia was not available at press time.

1. PUBLIC PROSECUTORS

Some statistics, however, have been published. For example, the Prosecutors' Office of the Republic of Latvia has provided the following information:

a. In 1996 the prosecutors verified information on a total of 2456 violations of law;

b. Of those cases, 226 concerned violations of laws on the rights and legal interests of individuals. Thus, the state authorities rejected the applications or did not respond to an application or a complaint from individuals. In 47 cases violations of law have been established. A prosecutor's warning was issued in one case, and protests were filed in 26 cases.

c. There have been 380 complaints of unlawful activities of officials of state and local government institutions (in 90 of the cases, violations of law have been established). Seven warnings and 21 protests have been filed;

d. In 1996, 104 administrative cases have been reviewed in court in the presence of the prosecutor. Sixty-four protests have been submitted against court judgements: fifty-one protests have been granted, while nine protests have been rejected.

2. CORRUPTION

There are two types of special devices in the Criminal Code devoted to the elimination of corruption in the administration: 1) conflict of interest provisious for certain administrative positions; 2) rules against bribery. According to the Prosecutors' Office of the Republic of Latvia the prosecutors have initiated 46 criminal cases on bribery in 1996. There have been no other cases connected with corruption.

The Chapter has been prepared on the basis of information provided by Anita Usacka

NOTES

1 *Official Gazette*, 1990, No. 20.
2 *Official Gazette*, 1991, No. 21.
3 *Official Gazette*, 1991, No. 42.
4 *Official Gazette*, 1992, No. 4.
5 Article 85 of the Satversme.
6 Article 81 of the Satversme and Article 14 of the Law "On Structure of the Cabinet of Ministers".
7 *Latvijas Vestnesis* (hereinafter referred to as *LV*) 1996, No. 80.
8 Article 47.
9 Article 71.
10 Articles 69, 70.
11 Article 78.
12 Article 42.
13 Article 43.
14 Article 44.
15 Article 41.
16 Article 42.
17 Article 41.
18 Article 48.
19 Article 45.
20 Article 46.
21 *LV*, 1994, No. 61.
22 Article 15 of the Law "On the Structure of the Cabinet of Ministers".
23 For example, the Instruction "The Procedure of Collecting Taxes and Duties in Hard Currency by the Department of Public Treasury" issued by the Ministry of Finance of the Republic of Latvia on February 18, 1994 (unpublished), and the Recommendation issued by the Ministry of Welfare on April 21, 1994 "On Payment of Pensions and Benefits at the Post Offices of Latvia" *Latvijas Vestnesis*, 1996, No. 96.
24 E.g. Instruction No. 39 of the Ministry of Welfare of the Republic of Latvia of February 8, 1996, "On Licensing Businesses Associated with Export, Import, Production and Sale of Medical Goods Medicines"; Instruction No. 77 of March 19, 1996, by the Ministry of Welfare "On the Licensing of Doctors"; Instruction "On the Conflict Committee of the State Sickness Foundation", issued by the Ministry of Welfare of Latvia on February 13, 1997.
25 *LV*, 1997, No. 52.
26 *LV*, 1997, No. 95.
27 *LV*, 1994, No. 61.
28 "Law on Local-Government", Article 41.
29 Article 1.
30 *LV*, 1996, No. 103.
31 *LV*, 1994, No. 57.
32 *LV*, 1994, No. 93.
33 *LV*, 1995, No. 23.
34 *LV*, 1994, No. 145.
35 *LV*, 1997, No. 73.
36 *LV*, 1995, No. 104.
37 *LV*, 1996, No.221.
38 *LV*, 1994, No. 130.
39 *LV*, 1993, No. 101.
40 *LV*, 1995, No. 146.
41 Article 54 of the Regulations.
42 *LV*, 1994, No. 65.
43 *LV*, 1996, No. 100.

44 *LV*, 1994, No. 72.
45 *LV*, 1995, No. 153.
46 *LV*, 1997, No. 46.
47 *Zinotajs*, 1993, No. 14.
48 *LV*, 1995, No. 156.
49 *LV*, 1996, No. 94.
50 *LV*, 1997, No. 49.
51 *LV*, 1997, No. 63.
52 *LV*, 1997, No.7/8.
53 *LV*, 1997, No. 27.
54 *LV*, 1997, No. 52.
55 *LV*, 1996, No. 199.
56 *LV*, 1997, No. 52.
57 *LV*, 1995, No. 148.
58 *LV*, 1996, No. 72.
59 *LV*, 1996, No. 165.
60 *LV*, 1994, No. 27.
61 *LV*, 1997, No. 88.
62 *LV*, 1995, No. 103.
63 *LV*, 1996, No. 223.
64 *Zinotajs*, 1992, No. 32.
65 *LV*, 1996, No. 189.
66 *Zinotajs*, 1991, No. 3.
67 *LV*, 1996, No. 177.
68 *LV*, 1997, No. 23.
69 *LV*, 1996, No. 120.
70 *LV*, 1994, No. 41.
71 *LV*, 1996, No. 87.
72 *Zinotajs*, 1993, No. 14.
73 *LV*, 1997, No. 1.
74 *LV*, 1995, No. 66.
75 *LV*, 1996, No. 14.
76 *LV*, 1997, No. 1. The law was passed on September 14, 1995, *LV*, 1995, No. 152.
77 *LV*, 1997, No. 108.
78 *LV*, 1997, No. 1 , adopted on December 20, 1990. *Zinotajs*, 1991, No. 11.
79 *LV*, 1995, No. 163.
80 *LV*, 1996, No. 100.
81 *LV*, 1997, No. 36/37.
82 *LV*, 1993, No. 105.
83 *Zinotajs*, 1992, No. 5.
84 *LV*, 1995, No. 137.
85 *LV*, 1996, No. 178.
86 *LV*, 1997, No. 104.
87 *LV*, 1997, No. 104.
88 *LV*, 1997, No. 104.
89 *LV*, 1995, No. 179.
90 *LV*, 1995, No. 191.
91 *LV*, 1996, No. 116.
92 *LV*, 1996, No. 116.
93 *LV*, 1994, No. 106.
94 *LV*, 1997, No. 12/15.
95 *LV*, 1996, No. 167.
96 *LV*, 1995, No. 104.
97 *LV*, 1996, No. 111.

98 *LV*, 1994, No. 132.
99 *LV*, 1996, No. 226.
100 *LV*, 1997, No. 23.
101 *LV*, 1997, No. 31.
102 *LV*, 1997, No. 3.
103 *LV*, 1997, No. 27.
104 Decision No. 04-01 97 "On the Conformity of the Regulation of the Cabinet of Ministers No. 23 of January 10, 1997, 'Amendments to the Law "On Regulating Business Activity in the Energy Sector'".
105 Verbatim report of the Saeima meeting of November 25, 1996, *Latvijas Vestenis*, 1996, No. 206.
106 The verdict of the Constitutional Court of Latvia on Case No. 04-01 97 was published in *Valdibas Vestnesis*, 1997, No. 113.

CHAPTER SEVEN
LITHUANIA

I. GENERAL DESCRIPTION OF THE ADMINISTRATIVE LEGAL SYSTEM

1. A BRIEF ACCOUNT OF THE HISTORY OF THE ADMINISTRATIVE LAW SYSTEM

1.1 Establishment of major state institutions

Administrative law today, as the leading branch of public law, has to meet the objectives, priorities, and challenges of modern society and the legal system, where it "should be not only an instrument organising the public administration but also the law that regulates the exercise of administrative power and provides control over its use".[1] Since 1990, when Lithuania declared its independence, some steps have been taken to redesign its constitutional, legal, and administrative system. However, the principles of administrative law and administrative process inherited from the Soviet administrative system of imperatives, commands, and strict subordination and unconditional obedience of citizens to the administrative authorities, remains, to a considerable degree, unaltered. Therefore, administrative law in Lithuania suffers from a conceptual as well as an institutional crisis. As a starting point, the substantive principles of administrative law, such as lawfulness, equality before the law, conformity to statutory purpose, proportionality and balance between public and private interests, objectivity and impartiality, protection of legitimate interests and vested rights, as well as transparency and openness, need to be properly reflected in new laws governing the administrative legal system.

The first important steps forming the core of the present Lithuanian administrative legal system were taken on March 11, 1990, when the Supreme Council of the Republic of Lithuania adopted the Act on the Restoration of the Independent State of Lithuania[2] and the Law "On the Reinstatement of the May 12, 1938, Constitution", which annulled the April 20, 1978, Constitution of the Lithuanian SSR, and other USSR legislation.[3] The May 12, 1938, Constitution of Lithuania was reinstated, suspending the acts governing the status and powers of the President, the Seimas (Parliament), the Assembly, the State Council, and the State Control Office (Audit Chamber). This was of primary importance because it constitutionally dissociated the State of Lithuania from the member states of the USSR and its legal system in general. The principles of independence set forth in the Act of the Restoration of the Independent State of Lithuania were constitutionally established.

On the same day the Supreme Council, by adopting the Law "On the Provisional Basic Law of the Republic of Lithuania", terminated the validity of the May 12, 1938, Constitution of Lithuania and simultaneously ratified the Provisional Basic

Law of the Republic of Lithuania.[4] This law established the new legislative, executive, judiciary, and controlling institutions of the Republic of Lithuania. Two years later, the Constitution of the Republic of Lithuania of October 25, 1992,[5] entrenched the principle of separation of powers (Article 5). According to this principle, the Supreme Council, which was later renamed the *Seimas* (a unicameral parliament), was vested with the highest legislative power. The President and the Government, headed by the Prime Minister, were proclaimed as the highest executive bodies. The functions of central executive were delegated to newly created or reorganised ministries, departments, and other administrative authorities. Local executive powers were vested in the local government bodies of the administrative units (city and county councils and their executive bodies). Finally, the higher (intermediate) level of executive powers was delegated to the Government representatives (now district governors).

The backbone of the judicial power was established as a four-tier court system consisting of the county and regional courts, the district courts, the Court of Appeal, and the Supreme Court. The prosecutors' powers were narrowed: whereas formerly the *procurators* were responsible (in addition to criminal prosecutions) for the supervision of the proper enforcement of the rights and interests of individuals and the lawful execution of administrative acts, these powers may now be executed by the prosecutors to a very limited extent. Today the procurators are mainly in charge of prosecution on behalf of the State, and the supervision of interrogative bodies.

Further, the State Control Office was vested with the power of supervision over the state property and the state budget. The Ombudsmen (Seimas' Controllers) were authorised to examine the complaints of citizens concerning abuse of powers. The Constitution also provided for the establishment of a Constitutional Court ruling on the conformity of laws and other legal acts with the Constitution.

The executive, judicial, and state control institutions were developed in their present form in 1993 and 1994 with the establishment of the Constitutional Court and the Ombudsman as well as with the re-establishment of the local governments and district governors. Although the Law on Courts provides for the establishment of special administrative, labour, commercial, and other courts, separate courts with jurisdiction over administrative law matters have not yet been established. Jurisdiction over certain cases of administrative offences and judicial review of administrative acts was delegated to the ordinary courts.

1.2 Adoption of procedural laws and codes

The adoption of procedural laws of the new administrative legal system was not started from scratch. The Basic Provisional Law and, later, the Law on the Enactment of the Constitution established that laws and legal acts adopted before the restoration of state independence and before the enactment of the Constitution were valid, provided that they did not contradict the Constitution. Therefore, all procedural laws regulating the administrative legal system may be divided into two groups: 1) laws adopted before the restoration of independence, and 2) laws adopted after the restoration of independence.

It should be noted that the administrative process was partly codified during the time of Soviet rule; namely, the procedure concerning administrative law offences was codified by the Administrative Law Offences Code in 1984. This Code is still applicable in Lithuania. Although many provisions of the Code have been amended since 1990 (the code has been amended 75 times), no essential revision, taking into account the principles of modern administrative law and process, has been made. The Code still regulates only the questions of administrative adjudication concerning cases of administrative law offences.

Lithuania does not have an Administrative Procedure Code covering the general matters of administrative procedure. A host of provisions on administrative procedure related to administrative acts and their internal review are dispersed among approximately 150 statutes, regulations, instructions, and other legal enactments regulating the activities of the administrative authorities or governing the subjects of public administration.

The procedural issues concerning the right to judicial review of administrative acts was provided for by the Civil Procedure Code (Chapter 21-1 as amended in 1996) prior to the restoration of independence. It should be noted that the number of still-valid procedural laws adopted before the restoration of independence has significantly decreased. However, as far as administrative procedural rules are concerned, there is an abundance of such legal acts, which are either unnecessarily detailed and complicated or too weak and superficial to be of practical use. To a considerable extent they are applicable only in very specific public administration areas, and the only justification for their preservation is that they are convenient to a particular administrative authority. Given that Lithuania ratified the European Convention on Human Rights[6] and that it is on its way toward accession to the European Union, such a lack of general, more or less universally applicable and transparent rules of administrative process constitutes a major problem.

2. THE STRUCTURE OF THE EXECUTIVE

The system of the executive power in the Republic of Lithuania consists of:

1. the President of the Republic, who is the head of State;
2. the highest executive power (the Government of the Republic);
3. central institutions of the executive power (ministries and other governmental institutions–departments, inspections, agencies);
4. higher (intermediate) institutions of the executive power (district governors);
5. local executive authorities (councils of administrative units and their executive bodies, prefects of the rural territories and villages).

2.1 The President

The President is the head of State elected by the citizens for a term of five years. The President represents the State and performs all the duties which he or she is charged with by the Constitution, the Law on the President of the Republic,[7] and other laws. The President makes annual reports in the Seimas about the situation in Lithuania and the domestic and foreign policies of the State. In the event that the President dies or is removed from office according to the impeachment procedure, or if the Seimas resolves that the President is unable to fulfil his official duties because of health reasons, the prerogatives of the President are to be temporarily passed over to the Seimas Chairman.

2.2 The government and the ministries

The functions of the government are defined by the Constitution, the Law on Government,[8] and the Standing Orders of the Government[9] and are implemented in such areas as: a) the protection of constitutional order, inviolability of the territory of the Republic, home/inter-nal affairs (the Government administrates the internal affairs of the country, including security and public order), b) foreign affairs, c) introduction of draft legislation and other legal acts, d) implementation of the laws of the Seimas and the decrees of the President, drafting the State budget, its execution and the report on its implementation, e) co-ordination of the activities of the ministries and other government institutions; establishment or abolition of Government institutions, f) the organisation of government in the higher administrative units (districts), and others. The Government is also entitled to file a petition with the Constitutional Court asking to investigate the compliance of the Lithuanian laws with the Constitution.

The Government is a collegiate body consisting of the Prime Minister, appointed by the President with the approval of the Seimas, and ministers appointed by the President upon a nomination by the Prime Minister.[10] If the Seimas does not approve the programme of the newly formed Government on two consecutive sessions, the latter must resign. The new Government is granted authorisation to act only after the Seimas approves its programme by a simple majority vote of the Seimas members present at the sitting.

The Government is collectively responsible to the Seimas for its general activities. It must present an account of the implementation of the Government's programme to the Seimas at least once a year. The ministers are responsible to the Seimas and the President and are directly responsible to the Prime Minister. The Government and individual ministers must account to the Seimas for their activities, if requested by the Seimas. At least one-fifth of the Seimas members may initiate an interpellation of the Prime Minister or a minister requiring explanation of the reasons for certain decisions of members of the Government. The Seimas may accept or reject a reply of the member of the Government. If no confidence in the

Prime Minister, minister or the Government as whole is voted (upon the initiative of at least one-fifth of the Seimas members), then the Prime Minister, minister, or the Government, as the case may be, must immediately resign.

The ministries are established by the Seimas on a recommendation by the Government. There are 17 ministries in Lithuania whose functions and activities are approved by Resolutions of the Government.[11] Some ministries may establish their divisions for management of particular areas. For example, the Ministry of Finance has established the State Tax Inspectorate, which operates through locally based territorial inspectorates.

2.3 Governors of districts

According to the Law on the Governing of the Districts,[12] the governors of districts are appointed by the Government on the nomination of the Prime Minister. The objective of establishment of this higher-level executive is to provide supervision ensuring that the Constitution and the laws are observed, and that the decisions of the Government and central executive bodies are implemented by the local governments in the territory of the district. There are 10 districts in Lithuania.

2.4 Councils of administrative units and their executive bodies

Executive powers at the local level are exercised by the councils, elected for a three-year term by residents of the administrative territorial units who are also citizens of the Republic.[13] The councils create executive bodies accountable to them for the direct implementation of laws, decisions of the Government, and acts of the local government. Article 120 of the Constitution states that "the local governments act freely and independently in accordance with the competence determined by the Constitution and the laws". This principle of self-government is guaranteed by the right of the councils to appeal to courts against violations of their jurisdiction. By adopting a law, the Seimas may grant local governments or the executive bodies created by them special functions, so long as this does not contradict the Constitution. Lithuania has 44 administrative units and 56 municipalities.

2.5 Relations between the local government and the central administration

The relations between the local government and the central administration are regulated by the Constitution, the Law "On the Basic Principles of Local Government", and other laws. The bodies of local government are independent from the central state institutions and possess full independence while deciding questions within their exclusive jurisdiction (as provided by the law). The compliance of the local authorities with the Constitution, the laws, and the decisions of the government is supervised by the district governors. The district governors ensure that the decisions adopted by the institutions of local government do not violate the rights of citizens or institutions and that the decisions of the central executive are implemented properly. The Government and the local government co-ordinate all questions concerning urban planning. The Government also supports the establishment and restructuring of local government offices and co-operates in the determination of the policies on common social security, health, education, and culture.

Article 2 of the Law "On Direct Administration in Local Government Territory"[14] establishes that "direct administration" may be introduced and result in: a) dissolution of a given local government council, b) release from office of officials appointed or elected to the council, and c) suspension of the validity of laws on local government. The right to introduce "direct administration" is entrusted to the Seimas, which can resolve the issue of dissolution of the council of local government by temporarily introducing direct administration and suspending the legal acts of the local government. The Law stipulates that direct administration may be introduced in the following cases: if the activity of the bodies of a local government contradicts the Constitution and the territorial integrity of the State; if a court establishes that local government bodies have grossly violated the laws or constitutional rights of citizens; if the council fails to form executive bodies within a period prescribed by the law; and if the executive bodies and the council do not abide by the rules provided for by Article 9 of the Law.[15] A reasoned decision of the Seimas to dissolve the council must be made on the basis of the conclusions presented by the specially formed commission of the Seimas. In the event that direct administration is introduced, the Government must appoint its representative (the district governor), who temporarily governs and administers the administrative unit until a newly elected council and a mayor take office.

3. ACTS ADOPTED BY THE PRESIDENT, THE GOVERNMENT, AND OTHER GOVERNMENT INSTITUTIONS

The President, the Government, and the other Government institutions adopt their legal acts in accordance with the Constitution, the laws, and the Government resolutions. In Lithuania the delegation of legislation to the President or the Government is not provided for by the Constitution. Legal acts passed by the Government in certain cases prescribed by law must be approved by the Seimas. Legal acts adopted by other institutions of executive power are not submitted to the Seimas for approval; instead, they are approved by the head of the institution. Acts regulating activities of central executive and, in certain cases, lower-level institutions are approved by the Government: for example, the Government approves the regulations governing the activities of ministries.

3.1 The Acts of the President

The President adopts *decrees*. The President's decrees on the appointment or recall of Lithuania's diplomats, conferring of the highest military ranks, and declaration of a state of emergency, require countersignature by the Prime Minister or an appropriate minister within three days after the decree has been passed. The Prime Minister or minister who has signed the presidential decree takes full responsibility for it. Generally, the President's decrees deal with individual matters. Over a period of five years the President has adopted over 1,300 legal acts.[16]

3.2 The acts of the Government

The Government of Lithuania adopts two types of legal acts: *resolutions* and *directives*. Government resolutions are passed at Government meetings by a majority vote of all Government members. Since 1990 the Government has adopted over 12,000 legal acts. Government resolutions usually address the most important issues of executive power. They establish particular norms and rules addressed to various executive institutions, officials, enterprises, citizens, organisations, etc. Various rules and regulations related to the central executive are approved by Government resolutions. Resolutions are signed by the Prime Minister and in cases when the resolution covers several spheres of administration, by the appropriate ministers as well. The Prime Minister or the appropriate minister must not refuse to sign a resolution adopted in accordance with the procedure prescribed by the law even if they voted against its adoption. The resolutions concern general normative matters.

Within his competence, the Prime Minister issues *directives* concerning the organisation of the Government's internal work and personnel matters. Generally, the directives deal with individual matters.

The directives differ from the resolutions insofar as the former are usually acts of individual application adopted on questions which do not require collegial consideration. They are adopted for implementation in a particular situation and for a limited term. The resolutions are of a general normative nature.

The heads of ministries and other Government institutions (departments, inspectorates, agencies, committees, councils) may adopt *instructions, rules, orders,* and other legal enactments on questions within their competence. *Orders* may be administrative acts of normative or individual nature. The Lithuanian administrative legal system has 60 administrative agencies of the executive, with the right to prepare and enact legal enactments.

Instructions are always acts of normative nature where the order of implementation of other acts is prescribed or where the procedure of carrying on material-technical operations is detailed.

Despite the above enactments, the ministers and heads of other Government institutions or other authorised officials may adopt administrative acts addressed to and binding on institutions, enterprises and organisations, as well as private persons. Directions may take various forms, including official letters, explanatory letters, statements and reports.

4. THE SYSTEM OF (JUDICIAL) INSTITUTIONS DEALING WITH ADMINISTRATIVE LAW ISSUES

As pointed out earlier, administrative courts have not yet been established in Lithuania. Therefore, jurisdiction over a narrow number of administrative law issues is delegated to the ordinary courts (unit and regional courts and, in certain cases, the district courts, and the Appellate Court). The rest of the administrative law cases fall within the jurisdiction of the administrative agencies. The institutional system that adjudicates on administrative law issues is very extensive, and its operation can be better encompassed by dividing all administrative law cases into two groups: administrative offences and other administrative acts.

Table 5 contains all 23 institutions dealing with administrative law offences.[17] These institutions can be grouped into:

- administrative agencies (the police, state inspections, and other authorised administrative agencies and their officials);
- unit, regional, and district courts;
- administrative commissions formed at the councils of local governments, and the prefects of villages and rural units.

Considering the allocation of cases among the institutions, and judging by the number of penalised persons (Table 3),[18] during 1996 approximately 96 per cent of all administrative law offences were adjudicated by administrative authorities. The courts have adjudicated only four per cent of these cases. The courts have exclusive jurisdiction over 85 types of administrative law offences: for instance, only the courts can adjudicate administrative law offences entailing the imposition of administrative arrest and penitentiary work.

The courts in Lithuania are entrusted with judicial review of administrative acts. However, this method of control over administrative acts is used much less frequently than internal review of administrative acts by administrative agencies. The question of jurisdiction in judicial review depends on the executive level of the administrative authority that has issued the administrative act. If the act in question has been issued by an authority of the central executive, judicial review falls within the jurisdiction of the district courts.[19] In case of a local executive act, the application has to be filed with the relevant unit or regional court.

Judicial review based on the Constitution is also generally defined by Article 269-1 of the Civil Procedure Code, which states that "a person who assumes that his or her rights and freedoms are violated or constrained by administrative acts of state institutions and their officials, whether by an action or failure to act, has the right to appeal before a court".

Table 1 (Lithuania). Number of persons against whom administrative penalties were imposed in 1996

Police	675,942
Other institutions	86,113
Total	762,055

Table 2 (Lithuania). Average amount of fines per person in 1996 (inlitas)

Agricultural Inspection	37
Hygiene Inspection	72
Fire Department	100
Environmental Protection	101
State Defence	104
Police	107
Quality of Goods Inspection	140
Labour Inspection	243
Ministry of Transport	247
Tax Authorities	524
SODRA	636
Customs	1190

The control over administrative acts is extensively dealt with by the administrative authorities through internal review procedures. According to the Constitution, the consideration of a citizen's appeal or petition is a duty of every state institution and its officials. This type of control over administrative acts is more convenient (because it is speedy, cheaper and informal). The administrative authority competent for such a review may be the one that took the administrative act in question or a superior authority. No special administrative appellate authority has yet been established. The right to internal review is provided for by various laws, statutes, regulations and other enactments regulating that a person whose rights and lawful interests may be adversely affected by an administrative act has the right to appeal to a superior administrative authority.

In many cases, to challenge an administrative act before a court, the laws require that such act have been the subject of a prior administrative complaint. If this requirement of internal review has not been met, the case submitted for judicial review may be suspended until the completion of the internal review over the act in question.

Quasi-judicial bodies dealing with the adjudication of administrative law issues may be established by special laws. However, they are very rare and applicable only within the court system, army, police, procurator's office, and other "closed institutions" or professions requiring specific expertise. Their activity is mostly to decide on the suitability of an official for a certain position or whether an official should stay in office after an instance of misconduct.

5. GENERAL PROCEDURAL LAWS

The procedural laws of the Lithuanian administrative law system can be grouped into codified and non-codified laws. The first group is represented by the Code of Administrative Law Offences, the Code of Civil Procedure, the Customs Code,[20] the Railway Transport Code,[21] and the Internal Roads Code.[22] Lithuania has no Administrative Procedure Code embodying the procedural principles and general problems of judicial, internal and external review of administrative acts. Nor has there been any successful legislative effort to adopt codified procedural laws over the last few years.

Concerning non-codified procedural laws, the problems of administrative procedure are, as a rule, addressed by numerous laws, statutes, regulations, instructions and other legal enactments. Due to the abundance of legal acts, their repeated amending, appending and frequent controversies in the complex period of the reform of the legal system, a number of procedural issues related to internal and external review of administrative acts are not properly regulated. The main principles of administrative procedure as related to the access to public services, right to hearing, legal representation and assistance, time limits, notice, statement of reasons and indication of remedies, as well as the execution of administrative acts, are either not regulated at all or only in a very vague manner. Since those principles are not properly guaranteed, one's opportunity to know and secure one's rights rests on shaky ground.

Until now no general procedural normative act has been adopted other than the Governmental Resolution of 1992 "On Procedure of Review of Citizen's Appeals, Complaints, and Proposals by the State Institutions and Officials".[23] It sets out certain rules of internal review of administrative acts. A new draft law on the Procedure for Review of Citizen Complaints, Petitions, Proposals and Appeals was approved by the Government in 1996 and submitted to the Seimas.

5.1 Administrative Law Offences Code: a general description

As already mentioned, the Administrative Law Offences Code is applicable only in adjudication of administrative law offences. It defines 215 administrative offences in the areas of management of the economy, administrative-political and sociocultural processes. Almost every article presents two to five forms of offensive acts which can incur the imposition of administrative sanctions upon a person who intentionally, negligently or by an act of omission has violated the rules prescribed

Table 3 (Lithuania). Number of administrative penalties by departments and institutions

Labour Inspectorate	1,625
State Defence	2,164
Customs	2,376
Courts	25,431
Fire Department	4,317
Agricultural Inspectorate	4,985
Tax Authorities	5,082
Hygiene Inspectorate	11,502
Quality of Goods Inspectorate	12,551
Environmental Protection	17,856
Police	675,942

Table 4 (Lithuania). Fines imposed in 1996 (in litas)

Police	72,267,034
Other institutions	13,305,855
Total	85,572,889

by the administrative laws. Other 140 articles concern the general procedural rules for instituting, investigating, and deciding on cases of administrative offences. The Code also regulates the questions of administrative liability and imposition of administrative penalties. Subject to administrative sanctions are a) private persons (citizens, legal residents or foreigners, except those with a status of diplomatic immunity), if they violate administrative acts; and b) officials, if they are in breach of their duties related to the execution of administrative acts falling within their jurisdiction. The latter category of subjects, however, does not cover those officials who issue, supervise, enforce or are responsible for the implementation of the administrative acts.

Administrative law offence adjudication procedure involves the following stages: 1) filling out a protocol establishing the administrative offence, 2) guarantees of adjudication in cases of administrative law offences; 3) procedural rights of the parties within the adjudicative procedures; 4) rules of adjudication; 5) decisions; and 6) appeal. The time limit for taking a decision on the imposition of an administrative sanction cannot be longer than two months from the date of unlawful conduct. The administrative penalties are a warning, fine, administrative arrest, penitentiary work, suspension or withdrawal of license, permit or certificate, compensatory seizure of properties used in the course or for the purposes of unlawful conduct, confiscation of goods or other valuables acquired through unlawful conduct, and removal from offices.

While reviewing the acts of administrative authorities, the courts follow the rules provided by the Civil Procedure Code. Judicial review has existed since the 1980s and is provided for by Chapter 21-1 of the Civil Procedure Code.[24] In its present form, judicial review is defined by the Constitution, which states that each citizen is guaranteed the right to appeal against the decisions of state institutions and their officers (Article 33.). Furthermore, the Constitution prescribes that the "actions and acts of local government councils and their executive bodies and officers that violate the rights of citizens and organisations may be appealed against in court" (Article 124). In fact, only after 1996, when the jurisdiction provisions of the Civil Procedure Code were amended, did the system of judicial review become relatively streamlined.

Judicial review is exercised in accordance with the rules of the Civil Procedure Code.

5.2 Appeal procedures

Generally, all administrative law decisions may be subject to appeal. Almost all administrative acts can be appealed before the courts. Some laws and statutes provide for an appeal of administrative act before a superior administrative authority. And even an appeal before the superior authority does not prevent a person from appealing an order of such a superior authority before a court. Exceptions can be provided only by a law. Only a few of the administrative acts are final and cannot be appealed in court. For example, a decision of the Commission on Privatisation related to the results of a public auction cannot be appealed in court; the same holds true for a refusal of the Medical Commission to issue a licence to practice a medical profession. These exceptions contradict the right of appeal guaranteed by the Constitution.

In administrative law offence cases, a decision made by an administrative authority can be appealed before the unit or regional court. An appeal of the decision of such a court can be taken to the district court, whose decision on the matter is final. Administrative law offence cases that have been decided by the unit court, the regional court, and the district courts (as a first instance) can be appealed before the Appellate Court, whose decision is final. Appellate-level procedures are governed by the rules on judicial review provided by the Civil Procedure Code (Articles 262-296).

The court reviews the appeal within 10 days after receipt. Appeals have to be lodged within 10 days from the date when the decision in the administrative law offence case has been made. The appellate-level court may rule:

- to revoke the administrative sanction and dissolve the case;
- to reverse a decision and forward the case for a new adjudication;

Table 5 (Lithuania). Structure of institutions

Institutions subordinate to the Seimas			
State Audit Control	Bank of Lithuania	Seimas Ombudsmen	State Lithuanian Language Commission
Government institutions			
Archives Department of Lithuania		State Competition and Consumer Rights Protection Council	Department of Statistics
Institutions subordinate to ministries			
Institutions of the Ministry of Environmental Protection	Institutions of State Energy and Nuclear Safety Inspectorate of the Ministry of Economy	Institutions of the Ministry of Finance, Customs Department, State Tax Inspectorate, Securities Commission, State Insurance Supervisory Service	Institutions of the Ministry of National Defence
Institutions of cultural heritage, Department of the Ministry of Culture	Institutions of agriculture and forestry ministries, National parks institutions, animal pedigree breeding, veterinary supervision, plant protection, land survey and geodetic survey, agricultural machinery state supervisory institutions	Institutions of state telecommunications	State Labour Inspectorate, SODRA
Ministry of Construction, Geological service, Construction supervision institutions	Ministry of Transport, railway, sea, inland, water, air, motor car and electric transport, State road, State motor roads supervision institutions	Ministry of Health, State Hygiene Inspectorate	Ministry of Internal Affairs, police, fire prevention supervision institutions
Municipal institutions			
Administrative commissions at the municipal councils		Village prefects of municipal area offices in rural localities	
Courts			
County courts	Regional courts	District courts	Appellate courts

- to refuse to review a decision, and
- to impose another administrative penalty (however, the court cannot impose a more severe sanction than the one imposed by the administrative agency.)

The decision of the court in a judicial review case may be appealed before the higher-level court (district court or the Court of Appeal) within 20 days from the day after the decision has been made.

The provisions of the special laws are very different regarding the time limits applicable to judicial review. Usually, a 30-day term is prescribed. The courts exercise judicial review according to the procedures of the Civil Procedure Code. The remedies that can be granted by the court in case of judicial review may be as follows:

- to grant the appeal and compel the state institution or its official to take certain actions eliminating the unlawful act;
- to grant the appeal and annul the challenged administrative act.

The court may also order the administrative authority to pay damages or compensate the aggrieved party.

The decision of the court in judicial review cases may be appealed before the higher-level court (district court or the Court of Appeal) within 20 days of the day after the decision has been made.

The procedures of appeal before the superior administrative authority (internal review) set forth different time limits, i.e., five days, 10 days or one month.

The procedural laws regulating administrative law offences contain several exceptions related to possible extensions of the term of detention of the offender and cases when a person can be penalised without filling out the protocol which is mandatory in all other cases.

6. OMBUDSMAN

The Seimas Ombudsmen's Office was established by the 1994 Law on the Seimas Ombudsmen. The significance of this enactment was that it provided for an external review of administrative acts.

The Ombudsmen's Office is an autonomous state institution comprised of the ombudsmen (appointed by the Seimas), the Board, deputies, departments and other structural subdivisions. Five ombudsmen are appointed by the Seimas for a four-year term from the candidates nominated by the Chairman of the Seimas. The ombudsmen investigate citizens' complaints concerning abuse of powers of state and local government officials or other authorised persons whose duties include the performance of organisational, managerial or administrative functions. The ombudsmen's jurisdiction does not encompass investigations of the activities of the President, the members of the Seimas, the judges of the Constitutional Court, the

Supreme Court and other courts, the procedural actions of the prosecutors, investigators or interrogators, the activities of the Prime Minister, the State Controller and the Government (as a collective institution), as well as of the local government councils and their boards (as collective institutions). The ombudsmen do not investigate complaints arising from legal relations of employment, and other complaints falling within the jurisdiction of the courts; in addition, they do not examine the reasoning and validity of the decisions and judgements of the courts.

A complaint must be submitted within three months after the action in question has been committed. Complaints filed after the expiration of the time limit, as well as anonymous complaints, are not investigated unless the ombudsmen decide otherwise.

At the ombudsmen's request, officials of state and local government institutions must immediately present information, documents and materials necessary for the ombudsman to carry out his duties. When adopting decisions on complaints against an official's abuse of his position or other bureaucratic violations, the ombudsman may not revise or revoke the official's decisions. Upon establishing that an official abused his position while adopting a decision, the ombudsman must apply measures to revoke the decision in the manner established by law. The ombudsman's recommendation to revise the unlawful decision of the official must be examined in the institution to which the official is accountable. The decision of the court to remove from office, on recommendation of the ombudsman, officials guilty of abuse of official power or bureaucratic prerogatives is obligatory for the employer and constitutes a ground for terminating the employment contract.

Complaints must be investigated and a response must be given within one month of the day of receipt of the complaint (if necessary, the period of investigation may be extended by the ombudsman up to one more month.)

If numerous or flagrant violations of law are established during the investigation, the ombudsman must notify the Seimas, the Government, or the corresponding local government council. Each year, by March 15, the ombudsman must submit a written report on his general activities during the previous calendar year to the Seimas. The report must be made public and debated on by the Seimas. The report must contain generalised information stating in which of the state and local government institutions the greatest number of violations committed by officials has been established, which statutory laws or other legal acts encourage abuse of official position, and what measures should be taken to reduce the abuse of official position.

According to Articles 224, 259 and 187-3 of the Administrative Offences Code, the ombudsman has the right to institute an administrative offence case (file a protocol and forward the case either to an administrative authority or the court) and initiate judicial review, internal review or disciplinary action. The ombudsman also has the right to demand information and documents related to an investigation of petitions and claims. Officials who fail to fulfil such a request may be penalised by administrative fines in the amount of up to 2000 litas (USD 500).[25]

The ombudsman review of administrative acts (external review) is an important form of control over the administrative authorities, as the ombudsman not only protects the rights and freedoms of private persons and reviews the lawfulness of administrative acts but also is vested with powers to express opinions as well as to make administrative and legislative recommendations.

7. OTHER FORMS OF SUPERVISION OF THE ADMINISTRATION: THE PROCURATOR AND THE STATE CONTROL

In the Lithuanian administrative system other forms of control over the administration may be executed by the procurators (prosecutors), State Control Office, and district governors. The procurator's status is very complicated. Although his powers are limited to prosecution and supervision of criminal investigation and situation, many people still apply to the procurators to secure the protection of their rights.[26]

The functions of the procurators are determined in Chapter 9 of the Constitution, "The Court". Thus, procurators are interpreted here as an integral part of the judicial power. However, this does not mean that procurators may administer justice as the courts do. Article 118 of the Constitution states that "the public procurators shall prosecute criminal cases on behalf of the State, shall carry out criminal prosecutions, and shall supervise the activities of the interrogative bodies". Neither this nor the other articles of the Constitution specify the function of general supervision over the administration.

Nevertheless, certain forms of supervision over the administration that can be applied by the procurator are established in Article 21 of the Law on the Procurator's Office. According to this law, the procurator's right to apply to the courts is inseparable from the procurator's official duties. Thus, while performing their function of criminal prosecution or while investigating appeals and petitions of citizens, the prosecutors may also submit a petition to the court to ensure the protection of other people's rights (including in the sphere of administrative law). The procurators have the right to apply to the court in relation to the protection of lawful state interests as well as in cases of violation of public law rules. In such cases they may order the administrative bodies, enterprises, institutions and other organisations as well as officials to submit documents and information necessary to start a civil case; still, they cannot supervise the lawfulness of executive acts.[27]

Chapter 12 of the Constitution determines the functions and framework of the activities of the State Control Office. This is a state body, authorised to exercise economic financial control. It supervises the legality of the use of state property and the implementation of the state budget. It is accountable directly to the Seimas, which performs parliamentary control over this institution. The State Control Office is not hierarchically subordinated to the Government.

8. THE SYSTEM OF PARLIAMENTARY COMMITTEES AND ITS ROLE IN THE SUPERVISION OVER THE ADMINISTRATION

According to the Seimas Standing Orders,[28] committees are formed at the first session of the newly elected Seimas. The Seimas committees are responsible and accountable to the Seimas for their activities. They must, within a reasonable time, consider questions submitted to them and give their opinion, as well as fulfil other tasks within the competence of the Seimas. Currently, there are 12 committees.[29] The basic powers of the committees are to:

1. consider draft laws, prepare opinions, and investigate questions submitted for committee consideration;
2. upon the request of the Seimas or on their own initiative, prepare drafts of laws and other legal acts, analyse the necessity of new laws and their amendments;
3. prepare and consider questions related to state, economic, social and cultural matters, and submit their proposals to the Seimas;
4. consider the Government program;
5. consider sections of the state budget and accounts of the budget implementation prior to the debate on the issue in a sitting of the Seimas;
6. consider proposals on the establishment and abolition of ministries and other state institutions;
7. when carrying out parliamentary control, hear information and reports of ministries and other state institutions concerning the implementation of the Lithuanian laws and other acts adopted by the Seimas;
8. investigate the proposals of voters and social organisations, and if necessary, transfer these proposals to the state institutions together with their own recommendations.

The decisions adopted by the committees are not binding on the state institutions: they are just recommendations. The committees inform the Chancellery of the Seimas and, if necessary, the Government about the proposals and recommendations sent to other institutions. After the receipt of the recommendations, all state institutions, with the exception of the courts, must consider them and report on the measures taken within 15 days of the receipt of the recommendation or within a term established by the committees themselves.

The committees are entitled within their competence to check how the Lithuanian laws are observed, as well as how the committees' recommendations and proposals are implemented. They have a right to invite the heads of state institutions, with the exceptions of the courts, to their meetings. Also, the committees have a right to request documents and written opinions from state institutions, and reports from officials.

II. DEVELOPMENTS IN ADMINISTRATIVE LAW DURING 1996-1997

INTRODUCTION

In the seven years of independence, the scope of administrative law regulation in Lithuania has changed remarkably, and the range of administrative activities has rapidly expanded. These changes have occurred as a result of Lithuania's transition to a market economy and its determination to harmonise its administrative law system with European Union legislation.[30] Laws, Government decrees, regulations, instructions of ministries and other enactments of Government agencies covered those areas of the economy and socio-cultural and administrative-political processes, that were not previously regulated. Almost all laws have been amended in accordance with a new and modern approach to the management of the public domain.

The changes in the regulative scope of administrative law, however, are still very chaotic. Most of them are more an expression of political will than carefully considered steps towards comprehensive administrative law reform. The principles and methods of application of administrative law today must be reconciled with the democratic principles of the rule of law. So far, paradoxically, the unrevised and outdated Soviet procedures of administrative law are extensively applied to regulate those public administration areas where radical democratic reforms have been introduced.

Furthermore, administrative law as an independent branch of public law also remains underdeveloped in Lithuania. Although a discipline of administrative law is being taught in various establishments of higher education, the course mostly covers the administrative liabilities and sanctions for violation of administrative laws. Since 1990, neither significant legal research results nor new administrative law textbooks have been published. Although a working group on drafting an Administrative Code was formed in 1991, its activities to date have been confined only to amendments to the Administrative Offences Code. A general revision of this Code will be started after the revision of the Criminal Code is completed (probably within the next three years). This is related to the rule that some minor criminal acts can be considered administrative violations incurring administrative liabilities, while some repeatedly committed administrative offences can entail criminal punishment.

So far, the problems of administrative law are caused mostly by a misguided approach to its basic principles. Many democratic principles of the relations between the administrative authorities and private persons have been established by the Constitution and repeated in many laws adopted within the recent few years. However, the mechanism of enforcement of these principles has not yet been properly tuned. The principle of unconditional obedience of citizens to administrative authorities, inherited from Soviet administrative law, and the very high level of penalisation for administrative law offences should not predominate in a democratic state. Table 1 illustrates that, during 1996, almost every fourth citizen of Lithuania has been penalised for an administrative law offence. The total amount of fines imposed in 1996 was 85,572,889 litas (over USD 21 million). These figures show that the average administrative fine per person in 1996 was 109 litas (approximately USD 25).

Furthermore, the bureaucracy has remained almost untouched by the instruments of responsibility for acts of misuse of power. Although the mechanism of state control has been improved, developing methods of judicial and internal review over administrative acts as well as establishing external review (the ombudsmen), administrative penalties are only rarely imposed upon officials. Mostly, the officials of administrative authorities are subject to political control over personnel. This control is exercised under the Law on Public Officials,[31] whose objective is to expose corrupt and ineffective administrative practice as well as instances of bureaucratisation.

According to Article 30 of the Constitution, material and moral damage inflicted on a person by the administrative authorities must be compensated. The basic rules for compensation are provided by the Civil Code (Article 485) and are to be enforced through civil litigation. The personal liability of an official is limited, usually, to three months' salary. Also, if an act of misuse of power does not constitute a criminal offence and does not inflict damages on a person, the official may be dismissed from office as a result of political control, or, in some cases, disciplinary action may be taken against him (procurators, policemen, military servants, etc.).

Administrative law should not only define the power or discretion that has been conferred on the administrative authorities, but also regulate how that power should be exercised, and what would happen if powers are exceeded or otherwise unlawfully exercised. Therefore, another problem of administrative law is that, as already mentioned, Lithuania lacks such regulations as a separate administrative procedure act, a code on administrative procedures or statute of administrative procedure rules. As a result, there are no unified: a) procedures employed by the administrative authorities in effecting administrative acts; b) general rules of adjudication, rulemaking, and investigation applicable to all administrative authorities, administrative acts and persons; and c) rules of review of administrative acts.

Those problems demonstrate the need to revise, first of all, all legal acts directly or indirectly governing the scope of administrative law regulation and re-elaborate the basic principles of substantive and procedural administrative law. The institutional reforms of the administrative legal system which have been introduced to date are not sufficient. The principle of rule of law must form the basis of the administrative legal system, requiring that the "government operates within the confines of the law; and that aggrieved citizens, whose interests have been adversely affected, be entitled to approach an independent court to adjudicate whether or not a particular action taken by, or on behalf of, the state is in accordance with the law".[32]

A. THE CONSTITUTION

The Constitution of the Republic of Lithuania was approved by the citizens in a referendum on October 25, 1992. The Constitution of the State is a legal act with supreme legal power on which the whole legal system of the State is based. It consists of a preamble, 14 chapters and final provisions and has 154 articles that establish the basic institutions of the State of Lithuania, the relations between the individual and the State, the main principles of national economy and labour, the basic principles of the State budget and finances, the State Control, the foreign policy and national defence and the procedures for amending the Constitution.

Under the Law on Enactment of the Constitution an attempt was made to avoid gaps and controversies in the legal system. Namely, Article 2 of this Law established that: "Laws, other legal acts or parts of acts which have been in effect on the territory of the Republic of Lithuania prior to the adoption of the Constitution, shall be effective provided that they do not contradict the Constitution and this law, and shall remain effective until they are either declared null and void or harmonised with the provisions of the Constitution".

Changes to the Constitution are reserved exclusively for the legislature. Since November 1992, when the Constitution was enacted, it has been amended twice. Both amendments were enacted in 1996. The first amendment extended the right of ownership over land to Lithuanian economic entities, foreign nationals and foreign economic entities (Article 47).[33] The second amendment concerned the formation of local government councils which are currently elected for a three-year term[34] (instead of a two-year term).

B. LEGISLATION AND REGULATION

Legislative powers are exercised only by the Seimas. Article 67 and Article 70 of the Constitution state that the Seimas enacts laws and may adopt other acts as well. Essential governmental and national questions may be decided by referendum. The right to initiate a referendum is vested within the Seimas (one-third of its members) and 300,000 citizens of the Republic.[35]

According to Lithuanian legal traditions and legal science, authoritative legal acts are divided into:

- laws (Constitution, constitutional laws, laws);
- regulations or executive acts (non-normative acts of the Seimas; resolutions and decrees of the Government; regulations, orders and instructions of ministries and other central and local government authorities; informal rules of administration, etc.) and
- judicial decisions.

Further, depending on their form and content, all legal acts can be grouped into the following categories: a) legislative and sub-legislative; b) normative (general), special (ad hoc), individual (private), and local (informal) acts.

Normative acts are those containing universally binding rules of a general nature. Individual acts contain an instruction given to a concrete person under concrete conditions to act in an appropriate way. Both can be adopted by the legislature, executive bodies, and sometimes by the courts.

A law is an original act adopted in the procedure prescribed by the Constitution and the Statute of the Seimas that expresses the legislator's will and that has supreme legal power. Therefore, a law can be amended or its validity nullified only upon the adoption of another law or the declaration of its contradiction with the Constitution by the Constitutional Court.

All other legal acts must be in conformity with the laws. This category of legal acts, known in other administrative legal systems as "regulations", is referred to by Lithuanian law as "sub-legislative acts", i.e. those which emanate from the executive bodies of the state. In order to be valid, these acts must be substantively intra vires (within the jurisdiction of the issuing authority), be constitutional, and be promulgated in conformity with the established procedure.

Executive acts, whether adopted by the Government or another administrative authority, are considered the acts of the administration. Such an act may not replace the law itself and create new legal rules of general nature competing with the norms of laws. It is an act of application and implementation of norms of law regardless of whether this act is of temporary (ad hoc) or permanent validity".[36] These features are characteristic for executive acts adopted not only by the executive bodies but by the Seimas as well (Article 70 of the Constitution). Executive acts of the Seimas may not contradict the Constitution or the laws enacted by the Seimas. Programme laws setting the economic and social agenda of the governing majority are also considered laws, although they do not establish concrete legal rules regulating the conduct of legal subjects.

1. LEGISLATIVE PROCESS

"Legislation" in Lithuanian legal science is considered the whole body of legally significant acts necessary for the adoption of a law. The process of legislation is regulated by the Constitution, the Statute of Seimas (the Chapter on Legislation), the Law on Drafting Laws and Other Normative Legal Acts,[37] and by several other laws. Over the last two years the legislation procedures have become relatively stable; at present, the legislative process includes the following stages:

- legislative initiative (Article 68 of the Constitution),
- consideration of a draft law by the Seimas,
- adoption of a draft law (Article 69 of the Constitution), and
- promulgation and enforcement of the enacted law (Article 70–72 of the Constitution).

The procedures of issuing sub-legislative acts by the Government and the other executive bodies include similar stages and are regulated by the Law on Government. The legislature frequently determines that certain sub-legislative acts must come into force only after having been approved by the legislature. Furthermore, very often the legal acts passed by executive bodies other than the Government are to be enacted only after the Government approves them.

The process of legislation starts with putting forward an initiative. Only the members of the Seimas, the President, and the Government enjoy the right to legislative initiative. If 50,000 Lithuanian citizens enfranchised to vote, so choose, they can also submit a draft law to the Seimas, and the Seimas must consider this draft. In practical terms, this right is realised by the submission of some concrete draft law to the Seimas or a written proposal concerning a new, substantial legislative project. Usually, after the right to legislative initiative is exercised, a working group or commission is formed to prepare a draft law. Working groups may include the officials as well as independent persons. Formally, such a working group must be approved by the Government. The first draft law must be reviewed by the respective ministries before it is submitted to the Government for its approval. Usually, experts are asked to provide their comments on the contents of the draft law, particularly on its consistency with the European Law. In April 1997 the Legal Bureau at the Ministry of European Affairs was formed to provide assistance on the matters of harmonisation of national legislation with European legal standards.

After the Government's approval has been obtained, the draft law must be submitted to the Seimas, where it is registered as a bill. The Seimas, at this stage, must initiate the consideration of the bill. According to the rules under the Statute of the Seimas, the bill is circulated among the Committees and Commissions of the Seimas, which review the draft law and provide their remarks, proposals, amendments and supplements to the contents of the draft law. At this stage, however, the legislature can consider only the draft law; the Constitutional Court has ruled that the filing of comments to the draft cannot be interpreted as a legislative initiative.[38]

The stage of discussion of the draft laws is governed, generally, by the Statute of the Seimas. Article 71 establishes the right of the President to refer the law back to the Seimas "for reconsideration"; Article 72 establishes the right of the Seimas "to reconsider and enact laws" that have been referred back by the President. After reconsideration of the draft by the Seimas, the law is to be deemed enacted if the amendments and supplements submitted by the President of the Republic are adopted, or if more than half of all the Seimas members vote in favour of the version prior to the presidential amendments (in case of a constitutional law–if at least three-fifths of all Seimas members vote for the unamended version) (Article 72 of the Constitution).[39]

Under the second part of Article 69 of the Constitution, laws shall be deemed adopted if the majority of the Seimas members participating in the sitting vote in favour of the bill.

The second part of Article 7 of the Constitution specifies: "Only laws which are promulgated shall be valid". Articles 70 and 72 of the Constitution provide a procedure for promulgation and enforcement of laws. In Article 4 of the Law on the Procedure for Promulgation and Enforcement of Laws and other Legal Acts of the Republic of Lithuania,[40] it is established that laws of the Republic of Lithuania become effective only after their signing and official promulgation in the official gazette *Valstibės Zinios* by the President of the Republic, unless the laws themselves establish a later enforcement date. Resolutions of the Government in which legal norms are established, amended or declared null and void become effective on the day following their signing by the Prime Minister and their official promulgation by the appropriate minister in *Valstibės Zinios.* Resolutions of the Government in which legal norms are not established, amended or declared null and void along with the directives of the Prime Minister, become effective from the day of their signing, unless the resolutions and directives themselves provide for a later enforcement date.

The power of laws or other legal acts is prospective. Otherwise, the law itself would lose its authority and would hamper the establishment of a stable legal order.[41] In the process of legislating, the adoption of retrospective norms is an exception. This occurs only when the law itself specifies its retroactive validity, or when the law nullifies (or mitigates) sanctions for acts or administrative liability for administrative law violations.

All laws and legal acts enacted in the Republic of Lithuania are to be registered with the Register of Laws and Legal Acts.[42]

Theoretically, legislation and regulation are to be harmonised. However, their practical interaction is characterised by a very high level of "legal inflation", i.e. a situation in which an unreasonably large number of sub-legislative acts (regulations) adopted by the Government and the administrative agencies exceeds the boundaries of power delegated to them by the law. For example, as of 1996 more than 600 laws have been adopted (including laws on amendments to already enacted laws) and over 3,000 government legal acts passed. A simple calculation shows that, on average, every law has been followed by four or five regulations. These figures do not include the "informal rules" of the administrative authorities or, as they are referred to in Lithuania, "local rules". Apart from some exceptional cases, those rules are enacted without a public notice, without an opportunity for the affected members of the public to comment on the proposal, and without publication. Therefore, "informal rules" often contradict the laws or the Government regulations as well as the constitutional rights and interests of the citizens.

The complexity of the transition to a market economy and liberal democracy brought about a number of laws and regulations of an ad hoc character in Lithuania. The legislative process is overwhelmed by the need to introduce temporary legal acts (laws) applied only to one legal relation or to groups of vaguely defined legal relations. Such acts are as a rule rendered inapplicable, since the legal relations meant to be regulated on their basis are already regulated by other legal acts of general validity. This certainly raises questions about the consistency of the laws with the Constitution and the other legal acts. Since 1993, such questions have frequently been addressed to the Constitutional Court of Lithuania, which has issued a number of rulings on the matter. In addition, many laws and sub-legislative acts have been revised through the mechanisms of political control over the legislature and the executive. However, these forms of control have not proved sufficient to ensure a consistent hierarchy of legislative and executive norms.

2. SUBSTANTIVE LAWS

2.1 The management of economy

2.1.1 LAWS ON PRIVATISATION

The first stage of privatisation in Lithuania, which focused on mass privatisation of state property through a voucher scheme, has been practically finished, and almost 80 per cent of the state capital slated for privatisation has been privatised.[43] The Law on Privatisation of State and Municipal Property of 1995 provided for a cash-based privatisation under equal conditions for both national and foreign investors. In January 1996, the State Privatisation Agency was created. This institution acts as a representative of the Government in the privatisation of state-owned property. The ministries and local governments are responsible for the preparation of the establishments, which are in their control, for privatisation. The State Privatisation Agency compiles all privatisation information, proposes to the Government to approve a suggested method of privatisation (public subscription for shares, auction, open tender, sale by direct negotiations or lease with an option to purchase), co-ordinates and administers the privatisation deals, and completes privatisation transactions. This institution is also responsible for publishing information on privatisation in the official gazette.

The Privatisation Commission elaborates the privatisation strategy and controls the implementation of the privatisation goals. In 1997 one more administrative authority was created to control the privatisation of strategic enterprises: the Department of Privatisation in the Ministry of European Affairs. It supervises and provides advice in the privatisation processes of 13 state-owned companies in such spheres as telecommunications, air transport, energy and heat supply.

2.1.2 LAWS ON THE OWNERSHIP AND MANAGEMENT OF LANDS

Part I of Article 47 of the Constitution establishes that: "Land, internal waters, forests, and parks may only be owned by the citizens and the state of the Republic of Lithuania". According to the Constitution, the land is a public asset whose main social function is to serve the welfare of the nation as a whole (Article 47 and Article 54). Rational and effective regulation of land ownership relations is to be balanced against the principle of integrity and indivisibility of the territory of the State of Lithuania (Article 10).

The major laws in this area were passed in the 1991–1995 period: the Law on Land Reform,[44] the Law on Lease of Land,[45] the Law on Tax on Land,[46] and the Law on Land.[47] The land reform is administered by agrarian reform agencies in the rural districts and by district privatisation commissions. At present, the pace of the land reform seems very slow, due mainly to debates over new legislative proposals regarding the restitution of property rights over land and other real estate property. The Law on Land establishes the basic rules for rational use of land, guarantees the protection of ownership of land, provides for exclusive ownership of certain lands and defines the land designated for agricultural purposes, forestry, conservation, as well as the problems of melioration and the basic principles of state land-use planing.

Despite the 70 new legal acts passed from January 1996, this area of the economy was further regulated by Constitutional Law No. 1392, passed on June 20, 1996,[48] as well as by the Constitutional Law on the Subjects, Procedure, Terms, Conditions, and Restrictions on the Acquisition into Ownership of Land Plots Provided for by Part 2 of Article 47. Under this Law the right to acquire land is granted to Lithuanian enterprises (national subjects) and foreign subjects if certain requirements prescribed by that Law are satisfied. Acquisition procedures require an applicant to obtain permission from the Government. The Law also identifies 14 categories of land excluded from private ownership (parks, recreation territories, agricultural land, resorts, special landscape territories, border zones, and others.). Before such permission is issued, the applicant must accept the obligation to undertake or complete reconstruction works on the land plot: the Government has the right to impose a fine if the new owner of land fails to do so. It is also important that the Constitutional Law will go into effect only after the European Agreement on the association of the European Union and its member states with the Republic of Lithuania has entered into force.

Under the same constitutional law, the local governments were granted the right to acquire property rights over land plots for non-agricultural purposes. However, these plots may be used only for construction and exploitation of buildings and facilities necessary for the implementation of the essential functions of the local government. Yet, at present, the local governments are not landowners: therefore they may not be considered land property owners like the State.[49]

Another change in this area came in December 1996, when the Agricultural Ministry and the Forestry Ministry merged into a new Ministry of Agriculture and Forestry.

2.2 Laws on environmental protection and natural resources

Until 1996, the Lithuanian Parliament passed a number of laws on the protection of the environment: the Law on Compensations for Environmental Pollution,[50] the Law on State Protection of Special Territories (Reserves),[51] the Law on Plant (Flora) Protection.[52] The former two laws establish the general procedures for compensating and paying for damage to the environment as well as the regulation of natural reserves and other protected areas. The latter law regulates the "activity of all legal and natural persons with respect to plant protection from diseases, pests and weeds and also establishes the procedure for registration, manufacture, import, trade, storage and state supervision of chemical and biological means for plant protection and vegetation control materials".

In 1994 the former Department of Environmental Protection was transformed into a Ministry of Environmental Protection. Since 1996, Lithuania has passed over 60 legal acts related to environmental protection. The major act in this area, the Law on Environmental Protection, was also passed in 1996.[53] It established the main rights and duties of the juridical and natural persons in this area and set out the basic principles and procedures of utilisation of natural resources. Under this Law, the following areas and resources enjoy special state protection and require special licensing procedures for their utilisation: protected territories, reserves, national and regional parks, natural reserves, protected zones, natural monuments, species of flora and fauna protected by the State. Furthermore, all natural resources must be registered. The Law also sets out some economic mechanisms of enforcement, financing and liabilities for violation of the environmental protection laws.

In September 1996 a Strategy Plan on Environmental Protection[54] was approved by the Seimas. The Ministry of Environmental Protection, which is responsible for the management of this area, has passed 36 acts since that time. One of its most recent documents is the Rules on Assessment of Pollution of March 19, 1997, No. 50.

2.3 Laws on finance

One of the major laws in this area was the Law on the National Currency, passed in 1991 and readopted in 1993.[55] The Law on the Bank of Lithuania was passed in 1994.[56] The Bank of Lithuania is established by and is accountable to the Seimas. It is governed by the Board of the Bank. Its main functions are to approve and manage the monetary policy, license credit institutions, establish standards of credit activities, and control and supervise credit institutions. Until 1996 the Bank of Lithuania had passed over 60 acts regulating the Lithuanian monetary policy.

The Law on Commercial Banks was passed in 1994.[57] However, by the beginning of 1996 it had been amended six times. Under this law, commercial banks must obtain a licence from the Bank of Lithuania. The main objective of the establishment and management of such banks as well as of their regulation by the Bank of Lithuania must be to secure a safe and efficient system of banks.

The Law on Budgeting of 1990[58] sets up the state budgetary structure, which consists of the state budget and independent budgets of the local governments. A uniform classification of revenues and expenditures must be elaborated by the Ministry of Finance. The state budget draft must be prepared by the Ministry of Finance, approved by the Government and enacted by a law.

All 16 types of taxes applicable in Lithuania[59] are regulated by the Law on Tax Administration of 1995.[60] All taxes are administered by the State Tax Inspectorate, subordinated to the Ministry of Finance. One of the most important recent acts in this area was Regulation No. 83 passed in May 1997, which, inter alia, covered the procedural arrangements of avoiding double taxation.[61]

2.4 Laws on transport

The latest changes in the transport management area are related to the integration of Lithuania into the Western European transportation system. Following the provisions of the Law on the Principles of Transport,[62] all transport (railway, motor vehicle, sea, inland water, air, etc.) is managed by the Ministry of Transportation through its agencies. As of 1996 Lithuania had passed approximately 85 acts regulating this area of the economy. In 1996 the main laws in this area were codified in the Railway Transport Code[63] and the Inland Water Transport Code.[64] The Law on Civil Aviation was adopted in 1996.[65] Under the Regulation on Passengers Carrying Transport of April 1997,[66] the State Traffic Inspectorates subordinated to the Ministry of Communication and to local government are vested with controlling powers.

2.5 Laws on customs

The most important new feature in this area of management of the economy is the draft Customs Code, enacted on January 1, 1998.[67] Currently, all customs-related matters are regulated by the Law on Customs and Law on Customs Tariffs.[68] The Customs of the Republic of Lithuania with its territorial inspectorates is the state controlling agency subordinated to the Ministry of Finance.

2.6 Laws on communication and mass media

A new Law on Communication came into force on January 1, 1996[69]. It established: a) "the rights and obligations of the State, enterprises, organisations and natural persons in the management and use of technical facilities of telecommunications; b) the rights of ownership over media; c) the regulation of operating telecommunications networks; d) the provision of postal and telecommunications services, as well as e) the general principles of responsibility for violation of the discussed Law". According to this Law, public media are regulated by the Seimas and managed by the National Council of Television and Radio, which is an independent public body.

Broadcasting is administrated by the Radio and Television Commission, which announces tenders and issues permits on broadcasting. The status and functions of this Commission are defined by the Regulation adopted on March 14, 1997.

At the end of 1996 the Law on the Provision of Information to the Public was passed.[70] Although this Law is very new, it has already been amended three times. This Law established a procedure of obtaining, processing, and disseminating public information. It also defined the rights, duties, and liabilities of public information producers, disseminators, owners of information agencies, and journalists. Under the Law, any person can approach a state agency and within 10 days, obtain information related to him or her possessed by the agency. The provision of such information is free of charge. Implementing this Law, in November 1996 the Government enacted the Resolution on Provision of Information on Citizens of Lithuania Possessed by State Agencies.[71]

2.7 Laws on urban organisation, planning, and construction

The Law on Urban Organisation and Planning came into force in January 1996.[72] It established the principles of urban planning and regulated the relations between individuals, legal persons (private corporations as well as public organisations), and the state agencies in matters concerning planning and construction. Since 1996 Lithuania has enacted other 11 legal acts closely related to the administration of this area. The most important acts are as follows:

1. Governmental Decree on Administration and Registration of Territorial Administrative Units;[73]
2. Governmental Decree on Regulation of Planning and State Supervision of Construction Works.[74] This regulation defined the responsibilities of the central agencies–the Ministry of Construction and Urban Development, the State Commission on Urban Planning and Construction, and of District Governor's Office with its local inspectorates on territorial planning and construction;
3. Governmental Decree on Public Consideration of Project Documentation on Urban Planning.[75] According to this Decree, such projects must be announced publicly for discussions before they are submitted for a final approval;
4. Law on Constructions of 1996,[76] which established the main principles and rules of all stages of construction work as well as the forms of supervision and licensing, control and inspection of construction activities. Under the Law, authorisation for construction is a quite complicated procedure, which starts with obtaining various consents and permissions from more than 15 different administrative authorities. The final approval is granted by the District Governor's Office or the Ministry of Construction and Urban Development, depending on the complexity of the project.

The Ministry of Construction and Urban Development has enacted over 30 legal acts regulating the questions of planning and construction since the beginning of 1996.

2.8 Laws on education

The Law on Education was passed in 1991.[77] It set out the structure of the education system and defined the objectives, activities, and management of education institutions, excluding only the higher education institutions. According to that Law the system of education (primary and secondary) includes state and non-state education institutions. State education institutions are established by the Ministry of Education or the District Governor's Office with the consent of the local government. Non-state education institutions are established by private or corporate persons, who must obtain a licence from the Government. The Ministry of Education (through its local agencies) is responsible for the management of the education system (except for the sphere of higher education). Since the beginning of 1996 the Ministry has enacted over 15 legal acts regulating the activity of the education institutions, their study programs and teachers' qualification. The procedures of establishment, reorganisation and liquidation of primary and secondary education institutions are regulated by Instruction No. 757 of the Ministry of Education.[78]

The higher education system is governed by the Law on Science and Education, passed in 1991.[79] Under the present arrangements, two scientific degrees may be conferred: Doctor (after completion of post-graduate doctoral studies) and Doctor Habilius (after the requirements of habilitation are met). Academic titles of Associate Professor and Professor are conferred if the qualification requirements (prepared by the institution under recommendation of the Council of Science and approved by the Government) are satisfied.

2.9 Laws on health care

The Law on the Health Care System was enacted in 1994.[80] Following the provisions of the global strategy "Health to Everybody in 2000", adopted at the 30th Session
of the World Health Assembly in 1997 in Ottawa, the Law established the national health care system, its institutional structure, defined the extent of legal regulation of health care, health strengthening and health recovery, fundamentals of establishment of the scope of health activities, organisation and management of individual and public health care methods, health promotion, conclusion of contracts concerning health activities, fundamentals of the liability for violations of legal norms of health care activities, and rights and duties of the residents and subjects of health activities. The responsibilities for control and supervision over the health care system are vested within the Ministry of Health Care. Until 1996 the Ministry had made over 100 enactments regulating the area of their responsibilities. In 1996 the Law on Health Care Institutions was passed.[81] That Law established the basic principles of the National Health Care System and designated the types of health care institutions, the rules governing their activities, reorganisation,

liquidation, state control measures, relations between health care institutions and patients, and the principles of liability for violation of the Law. Only those institutions accredited for individual or public health care and which have obtained a document (licence, accrediting certificate) from the State Service Accrediting for Health Care Activities at the Ministry of Health are allowed to provide health care services. Doctors or physicians must be licensed to practice by the Ministry of Health Care.[82] A refusal to issue a licence, permit or accrediting certificate must be reasoned.

A new Law of Health Insurance was passed in 1996.[83] The provisions of the Law introduce a new mandatory health insurance system and govern its formation, operation and administration. Although the Law has been applicable only since July 1, 1997, it is already amended, and a draft on other 18 amendments and additions is pending in Parliament. Under the Law on Compensation Damages Incurred to Patients,[84] damages shall be assessed by the Commission on Evaluation of Damages, which is subordinated to the Ministry of Health.

From 1996 until July 1997, more than 10 new laws were enacted to regulate the health care including the Law on Economic Sanctions for Violation of Health Care Legal Acts,[85] the Law on Medical Practice of Physicians,[86] the Law on Dental Care (Assistance),[87] the Law on Human Tissue and Organ Donation and Transplantation,[88] and the Law on Supervision of Drug- and Alcohol- Addicted Persons.[89]

Sanitation control is regulated by the Law on the Health Care System and the Law on Local Government. In implementation of those laws, the Regulation of Sanitary Control adopted by the governmental states that every local municipality through its special Sanitary and Hygiene Inspection executes sanitary control in the territory of the municipality. Several specific legal acts have been adopted to govern sanitary control of special industrial or environmental subjects.

2.10 Laws on the management of historical heritage

Depending on the matters concerned, this area is managed by the Department of Preservation of Cultural Heritage, the State Commission on Preservation of Monuments, the State Archives Department, or the Municipalities or District Chief Offices.

2.11 The management of administrative-political processes

2.11.1 LAWS ON NATIONAL SECURITY

The Law on Fundamentals of National Security[90] was passed in 1996. It established the principles and institutional system of national security. The Law on Military Service was also passed in 1996.[91] Mobilisation is governed by the recently adopted

Law on Mobilisation.[92] Military and defence affairs are administered by the Ministry of State Security through its territorial divisions. State security issues are in the jurisdiction of the Department of State Security, whose activity is governed by the Law on the State Security Department.[93] The Lithuanian police is regulated by the Law on Police of 1990.[94] Since 1990 there have been many attempts to reform the Lithuanian police; however, all projects have failed conceptually, and the changes proposed related only to "technical rearmament of the police force" and did not address police management. Yet in June 1997 the police apparatus was significantly restructured.[95] The new system of the police bodies consists of the Police Department, Tax Police Department, Border Police Department and Special Investigation Service. All those departments are subordinated to the Ministry of Internal Affairs. Execution of the functions of these departments is carried out through municipal and local divisions of the departments. The General Commissar appointed by the Minister of Internal Affairs is the head of the police force. Police forces are also divided into traffic police, criminal police, transport police and security police.

2.11.2 LAWS ON MEETINGS, MANIFESTATIONS, AND STRIKES

The Law on Meetings was adopted in 1993, and no other legal acts nor any amendments to legislation in this area have been enacted since. The right to initiate strikes is provided by the Law on Collective Bargaining and the Law on Trade Unions, but no special legal act regulating other forms of industrial action has been passed. More than 20 laws provide for restrictions on strike action in certain areas of government and administration.

The Chapter has been prepared on the basis of information provided by Ramunė Dulevičienė, Audrius Bukaveckas and Antanas Bukauskas

NOTES

1 *Principles of Administrative Law Concerning the Relations between Administrative Authorities and Private Persons*, - A Handbook prepared by the Directorate of Legal Affairs, Strasbourg, 1996, p. 5.

2 No. I-12 of 11. 03. 90, - published in the official gazette *Valstibės Zinios*, 1990, No. 9, pub. No. 222. Hereinafter a reference to *Valstybės Zinios* is abbreviated as *VZ*.

3 No. I-12 of 11 03 90, -*VZ*, 1990, No. 9, pub. No. 222.

4 No I-14 of 11. 03. 90, - *VZ*, 1990, No. 9, pub. No. 224, annulled on 06. 11. 92 when the Constitution was enacted.

5 The Constitution of the Republic of Lithuania was approved in a referendum on October 25, 1992 and adopted by Law 06. 11. 92, - *VZ*, 1992, No. 33, pub. No. 1014.

6 Law No. I-865 of 27. 04. 95, - *VZ*, 1995, No. 37, pub. No. 913.

7 No. I-56 of 26. 01. 93, - *VZ*, 1993, No. 5, pub. No. 89.

[8] No. I-464 of 08. 06. 94 - *VZ*, 1994, No. 43, pub. No. 772.

[9] No. I-728 of 11. 08. 94, - *VZ*, 1994, No. 63, pub. No. 1238.

[10] In the period 1990-1997 Lithuania had eight Prime Ministers and Councils of Ministers.

[11] The ministries are the Ministry of Environmental Protection, Ministry of European Affairs, Ministry of Finance, Ministry of National Defence, Ministry of Culture, Ministry of Communications and Information, Ministry of Social Security and Labour, Ministry of Construction and Urban Planning, Ministry of Transport, Ministry of Justice, Ministry of Health, Ministry of Economy, Ministry of Education and Science, Ministry of Foreign Affairs, Ministry of Public Administration Reforms and Local Government Affairs, Ministry of Internal Affairs and Ministry of Agriculture and Forestry.

[12] No. I-707 of 15. 12. 94, - *VZ*, 1994, No. 101, pub. No. 2015.

[13] Constitutional Law No. VIII-32 of 12. 12. 96 on Amendment of Article 119 of the Constitution of the Republic of Lithuania - *VZ*, 1996, No. 122, pub. No. 2863.

[14] *VZ*, 1995, No. 31, pub. No. 701.

[15] New amendments to the Law on Local Government were adopted by Law No. VIII-144 of 13. 03. 97, - *VZ*, 1997, No. 41, pub. No. 996.

[16] This and other illustrations are based on updated information contained in the computerised programme "LITLEX", created by the Centre of Legal Information at the Ministry of Justice.

[17] *Materials of the Conference on Prevention of Crimes, organised in Vilnius on October 24, 1996* - published by the Law Institute, 1996.

[18] This information was publicised in the Conference on the Role of the Seimas in the Prevention of Corruption, organised in February, 1997 by the Council of Seimas in co-operation with the Konrad Adenauer Fund.

[19] Law No. I-1445 of 09. 07. 96, - *VZ*, 1996, No. 67, pub. No. 1606.

[20] Will be enacted as of 1998.

[21] No. I-1361 of 04. 06. 96, - *VZ*, 1996, No. 59, pub. No. 1402.

[22] No. I-1628 of 19. 11. 96, - *VZ*, 1996, No. 119, pub. No. 2772.

[23] No. 774 of 16. 10. 92, - *VZ*, 1992, No. 32, pub. No. 995.

[24] The Code was enacted in 1964, Chapter 21-1 was enacted before 1990. The Code has been amended 32 times; Chapter 21 -1 was amended by the Law on Amendments to the Civil Procedure Code No. I- 1445 of 09. 07. 96 - *VZ*, 1996 No. 67, pub. No. 1606.

[25] No. VIII-216 of 08. 05. 97 - *VZ*, 1997, No. 41, pub. No. 996.

[26] Rulings and Decisions of the Constitutional Court, 1994, No. 2, p. 23.

[27] Rulings and Decisions of the Constitutional Court, 1994, No. 2 , p. 24.

[28] No. I-.I-399 of 17. 02. 94 - *VZ*, 1994, No. 15, pub. No. 249.

[29] The following committees have been set up: economics, budget and finance; environmental protection; village affairs; national defence; labour and social affairs; health affairs; education, science and culture; law and order; foreign affairs; administration reforms and local government; human rights, minorities and legal affairs (in the area of integration with the EU).

[30] On June 20, 1996, the Seimas (Parliament) ratified the Association Agreement with the European Union.

[31] No. I-836 of 04. 04. 95, - *VZ*, 1995, No. 33, publ. No. 759, amended three times.

[32] Jeremy Pope, *Transparency International*, (TI), Berlin, 1996, p.49.

[33] Law No. I-1390 of 20. 06. 96, - *VZ*, 1996, No. 64, publ. No. 1501.

[34] Law No. VIII-32 of 12. 12. 96, - *VZ*, 1996, No. 122, publ. No.2863.

[35] Law No. I-1505 of 22. 08. 96 on Amendment of the Law on Referenda of 1989, - *VZ*, 1996, No. 86, publ. No. 2044.

[36] Ruling of January 19, 1994, - Rulings and Decisions of the Constitutional Court of the Republic of Lithuania, No. 2, 1994 (hereinafter this issue is referred as "RD of the Constitutional Court").

[37] No. I-872 of 02. 05. 95, - *VZ*, 1995, No. 41, publ. No. 991.

[38] Ruling of January 19, 1994 - RD of the Constitutional Court, 1994, No. 2.

[39] It should be noted that in 1997 the President vetoed several laws, such as the Law on Restoration of Property Rights, the Statute on Bankruptcy, etc.; however, the Seimas does not always take into account the proposals of the President and usually re-enacts the vetoed laws.

[40] No. I - 119, - *VZ*, 1993, No.12, publ. No.296.

41 Ruling of March 16, 1994, - RD of the Constitutional Court, 1994, No. 2, p. 39.
42 No. I-875 of 02. 05. 95, - *VZ*, 1995 No. 41, publ. No. 992.
43 A Review prepared by the Lithuanian State Privatisation Agency, 1997.
44 No. I-1607 of 05. 07. 91, - *VZ*, 1991, No. 24, publ. No. 635, amended 11 times.
45 No. I-354 of 23. 12. 93, - *VZ*, 1994, No. 3, publ. No. 41.
46 No.I-2675 of 25. 06. 92, *VZ*, 1992, No. 21, publ. No. 612.
47 No. I-446 of 26. 04. 94, *VZ*, 1994, No. 34, publ. No. 620, last amendment made on 24. 09. 96, No. I-1540.
48 *VZ*, 1996, No. 64, publ. No. 1503, amended on 17. 02. 97, No. 121.
49 Ruling of Sept. 25, 1996 "On the Compliance of the Norms of Law on Land Regulating the Rights of Institutions of Local Government in the Sphere of the Possession of State Land with the Constitution", - RD of the Constitutional Court, 1996, No. 7, p. 24.
50 No. I-1188 of 02. 04. 91, - *VZ*, 1991, No. 12, publ. No. 309.
51 No. I-1013 of 09. 11. 93, - *VZ*, 1993, No. 63, publ. No. 1188.
52 No. I-1069 of 19. 10. 95, - *VZ*, 1995, No. 90, publ. No. 2013.
53 No. I-1352 of 28. 05. 96, - *VZ*, 1996, No. 57, publ. No. 1335.
54 Act of the Seimas No. 1550 of 15. 09. 96, - *VZ*, 1996, No. 103, publ. No. 2347.
55 No. I-1949 of 09. 11. 91 and No. I-199 of 01. 07. 93, - *VZ*, 1991, No. 33, publ. No. 896; *VZ*, 1993, No. 27, publ. No. 623.
56 No. I-678 of 01. 12. 94, - *VZ*, 1994, No. 99, publ.No. 1957.
57 No. I-720 of 21. 12. 94, - *VZ*, 1995, No. 2, publ. No. 33.
58 No. I-430 of 30. 07. 90, - *VZ*, 1990, No. 24, publ. No. 596.
59 I.e. income tax of natural persons, corporation tax, value added tax, excise duties, custom duties, land tax, real estate tax, taxes of natural resources, taxes on oil and gas, taxes on environmental pollution, consulate taxes, stamp duties, sales tax, payments to the road fund, inheritance and gift tax, and taxes on state land and state water.
60 No. I - 974 of 28. 05. 95, - *VZ*, 1995, No. 62, publ. No. 1525.
61 No. 71 of 15. 05. 97, - *VZ*, 1997, No.43, publ. No. 1070. The Republic of Lithuania has signed the Treaties on Avoiding Double Taxation with Belarus, Denmark, Czech Republic, Latvia, Estonia, China, Norway, Sweden, and Finland.
62 No. I-1863 of 08. 10. 91, - *VZ*, 1990, No. 30, publ. No. 804.
63 Enacted by the Law No. I-1361 of 04. 06. 96, - *VZ*, 1996, No. 59, publ. No. 1402.
64 Enacted by the Law No. I-1534 of 24. 09. 96, -*VZ*, 1996, No. 105, publ. No. 2393.
65 No. I-1323 of 02. 05. 96, - *VZ*, 1996, No. 48, publ. No. 1140.
66 Governmental Decree No. 150 of 28. 04. 97, - *VZ*, 1997, No. 40, publ. No. 981.
67 Code adopted by the Law No. I-1292 of 18. 04. 96, - *VZ*, 1996, No. 52, publ. No.1239.
68 No. I-140 of 29. 04. 93, amended four times, and No. I-138 of 27. 04. 93, amended five times.
69 No. I-1109 of 30. 11. 95, - *VZ*, 1996, No. 102, publ. No. 2280.
70 No. I-1418 of 02. 07. 96, - *VZ*, 1996, No. 71, publ. No. 1706.
71 No. 1425 of 29. 11. 96, - *VZ*, 1996, No. 118, publ. No. 2746.
72 No. I-1120 of 12. 12. 95, - *VZ*, 1995, No. 107, publ. No. 2391.
73 No. 651 of 03. 06. 96, - *VZ*, 1996, No. 54, publ. No. 1277.
74 No. 370 of 16. 04. 97, - *VZ*, 1997, No. 34, publ. No. 851.
75 No. 1079 of 18. 09. 96, - *VZ*, 1996, No. 90, publ. No. 2099.
76 No. I-1240 of 19. 03. 96, - *VZ*, 1996, No. 32, publ. No. 788.
77 No. I - 1489 of 25. 06. 91, - *VZ*, 1991, No. 23, publ. No. 593, amended four times.
78 No. 757 of 03. 07. 96, - *VZ*, 1996, No. 80, publ. No. 1914.
79 No. I-1052 12. 02. 91, - *VZ*, 1991, No. 7, publ. No. 191.
80 No. I-552 of 16. 07. 94, - *VZ*, 1994, No. 63, publ. No. 1231.
81 No. I-1367 of 06. 06. 96, - *VZ*, 1996, No. 66, publ. No. 1572.
82 Law No. I- 1557 of 15. 09. 96, - *VZ*, 1996, No.102, publ. No. 2315.
83 No. I-1344 of 21. 05. 96, - *VZ*, 1996, No. 55, publ. No. 1288.
84 No. I-1562 of 03. 10. 96, - *VZ*, No. 102, publ. No 2317.
85 No. I-1572 of 08. 10. 96, - *VZ*, 1996, No. 104, publ. No. 2365.

[86] No. I-5558 of 25. 09. 96, - *VZ*, 1996, No. 102, publ. No. 2316.
[87] No. I-1246 of 28. 03. 96, as amended by 25. 09. 96, - *VZ*, 1996, No. 35, publ. No. 855.
[88] No. I -1626 of 19. 11. 96,-VZ, 1996, No. 116, publ. No. 2696.
[89] No. VIII-156 of 03. 25. 97,-*VZ*, 1997, No. 30, publ. No. 711.
[90] No. VIII-49 of 19. 12. 96,-*VZ*, 1997, No. 2, publ. No. 16.
[91] No. I-1593 of 12. 10. 96,-*VZ*, 1996, No. 106, publ. No. 2427.
[92] No. I -1623 of 19. 10. 96,-*VZ*, 1996, No. 116, publ. No. 2695.
[93] No. I-380, 20. 01. 94,-*VZ*, 1994, No. 11, publ. No. 163.
[94] No. I-851 of 20. 01. 91, - *VZ*, 1991, No. 2, publ. No. 22, amended four times.
[95] Law No. VIII-356 of 01. 07. 97 amending the Law on Police, - *VZ*, 1997, No. 69, publ. No. 1734.

CHAPTER EIGHT
POLAND

I. GENERAL DESCRIPTION OF THE POLISH ADMINISTRATIVE LAW SYSTEM

1. HISTORY OF THE EVOLUTION OF THE POLISH ADMINISTRATIVE SYSTEM: THE POLISH CONSTITUTIONS

The evolution of the modern Polish administrative law system began with the adoption of the country's first Constitution on May 3, 1791. The adoption of this document streamlined the processes of administrative centralisation and stabilisation of the Polish state during the second part of the 18th century. Unfortunately, this Constitution was doomed to have a limited historical significance. By 1795 Poland, partitioned among the Russian, Austrian and Prussian empires, had ceased to exist as an independent state. Only after the First World War did Poland regain its independence. Between the two world wars Poland adopted two constitutions, in March 1921 and then in April 1935. This period in Poland's history and legal order ended after the Second World War and the establishment of communist rule in the country.

The present Polish legal order was established after the political transformation in Eastern Europe in 1989. The first important step was the enforcement, on October 17, 1992, of the so-called "Small Constitution",[1] which outlined the powers and structure of the major institutions in the country. It was, however, a temporary substitute for a basic law since it did not provide a bill of rights and left a great number of constitutional issues to be settled by an entirely new Constitution. The old communist Constitution[2] of July 22, 1952, therefore remained partly in force to prevent a legal vacuum in the areas left open by the "Small Constitution".

The Small Constitution was repealed with the adoption of the new Polish Constitution in the spring of 1997. The procedures and rules of drafting of the new Constitution were established by the constitutional statute of April 23, 1992[3]. According to this statute both chambers of the National Assembly, the Seym and the Senate, had to adopt the new basic law. Apart from this statute, the Assembly had to abide by its Resolution of September 22, 1994: Rules and Regulations of the National Assembly for the Adoption of a Constitution.[4] The procedure for constitutional adoption established by these documents is as follows. First, the law provides for the establishment of a Constitutional Committee, which is entitled to prepare drafts of a new Constitution and put them forward to Parliament for discussion. (The Constitutional Committee issued a Resolution on January 18, 1994, on the rules and regulations of its work.)[5] Second, after the National Assembly has debated the constitutional drafts, the bill can only be accepted by a two-thirds majority when at least half of the National Assembly members are present. After Parliament adopts it, the Constitution is then sent to the President, who may introduce amendments. The National Assembly must then pass the Constitution, with any presidential amendments, by a two-thirds majority in the presence of at least half of its members. The Constitution is then voted on in a referendum called by the President and carried out under the rules of the Statute on Referenda of June 29, 1995.[6] The Constitution is considered approved if the majority of citizens participating in the referendum vote for it.

Following this procedure, a draft of a new Constitution of the Republic of Poland was accepted by the National Assembly in April 1997. The referendum validating the Constitution took place on May 25, 1997. The Constitution entered into force three months after its promulgation.

2. ESTABLISHMENT OF THE BASIC ADMINISTRATIVE INSTITUTIONS

Prior to the Second World War administrative procedure in Poland was governed by a Decree on Administrative Procedure of the President of the Republic adopted on March 22, 1928. New legislation, the Code of Administrative Procedure, was only issued on June 14, 1960.[7] The Code did not provide for separate administrative courts, and it was only in 1980, after the adoption of the Statute on the High Administrative Court, which amended the Code of Administrative Procedure,[8] that the first separate administrative court, the High Administrative Court, was appointed. This statute introduced some important changes in the development of administrative procedure and brought it closer to the civil procedure before common courts.[9]

3. STRUCTURE OF THE BASIC ADMINISTRATIVE INSTITUTIONS

The Seym and the Senate are the highest legislative bodies in Poland, while the President and the Council of Ministers are the highest executive bodies in the country. The Council of Ministers, the Government, is politically accountable before Parliament. Generally the Seym exercises control over the government in cases of national importance. The Council of Ministers is accountable before the Seym for the implementation of the annual budget of the country and is also responsible for the acts of all governmental administrative bodies.

No later than 14 days after the appointment of the new President, and prior to the establishment of a new Council of Ministers, the Prime Minister of the Council presents the programme and members of the new Government to the Seym. The Seym then votes for the appointment of the Government via a majority of votes when at least half of the Members of the Diet (Seym) are present.

The Government can issue decrees, but these do not have the same power as statutes, e.g. decrees cannot be issued that purport to change the constitution or electoral law. These decrees, passed by the Council of Ministers, do not need parliamentary approval and, like statutes, are signed by the President. The President can apply to the Constitutional Tribunal to give an approval that a decree does not infringe the law. This involves the same procedure as at the approval of a statute. The President also has a right to refuse to approve the decree, although the Small Constitution does not state in which cases, and he may, therefore, return it, within 14 days, to the Council of Ministers. After such a presidential refusal, the only option left to the Council of Ministers is to apply to the Seym using the decree as a governmental proposal for a statute. This procedure does differ, however, from that applied in issuing a statute, because the President cannot refuse to confirm a statute if the Constitutional Tribunal finds that a statute is in accordance with the law. The Seym can vote against the government on a motion tabled by the group of at least 46 members of the Seym.

The Small Constitution states that the President is the head of state of Poland, representing it both inside and outside the country. He is accountable only before a special court, the Court of State, for breach of the Constitution or statutes or for committing a crime. The National Assembly alone has the authority to deal with accusations made against the President (upon a motion of one quarter of the Members of the Assembly approved by a two-thirds majority of votes).

4. RELATIONS BETWEEN THE CENTRAL AND THE LOCAL ADMINISTRATION

Only one article in the Small Constitution, Article 68, involves a general rule about the relations between central and local government administration. It states that a voivode is an administrative body, belonging to the governmental administration and represents the Council of Ministers in a voivodeship (territorial unit). A separate section in the Small Constitution is devoted to self-government.[10] In Poland there are two parallel local administrations: central local government and self-administration of the communes. The central government administration creates its local units: regions and voivodeships. A voivodeship consists of a few regions. As mentioned above, the voivode is an administrative organ and head of a voivodeship. A commune is a union of people living on one territory. According to the statute on self-government, a commune is a legal person acting through its organs: i.e. a board of the commune and president of the board of the commune. Organs of the commune act in every sphere of government administration.

According to Article 71, the organs of the commune, within the scope of the authority granted to them by different statutes, fulfil the tasks of the local government administration. This rule derives from the statute of March 8, 1990, about self-government,[11] which also states that the Prime Minister and the voivodes have to supervise the acts of organs of the commune and that the regional accounting chamber is responsible for the control over the implementation of the commune budget. Every legal act issued by the organs of the commune has to be presented to the voivode. The supervisory body is entitled to take action on declaring the invalidity of the act. The tasks of government administration which the organs of commune are obliged to carry out are listed in the statute of May 17, 1990. This statute deals with the division of power between the organs of the commune and the organs of local government administration.[12]

5. ACTS OF THE ADMINISTRATION

5.1 Acts of the Council of Ministers

According to the Small Constitution the Council of Ministers issues decrees implementing statutes, which are based on authorisations contained in the statutes, but subordinate to them. The Government also issues resolutions in the implementation of its constitutional rights. The Seym can delegate its power to the Council of Ministers to issue decrees, which have the same legal power as statutes.[13]

5.2 Acts of the President

The Small Constitution states that the President issues decrees and orders subordinated to statutes to implement the statutes, based on legal authorisations from the statutes. He also issues different types of orders (based on a general authorisation given in the Small Constitution) to fulfil his constitutional rights and duties. Presidential legal acts have to be countersigned by either the Head of the Council of Ministers (PM) or by a minister who applies to the President to issue a legal act. According to a clause in the Small Constitution, in some cases the presidential acts do not have to be approved (countersigned) by the Prime Minister or a minister.

5.3 Acts of Ministers

According to the Small Constitution a minister is head of a department: the tasks of ministers are stated in laws. He issues decrees and orders subordinated to statutes. On application of the Prime Minister, the Council of Ministers is entitled to annul a decree or an order of a minister.

6. ADMINISTRATIVE JUDICIAL HIERARCHY

6.1 The High Administrative Court

There is only one administrative court in Poland, the High Administrative Court (NSA), which has been in existence since 1980. There were no administrative courts in Poland from the end of the Second World War until 1980. The High Administrative Court was established by the statute of January 31, 1980, and by an amendment to the Code of Administrative Procedure. The newest act establishing the internal organisation, scope of jurisdiction and procedure before the High Administrative Court was issued on May 11, 1995.[14] The administrative process has one instance (level). The court decides about citizens' claims in almost all individual administrative cases, with some exceptions (see below). The court has subsidiary units in different cities, but they are created for functional reasons and are part of the NSA. In some types of cases common courts decide on appeals against administrative acts as well.

6.2 Jurisdiction of the Court

The jurisdiction of the High Administrative Court is based on the rule of protection of individual rights, which means that the court takes an action only on the claim of an individual. The court does not decide on general normative administrative acts such as decrees and orders, although it adjudicates if a citizen's rights have been violated by an individual administrative act issued on the basis of an illegal general law. The High Administrative Court is competent in the adjudication of administrative acts issued by the following administrative organs:

1. central administrative organs, such as ministers and presidents of the central offices;
2. territorial organs of governmental administration (voivodes and chiefs of the region offices);
3. organs of communes;
4. other organs if they are competent in cases of public administration.

The NSA also adjudicates on legal local regulations issued by the organs of communes or the governmental administration. These acts (resolutions) are binding on all people living on the territory of the commune or in one governmental administration division unit: they are therefore not individual but rather general (normative) legal acts. This is partly contradictory to the doctrine of Polish administrative law, which states that Polish administrative jurisdiction adjudicates the lawfulness of individual acts only.

According to the statute on the High Administrative Court, the following legal acts belong to the scope of jurisdiction of the Court: administrative decisions and other administrative acts, including executive resolutions of the organs of communes and acts of organs of governmental administration; local legal regulations and acts of inspection over communes done by the organs of governmental administration. All of the units of the High Administrative Court have the same scope of jurisdiction. Additionally, the NSA is authorised to adjudicate litigation regarding separation of power between the organs of communes and the organs of local governmental administration, as well as decisions of the appeal body of the communes. It also adjudicates on citizens' claims in cases when the administrative organ should have issued a decision but has not, and in cases specified in other specific statutes. The scope of the NSA's jurisdiction is based on a general clause in its governing statute which is limited by a clause of negative enumeration: the following cases are excluded from its jurisdiction:

1. cases belonging to the scope of jurisdiction of other courts and the Commission of Appeal of the Patent Agency;
2. cases regarding subordination between administrative organs, and official subordination in the special services and the army;
3. disciplinary cases, refusal of appointment to perform functions in administrative organs, visas and permission for foreigners to stay on Polish territory;
4. some types of administrative cases which are adjudicated by the sections of common courts (in particular, cases regarding national security system and anti-monopoly cases).

Further, according to the statute of April 18, 1985, (adjudication of labour law and national insurance system cases by the common courts),[15] and the statute of November 25, 1986, (organisation and financing of the national insurance system),[16] common courts of voivodeship (their sections of labour law and national security in particular) adjudicate appeals from decisions issued by the sections of Agency of the National Insurance System. The common courts of voivodeship are appellate courts for decisions of the Agency of National Insurance System. The courts apply the rules established in the Code of Civil Procedure of November 17, 1964.[17] There is a separate civil law procedure of judicial review in labour law and national insurance cases as well.

According to the statute of February 24, 1990, (action against monopoly),[18] recourses from decisions of the Anti-Monopoly Office (the central administrative body in this area) are adjudicated by the common Court of Voivodeship in Warsaw. There are also other particular cases, e.g. in water law, when a party can apply to a common court.

6.3 Special quasi-judicial administrative bodies adjudicating cases requiring administrative expertise

Some professions, such as doctors, nurses and pharmacists, are given special responsibilities and enjoy special administrative legal status. The rules of administrative supervision and control in these specific areas are more liberal: the practice of the state is to regulate them through the establishment of professional self-government. Therefore, there are special courts of professional responsibility, which are also the bodies of professional self-government. As an illustration, the arrangements concerning the medical profession will be briefly described here; a more detailed analysis of the recent changes in this area is provided in the second part of the chapter.

The rules of doctors' responsibility are established by the statute of May 17, 1989, (doctors' chambers, doctors' self-government),[19] and a decree of the Ministry of Health and Social Help of September 26, 1990, on the proceedings with regard to doctors' professional responsibility.[20] The rules of the statute about doctors' chambers provide professional responsibility before special doctors' courts. The governing body is responsible when a doctor acts in breach of both the rules of professional ethics and the rules of practising as a doctor; these are derived from the statute governing the profession (a new one has not yet come into force, while the old one dates from 1950–see below), a Code of Doctors' Ethics, the statute on doctors' chambers and the statute of August 30, 1991, on health care institutions.[21] For infringement of the above rules a doctor can be punished with reprimand, or his right to practice can be suspended or revoked. Special professional courts have been created based on the rules of the statute about doctors' chambers. A spokesman of professional responsibility is appointed to investigate at a first stage, before the case reaches the court. Once the case reaches the court, the spokesman acts as a "prosecutor".

There are two instances of professional courts: regional doctors' courts, as a court of first instance, and a Main Doctors' Court, as an appeal court for decisions taken by the regional courts. The final tier to which proceedings concerning a doctor's breach of professional conduct can be taken is the Supreme Court. Decisions of suspension or deprivation issued by the Main Doctors' Court at appeal may be reviewed before the Supreme Court.

7. GENERAL PROCEDURAL CODES AND LAWS OF ADMINISTRATIVE LAW

The Code of Administrative Procedure was issued on June 14, 1960, and is still in force.

7.1 Appeal before administrative agencies: internal administrative appeal

The procedure for appeal of administrative acts is regulated by the Second Section of the Code of Administrative Procedure. Articles 127–140 of the Code relate to recourses from administrative decisions, providing for substantive settlement of a case. Articles 141–144 of the Code govern appeals from other decisions, i.e. those of a procedural nature which were issued by an administrative organ during administrative proceedings. The first form of recourse is general: it is vested in a party in any decision giving substantive settlement of a case. The second form, an appeal from procedural administrative decision, can be lodged by a party or others (a witness, an expert), but only against decisions issued during administrative proceedings. The Code of Administrative Procedure states which of the above decisions can be appealed: there are not many instances, but examples include decisions with which an agency refuses to begin an administrative procedure or to give access to a proceeding to a social organisation representing another person, decisions refusing the renovation of a fixed time limit for recourse or appeal (excluding final decisions), decisions suspending proceedings, decisions explaining doubts in a decision and decisions regarding the costs of proceedings. The Code states that if the rules do not authorise a party to lodge an appeal from a decision issued during proceedings, it can nevertheless be lodged together with a recourse from a decision regarding the substantive matter. The fixed time limit for recourse is 14 days and seven days for appeal, counting from the day when the decision was delivered or orally announced to a party. According to the Code of Administrative Procedure, the procedure for both recourse and appeals is two-tiered (two instances), and the rules of the Code regarding recourse are also applied for appeals.

The appeal of a decision is decided on by the administrative organ superior to the organ that has issued the decision. If the main administrative authority (e.g. minister) who has no superior authority over him has issued a decision at first instance, then recourse is not possible. A party can apply to the main authority which has taken the decision for further consideration of the case. The above rule also applies to the decision issued in the first instance by the board of appeal acting at the Seym of a commune, which is the superior body for the council of commune and board of commune.

First, however, the recourse should be lodged with the organ of first instance, which can change or annul its decision if a recourse has been lodged by all parties and the organ ascertains that a recourse is worth taking into account. If it is ascertained that this is not the case, he sends the recourse to a superior organ of second instance within seven days. The organ of second instance has three options: 1) to sustain the decision of the organ of first instance, 2) to annul the decision and decide about the matter or discontinue the case before the organ of first instance, 3) or discontinue the appeal.

7.2 Judicial review of administrative acts

Since 1980 the Code of Administrative Procedure has provided for judicial review before the High Administrative Court (NSA) from almost every administrative act. The Code established the scope of jurisdiction of the NSA and the procedure before the Court.[22] These rules lost all legal force on October 1, 1995, the date when the rules of the statute about NSA were introduced, and are currently binding only where complaints were lodged with the NSA before October 1, 1995. The procedure before the NSA is presently generally regulated by the statute about the High Court. It states which rules of the Code of Administrative Procedure are applied before the High Administrative Court (e.g. general principles of administrative procedure, time limits, stay of proceedings). The rules of the Code of Civil Procedure are also applied subsidiarily (i.e. if a specific law does not provide other procedures) when there is no regulation either in the statute on the High Court or in the Code of Administrative Procedure.

The statute provides for a particular procedure before the NSA. A complaint can be lodged by anybody who has a legal interest for doing so: 1) prosecutor, 2) ombudsman, or 3) social organisation or individual. A complaint can be lodged only when a decision has been finalised, which means that it must have already been appealed before an administrative organ of second instance. The only exception is when a public prosecutor or ombudsman complains. A complaint has to be lodged within 30 days from the day of deliverance of the final decision to a party or from the day when a party learned about the act. It is not possible to complain to the NSA if the administrative organ has taken an action to change, annul or to state the invalidity of an act. Complaints must be lodged directly with the High Administrative Court, which directs the complaint to the organ issuing the relevant decision as last instance. The organ is obliged to answer the complaint. Until the first trial the administrative organ can satisfy the complaint. The administrative organ issuing the decision is a party in the procedure. The High Administrative Court considers the case generally at a trial: it is not involved in the particulars of a complaint and only judges if any rule of material or procedural law has been broken.

7.4 Judicial remedies

When a complaint is made, the High Administrative Court can either take action or disregard it. At the preliminary procedure the Court can dismiss a complaint if it is inadmissible, if a party does not obey the fixed time limit of 30 days in which to complain, or if a party does not make amendments in accordance with decisions rejecting complaints. The Code of Administrative Procedure sets out the occasions when a complaint will be inadmissible. The most important are when a case does not belong within the scope of jurisdiction of the NSA, a claim is made by a person who is not a party, when other legally proscribed forms of recourse have not been exhausted or the same decision between the same parties has been already considered by the Court. Complaints may be rejected due to a lack of letters of attorney or proof of entry registration. The Court can reinstate a term "for important reasons" and may take three forms of action when faced with a complaint: it may annul a decision, state the invalidity of a decision or note the incompatibility of a decision with the law. The above possibilities differ from each other in relation to types of infringement and procedural effects, but they do actually give the same final result, i.e. a decision has been dissolved. The Court annuls a decision when the decision has been taken by infringing material or procedural law. The Court notes the invalidity of a decision when one of the reasons stated in the Code of Administrative Procedure has occurred. Some of these reasons have already been mentioned while explaining the inadmissibility of a complaint. The Court ascertains the incompatibility of a decision with the law where they cannot proclaim that a decision is invalid because of lapse of time (10 years after deliverance or announcement of a decision to a party) or when a decision caused an irreversible legal outcome.

The Court can take five other steps: it may 1) state the invalidity of the act which is the source of local regulations, 2) annul an act of supervision over an organ of commune, 3) issue a decision stating or conferring rights to a party (when a complaint regards an administrative act as different from an administrative decision), 4) indicate an organ competent in a case, and, finally, 5) bind an administrative organ to issue a particular administrative act.

The Court can also fine an administrative organ when it ascertains that the organ has not carried out the decision of the Court. In addition, and in this case only, if all the legal and factual circumstances of a case are unquestionable, the Court can decide about the existence or non-existence of a right. The statute[23] states that a person who sustains a loss because an organ has not carried out a decision of the Court can claim indemnity against the non-complying administrative organ. The Court informs the organs, or their superiors, about serious infringements of law and of the non-fulfilment of the Court's decree.

The Court also decides about restitution of the costs of procedure to a party from an organ who has issued a decision. The Code of Administrative Procedure provides exceptions in the procedure in relation to tax organs in tax cases and organs of the national security system. The main features of the procedure in cases regarding national security have been presented above. The Code of Administrative Procedure states that in these cases the rules of administrative procedure are applied, with some exceptions provided by the statute about organisation and financing of the social security system[24] and the Code of Civil Procedure.[25]

8. OMBUDSMAN

The institution of Ombudsman has existed in Poland since November 1987 and was established by statute on July 15, 1987.[26] The latest changes in the statute were made on August 24, 1991. It is also stated in the rules of the "old" Constitution in 1952 that the Ombudsman guards the rights and liberties of citizens. The Ombudsman is appointed by the Seym, with the Senate's approval, for a four-year period. He is not dependent on any governing body but responsible only to the Seym. He presents annual reports to the Seym and Senate about his activities and the state of observance of the law in the country. He investigates to ensure that the organs and organisations do not infringe the rights and liberties of the citizens.

Where the Ombudsman finds that the law has been broken he can apply to the organs of inspection or prosecutor. He can make an application to the Seym requesting that the Highest Audit Chamber carry out an inspection, and he may also lead an inspection himself. The Ombudsman is entitled to inspect any authority, including the organs of social organisations. His main role within the administrative procedure is to apply to take administrative action and judicial review against administrative decisions. He can also make statements about acts of administrative organs and direct them to the supervisory body. These statements also include disciplinary cases. The organs are obliged to co-operate with the Ombudsman and notify him about all amendments they make after his application. The Ombudsman can also apply to the authorised organ to take initiative of issuance or change of the law. He may apply to the Constitutional Tribunal for verifying that a statute is in accordance with the Constitution.

9. OTHER FORMS OF SUPERVISION OVER THE ADMINISTRATION

Supervision over the administration is carried out, firstly, by administrative organs accountable before the main administrative authority and, secondly, by organs independent from the administration. The first group are mainly various inspectorates accountable before the ministers, i.e. members of Government.[27] The ones involved here are the State Sanitary Inspection, State Commercial Inspectorate and the State Fire Brigade. Within this first group the Treasury Inspectorate and the Regional Accounting Chambers are worth noting. The former was established by statute on September 28, 1991.[28] It is accountable to the Ministry of Finance. One of its main tasks is to inspect the expenses of the organs of governmental administration.

The statute of March 8, 1990, about self-government[29] states that Regional Accounting Chambers supervise the financial economy of a commune and are accountable to the Prime Minister of the Council of Ministers. The statute regarding the Regional Accounting Chambers was issued on October 7, 1992.[30]

Within the first group of supervision it is necessary to mention the public prosecutors. Since the change to the statute of June 20, 1985, (about public prosecutors)[31] on March 22, 1990,[32] public prosecutors have been included under the jurisdiction of the Ministry of Justice. This is related to the fact that the Minister of Justice is also a General Prosecutor. Public prosecutors control whether a decision issued by an organ of governmental administration or an organ of local administration is in accordance with the law. The Code of Administrative Procedure states that they can order an administrative organ to start certain administrative proceedings and can also take part, at any stage, in an administrative procedure that has already occurred. Furthermore, public prosecutors can lodge complaints with the High Administrative Court. According to the Code they may lodge objections against a decision when it is invalid, for reasons mentioned in the Code, when the decision is incompatible with the law, e.g. where there has been an infringement of material or procedural law, or when a procedure should be renewed for reasons given by the Code of Administrative Procedure.

In the second group of supervisory bodies the Highest Audit Chamber and State Labour Inspectorate are particularly noteworthy. The latter Inspectorate acts on the basis of a statute on March 6, 1981.[33] It is accountable before the Seym.[34] The Highest Audit Chamber was established in 1949. It was initially accountable to the Government, but on October 8, 1980, the Constitution of 1952 was changed, and since then the Chamber has been accountable only to the Seym. The last statute regarding the Organisation, Tasks and Acts of the Highest Audit Chamber, was issued on December 23, 1994.[35] The Chamber supervises 1) all organs of governmental administration and administration of communes, 2) state and communal co-operations and unions, e.g. the Constitutional Tribunal, Supreme Court, High Administrative Court, Chancellery of Seym and Senate, 3) organisations and subjects which carry out tasks of administration, 4) organisations and other subjects which carry out orders of state and commune or 5) those which use the financial means from the central budget or budget of commune. The objective scope of the activity of the Highest Audit Chamber is to inspect the carrying out of a central budget, statutes and other acts, regarding financial, economic, organisational and administrative aspects. The criteria of inspection of the Highest Audit Chamber are lawfulness, purposefulness and straightforwardness. Together with others, the Chamber presents to the Seym its analysis of the budget, as well as financial and political opinion before a vote of confidence in the Government, related to budgetary issues.

10. PARLIAMENTARY COMMITTEES

The committees of the Seym are created on the basis of the resolution of the Seym on July 30, 1992 (The Rules of the Seym).[36] The role of the committees is to prepare draft statutes and give opinions on different matters as requested by either the Seym or its President. The committees are appointed to undertake inspections to ensure that the statutes and resolutions of the Seym are carried out. They are entitled to inspect the main authorities of state administrative organs and organisations. The Seym appoints 24 ordinary standing committees and can also appoint extraordinary committees if necessary. The Seym establishes the purpose, rules and procedure of extraordinary committees. The Small Constitution also provides for the establishment of extraordinary committees, appointed to investigate pressing matters.

During the investigation a committee applies the rules of the Code of Penal Procedure;[37] for example, it is entitled to hear a suspected person. According to the resolution of the Seym on March 31, 1995, concerning an amendment to the Rules and Regulations of the Seym of the Republic of Poland[38] a member of the Diet cannot be a member of a committee which inspects an administrative organ where the member acts as a minister, secretary or vice-secretary of state. This regulation is derived from a new statute issued on May 9, 1996, (holding a seat in the Seym and Senate).[39] The Senate can also appoint committees on the basis of the resolution of November 23, 1990, (Rules and Regulations of the Senate).[40]

II. DEVELOPMENTS IN ADMINISTRATIVE LAW DURING 1996-1997

INTRODUCTION

1996 and the first part of 1997 brought many changes in administration at the central and local level and also in many fields of administrative activity. The number of laws and other legal acts issued in 1996 exceeds the number issued in 1995.

Generally 1996 was a year of reforms. Some have already been introduced, i.e. the "reform of Centrum (central administration)", some are being drafted and introduced more slowly, e.g. reform of the national security system, and others are in the process of being planned, e.g. the reform of health care institutions. There were various events connected with the process of privatisation: issuance of the statute about commercialisation and privatisation of state establishments, distribution of the universal sharing certificates which provide a right to bc a shareholder in companies arising after the privatisation process, etc. This chapter only concerns developments in 1996 and part of 1997: draft rules are therefore not included.

Poland's social security system is very old, and the necessary reform of the system will take a long time. Nowadays everyone has to pay a premium of 45 per cent of their salary for the social security system. Then, after retirement, everybody obtains a pension from the State on a scale which corresponds to the salary earned. The system is organised in such a way that present employees pay for the pensions of retired employees. Pensions, however, are so small now that the people who worked for their whole life and paid for the national insurance system are not able to survive on them alone. Under the new system everybody will decide how much money they will receive after retirement. The system of premiums will change; for example if an employee wants to get more than a basic pension from the state he may pay for special funds.

The Agency of National Security System controls the Fund of National Security where all income from insurance premiums is gathered. The organisation and financing of the national security system by the agency is governed by statute.[41] The Council of Ministers has issued a resolution enacting the Inter-Departmental Commission for the Reform of Social Security.[42] The Inter-Departmental Commission acts as a governmental body. The Minister of Labour is a President of the Commission and Plenipotentiary of Government for Reform of Social Security. The Plenipotentiary presents draft rules regarding the reform of social security to the Commission, prepares experts' opinions and gives professional advice to the organs of governmental administration regarding their acts connected with reform of social security.

In 1996 Parliament began the "reform of Centrum" by issuing several statutes discussed below in Section II B. The "reform of Centrum" provides changes in the administrative system at central level. As critics have said,[43] the reform has not changed the obsolete system of central administrative authorities. Its main thrust has been to change the scope of activity of several ministers by joining the competencies of some ministers and also creating new ones. The reforms have sustained the strong position of a minister as an organ of central administration but have not provided any clear distinction between the role of a minister as a member of the Government and his political role as an individual. According to critics the reforms do not meet European standards and are rather superficial. The same critique says that there is a need for a strong Government in Poland. In order to fulfil its political tasks the Government needs strong machinery consisting of qualified officials. The ministers should only supervise offices and institutions and should not undertake concrete administrative tasks. In every ministry there should be a section of horizontal co-operation between all offices in Government service. Every ministry should have an adviser who co-operates with the advisers of other ministers. The newly appointed Prime Minister's Office should act as co-ordinator of the whole administration attending to Government. The number of ministers and the scope of their competencies and offices subordinated to them is rigid, and a number of critics have argued that the Prime Minister should have greater freedom when he creates a new Government.

The reform of Centrum mainly consists in reform of the functioning of the economy and public administration. It has been introduced by a few statutes:

1. Statute of August 8, 1996, (rules introducing the statutes reforming functioning of the economy and public administration).[44] According to the statute the following ministers have been eliminated: a) Minister of Industry and Commerce, b) Minister of Property Transformation, c) Minister of Co-operation with the Foreign Lands, d) Minister of Territorial Planning and Constructions, e) Minister - Chief of Office of Council of Ministers, f) Minister - Chief of Central Office of Planning, and g) Minister of the Interior. Their tasks have been taken over by three newly created ministers: Minister of the Interior and Administration (taking over from the bodies mentioned above in d, e, g, and the Office of the Council of Ministers), Minister of Economy (a, c, f), and Minister of State Treasury (b). The Central Planing Office and Office of Council of Ministers have been abolished and the President of Office of Housing and Development of the Cities, the Main Geodesist of the Country, and the Chancellory of the Prime Minister have been set up instead. The statute discusses the creation of the new Government committees: the Committee of European Integration, Governmental Centrum for Strategic Studies and the Board of Special Services, which replaces the Political Advisory Committee acting at the Ministry of the Interior.

2. On the same date other important statutes were issued concerning the organisation and course of work of the Council of Ministers, and the scope of activity of ministers.[45] One of these statutes established the Office of the Prime Minister. This has taken over some of the tasks of the Office of Council of Ministers, which, as mentioned above, was abolished. The main function of the Office of Prime Minister is to attend to the Council of Ministers and the Prime Minister, the Vice-Prime Ministers, standing committees of the Council of Ministers and the Board of Special Services. The Office is controlled by the Chief of the Office of the Prime Minister

and subordinate to him. The statute does not repeal the resolution of the Council of Ministers on February 12, 1991, which concerns the rules and regulations of the work of the Council of Ministers.[46] According to the rules of the statute,[47] these regulations are binding until the Council of Ministers issues new rules and regulations regarding its work. The statute has also introduced rules on the scope of tasks and competencies of new ministers and committees.

3. Statute of June 21, 1996, on the post of Minister of the Interior.[48]

4. Statute of June 21, 1996, on the post of Minister of the Economy[49] and statute on August 8, 1996, about the post of Ministry of State Treasury.[50] The latter statute regulates the scope of the minister's competence, especially in relation to managing property of the State Treasury, initiating privatisation processes, protecting the interests of the State Treasury, and controlling state legal persons (state establishments) and state unions which are not considered legal persons. Furthermore, according to the statute introducing the statutes reforming the functioning of the economy and public administration,[51] the Minister of State Treasury now has the tasks and competence of the former Minister Property Transformation and in particular he has the competence to privatise state enterprises. In the same law[52] the tasks and competence concerning the management of shares belonging to the State Treasury, which were previously performed by other ministers, have been transferred to the Minister of State Treasury. He also represents the State Treasury in legal transactions (contracts) involving property of state enterprises. These contracts are part of the privatisation processes (see section B 2.1 below). Finally, the statute establishes an Agency of Privatisation.[53] The main tasks of the Agency and its organisation are discussed in section II B 2.1 and 3 below.

6. Statute of June 21, 1996, on the post of Ministry of Finance and treasury offices and chambers.[54]

7. Statute of August 8, 1996, on the Committee of European Integration.[55]

8. Statute of August 8, 1996, on the Governmental Centrum of Strategic Studies.[56]

9. Other changes to the most important statutes regarding the functioning of the economy and public administration were made by the statutes on August 8, 1996.[57]

10. Statute of December 20, 1996, (amendments to the statute on commercialisation and privatisation of state establishments).[58]

In addition, the statute of August 8, 1996,[59] (amendments to the statute of March 22, 1990, on the organs of central local government administration)[60] introduced relevant amendments in order to accommodate the central-level changes at the local level. The changes provided by the statute include a clarification of the position of the head of central office of local administration as well as the status of other persons and bodies in the central administrative organs (the previous regulations were ambiguous as to the precise meaning of "central organs"). The legislators have now made it clear that "other persons", unlike the heads of offices, may be entitled to perform rights and duties of government organs of local administration.

The changes provided by the statute[61] relate primarily to an increase in the competencies of the voivode, an organ of local government administration in the region. According to the statute, they are competent to formulate the particular policies of government in their regions. The statute that makes these changes, just like the statute about organs of government administration,[62] states that voivodes co-ordinate and supervise carrying out the tasks deriving from these purposes. Under this statute, and also under the statute on local government [63] mentioned above, the organs of the commune may fulfil the tasks belonging to the government administration. A duty to fulfil these tasks may derive from the law or from the special agreements between the organs of commune and organs of government administration. Voivodes must co-operate with organs of communes in relation to matters important for a region, especially concerning social politics, economy, territorial organisation and planning and protection of environment.[64] This statute also introduced the power entitling the voivodes to give instructions to the organs of autonomy but only in strictly enumerated cases. These cases are threat of human life and health, natural environment, preservation of public order and safety of the State, protection of citizens' rights and prevention of disasters. They are also entitled to give instructions to the organs of government administration, including special administration. The statute which made alterations to these provisions established a special procedure under which a voivode is obliged to inform a "proper minister" about their instructions. The minister may stop the implementation of an instruction. The competencies of voivodes in relation to the organs of special administration are being built up first of all by the right to give instructions, influence acts of organs of special administration and by giving more rights to decide in personal matters. A voivode is now entitled to require that disciplinary action be taken against an employee of special administration in a region concerning breach of the law in cases regarding, for example, a threat to human life and health or natural environment. It is also entitled to give an opinion about the candidates for heads of organs of special administration. Additionally a voivode can now also apply for the dismissal of the chiefs of organs of special administration. The organs of special administration are obliged to obtain the agreement of a voivode concerning every piece of legislation or individual act they issue, to obey his instructions and, on his application, to inform him of their present activities. The scope of competence of voivodes has also been increased by the subordination of the special services and inspections to him. The statutes state that these special services and inspections are regional units; they operate under the authority of the voivode and fulfil tasks given them by a particular law.

The voivode appoints the heads of special services and inspectorates after consultations with the relevant minister. The statute also contains provisions regarding the relations between the voivode and organs both superior and inferior to him, i.e. vice-voivodes, general directors of offices of regions, chiefs of administrative units of the regions and heads of inspections and special services, all of whom help him to fulfil his tasks. The statute subordinates voivodes directly to the Prime Minister and the Council of Ministers. Furthermore, a minister of administration is now competent to establish, by an order, the rules of management and organisation of a voivode's work and office in a region.

The scope of tasks allotted to voivodes has also been increased by obliging them to fulfil tasks regarding the defence and security of the state and co-operation with organs of other countries in relation to cross-border and international, inter-regional co-operation. The rules of this co-operation will be established by the Minister of Foreign Affairs. A new moment introduced by the statute is that the voivodes are founding organs (principals) of state enterprise.

According to the Law of September 25, 1981, on State Enterprises,[65] a founding organ is an organ which creates an enterprise and has special competence over its control and supervision. According to the statute, the organs of an enterprise consist of a general assembly of employees, board of employees and director. According to the statute of September 25, 1981, on governing organs of autonomy of enterprises, the general assembly of employees and board of employees are the self-governing organs of an enterprise.[66] The founding organ has the power to appoint the first director of a new enterprise and dismiss directors in cases provided by the statute. The rules and regulations of some enterprises have to be accepted by a founding organ, and in all cases they decide about the merger, division and liquidation of an enterprise. Founding organs may only be the main and central organs of state administration, the National Bank of Poland, and other banks.[67] Only in certain statutorily specified cases[68] can organs of state administration, other than those already mentioned, found an enterprise. Even then they can only do so after obtaining the approval of a main/central administrative organ.

Another new piece of legislation[69] states that the voivode represents the State Treasury. The scope and rules of this authorisation are provided in different laws. Furthermore, the statute states that chiefs of state entities, e.g. state enterprises, state agencies and state units, are obliged to inform the voivode, if so requested, about the situation and activity of the units which he controls. In corporations where the State Treasury is a shareholder, the voivodes give opinion about the candidates to supervisory and governing bodies. They also have the right to propose a candidate to the supervisory body.

A. THE CONSTITUTION

A majority of voters approved the Constitution in a May 25, 1997 constitutional referendum. Complaints were, however, lodged asserting the invalidity of the referendum. According to the relevant statute,[70] the Supreme Court must adjudicate these complaints and, within 60 days from the day of the referendum in question, must issue a resolution on its validity. Initially, the Supreme Court judges appeared to be divided on this issue. The main problem was that those participating in the referendum were only around 40 per cent of those entitled to vote. The Small Constitution says that the result of a referendum is binding if a majority of those entitled to vote took part in it. Similarly the statute on drafting and adopting the Constitution[71] says that the Constitution is considered accepted if a majority of those taking part in the referendum voted for it.[72] In the end, however, the Court upheld the validity of the referendum.

The Constitution has been the focus of political and social debate since 1995. The main points of dissension concern the relationship between Church and State, the position of the Catholic Church and religion at school, the situation of minorities in Poland and other citizens' rights.

The Constitution establishes the main rules of the political and economic system, and the liberties, rights and obligations of citizens (individual, political, economic, social and cultural). The Constitution lists the sources of internal law, including international agreements ratified by Poland. Where there are conflicting rules, international agreements which have been accepted by the Seym are given priority over domestic statutes. The Constitution also states that the Republic of Poland, on the grounds of an international agreement, can in some cases transfer competencies of organs of the State to international organisations. The objections instituted against this rule of the Constitution appear justified. This rule has great importance for Poland, in view of the process of European integration, but by itself it is too enigmatic and vague (e.g. the terms "international organisation", "international organ", and "some cases" are not properly defined). The Constitution also regulates the prerogatives and method of formation, appointment and dismissal of the main authorities in the country, e.g. the Seym, Senate, President, the Council of Ministers, and the courts (the common courts, the Supreme Court, High Administrative Court, Constitutional Tribunal), and the organs of state control and supervision and protection of law (Highest Audit Chamber, Ombudsman, State Council of Radio and Television).

1. THE POWERS OF THE PRESIDENT OF THE REPUBLIC

In comparison to the Small Constitution, the new Constitution did not introduce many amendments. According to the new electoral provisions, a candidate for the presidential post is to be proposed by a group of 100,000 citizens who have an active right to vote in general elections. The Supreme Court decides on the validity of presidential elections.

Another new feature is the established by the new Constitution advisory body to the President, which was not provided for by the Small Constitution. The new basic law also has introduced some amendments regarding the presidential veto on legislative acts. New statutes, adopted by the Seym and approved by the Senate, go to the President who under the new arrangements has 21 days (compared to 30 in the Small Constitution) to sign it. The President has a right to come to the Constitutional Tribunal to ascertain that a statute is in accordance with the Constitution. If the Constitutional Tribunal decides that a statute is not in accordance with the Constitution, the President shall refuse to sign it. According to the new Constitution, the President should sign a statute if the Constitutional Tribunal has decided that only some of its provisions are in contradiction to the Constitution, provided that these provisions are not inseparable from the whole statute. The President may sign the new statute without these provisions, or he may direct the statute back to the Seym to remove them.

The President may also, without directing a new statute to the Constitutional Tribunal, return it to the Seym. The Seym must then vote again for the new statute and may reject the presidential veto with a three-fifths majority when at least half of the members of the Diet are present. The Small Constitution permits a two-thirds majority of the Seym to reject the presidential veto.

2. THE POWERS OF THE GOVERNMENT

In general, the scope of competence and tasks of the Government has not been increased in the new Constitution. It is noteworthy, however, that control over the defence of the State and the annual number of recruits in particular has been transferred under the Government's jurisdiction. Furthermore, the Constitution no longer gives the legal force of a statute to Government decrees.

More changes have been made concerning the members of the Government. The Constitution now clearly states the competencies of the Prime Minister, who controls the work, generally, of the Council of Ministers and, individually, of each member of the Council. Important changes have been made with regard to the responsibility of members of the Council of Ministers (ministers and presidents of committees), who are now jointly accountable before the Seym for the Council of Ministers' actions and individually accountable for acts belonging to their competencies or acts ordered by the Prime Minister. Like the President, members of the Council are responsible before the Tribunal of State for infringement of the Constitution or statutes and for crimes connected with abuse of office. The Seym votes to call a minister to account on the application of at least 115 members of the Diet with a three-fifths majority of all members of the Diet. The Constitution provides amendments in the stages of appointment of Council of Ministers. Also the President may not now dismiss the Council of Ministers even if the Prime Minister himself resigns.

The new Constitution appoints politically neutral civil servants to fulfil tasks of the State. The head of the civil service is the Prime Minister. According to the statute of July 5, 1996, on the civil service,[73] employees of the civil service work in offices of Government administration.

Regarding regional autonomy, the new Constitution warrants support from the public budget in the form of subsidies, and independence to establish local taxes and other levies. Statutes can impose, on the organs of the communes, public tasks belonging to organs of state administration only in case of justifiable public necessity. Certain matters, e.g. supervision over organs of the commune and the communes' right to unite, which were previously regulated by the statute on self-government, are now also regulated in the Constitution. Other matters regulated by the new Constitution are public finances, state of emergency and amendment mechanisms.

B. LEGISLATION

1. PROCEDURAL AND GENERAL ORGANISATIONAL LAWS

1.1 Self-government

Important changes have taken place in the area of regional autonomy. A new statute on the economy of communes was issued on December 20, 1996[74]: it regulates the forms of economic activity in which a commune can be engaged. This statute has amended, among others, the statute of March 8, 1990, on self-government.[75] The draft was prepared by members of the Diet in 1994: the first draft prepared by the Seym and Government was rejected by the Seym in 1991.

The authors of the draft aimed to correlate new rules with the rules of the statutes governing economic activity[76] and the statute on public procurement.[77] According to the new law, self-government is allowed only in forms provided by law. This is a very important change from existing regulations because previously only two statutes contained rules regarding the economic activity of communes: the statute of March 8, 1990, on self-government and the statute of May 10, 1990, introducing the statute about self-government and the statute about employees of self-government.[78] The regulation was very general: a commune was entitled to create units, including commune enterprises, to fulfil its own tasks. The statute of May 10, 1990, stated that communal enterprises were only transitional forms of the activities of communes. The decision about changing the form of economic activity had to be taken by the board of the commune, but the statute did not specify a fixed time limit for the establishment of new, market-oriented enterprises by these bodies. Nevertheless, the creation of communal enterprises broke the State monopoly in the economy. They were created by the transformation of the State enterprises where founding organs were the local organs of State administration. Also the rules of the old statute on state enterprises[79] were to be applied in relation to communal enterprises, thus transforming them into separate legal persons.

The statute on the economy of communes introduces three forms of municipal economic activity: communal budget establishments, corporations with limited responsibility of shareholders, and business corporations. The commune is entitled to create communal budget establishments and corporations or to enter corporations already being established by other persons. Furthermore, if the board of a commune did not take a decision about the form of activity of communal enterprises before June 30, 1997, the enterprises were to be transformed by law into a one-person communal corporation. The statute also allows a commune to make their one-person corporations accessible to other persons and to transform budget establishments into one-person communal corporations. To avoid corruption, the statute[80] establishes a ban on participation of members of the board of the communes in the boards of the communal corporations.

The statute regulates more liberally the types of activity that a commune is allowed to lead. Prior to the changes, the statute about self-government stated that the commune is obliged to fulfil tasks of a public character (e.g. building public roads, streets, and bridges: keeping areas clean; protecting public health), and in practice it was only allowed to lead economic activity regarding these tasks. Now the new regulation permits communal economic participation in other activities. According to the legislators, "other activity" means everything that is not "currently" addressing public demands and needs. The statute also establishes the conditions under which such extra-public activity can be led, e.g. failure to provide for public needs, unemployment on the territory of the commune, etc. Another piece of legislation[81] permits a commune to contract with other persons for the fulfilment of communal tasks. In the opinion of some analysts,[82] such contracts will de-monopolise the economy of communes and encourage competition; a commune will ensure financial and technical help for its contracts' partners, help to develop the private sector and guard against unemployment.

1.2 Amendments to the Code of Civil Procedure

Important changes were introduced to the Code of Civil Procedure, which influenced the procedure before the High Administrative Court. The amendments to civil procedure, concerning alterations in the Code of Civil Procedure, were enacted by several pieces of legislation and regulation: the statute of March 1, 1996, resolutions of the Presidents of Republic of Poland, the Bankruptcy Law and the Composition Agreement, the Code of Administrative Procedure, a statute on court fees in civil cases, and others.[83] All this legislation introduced significant new features in the organisation of the judicial system, particularly in the number of judicial instances (levels). Previously, in civil procedures: a) district courts were courts of first instance; b) region courts were an instance of appeal for cases adjudicated by the district courts; c) courts of appeal (which covered wider districts than the districts of region courts) were an instance of appeal for cases adjudicated by region courts.

Also, prior to the changes, under the Code of Civil Procedure, the Minister of Justice, the First President of the Supreme Court, the Ombudsmen and (in labour law and social insurance cases) the Minister of Labour, could lodge an extraordinary appeal against the final sentence of the Supreme Court. An extraordinary appeal could be lodged when the sentence flagrantly and seriously infringed the law or interests of the Republic of Poland.

Following the Code's amendment, anyone represented by a lawyer has a right to lodge a cassation appeal at the Supreme Court. Cassation is an ordinary remedy at law: the Supreme Court is now a court of third instance. Cassation can be lodged against the sentence of the court of second instance. The rules regarding extraordinary appeal have been repealed. However, the new regulation states that extraordinary appeal can be lodged against sentences of the NSA: in these cases, as well, the procedure of cassation provided in the Code should be applied. This means that extraordinary appeal is still applied only regarding decisions of the High Administrative Court. Moreover, the legislators have not repealed the rules of the statute on the NSA[84] regarding extraordinary appeal against its sentence decisions.

2. SUBSTANTIVE LEGISLATION

2.1 Privatisation Laws

A new statute was issued on August 30, 1996, on the commercialisation and privatisation of state establishments,[85] replacing the statute of July 13, 1990, on privatisation of state establishments.[86] Some of the provisions of the new statute have been binding since October 7, 1996 (the date of publication of the statute), while the rest of the rules came into force on April 8, 1997, as provided by two laws, amending the statute on commercialisation and privatisation.[87] The main change regards the stages of privatisation. In previous statutes on the privatisation process two types of privatisation were provided for: capital privatisation and liquidation privatisation.

Capital privatisation means that state establishments are being transformed into companies with exclusive participation of the State (the State Treasury) and then shares in the corporations are made available to third persons after economic-legal analysis. These companies are legal successor of the establishments: they take over ex lege the establishments' capital and employees and can found joint stock companies as well. Employees are entitled to buy 20 per cent of the shares at a discounted price. Transformations of state enterprises under this procedure were carried out by the Minister of Transformation Processes on application of the organs of the enterprise or its founding organ.[88] Each case required the agreement of the director and workers' board of the enterprise (representative organ of the employees).

In relation to the second type of privatisation, three possibilities of liquidation of enterprises were provided:

a. alienation of an enterprise or its parts,
b. transfer of an enterprise or its part to another company,
c. change of the business activities of the enterprise or its parts in order to make it profitable (including leasing of property).

The present statute on commercialisation and privatisation provides similar options.[89] The difference is that the transformation of an enterprise into a one-person company with exclusive participation of the State is now considered as a first stage of privatisation, either direct or indirect; it in practice amounts to a commercialisation of the enterprise. Privatisation is the second stage, but may be the only stage if direct privatisation is involved. The statute of August 30, 1996, distinguishes two types of privatisation which are almost the same as those previously established by the statute of July 13, 1990.[90] The second stage of capital privatisation is now called "indirect privatisation," and liquidation privatisation is now called "direct privatisation". Direct privatisation can be done by disposing of all material and immaterial components of an enterprise or company.

The statute further introduces changes in the scope of competencies of the organs entitled to initiate the commercialisation process. The same organs are entitled to lodge an application as before–the founding organ, the director, the workers' board–but if the founding organ applies for transformation the acceptance of the director and the workers' board is not required. Additionally the Minister of State Treasury (the post which replaced that of Minister of Property Transformation) is now entitled to initiate commercialisation by himself. Another novelty is that transformation of an enterprise into a corporation is also permitted for purposes other than privatisation, which means that corporations may exist for longer than the two years previously allowed. In practice, in most cases it was impossible to privatise a State corporation within two years.

Commercialisation has been intentionally made different from privatisation by requiring the Council of Ministers' acceptance. Employees are entitled to receive 15 per cent of shares of the company for free (previously it was 20 per cent at half price) irrespective of the manner of privatisation. Previously those employed in enterprises whose business activity was to be changed, not excluding leasing of property, had no right to buy shares at half-price.

The new statute has also modified the way of functioning of the organs of one-person state corporations. The general principle is that the rules of the Commercial Code are applied,[91] although the statute provides some different arrangements. The Minister of State Treasury acts as a shareholder, having competencies deriving from Article 388 of the Commercial Code and making certain decisions on his own (e.g. changes of the rules of the corporation and appointments of Supervisory Board and Board of Directors). The workers have a right to choose two-fifths of the members of the Supervisory Board. If a corporation employs an average of 500 workers per year, the workers are entitled to choose one member of the Board of Directors. A further change is that the director of an enterprise now becomes president of the Board of Directors, provided he agrees to that; previously, under the rules of the statute on privatisation,[92] the director was ex lege dismissed. After privatisation, the State (represented by the Minister of State Treasury) is authorised by the statute to approve the so-called "managerial contract", signed by the Supervisory Board, with the new person or entity controlling the corporation.

Although there are other amendments provided by statute differing from the rules of the Commercial Code, it is not possible to mention them all here. The conception of one-person boards controlling corporations based on separate contracts matches European standards. An innovation is the idea of commercialisation together with conversion of debts. This takes place when the funds of an enterprise are lower than the minimal founding capital provided by the Commercial Code. In this situation, the statute states that the creditors of the enterprise become shareholders of the company, with the total value of shares designated to one creditor being one-third of the value of the debts to him. Further, the one-person companies of the State Treasury are now entitled to found different types of commercial corporations: not only joint-stock but also limited-liability companies.

The statute which amended those statutes connected with the reform of functioning of economy and public administration[93] also authorised the Council of Ministry to issue decrees for the establishment of state enterprises and one-person state corporation, which are especially important for the state economy. Privatisation of these enterprises and corporations requires the approval of the Council of Ministers. There are also some amendments provided by statute regarding the functioning of the organs of corporations of special importance for the State economy. The statute states that the composition of supervisory boards and regulations of these corporations have to be approved by the "relevant minister". Basically this means that instead of the Minister of Treasury, who appoints the Supervisory Board, other ministers, e.g. of Finance, Economy, Administration and Communication, also decide about the composition of supervisory bodies in corporations of special importance for the state economy. No such decree has been issued during the period under review.

The general aim of the new statute on privatisation[94] is to speed up the privatisation process. The territorial departments of the Ministry of State Treasury are the authorities responsible for privatisation in the regions, while the Ministry co-ordinates the process. Its accessory body is the Agency of Privatisation, accountable to the Minister of State Treasury. The Agency acts on the basis of statutes relating to the Ministry of State Treasury,[95] and regulations on the organisation and works of the Agency established by the decree of the Prime Minister of April 3, 1997,[96] and issued on application of Minister of State Treasury and also the statute about commercialisation. The decree of the Prime Minister has been issued under legal authorisation deriving from the statute about the Ministry of State Treasury. (The decree is discussed in Part C 2.) The statute states that the Agency of Privatisation is a state entity supervised by the Ministry of State Treasury. The Agency controls the privatisation of state enterprises on behalf of the State Treasury, under authorisation by the minister.

New amendments have altered legislation connected with reforming the functioning of the economy and public administration and also changed the statute on commercialisation and privatisation of state enterprises.[97] Thus it is the Agency of Privatisation rather than the Ministry of State Treasury that represents the Treasury in its one-person corporations, sells shares of corporation to other persons and transfers rights deriving from shares to the Ministry, if the shares have not been sold within three months of becoming available.

The relations between the reform of central administration and the statute on commercialisation and privatisation[98] have attracted criticism, especially concerning the competencies of the Ministry of State Treasury deriving from Statute No 106, 96/493.[99] Article 5 of the Statute states that the Ministry may create, liquidate, join, divide and transform state entities; appoint their organs, and lodge objections against legal acts of state legal persons in connection with controlling their property.

The entities must notify the Minister about every transaction worth over ECU 50,000. If the Minister does not agree, the organs of the state entities may lodge an appeal with the Minister. If he refuses to overturn his decision, they can make a claim to common court. If the entity does not notify the Minister about the privatisation, the transaction is not valid.

The state enterprises and one-person state corporations created after commercialisation are state entities (including also banks and insurance agencies). The criticism of the arrangement as a whole has focused on the role of the Minister of State Treasury and the broad scope of his jurisdiction as capable of slowing down privatisation. Yet the statutes on the Minister of State Treasury authorise the Council of Ministers to release some state legal persons from the duty to notify the Minister about their transactions by a decree. The Council of Ministers has not issued such a decree over the reviewed period.

2.2 Health care

In this area, a new statute on the medical profession and an important statute on health insurance were adopted. Mass protests by doctors in public hospitals have pointed up the critical situation facing Polish health care institutions. The law on collective bargaining ofMay 23, 1991,[100] forbids strikes that cause a threat to human life or health. Accordingly, doctors carried out limited protest actions: in some hospitals they provided only urgent and absolutely necessary medical treatment. A peculiar feature of the doctors' bargaining situation was that they could not conclude collective labour agreements for all public health care institutions because the Doctors' Trade Union did not fulfil the conditions of the Labour Code to represent the doctors in the whole country. In Poland, these conditions are only fulfilled by the Solidarity and OPZZ trade unions.[101]

A new statute on the medical profession was adopted by the Seym on December 5, 1996, but was published only on March 26, 1997.[102] The procedure by which the statute was issued was long and complicated. The rules were drafted by the Main Doctors' Chamber, which is the highest self-governing authority in the profession.

At first, according to the procedure of the Small Constitution, after the statute has been adopted by the Seym, it is to be sent to the Senate. Within 30 days the Senate can accept the statute, lodge its amendments or refuse to accept it. Next, the Seym can reject the Senate's resolution on refusal or amendments with majority vote. Following this procedure, after the approval of the Seym, the statute on the medical profession was sent to the Senate, where the Marshal of the Senate, according to the rules and regulations of the Senate, sent it to the Committee of Social

Policy and Health and the Committee of Initiative and Statutes Works. The Committees proposed a number of amendments. For the most part they regarded the character of the medical profession as including medical and scientific experiments, the rules of carrying out the profession, rules of practice after graduation, and receiving the right to carry out the profession. The committees also proposed that the medical profession should become a "free profession". On December 20, 1997, the Senate rejected the statute. The Senate's veto was overruled by the Seym, and the statute was finally adopted without the Senate's amendments. The new statute on the medical profession replaced the old one of October 28, 1950,[103] and the decree of the President of Republic of Poland of June 10, 1927, on dentist practice.[104] There had been a consistent body of opinion declaring the need for a new statute. One new feature is that one statute regulates the status of both doctors and dentists. It strengthens the position of doctors' self-government. This, however, was also a major point of criticism in relation to the statute.[105] The organs of doctors' self-government are entitled to confer a right to carry out the profession after appraising if all legal requirements have been fulfilled, although not all of them are clearly stated in laws and regulation. They are also entitled to periodical verification of medical skills and qualification. A doctor is obliged to inform the doctors' board when he stops practising. An acceptance by the regional doctors' board is also necessary if he wants to start private practice. The new statute regulates the conditions of carrying out a medical profession by foreigners as well.

Another new feature is the regulation regarding the admissibility of medical experiments and medical treatment only upon patients' agreement, the carrying out of scientific experiments, and the scope of the doctors' duty to provide medical aid. Such a duty occurs whenever a delay may cause loss of life, health, damage to the body of a person or in any matter of great urgency. In such situations a doctor, like inspectors and officials, has the status of a public functionary. The statute also states that there is a duty to keep the secrets of a patient even after his death. Almost all of the rules of the statute became binding on September 26, 1997.

The other important piece of legislation in this area was the statute of February 6, 1997, on common health insurance.[106] This is a new feature in the Polish legal system and, probably, a reaction to the doctors' "strikes", which have led to a critical situation in the health care institutions. The gist of the statute is that every person in the country has to pay a premium of 10 per cent of their income for health insurance. The statute sets up new institutions: common health insurance societies. The main tasks of these societies is to collect the premiums for health insurance, to control the funds and to conclude contracts with health care institutions and doctors to carry out health services. The statute distinguishes between regional societies and branch societies, which unite in the National Union of the Societies. The statute goes on to provide for representation of beneficiaries in the organs of the society. The organs of the society issue administrative decisions regarding rights to benefits of citizens: a beneficiary may appeal this decision to the common court section of labour and social insurance. The legal regulation is similar to cases of social security benefits.[107] The statute also regulates the rules of refunding payment for medicines, in which the societies co-operate with pharmacies. The statute will enter into force on January 1, 1999. In the transitional period the organs which funded the health care institutions, under the provisions of the statute on health care institutions,[108] will transform themselves into independent unions. The Minister of Health and Social Aid is responsible for issuing the necessary sub-legislative regulation for the implementation of the statute: such regulation has not been adopted during the period under review.

C. REGULATION

1. REGULATION ON PRIVATISATION

In keeping with the legal authorisation by the statute on the Ministry of State Treasury the Prime Minister has issued a decree on the rules of the Agency of Privatisation.[109] The decree defines the Agency as a state legal person with residence in Warsaw. Following the principles of statute N33, 97/199,[110] in the decree the Prime Minister has established the tasks, organs and finances of the Agency. The rules and regulations of the Agency determine that it controls the privatisation of companies with shares held by the State Treasury, privatisation of state enterprises and corporations of special importance for the state economy[111] (under authorisation by the Council of Ministers on application of the Minister of State Treasury), and other acts of privatisation under authorisation of the Minister of State Treasury and upon the approval of the Prime Minister.

The Prime Minister's decree further establishes the structure of the organs of the Agency and their competencies, i.e. the President of the Agency, the directors of departments and directors of territorial sections, the Supervisory Board, its territorial structures and the Office of President of the Agency as an assisting unit. The rules also regulate the types of independent activity which the Agency is entitled to run, e.g. preparing and carrying out direct privatisation of state enterprise on the order of their founding organs, privatisation of communal enterprises, publications, dissemination of information and courses regarding privatisation, as well as other activities connected with the management of State property. Separate from the rules and regulations of the Agency are the rules of economy of the Agency, its funds and particular rules concerning the salaries of the Agency's employees.

D. COURT DECISIONS

The judgement of any court in Poland consists of a sentence and grounds (reasoning). Judgements of common courts are not officially published.[112] During a trial a judge reads the sentence of a decision to the interested parties. According to the Code of Civil Procedure, a party is entitled to lodge a motion for grounds (reasons) with the court of first instance, within a week of the decision. The court of appeal is obliged to issue grounds for its decision within two weeks of announcing it. If the decision of the court was announced orally, a reasoned decision is delivered to the parties only if they request it. If a decision has not been announced, the court is obliged to deliver a decision with grounds to the parties. Similarly, the Supreme Court is obliged to issue grounds for its judgement within four weeks. The rules regarding giving reasons are the same as in appeal proceedings. According to the statute about the High Administrative Court,[113] the NSA is obliged to issue the grounds for its decision within 30 days from passing sentence. A judgement is to be delivered to the parties, although the statute does not state a time limit. According to the statute of April 29, 1985, on the Constitutional Tribunal,[114] the judgements of the Tribunal are written and it is obliged to issue grounds for its decision. The statute also states that the Tribunal must publish a collection of its judgements. The judgements of higher courts are also published in collections. These collections are generally accessible to the public (e.g. in libraries):

Supreme Court - *Jurisdiction of the Supreme Court* and *Jurisdiction of Polish Courts;*

High Administrative Court - *Jurisdiction of the High Administrative Court;*

Constitutional Tribunal - *Jurisdiction of the Constitutional Tribunal,* official collection, issued by an office of Constitutional Tribunal.

The published judgement must include a signature of a judge, the composition of the bench, the name and position of the applicant, indication of the subject of a case, the sentence and the grounds.

In 1996 the Constitutional Tribunal considered 100 applications. This is the highest number of applications since the Tribunal was created 11 years ago. The Tribunal issued 33 judgements and formulated 11 interpretations of the law. Most of its judgements involved local government, communal property, finances and tasks completed on orders of the organs of government administration. Many cases regarded management of land, real estates and construction law. Some judgements concerned politically sensitive matters, e.g. the constitutional referendum and the process of privatisation.

Decision No 1. The resolution of the Constitutional Tribunal of February 13, 1996, concerned the binding interpretation of the rules of the statute on referenda: the case was initiated on the application of the President of the High Administrative Court. The problem was which rules of referendum should be applied in any particular instance. A look at the rules that guided the Tribunal's resolution helps to unterstand the matter. In the statute on referenda,[115] Article 2, passage 2 states that there are two possible ways of organising a referendum: to ask one question to which citizens may answer "yes" or "no", or to propose several possible solutions and give citizens a choice between them. Then, in Article 9, passage 1 the statute states that the result of a referendum is binding when more than half of those entitled participate in it. Article 9, passage 2, point 1 states that a referendum decides a matter if the majority of votes were "for" one of the two proposed solutions.

The question was: if the rule of Article 9, passage 2, point 1 also includes the first possible way of referendum, i.e. choice of "yes" or "no": in other words, should "majority of votes" mean that those voting "for" simply outnumber the votes for the other solution (or "against"), or should the positive votes outnumber the negative ones plus the invalid votes as well? The answer of the Constitutional Tribunal was that Article 9, passage 2, point 1 is also applicable when citizens decide on a matter by choosing "yes" or "no". The Tribunal further held that the term "majority of votes" means ordinary majority (without counting the invalid votes).

Decision No 2. In a judgement of October 28, 1996, the Constitutional Tribunal decided that an order of the Ministry of Finances was incompatible with Article 8, passage 1 of the statute of December 19, 1980, on tax obligations.[116] The judgement was issued on a legal question asked by the section of the High Administrative Court. The Tribunal decided that the Ministry of Finances exceeded its legal authority derived from the statute on tax obligations. Under the law, the minister was entitled to issue an order renouncing the collection of some tax, if the time limit for payment had not yet expired; instead, he issued an order lifting the duty to pay outstanding tax, for which the fixed time limit for payment had already been expired. His act was also contrary to Article 56, passage 2 of the Small Constitution, which states that orders of ministers and other central organs can only be issued within the scope of their legal authority under a statute and only to implement a statute. Referring to its earlier judgements, the Tribunal decided that orders can be issued only on the basis of clear, not implied, delegation, and cannot be discordant with the norms of the Constitution and all binding statutes dealing at least partially with matters regulated by the order.

Decision No 3. Judgement of the Tribunal on December 11, 1996, issued on the application of the Doctors' Trade Union. The Doctors' Trade Union applied to the Constitutional Tribunal for verification whether the restrictions imposed by the Labour Code on trade union rights to collective agreement regarding doctors' salaries, are consistent with Article 1 of the Small Constitution ("The Republic of Poland is a state of law"), Article 64 of the "old" constitution still in force ("All citizens of Poland are equal before the law"), and the statute of May 2, 1991, on trade unions.[117] The statute states that trade unions represent and defend workers', rights. It also authorises all trade unions to conclude collective contracts and agreements. According to Article 241,16 of the Labour Code, collective agreements involving employees of more than one establishment can be concluded by all trade unions representing those employees. If they cannot agree, then only those trade unions with at least 500,000 workers, or the greatest number of workers for whom a collective agreement is contracted, are authorised by the law to contract. The Doctors' Trade Union did not fulfil these requirements, and it was therefore not entitled to negotiate and contract better conditions of work and salaries with the State, represented by the Minister of Health. The Constitutional Tribunal decided that the rules of the Labour Code on the right to become a party to collective agreements conflict with the Small Constitution, the "old" constitution and the statute on trade unions.

Decision No 4. A very interesting decision was taken by the Constitutional Tribunal on November 26, 1996, concerning the relation between the jurisdiction of the High Administrative Court and the interpretation of statutes by the Constitutional Tribunal. Interpretations of statutes by the Constitutional Tribunal are binding on every authority, including the courts. In this case there was a divergence of opinion among an administrative authority, a ministry, and the High Administrative Court over a statute regarding finances. The Tribunal found that a "real" divergence may exist only between organs of equal standing applying legal rules, but not between an executive body and a court that supervises its activities. The judgement of an administrative court, regarding the legal basis for administrative decisions, is always binding on the administrative organs which issue these decisions. In the particular case, many judgements of the High Administrative Court had been issued with regard to the objected statute. The Constitutional Tribunal held that there was no need to issue its own interpretation of rules where the interpretation of the High Administrative Court is clear and stable, and there were no doubts as to the applicable legal rules. Although Article 33/a, passage 1 of the Small Constitution authorises the Tribunal to issue interpretations on every rule, this competence is not limited by any particular circumstance, although its scope always depends on the concrete context of the functioning of a rule and the understanding of the rule by the courts.

In 1996 the number of complaints adjudicated by the High Administrative Court increased in comparison with 1995. A total of 45,838 complaints, mostly by individuals, came before the Court, contrasted with 39,741 in 1995. The High Administrative Court admitted 36.2 per cent of the complaints and dismissed 63.8. The ombudsman directed four complaints to the NSA. The complaints involved acts of main and territorial organs of government administration and organs of the communes. In substantive law terms, the largest category consisted of complaints in tax and customs cases. The other complaints concerned mainly territorial planning, construction, citizenship and administrative statutes, housing, ownership and management of lands, expropriation and social support. A total of 38,600 complaints have been settled, whereas 33,030 were settled in 1995.[118]

The Court has taken decisions regarding prosecutor complaints to the Court about resolutions taken by the board of communes. A board of a commune claimed that before the prosecutor complained about the incompatibility between a municipal resolution and the law, he should have asked the board to remedy the alleged violation. On this issue, however, there was a conflict between the rules of the statute on public prosecutors and the statute on the High Administrative Court. The Court decided that a prosecutor is not obliged to ask the communal board to remedy the violation prior to complaining to the Court.

In cases involving medical responsibility the NSA has taken a noteworthy decision regarding the "legal validity" of the doctor's opinion. The Court decided that the opinion of a medical scientific institution is an expert opinion and not an administrative decision of an organ of higher instance. Therefore it can be reexamined and eventually overturned by ordinary health-care institutions. In another case from 1996, the NSA decided that the senior doctor of a voivodeship decides about the medical specialisation of the staff and health-care institutions under his jurisdiction. The private preferences of the medical staff are not to be taken into consideration, which is, in the opinion of some critics, contradictory to the constitutional principle of freedom of work.

The High Administrative Court also expounded the main principles of application of expropriation. First of all, the Court held that the conditions of expropriation deriving from the statute of April 29, 1985, on the management of lands and expropriation[119] should be interpreted and applied strictly. Furthermore, during 1996 the NSA paid special attention to consideration of international agreements and the rights of a party to honest and quick proceedings; another important issue dealt with by the Court was the problem of arbitrariness of administrative discretion. Also, in 1996 the Court started to apply Article 49 of the new statute on the NSA. It states that the Court, adjudicating by a three-judge panel, can turn to the President of the Court for an explanation of matters where there is a legal doubt of some sort. Legal explanations are issued by a seven-judge panel of the High Administrative Court and are binding on three-judge panels.

At present the Court has more cases to settle than before because the complaints go directly to the Court, and then, according to the statute on the NSA, the administrative organ that issued the decision is obliged to answer the complaint within 30 days. However, in many cases the administrative organs violate the deadline—as a result, it sometimes takes several years to settle a case.

E. THE WORKINGS OF OMBUDSMAN, AUDIT CHAMBER, PARLIAMENTARY COMMITTEES

1. OMBUDSMAN

In 1996 over 2,000 cases kept coming into the Office of the Ombudsman each month: 2,400 cases were considered in the 12-month period. Approximately 30 per cent of the cases were taken up each month. Among these, in over 55 per cent the ombudsman simply indicated the body of appeal which the applicant could address, 2.5 per cent of the cases were not taken into consideration, and the rest of the applications were directed to other organs. The ombudsman applied to the Constitutional Tribunal and the Supreme Court only once or twice a month. During the last quarter of 1996, out of 2,021 cases considered, a ruling in favor of the applicant was obtained in only 13.6 per cent; 61.4 per cent were refused because of lack of reasons, and 24.7 per cent were refused because of expired time-limitations, irreversible legal outcomes, or lack of evidence. In 0.1 per cent a decision by the ombudsman was not necessary or required, and 0.2 per cent have exhausted the possible remedies available through the ombudsman.[120] Most of the cases concerned national insurance, labour, housing, economic cases, taxation, banks, customs, insurance, consumers' rights, administration of justice, army, police, and public services.

The application of the ombudsman to the Constitutional Tribunal on April 26, 1996, was publicly debated. The Tribunal decided that a provision of the statute of April 30, 1993, on National Investment Funds[121] was not in accordance with the constitutional principle of equality of people before the law and social justice. According to this provision only Polish citizens with a permanent residence were entitled to obtain a universal share certificate (voucher) in the process of privatisation; consequently, the homeless and people without permanent residence due to often or unexpected change of accommodation were deprived of the right to obtain the certificates. (Universal share certificates were distributed by the Government among all adult citizens to secure participation in the programme of universal [mass] privatisation, established in 1993. The certificates, currently being changed into shares, guarantee shares in the National Funds, which are shareholders in the privatised corporations.)

2. AUDIT CHAMBER

In 1996 the following matters were the main subjects of inspection by the Highest Audit Chamber: the privatisation processes, the implementation of governmental programmes on health care, the implementation of public tasks by the organs of government administration, financing and carrying out of the tasks of government administration by the organs of communes and voivodes in the area of culture and art, appropriations of special financial resources from the central budget to state educational establishments, and the operation of state museums. The Chamber also examined the Report of the Committee on Economic Policy, Budget and Finance on the implementation of the budget. In 1996, the Highest Audit Chamber, together with other inspectorates, inspected high schools and universities, bodies of government and communal administration, the President of the National Bank of Poland, and the Polish Television. Between January and September 1996, a total of 1,963 complaints and applications came into the Highest Audit Chamber: 45.3 per cent of these were individual complaints, 2.9 per cent were complaints of groups, 4.7 per cent were initiated by members of the Diet (Seym) and the Senate, and 19.8 per cent were anonymous.[122] Most of the complaints addressed corrupt practices and waste of public property in industrial establishments, health-care institutions, educational and cultural institutions; the functioning of administrative offices with regard to decisions on territorial planning and construction; housing; the pension system; social aid; employment cases; and the inappropriate functioning of the finance and credit system, particularly in relation to privatisation. Five per cent of the complaints involved privatisation, especially the determination of the price of state establishments, appointment of organs of liquidating (usually directors of establishments), and rights of workers. In 1995 and 1996 the Chamber directed 141 cases to the prosecutors. Out of these, over 30 cases were dismissed by the prosecutors primarily because the penalty had been wrongly determined by the Chamber: in this relation, there were problems with the interpretation of the penal rules and the methods of investigation. The Highest Audit Chamber investigates only facts of infringement and does not consider the subjective side of a crime (personal guilt). Also the inspections of the Highest Audit Chamber are usually held three to five months after a crime is committed, and it is very difficult to collect evidence.

3. PARLIAMENTARY COMMITTEES

In Poland it is very difficult to obtain statistical data on the work of all parliamentary committees. The only committee whose reports have been systematically published is the Constitutional Committee of the National Assembly.[123] As of February 1997, the committee had met about 100 times.

The work of two other committees should be also mentioned. Firstly, the Committee on Constitutional Responsibility was appointed in 1995 to prosecute persons connected with the introduction of martial law in 1981 in Poland. The Seym, however, dismissed a motion of the Committee on the prosecution of these people, and therewith the proceedings instigated by the Committee were discontinued.

Secondly, a committee connected with a motion of the Minister of the Interior on crimes against State security by the Prime Minister was set up in 1995. The Minister of the Interior directed an application to the Public Prosecutor's Office in the Army. The Office instituted an inquiry as to whether the Prime Minister had co-operated with the Russian secret services. One of the main tasks of the Committee, appointed by the Seym in December 1995, was to examine if the Minister of the Interior and the Office of Protection of the State, subordinated to the Minister of the Interior, had acted in accordance with the law. During the investigation and after the hearing of a number of officials, the Committee found that the materials and evidence in the case had not been properly collected by the Office of Protection of the State. Moreover, the Minister had broken the law, because he had tried to investigate the Prime Minister on his own and had not given him immediate notification. The Committee concluded that the Minister of the Interior could be prosecuted, and the Seym approved the report of the Committee. [124]

The Chapter has been prepared on the basis of information provided by Justyna Stencel

NOTES

1 *Gazette for Current Law* (hereinafter *G.f.C.L.*) 92, Number 84, position 426, changes: *G.f.C.L.* 96, No. 106, pos. 488.

2 *G.f.C.L.* 76, No. 7, pos. 36 with amendments.

3 *G.f.C.L.* 92, N.67, pos. 336;changes: *G.f.C.L.* 94, No. 61, pos. 251.

4 *G.f.C.L.* 94, No. 54, pos. 453; changes: *G.f.C.L.* 96, No. 7, pos. 75.

5 *G.f.C.L.* 94, No. 8, pos. 62.

6 *G.f.C.L.* 95, No. 99, pos. 487, with amendments.

7 *G.f.C.L.* 80, No. 9, pos. 26, with amendments.
8 *G.f.C.L.* 80, No. 4, pos. 8, with amendments.
9 Prof. Zbigniew Janowicz, *Comments for Code of Administrative Procedure*, Wydawnictwo Naukowe PWN, Warszawa-Poznan, 1992.
10 Section 5, Articles 70-75.
11 *Gazette for Current Law* 90, Number 16, position 95.
12 *G.f.C.L.* 90, No. 34, pos. 198.
13 For details see section 2 above.
14 *G.f.C.L.* 95, No. 74, pos. 368.
15 *G.f.C.L.* 85, No. 20, pos. 85.
16 *G.f.C.L.* 89, No. 25, pos. 137.
17 *G.f.C.L.* 64, No. 43, pos. 296, with amendments.
18 *G.f.C.L.* 95, No. 80, pos. 405.
19 *G.f.C.L.* 89, No. 30, pos. 158.
20 *G.f.C.L.* 90, No. 64, pos. 406.
21 *G.f.C.L.* 91, No. 91, pos. 408.
22 Section VI of the Code of Administrative Procedure.
23 *G.f.C.L.* 95, No. 74, pos. 368.
24 *G.f.C.L.* 89, No. 25, pos. 137.
25 *G.f.C.L.* 4, No. 43, pos. 296, with amendments.
26 *G.f.C.L.* 91, No. 109, pos. 471.
27 The contributor has already given an account of some of these inspectorates in her paper for the Administrative Law Project 1996, "Investigation into restaurants: practices related to health, cleanliness and safety", published in *Administrative Justice in Central and Eastern Europe*, Budapest 1998.
28 *G.f.C.L.* 91, No. 100, pos. 442.
29 *Gazette for Current Law* 90, Number 16, position 95.
30 *G.f.C.L.* 92, No. 85, pos. 428.
31 *G.f.C.L.* 94, No. 19, pos. 70.
32 *G.f.C.L.* 90, No., pos. 121.
33 *G.f.C.L.* 85, No. 54, pos. 276 with amendments.
34 For further details see "Investigation into restaurants: practices related to health, safety and cleanliness" within the Administrative Law Project in 1996, published in *Administrative Justice in Central and Eastern Europe*, Budapest, 1998.
35 *G.f.C.L.* 95, No. 13, pos. 59.
36 *Polish Monitor* 92, No. 26, pos. 185 with amendments.
37 *G.f.C.L.* 69, No. 13, pos. 945.
38 *Polish Monitor* 95, No. 18, pos. 213.
39 *G.f.C.L.* 96, No. 73, pos. 350.
40 *Polish Monitor* 93, No. 20, pos. 198.
41 *G.f.C.L.* 89, No. 25, pos. 137.
42 *Polish Monitor* 96, No. 45, pos. 435.
43 M. Kulesza, "Draft reform of centrum", *Republic of Poland* 1996, No. 63.
44 *G.f.C.L.* 96, No. 106, pos. 497.
45 *G.f.C.L.* 96, No. 106, pos. 492.
46 *Polish Monitor* 91, No. 7, pos. 47.
47 *G.f.C.L.* 96, No. 106, pos. 497.
48 *G.f.C.L.* 96, No. 106, pos. 491.
49 *G.f.C.L.* 96, No. 106, pos. 490.
50 *G.f.C.L.* 96, No. 106, pos. 493.
51 *G.f.C.L.* 96, No. 106, pos. 497.
52 *G.f.C.L.* 96, No. 106, pos. 492.
53 *G.f.C.L.* 96, No. 106, pos. 493.
54 *G.f.C.L.* 96, No. 106, pos. 489.
55 *G.f.C.L.* 96, No. 106, pos. 494.

56 *G.f.C.L.* 96, No. 106, pos. 495.
57 *G.f.C.L.* 96, No. 106, pos. 496.
58 *G.f.C.L.* 96, No. 156, pos. 775.
59 *G.f.C.L.* 96, No. 106, pos. 498.
60 *G.f.C.L.* 90, No. 21, pos. 123 with amendments.
61 *G.f.C.L.* 96, No. 106, pos. 498.
62 *G.f.C.L.* 81, No. 24, pos. 123 with amendments.
63 *G.f.C.L.* 90, No. 16, pos. 95.
64 *G.f.C.L.* 96, No. 106, pos. 498.
65 *G.f.C.L.* 91, No. 18, pos. 80 with amendments.
66 *G.f.C.L.* 81, No. 24, pos. 123 with amendments.
67 See the Statute on State Enterprises i.e. *G.f.C.L.* 91, No. 18, pos. 80 with amendments.
68 *G.f.C.L.* 91, No. 18, pos. 80 with amendments.
69 *G.f.C.L.* 96, No. 106, pos. 498.
70 *G.f.C.L.* 95, No. 99, pos. 487 with amendments.
71 *G.f.C.L.* 92, No. 67, pos. 336;changes: *G.f.C.L.* 94, No. 61, pos. 251.
72 See section D 1 below.
73 *G.f.C.L.* 96, No. 89, pos. 402.
74 *G.f.C.L.* 97, No. 9, pos. 43.
75 *G.f.C.L.* 90, No. 16, pos. 95 and see section I 2 above.
76 *G.f.C.L.* 97, No. 9, pos. 43.
77 *G.f.C.L.* 94, No. 76, pos. 344 with amendments.
78 *G.f.C.L.* 90, No. 32, pos. 191 with amendments.
79 *G.f.C.L.* 91, No. 18, pos. 80 with amendments.
80 *G.f.C.L.* 96, No. 89, pos. 402.
81 *G.f.C.L.* 97, No. 9, pos. 43.
82 Robert Pietrzak, "Comments on the Statute on Economy of Communes," *Comments to G.f.C.L.* 97.
83 *G.f.C.L.* 96, No. 43, pos. 189.
84 *G.f.C.L.* 95, No. 74, pos. 368.
85 *G.f.C.L.* 96, No. 118, pos. 561.
86 *G.f.C.L.* 90, No. 51, pos. 298 with amendments.
87 *G.f.C.L.* 96, No. 156, pos. 775 and *G.f.C.L.* 97, No. 32, pos. 184.
88 See section B 1 above.
89 *G.f.C.L.* 96, No. 118, pos. 561.
90 *G.f.C.L.* 90, No. 51, pos. 298 with amendments.
91 *G.f.C.L.* 34, No. 57, pos. 802 with amendments.
92 *G.f.C.L.* 90, No. 51, pos. 298 with amendments.
93 *G.f.C.L.* 96, No. 156, pos. 775 cited in preceding section (II B 1).
94 *G.f.C.L.* 96, No. 118, pos. 561.
95 *G.f.C.L.* 96, No. 106, pos. 493.
96 *G.f.C.L.* 97, No. 33, pos. 199.
97 *G.f.C.L.* 96, No. 156, pos. 775, already cited above (see II B 1 b (9).
98 Jerzy Jacyszyn, "On the Statute on Commercialisation and Privatisation of State Establishments", *Notary* 97, No. 2.
99 *G.f.C.L.* 96, No. 106, pos. 493.
100 *G.f.C.L.* 91, No. 55, pos. 236.
101 For the application of the Doctors' Trade Union to Constitutional Tribunal see section D 1 below.
102 *G.f.C.L.* 97, No. 28, pos. 152.
103 *G.f.C.L.* 50, No. 50, pos. 458.
104 *G.f.C.L.* 34, No. 4, pos. 32.
105 Lech Paprzycki, "Comments for the statute about doctor's profession," *Comments for the Gazette for Current Law 97.*
106 *G.f.C.L.* 97, No. 28, pos. 153.

107 For instance, an appeal from a decision of the organs of the Agency of the Social Insurance System to common court – section of labour and social insurance. For further details see the contributor's paper "Inspection into restaurants, practices related to health, safety and cleanliness: Formal and Informal Rule-Making," *Administrative Justice in Central and Eastern Europe*, Budapest 1998.
108 *G.f.C.L.* 91, No. 91, pos. 408.
109 *G.f.C.L.* 91, No. 108, pos. 470, with amendments.
110 *G.f.C.L.* 97, No. 33, pos. 199.
111 For details on state enterprises and companies where the State Treasury is a shareholder see section B 2 above.
112 For the judicial system in Poland see section B 1.
113 *G.f.C.L.* 95, No. 74, pos. 368.
114 *G.f.C.L.* 93, No. 108, pos. 486, with amendments.
115 *G.f.C.L.* 95, No. 99, pos. 487, with amendments.
116 *G.f.C.L.* 93, No. 108, pos. 486, with amendments.
117 *G.f.C.L.* 91, No. 55, pos. 234.
118 *Bulletin of High Administrative Court* (for internal use only).
119 *G.f.C.L.* 91, No. 30, pos. 127, with amendments.
120 *Bulletin Of The Ombudsman '97.*
121 *G.f.C.L.* 93, No. 44, pos. 202.
122 *Bulletin of The Highest Audit Chamber, 97.*
123 See Part I.
124 *Parliament Review 96, 97.*

CHAPTER NINE
ROMANIA

I. GENERAL DESCRIPTION OF THE ADMINISTRATIVE LEGAL SYSTEM[1]

1. BRIEF HISTORY OF THE ADMINISTRATIVE LEGAL SYSTEM

The history of modern administrative law in Romania began with the adoption in the 19th century of the Organic Regulations, the basic laws of the two autonomous Romanian principalities, Wallachia and Moldavia. The Regulations were a result of negotiations between Russia and the Ottoman Empire, the two great powers that fought a number of wars for supremacy in the Balkans throughout the century. The Organic Regulations introduced the first principles of modern Romanian constitutional law, primarily the principle of separation of powers.[2] As a branch of public law, administrative law underwent major developments between the adoption of the Organic Regulations and the legislative reforms of Alexandru Ioan Cuza of 1864. The Law on the Council of State, of February 11, 1864, established the Council of State as a specialised jurisdiction for administrative disputes, following the French model of Conseil d'Etat. This body functioned for only two years, between 1864 and 1866. The 1866 Constitution abolished the Council of State. This was the only period in Romanian history when a specialised administrative jurisdiction existed. Since then, administrative disputes have been exclusively in the competence of the ordinary courts.

The legal literature[3] divides the history of administrative law in Romania into six periods. The first one was from 1864 until 1866. The second one lasted from 1866 until 1905 and is characterised by the elaboration of general procedures for resolution of administrative disputes in the ordinary courts. The third period was between 1905 and 1948. This period is characterised mainly by the introduction of special regulations on the competence of courts in administrative law disputes[4] and by the constitutionalisation of the institution of administrative contentious. The fourth period lasted from 1948 until 1965 and during it the "administrative contentious procedure" (judical review of administrative action) was abolished. The fifth period, between 1965 and 1990, is characterised by the introduction of some new procedural rules of administrative adjudication in the ordinary courts. The reforms of 1990, and especially the adoption of Law 29/1990 and the 1991 Constitution, marked the beginning of the sixth period.

2. ESTABLISHMENT OF THE MAJOR INSTITUTIONS IN THEIR PRESENT FORM

The Constitution of the Republic of Romania was adopted on November 21, 1991: it laid the foundations for the establishment of the country's present-day administrative institutions. The Constitution was adopted by an overwhelming majority of representatives: 414 votes for and 95 against. It was officially published in the Official Gazette[5] No. 233 of November 21, 1991 and was approved by referendum on December 8, 1991.

3. MAJOR PROCEDURAL CODES AND LAWS

The most important procedural code is the Code on Civil Procedure,[6] which was adopted on September 9, 1865, promulgated on September 11, 1865, and entered into force on December 1, 1865. The foreign sources used in the drafting of the Code were the 1819 Civil Procedure of the Geneva Canton and the 1806 French Civil Procedure. The Code was applied in the beginning only in Wallachia and Moldavia (the "Old Romania", formed in 1859), and was extended to Transylvania following the 1918 unification. The most important modification of the code was brought about by Decree 1228 of May 15, 1900. It was followed by three successive laws for speeding up the procedure, adopted on May 19, 1925, July 11, 1929, and June 23, 1943. The most important recent modification was carried out through Law 59/July 23, 1993.[7]

The second most important procedural code, the Code on Criminal Procedure, was adopted on November 12, 1968 and became effective on January 1, 1969. It was amended in 1970 and 1971. Substantial amendments were made by Law 6/1973 and Decrees 203/1974 and 218/1987. The code was substantially amended again after 1990, the most important amendments being introduced by Law 45/July 1, 1993,[8] and Law 141/November 5, 1996.[9]

Law 92/1992 on the Organisation of the Judiciary was published in the Official Bulletin 197/August 13, 1992 and entered into force on the day of its publication. It provides for the rules of composition and functioning of the judiciary, the Public Minister, as well as for the status of judges and prosecutors, the Superior Council of Magistracy, and the administrative and auxiliary staff. Another essential law is Law 29/November 7, 1990 on Administrative Judicial Review.[10] This is the basic judicial institution which regulates disputes between public administrative bodies and any other subject of law.

4. STRUCTURE OF THE EXECUTIVE

The 1991 Constitution establishes a semi-presidential system[11] of government. The highest executive bodies are the President of the Republic and the Government[12] headed by the Prime Minister.

4.1 The President

The President is elected through a direct, universal, equal, secret and freely expressed vote[13] for a four-year mandate. He can be re-elected only once. His main prerogatives are in the following areas: legislation, organisation and functioning of public bodies, appointments, defence of the state and public order and foreign policy.[14] In the area of legislation, the President promulgates the laws and has the right to ask the Parliament, once, for reconsideration of a bill.[15] He signs the laws before publishing and has standing before the Constitutional Court for preliminary constitutional review.[16] Further, he presents messages to the Parliament concerning the principal political problems of the nation,[17] consults the Government with regard to important and urgent matters,[18] participates in the sessions of Government and heads them under certain conditions,[19] and is entitled to organise referendums after consulting the Parliament.[20] His appointment and removal powers are quite important. He has to nominate a candidate for Prime Minister, after consulting the party that has an absolute majority in Parliament or, if there is no such party, after consulting all the political parties represented in Parliament.[21] He also appoints the Government on the basis of a confidence vote of the Parliament[22] and appoints and removes ministers, in case of reshuffling of the Government or vacancy of office, at the proposal of the Prime Minister.[23] The President also appoints three out of the nine judges of the Constitutional Court.[24]

The most important presidential prerogative connected with the Parliament is the power to dissolve it. This happens if the Parliament fails to grant its confidence vote for the forming of a Government in 60 days after it has been first asked, and only if at least two successive proposals have been made. The power of the President is discretionary: in constitutional terms he may dissolve Parliament, but he also has to consult with the presidents of the two chambers and the leaders of the parliamentary groups.[25] The President is the chief commander of the army and head of the Supreme Council of Defence. He is the one official entitled to declare mobilisation of the army with the prior approval of the Parliament.[26] If the country is attacked, he has to take measures for its defence and send a message to the Parliament.[27] The President is also responsible for declaring a state of emergency and state of siege.[28]

The President's prerogatives in the field of foreign policy include the signing of treaties previously negotiated by the Government,[29] appointing and recalling diplomats as well as establishing the status of Romanian diplomatic missions.[30] He also has other traditional presidential prerogatives, such as granting of pardons and conferring decorations and honorary awards.[31]

4.2 The Government

The Government is in charge of domestic and foreign policy, as outlined in its program previously approved by the Parliament; it is also responsible for the general management of the public administration.[32] The governmental program, together with a list of proposed ministers, are debated in a plenary session of the Parliament and have to be approved by simple majority.[33] The Government is politically responsible only before the Parliament. Each member of the Government is politically accountable for his own activity, as well as for the whole activity of the Government.[34] Parliamentary control over the Government is exercised in the following forms: presentation of information,[35] questions and interpellations,[36] motion of censure (vote of no confidence),[37] and vote of confidence.[38] The legal regime of questions and interpellations is set out in the Regulations of each parliamentary chamber.[39]

Article 148 of the Regulation of the Chamber of Deputies and Article 130 of the Regulation of the Senate establish the basic procedures for parliamentary questions. A question is a simple request for the following type of information: whether a fact is true, whether a piece of information is correct, whether the Government or another body of public administration intend to communicate to the Chambers the information already requested, or whether the Government will take a particular measure in view of a specific problem.[40] Article 156 of the Regulation of the Chamber of Deputies and Article 134 of the Regulation of the Senate define interpellations as requests to the Government or one of its members[41] concerning explanations of important problems in its domestic or foreign policy.

Interpellations are much more important than questions, because they may entail a motion[42] expressing the position of the Chamber *vis-à-vis* the object of the interpellation. Articles 112 and 113 regulate the most important mechanism of the Government's accountability before Parliament: the motion of censure. It may be initiated by a fourth of the total number of deputies and senators and is adopted by an absolute majority vote.[43] If the motion is rejected, the deputies and senators that initiated it cannot file another motion in the same session.[44] There is one exception to this rule, for the cases when the Government itself provokes a motion. This happens if the Government takes the responsibility, in a plenary session of the two chambers, for a program, a declaration of its general policy or a bill.[45] The Government is dismissed if in three days a motion of censure is adopted, but if this does not happen, the program, declaration or bill are considered adopted.[46]

5. RELATIONS BETWEEN CENTRAL AND LOCAL ADMINISTRATION[47]

The Constitution devotes four articles to regulating the general regime of local public administration. Article 119 establishes two major constitutional principles: the principle of local autonomy and the principle of decentralisation of public services.[48] The principle of local autonomy is realised by the local councils and the local mayors[49], locally elected as prescribed by a special law. They function as autonomous administrative bodies in charge of local affairs[50] and are not in any hierarchical relation to any administrative authority at the county or central level.[51] The county council is also locally elected and functions as a co-ordinator of the activities of local councils with respect to the carrying out of public services in the whole county.[52] The local representative of the Government is the prefect. He is the head of the decentralised public services of the ministries and other central bodies.[53] His most important relation with the local authorities is the control of the legality of the administrative acts adopted by the county council, the local council or the mayor.[54]

6. NORMATIVE ACTS OF THE EXECUTIVE

The President of the Republic adopts *decrees* in conformity with Article 99 of the Constitution which have to be published in the Official Gazette. These decrees passed in the exercise of specific presidential prerogatives[55] have to be countersigned by the Prime Minister. The legal regime of the decrees is debated in the legal doctrine, since some authors[56] grant them normative character, while others specifically deny them this character.[57]

The Government can adopt *decisions*, which can be individual or normative; *statutory orders*, which can be only normative (since they are passed in the exercise of delegated legislation); and acts with an exclusively political character.[58] The most common governmental act is the decision adopted for the implementation of laws (*secundum legem* and *praeter legem*). There is no need for parliamentary approval of governmental decisions.

Legislative powers can be delegated to the Government but not to the President. Regulation of the delegation of legislative powers is provided by Article 107, 3 and Article 114 of the Constitution. According to them, Parliament can adopt a special enabling law authorising the Government to pass statutory orders in areas which are not within the domain of organic laws.[59] This means that the Government can adopt only statutory orders that are within the area of ordinary laws. The enabling law has to establish the field and the date up to which the Government can adopt statutory orders. Furthermore, there is a distinction between statutory orders that require Parliamentary approval and those that do not. If the enabling law requires it, the statutory order has to be approved until the end of the enabling term; otherwise the order loses its effect. The Government can adopt emergency statutory orders[60] in exceptional circumstances, but they become effective only after they have been submitted to Parliament for approval.

Both decisions and statutory orders have to be signed by the Prime Minister, counter-signed by the ministers obliged to execute them, and published in the *Official Gazette*.[61]

The Constitution limits itself to regulating the acts of the two heads of the executive, the President and the Government. The jurisdiction of ministers is, however, specifically recognised in Article 106, 1, which makes a distinction between the activity of the Prime Minister and that of other members of the Government. It stipulates that the Prime Minister has to respect the substantive competence of other ministers. The legal doctrine[62] acknowledges the right of ministers, other heads of specialised central bodies, and of central bodies which are directly subordinated to ministries to adopt acts that have normative force[63] and are integrated in the hierarchical system prescribed by the Constitution. The legal force of an act depends on the issuing body's position in the administrative hierarchy. There is considerable debate on the right of the heads of autonomous bodies to adopt normative acts (e.g. the ombudsman).

7. ADMINISTRATIVE LAW COURTS AND JUDICIAL HIERARCHY

7.1 Structure of the judicial system

There are no separate administrative law courts in Romania and, apart from military courts, the court system is unitary. The lowest-level courts, the administrative sections of tribunals, Courts of Appeal and the Supreme Court of Justice have the competence to deal with administrative disputes.[64] The court system is structured to incorporate four levels: courts, tribunals, Courts of Appeal and the Supreme Court of Justice. The lowest courts decide on administrative disputes which special laws render within their jurisdiction.[65] The first regular instance for administrative disputes is the tribunal.[66] Article 17 of Law 29/1990 established administrative law panels (sections) at the tribunals, the Courts of Appeal, and the Supreme Court of Justice. This is the first time since the Council of State of 1864 when specialised sections for administrative disputes have been created within the court system.[67]

Tribunal decisions can be appealed at the Supreme Court of Justice, so the procedure for administrative disputes involves adjudication on two levels–the tribunals and the Supreme Court.[68] The Courts of Appeal, in their turn, are also given a first-instance competence in very specific areas.[69] Their decisions can also be appealed at the Supreme Court.

7.2 Scope of jurisdiction of the different levels of courts

The lowest courts, as mentioned, decide at the first and last instance on complaints against the decisions of public authorities and other bodies with jurisdictional activity, under conditions prescribed by law.[70] A systematic interpretation[71] of the legal texts in force divides the first-instance competence between the tribunals and the Courts of Appeal in the following way. The tribunals decide on administrative disputes that arise from administrative acts issued by mayors; the local councils; institutions and commercial companies created by the decisions of the local council; local bodies subordinated to the county bodies; lowest courts; local branches of certain public bodies. Article 3, 1 of the Code on Civil Procedure transfers to the competence of the Courts of Appeal all administrative disputes arising from acts of public central bodies, prefects, decentralised public services, ministers and other central authorities, public bodies at county level, and the administration of the city of Bucharest.

7.3 Special quasi-judicial bodies for adjudicating cases requiring professional expertise

The Court of Audit is an example of a quasi-judicial body. It is regulated by Article 139 of the Constitution and exercises control on the formation, administration and use of the financial resources of the state and the public sector in general. The Court also has jurisdictional powers, as approved by law, and reports annually to Parliament on the accounts of the national public budget administration, including cases of mismanagement. At the request of the Chamber of Deputies or the Senate, the Court checks the management of public resources. The members of the Court are independent, irremovable and are also subject to the general conflict-of-interest rules applicable to judges.

8. GENERAL PROCEDURAL CODES AND LAWS OF ADMINISTRATIVE LAW

There is no code of administrative procedure. The procedural laws are Law 29/1990 on Administrative Disputes, as a special law, and the Code on Civil Procedure, as a general law. Law 29/1990 was one of the first major laws to be adopted by the new regime. Among the intentions of the legislators was to revive the strong administrative tradition of the inter-war period[72] in an effort to guarantee the principle of separation of powers. The law has been amended twice: implicitly, when the 1991 Constitution was adopted, and in 1993, when Law 59 for the modification of the Code on Civil Procedure was adopted. Law 29 has the following main features:[73] first, it grants access to a court only when there is a right at stake, not just a simple interest; second, the courts can annul illegal administrative acts and give compensation.

Law 29/1990 is a special law and stipulates the exceptional legal regime of administrative regulation, in contrast with the ordinary substantive and procedural regulation. The Code on Civil Procedure is responsible for addressing all issues left open by the special law, mainly procedural aspects.

8.1 Appeal before administrative agencies

Article 47 of the Constitution establishes the citizen's right of petition. Citizens have the right to apply to public authorities by petitions formulated only in the name of the signatories. The public authorities are bound to answer to petitions in terms and under conditions as established by law.[74] According to Article 48, any person aggrieved in his legitimate right by an administrative act or failure of a public authority to consider his application within the legal term is entitled to the acknowledgement of his right, annulment of the act and remedies for the damage. This constitutional provision is at the basis for both contentious and non-contentious administrative procedure.

An essential condition that has to be fulfilled before going to court is the so-called prior administrative action.[75] Article 5 of Law 29/1990 sets the framework for this preliminary procedure. Before asking the court to annul an act or to oblige an administrative body to issue an act, the aggrieved person must petition the body within 30 days from the day the act has been issued. The same term of 30 days applies if the authority has not given any answer to the petitioner. The authority is obliged to decide on the petition within 30 days. If the person is not satisfied with the decision, he can either appeal it to the next highest authority or go directly to court.

The petition to the court must also be made within a 30-day period. The aggrieved person also has standing before a court if the administrative authority has not decided the petition within the prescribed time limit. In all cases, the action in court cannot be started later than a year from the day the administrative act was initially communicated to the petitioner.

8.2 Acts that cannot be appealed within the administrative hierarchy

The Law on the Contentious Administrative Procedure 29/1990 establishes prior administrative action as mandatory. Courts reject any complaint that has not fulfilled this basic condition. Consequently, if the complainant has not first tried to solve his problem through administrative appeal, he would in practice have no access to a court. Acts that are not subject to judicial review are also not subject to administrative appeal, as well as the purely internal administrative acts, the so-called technical-administrative acts, that have an exclusively internal application.[76] Nevertheless, the acts on which a final administrative decision have been based are subject to review, but only together with the principal act.

8.3 Procedure for judicial review before a court

Law 29/1990 stipulates two procedural methods to seek review of an administrative act. The first one is the common method of administrative contentious procedure: any aggrieved person has standing before the court, after the exhaustion of prior administrative action and respecting the terms prescribed by Law 29/1990. Article 4 of the same law provides for another possibility: the so-called jurisdictional-administrative acts[77] can be attacked by way of appeal after the exhaustion of all jurisdictional-administrative procedures. The appeal must be made within 15 days from the communication of the answer to the aggrieved person to the Administrative Section of the Supreme Court of Justice. The decision of the Court is final.

Article 122, 4 of the Constitution stipulates the possibility for the Prefect to challenge an act of a County Council, Local Council, or a Mayor before the court, where he thinks the act unlawful. The act attacked shall be suspended de jure.

Other possibilities of seeking judicial review can be found in various special laws, for example Law 48/1992 on Media Regulation: "disputes arising out of the denial to issue an act of authorisation for media operation shall be resolved in conformity with the law on administrative judicial review". In these cases there is no requirement for prior administrative action.[78] The parties which have standing before the court are the aggrieved physical or legal persons. Some special laws also mention that "all the interested persons" have standing. These persons must still fulfil the basic standing conditions set by the Code on Civil Procedure.

The provisions of Law 29/1990 must be read together with the provisions of the Code on Civil Procedure. The procedure is generally speedy as the decision is taken by a panel of two judges.[79] There is a court fee for filing a complaint, although the tendency is to abolish the fees or making them symbolic. The documents that have to be submitted with the complaint include the administrative act challenged or the denial of the administrative authority, or in case there was no answer within the time limit prescribed by law, the copy of the petition.[80]

In certain cases, to prevent imminent damage, the plaintiff can ask the court to suspend the execution of the act until the final judgement. The court has to reach a decision on this urgently, even without summoning the parties. This judgement is executed de jure.[81]

8.4 Acts excluded from judicial review

The exceptions from judicial review are regulated by Article 2 of Law 29/1990. The first category are acts of government, i.e., the acts concerning the relation between the Parliament or the President and the Government.[82] This category includes, according to the interpretation of the doctrine[83] and jurisprudence,[84] all the acts issued by Parliament and the President vis-a-vis the Government, and all the non-political acts of the Government vis-a-vis the other two bodies.

Another category are the administrative acts issued by the bodies of the Parliament.[85] These acts are excluded due to their connection to Parliament, despite their administrative character.

Further exceptions from judicial review include the administrative acts concerning the internal and external security of the state, as well as the administrative acts issued in connection with the interpretation and execution of international acts in the internal legal system.[86] The last thesis excepts from judicial review the urgent measures taken by the executive bodies for the prevention or elimination of the effects of events that present public danger. The law divides such events into two categories: state of necessity and natural disasters (such as fires and epidemics.)[87]

Acts of the armed forces are also excluded from judicial review.[88] The law makes no distinction between administrative and other acts of the armed forces. Other exclusions from judicial review are administrative acts whose annulment or modification is regulated by special procedures in special laws,[89] as well as the administrative acts of the state as a private body, issued for the administration of its private domain.[90] The last category of exclusions from judicial review is the administrative acts adopted in the exercise of hierarchical control.[91]

II. DEVELOPMENTS IN ADMINISTRATIVE LAW DURING 1996-1997

A. THE CONSTITUTION

The Constitution was adopted on November 21, 1991, and has not been amended since then.

B. LEGISLATION[92]

1. PROCEDURAL AND GENERAL ORGANISATIONAL LAWS

1.1 The organisation of the judicial system

One of the major changes in the organisation of the judicial system was brought by Law 79/July 12, 1996 amending the Law of the Supreme Court of Justice No. 56/1993.[93] The amendments introduced by this law have been long advocated by the Supreme Court judges, mainly for the sake of efficiency. The law sets up a nine-judge panel headed by the vice-president of the court as an intermediary link between the sections and the plenary court. The panel has a separate competence from both the plenary court and the five sections of the court (civil, criminal, commercial, administrative and criminal). The nine-judge panel is competent to judge appeals against the decisions issued by the sections of the Supreme Court at first instance, as well as the annulment appeals against the definitive decisions of the sections. The competence of the plenary court has changed as a result of the introduction of the nine-judge panel. It now decides the annulment appeals against the ordinary appeals of the nine-judge panel, the appeal in the interest of law, the petitions concerning changes in the jurisprudence of the courts and the petitions to the Constitutional Court for abstract preliminary review.

1.2 The general procedures for appeal and judicial review of administrative action

Law 35/March 13, 1997 on the Organisation and Functioning of the Peoples' Advocate[94] Institution introduced a new form of control over the administration.[95] This is a law that has been expected for some time now. It defines the aim of the institution, in conformity with the Constitution, as defending the rights and liberties of citizens in their relations with public authorities. The Peoples' Advocate is independent from any public authority and cannot be subject to any imperative or representative mandate. He is elected by the Senate[96] for a four-year period and can be re-elected only once. The eligibility conditions are the same as for the judges of the Constitutional Court.[97] There are also two Deputies of the Peoples' Advocate, selected by him with the approval of the Senate's Committee on legal issues, nominations, validations, discipline and immunities. The Peoples' Advocate co-ordinates the activity of the institution, receives and distributes the petitions, supervises their resolution, represents the institution, hires the staff and exercises disciplinary authority. The institution issues a report, which must be published, on its activity every year or at the request of Parliament. The report can also present recommendations on the amendment of legislation, or other measures for the protection of citizens' rights and liberties.

The Peoples' Advocate can also issue special reports on grave legislative omissions or cases of corruption. In the exercise of his functions he issues recommendations which are beyond the control of both Parliament and the judiciary. The Peoples' Advocate exercises his prerogatives ex officio or at request. Anybody, regardless of citizenship, age, gender, political affiliation, religion, can petition the Advocate. A special provision is dedicated to the obligation of the public authorities concerned to allow prisoners, army conscripts or officers to petition the Peoples' Advocate, "with the exception of cases determined by the law". The petition has to be written and must demonstrate an unlawful act of the administration. Anonymous petitions, or petitions whose object is older than a year, are not admissible. The Peoples' Advocate is not entitled to investigate acts of the Parliament and its two Chambers, deputies and senators, the President of the Republic, Government, Constitutional Court, the President of the Legislative Council,[98] and the judiciary. There is no fee for petitioning. The Peoples' Advocate can reject the petition, especially prima facie unfounded petitions, and provide reasons for doing so, or can ask for further information. If, after investigations, it is proved that the petition is in the competence of the Public Ministry, pending before court, or has as its object a judicial error, the Peoples' Advocate informs the chief Public Prosecutor or the Superior Council of the Magistracy,[99] who have to communicate their conclusions on the case to the People's Advocate. The Peoples' Advocate has the right to investigate, gather all necessary information, including that which is secret, hold hearings and examine documents. The public authorities have an obligation to give all assistance possible plus all information and documents requested to the Peoples' Advocate. The public character of his activities can be made confidential at the request of the petitioner or where there are justified reasons.

If the petition is justified, the Peoples' Advocate will request, in writing, the public authority concerned to reconsider or revoke the act, to pay damages and to restore the previous legal status of the aggrieved party. The public authority has 30 days to comply with the recommendations. In the event of non-compliance, its superior authority is informed, and a new term of 45 days starts. The Government is informed in the last instance, and where it too fails to act Parliament is notified. It can take any measures it considers appropriate.

1.3 Other procedural laws

Law 25/April 12, 1996 amending Law 70/1991 on Local Elections[100] was passed as a result of the adoption of permanent electoral lists and permanent electoral cards. It establishes the electoral bodies and the procedural steps to be taken before, during and after local elections. The electoral bodies are, in hierarchical order, the Central Electoral Bureau (CEB), the electoral bureaus of the districts and the electoral bureaus of the sections. They must all consist of lawyers, who are chosen by the drawing of lots.

The CEB is composed of seven judges of the Supreme Court of Justice chosen by the drawing of lots during public session. The CEB is in charge of the general supervision of legality of the elections. Its jurisdiction includes the consideration of petitions, other than those already given in the competence of the lower bureaus, concerning the organisation and progress of the elections as well as consideration of petitions alleging electoral fraud. In the exercise of its functions, the CEB takes decisions which are pronounced in public session and are announced by the public media. The decisions are binding for all electoral bureaus and bodies with electoral functions in the country. The decisions of the CEB, which interpret provisions of this law, are published in the Official Gazette. Appeals against CEB's decisions are made before the Supreme Court of Justice, within two days since communication of the decision to the parties. The Supreme Court's decision is final. The law also stipulates a special speedy procedure for citizens' petitions against any kind of mistakes in the electoral lists. The mayor in charge of the electoral list has to take a decision on the petition by means of a disposition. An appeal against the disposition can be made before a court within 24 hours from communication. The court has three days to resolve the case. The decision of the court is final, directly enforceable and communicated to the parties within 24 hours.

Another special procedure is stipulated for petitions against nominations by citizens, political parties, political or electoral alliances. The time limits are, once again, very short. The competent body is the court or tribunal in whose territorial competence the candidate has been registered. The decision of the court or tribunal is not communicated to the parties, but there is a possibility of appeal. The decision on the appeal is final and irreversible. Other provisions of the law establish the order of making public declarations, free access to media and a set of regulations concerning the national minorities. The political parties of the national minorities have media access if they participate in the elections in a manner proportional to their number in the city or county. Access to the private media has to be based on contracts; every private media should impose the same airtime fees for each party. The national minorities' political parties have to request media access (to both public and private media companies) within five days from the beginning of the electoral campaign: otherwise they lose this right. These provisions of the law are applicable only to the national minorities' parties, and since they set up unjustifiably stricter conditions for participating in the campaign, they seem to be discriminatory.

2. SUBSTANTIVE LEGISLATION

2.1 The management of the economy

2.1.1 LAWS ON PRIVATISATION

Law 66/July 3, 1996 concerning the reorganisation of the Romanian Savings House (CEC) as a joint-stock company[101] was passed as part of the national financial reform. The Savings House was the institution where citizens deposited their savings before the political transition of 1990. This state institution preserves its character: the state is its only shareholder, its president and vice-president are nominated by the Prime Minister, and the company continues to be mainly a savings bank.

Law 133/October 28, 1996 on the transformation of the Private Property Funds into companies of financial investment[102] was another important measure in the sphere of economic management. The Private Property Funds (PPF), together with the State Property Fund (SPF), are the principal managers of the privatisation process.[103] They were initially organised as commercial companies. This law modifies their status into companies of financial investment, which means that they have to be organised as stock companies, in conformity with Law 31/1990.

2.2 Laws on the environment

Law 26/April 24, 1996, known as the Forest Code,[104] was one of the major pieces of legislation adopted in the sphere of environmental management. It establishes the general legal regime of forests as well as the national autonomous administration of forests functioning on the basis of economic management under the authority of the Ministry of Waters, Forests and Environment. The Ministry has the power to act in the following spheres: the management of forest land held by the state; ecological reconstruction; regeneration and preservation of forests; and the security of forests and public services. Among the important provisions of the law is the obligation of the owners of private forests to follow the regime of public forests in many important aspects. The owners have to take care to regenerate the forest within two years after cutting: otherwise the national administration will do so at the owners' expense. The owner can petition the administration. The administrative decision can be appealed in court within 30 days from the day of issue. If the administration's decision is not appealed it is directly enforceable. The owners of private forests also have to accept the national administration's inspections. The quantity of wood that can be exploited from forests is established annually by a law. Any damage to forests is to be compenstated for in full by the perpetrators, aside from the administrative or criminal sanctions. The state has the right of preemption.

Furthermore, Law 107/September 25, 1996 on waters[105] established the general legal regime of waters. The regulation of the utilisation of waters is an exclusive right of government, regardless of the form of ownership over the waters. The national autonomous administration in charge is called "Romanian Waters", under the authority of the Ministry of Waters, Forests and Environment. The administration is helped by the Committee of Water Basins, a national body composed of 15 members, drawn from the Ministry of Waters, Forests and Environment, the Ministry of Health, local administration, the office for the protection of consumers, interested non-governmental bodies and consumer representatives. The committee co-operates with the national administration in the application of the national strategy and policy for the management of waters. The committee's authority includes media relations and the publicity of public policies. An article in the law is dedicated to the public's participation in the policy-making process. Before taking any decision, the Ministry and the administration are obliged to take into consideration the interests and opinions of the public or, as the case may be, of those directly concerned with the project. Publicity is mandatory: it can be achieved through the electronic media, newspapers, public debates and other means. Both the decision of the agency and the reasons for it have to be published. The ordinary law for administrative disputes applies where disagreements occur.[106] The management of certain waters can be entrusted to private persons, on the basis of authorisations issued by the Ministry. The Ministry decides on the procedure for issuing such authorisations as well as on the notification rules. The decision of modification, suspension or withdrawal of the authorisation has to be reasoned. An authorisation for the protection of the environment (preliminary impact assessment) is also usually required prior to the authorisation for management of waters. The intentional pollution of waters is a criminal offence. The law sets out special categories of offences and crimes concerning the regime of waters.

2.3 Laws on finance

Law 72/July 12, 1996 on public finance[107] regulated the formation, management and control of the financial resources of the state, local public bodies and public institutions. The Romanian budgetary system is unitary and is composed of the national budget, local budgets, special funds, the state treasury, and the budgets of other autonomous public institutions. The principal controlling bodies are the Court of Audit and the Ministry of Finance. The Government is in charge of the drafting and execution of the national budget, whilst the Parliament approves it.

The basic budgetary principles are: unity, generality, balance, realism, annual character, and publicity. The responsibilities in the management of public finance are divided between the Ministry of Finance and the National Bank of Romania. It is forbidden to meet governmental expenses by monetary emission or direct financing by banks. The formation and use of financial resources by the state outside the budget is forbidden. Taxes, regardless of their name and type, are established only by law. The local bodies (each commune, city, Bucharest's administrative divisions, and county) form and manage their budget. There is no hierarchical relation between the municipal and county budgets. If the local resources are not enough they may require help from the state budget. The annual budgetary law provides for purpose funds to be transferred to the local budgets. The government has to take measures to stimulate local initiative. Local taxes are established by the local councils within the limits prescribed by law.

Law 135/October 28, 1996 authorised the National Bank to give credits to some commercial banks in order to cover the requests for withdrawal from Dacia Felix Bank and Credit Bank.[108] These two institutions faced an insolvency crisis, and in order to meet public demand and to avoid citizen unrest Parliament ordered the National Bank to open a line of credit to cover the citizens' requests for withdrawal from the insolvent banks.[109]

2.4 Laws on traffic

Law 129/October 16, 1996 on railway transportation[110] established the state's monopoly on railway transportation. Railways are managed by the autonomous public body the National Society of Romanian Railways (SNCFR), which is under the authority of the Ministry of Transport. Although SNCFR is the principal authority in charge of the management of railways, the law stipulates the possibility of local railroad exploitation by private companies, with the authorisation of the Ministry of Transport and the Ministry of Defence. The Ministry of Transport is responsible for the control, supervision, research, authorisation and security of railroad traffic as well as for the normative regulation in this area. SNCFR established its own internal structure and is headed by a council of administration both of which, respectively, have to be approved and nominated by the Ministry. Besides the specific functions connected with the management of the railways and the rules of transport, SNCFR can be involved in and administer other commercial, tourist, research, educational, health care and media activities related to its main area of competence.

2.5 Laws on communication and media

The free circulation of information and the secrecy and inviolability[111] of telephonic and other forms of communication was guaranteed by Law 74/July 12, 1996 on telecommunications.[112] The Ministry of Communications, which has the competence to issue licenses, is the state body in charge of the management and control in this area. The law distinguishes between the licensing of public operators or the purveyors of basic telecommunications services and the private sphere.

In the first category, licenses can be granted only to Romanian legal persons. The Ministry decides on the number and the type of licenses (partial or full). Licenses can be granted either through auction or directly by the Ministry. The procedure, which has to be objective and transparent,[113] is also established by the Ministry. The Ministry has to justify the direct granting of a license. This happens in the cases and periods for which there was an exclusive right of a basic telecommunications service, for technological reasons, and if there was only one person present at the auction. The conditions of participation in the auction have to be published in the national and local newspapers. The most important conditions to be fulfilled for the granting of a license are certain technical requirements, financial capacity, compatibility with the communication system of the country as well as the impact on the competition. The license only lasts temporarily (between five and 15 years) and can be partially or totally, temporarily or permanently withdrawn after prior warning. The Ministry has to check the holder's statements and complaints within 30 days. Any conflicts between the Ministry and the holders of a license are resolved in conformity with the law on administrative contentious 29/1990: the same is valid for conflicts between citizens, holders of licenses and the Ministry. The law enumerates the rights and duties of the holders but these can be amended by mutual agreement and the actual license stipulates only those rights and duties chosen by the Ministry.

In the private sphere both Romanian and foreign legal persons can be authorised to operate a telecommunications enterprise. The Ministry may not issue authorisations when there is proof that the project endangers the security or health of the users or the confidentiality of the communication. Another reason for refusing to grant an authorisation may be the lack of available frequencies. An order of the Ministry establishes the procedure by which authorisations are issued. The authorisation is personal and cannot be transferred. The law stipulates some anti-monopoly rules, including one much-debated provision according to which the Ministry can nullify an inter-connecting agreement between holders of licences if it considers that the agreement endangers the effective competition on the telecommunications market. This law is, in general, characterised by the lack of guarantees for procedural fairness and gives overwhelming discretion to the Ministry.

2.6 The management of socio-cultural processes

2.6.1 LAWS ON URBAN ORGANISATION, PLANNING AND CONSTRUCTION

Law 114/October 11, 1996 on residence and accommodation[114] was one of the most important laws to be adopted in 1996. The reason is that, previously, residence was regulated by the restrictive Law 5/1973 and the Decision of the Council of Ministries 860/1973, two examples of the most retrograde communist legislation. Law 114 is based on the principle of free and unconstrained access to accommodation and residence, which is considered to be a right of every citizen. It is a major national objective, assigned to both central and local public administration, to encourage free choice in residence. The law establishes the social, economic, technical and legal aspects of construction and the use of accommodation and residential areas. Important provisions of the law include those concerning the subvention by the state, through the local councils, of the construction of flats for some special categories of persons.[115] The local councils approve or reject the request and establish the priority order. Although the law does not have special provisions for recourse to justice, the general principle of access to justice applies, in conformity with the constitution and the law on the administrative contentious. The dwellings built in this way cannot be sold before the debts to the state are paid off. CEC (Romanian Savings House) has to give credit for the construction, purchase, repair and rehabilitation of dwellings. Together with the Ministry of Finance it has to establish the credits and rules that will apply on an annual basis.

A very important part of the law, which derogates from the Civil Code,[116] deals with rent contracts, i.e. contracts with a special character. Other provisions of the law establish the maximum level of the rent for a state dwelling, the rules for the management of dwellings and the rules for some particular types of dwelling. The annex to the law provides the minimal surfaces and conditions a place has to fulfil in order to be considered a dwelling, as well as the model regulation for associations of owners.

Law 125/October 16, 1996, amending and supplementing Law 50/1991 concerning the authorisation of construction and other measures for securing accommodation,[117] altered the regulations concerning the issue of authorisations for construction. Authorisation has to be issued within 30 days from the day the request, the legal permits and the technical documentation have been submitted. If the technical documentation is not complete it will be returned for the necessary completion.

2.6.2 LAWS ON THE MANAGEMENT OF HISTORICAL HERITAGE

Law 16/April 2, 1996 on the National Archives[118] determined that the National Archives is a budgetary unit within the Ministry of the Interior. It manages, supervises and protects the national archival fund as well as giving expert assistance and ensuring the unitary development of all archive operations in the country. A scientific advisory council operates within the National Archives. The law sets up norms for the evidence, selection, keeping and use of archive documents. The National Archives has the right of pre-emption for all documents classified as having archival value. All documents older than 30 years are declassified upon the approval of the National Archives. Approval will not be given where the revelation of documents may affect national security or the rights and liberties of people. A list of terms for documents with special status is established by an annex to the law.[119]

2.7 The management of administrative-political processes

2.7.1 LAWS ON NATIONAL SECURITY

Law 17/April 2, 1996 on the legal regime of firearms and ammunition[120] established a very restrictive legal regime for the ownership and use of arms and ammunition. There is a state monopoly over military armament and ammunition. This includes their possession, control and commercialisation and, hence, the Ministry of Interior controls the ownership, carrying, and use of arms and ammunition. It also establishes the number of arms that can be owned by a person, i.e. no more than two firearms of the same calibre per person, as well as the quantity of ammunition. The law, therefore, limits the range of persons and the uses of arms. The application of the law differs according to whether the individual involved is a Romanian or a foreign person. The police issue the permit for carrying arms and may suspend or revoke it. Any complaint in such matters is to be solved by the court in conformity with the law on Administrative Contentious.

Legal persons are subject to a more restrictive regime. Possession and use of arms should be part of their system of protection. The law also sets up the rules for use of arms by the military. The commercialisation of arms and ammunition is possible, for companies, only with the authorisation by a court upon authorisation of the Ministry of the Interior.

Law 46/June 5, 1996 on civil and military defence training[121] concerned the regime of obligatory military service and other forms of training for defence. There are two types of military service: regular and reduced. The reduced term (half the normal duration) is for graduates of universities or any other institution of higher learning. For conscientious objectors the law provides for the possibility of alternative military service,[122] lasting twice as long as regular military service. The implementation of this provision is established by a government decision, and it is always possible to switch back to regular service. The body in charge of conscription is the local military commission. Petitions against the commission's decisions are solved by a special regional commission. The commission's decision is final.[123] The medical conclusions of the commission can be revoked only by the Central Commission of Medical-Military Expertise.

2.7.2 LAWS ON CITIZENSHIP AND ADMINISTRATIVE STATUS

A personal numerical code was introduced for the first time in Romania, as the only identifier for all systems that process data concerning physical persons, by Law 105/September 25, 1996 on the means of identification and identity cards.[124]

Law 119/October 16, 1996 on documents concerning the civil status of persons[125] established the competence of state organs, the rules concerning birth, marriage and death certificates and various rules of private international law concerning both Romanian citizens abroad and foreigners in Romania. It has been harmonised with Law 105/1992 concerning private international law relations.

2.7.3 LAWS ON THE RESIDENCE OF FOREIGN NATIONALS ON THE TERRITORY OF THE COUNTRY; REFUGEES

Law 15/April 2, 1996 on the status of refugees in Romania[126] defines as a refugee a foreigner who proves that they have justified fears that in their country of origin they may be persecuted on the basis of race, nationality, religion, affiliation to a certain social group or other political reasons. The refugee status can be also given, for humanitarian reasons, to persons who do not satisfy the requirements above. Refugees are subject to the Romanian legislation and the international conventions on refugees' status. Among the conditions that justify the refusal of refugee status is danger to national security or public order which the person involved may represent due to his affiliation with a certain group or organisation.

Refugee status is granted by a commission nominated by the Government, consisting of representatives of the Ministry of Interior, the Ministry of Foreign Affairs, and the Ministry of Labour and Social Protection. The representative of the UN High Commissioner for Refugees in Romania may be present. The commission must justify, i.e. provide reasons for, any negative decisions in writing. The person may take this decision to court within 10 days of its issue. The court procedure in such cases has been accelerated and consists only of a two-judge panel and a prosecutor. The decision of the court may be appealed within five days, and the appeal decision is final and irrevocable. Various rights are vested in the individual making use of this court action: for example, there are no legal fees, the petitioner has a right to counsel, and he may obtain a translator free of charge and request that the proceedings be conducted in secret.

One of the most important rights and duties of refugees stipulated by the law is the obligation to receive primary education in Romania plus all other levels of education in conformity with the rules for foreigners. Refugees also enjoy religious liberty, free access to justice and administrative assistance. If refugee status is lost the person is subject to the legal regime of foreigners in Romania.

2.8 Other important laws

For the first time in Romanian history, Law 7/March 13, 1996 on real estate publicity[127] establishes a unitary system of recording land property and making the information on ownership public.[128]

Political parties are defined by Law 27/April 26, 1996 on political parties,[129] amended by the Emergency Statutory Order 3/June 25, 1996,[130] as associations of Romanian citizens who have the right to vote and participate freely in the formation and exercise of their political will. The parties are viewed as legal persons of public law. It is forbidden to establish political parties which defame the country and the nation, instigate wars of aggression, incite and propagate national, racial, class or religious hatred, discrimination, territorial separatism,[131] or public violence, as well as any obscene conduct contrary to morality. Also forbidden is the establishment of political parties or organisations which, by their aims or activity, militate against political pluralism, the principles of the rule of law, or against the sovereignty, integrity or independence of Romania. Political parties associated with foreign organisations which issue binding instructions are also outlawed.[132] The constitutionality of political parties is decided by the Constitutional Court. Political parties cannot organise military or paramilitary units or activities. They cannot receive donations from public institutions, autonomous public bodies, companies and banks with more than 50 per cent state capital or foreign states or organisations (with certain exceptions stipulated by law). All political parties receive an annual subsidy from the state budget. The possible uses of this subsidy are established by law. The Court of Audit is in charge of controlling the legality of the financial operations of political parties.

Finally, Law 140/November 5, 1996 amending the Criminal Code[133] introduced important amendments which will hopefully bring to an end some of the most heated criminal law controversies after 1989 such as the notions of public goods, public interest or civil servant.[134]

The well-known Article 200 of the Criminal Code was also amended, and homosexual relations that occur in public or produce a public scandal are now punished by imprisonment from one to five years. This seems to conflict with the requirements of the Council of Europe, and in this respect Romania is considered one of the countries with the most restrictive regulations. The instigation and promotion of homosexuality are also punished by imprisonment from one to five years. Among the other new provisions is Article 309: transmission of AIDS by someone who knows that he is infected is punished with imprisonment from five to 15 years.

Article 246 penalises civil servants who, in the exercise of their duties, knowingly do not fulfil an act or fulfil it wrongly, with the result of damaging the legal interests of a person. Furthermore, Article 247 inculpates discrimination, by a civil servant, on the basis of nationality, race, gender or religion. Article 250 incriminates the abusive behaviour of a civil servant, either by offensive speech or by violence. Generally speaking, sentences and sanctions have been stiffened for almost all crimes by the new amendments.

C. REGULATION:[135] DECISIONS OF THE GOVERNMENT

1. STRUCTURE AND PREROGATIVES OF THE GOVERNMENT: PROCEDURAL ASPECTS

Decision 935/October 8, 1996 on the organisation and functioning of the prefectures[136] defines prefectures as public institutions with legal personality. The prefecture contributes to the realisation of the governmental policies and objectives in the counties. The prefect alone can exercise legal prerogatives and has under his authority and supervision a technical expert apparatus. With regard to the activities of local administrative bodies, the apparatus has the following functions: a) to examine the legality of the administrative acts of local or county administrative bodies and make proposals for the elimination of instances of illegality; b) to report on investigated administrative acts, as well as on the execution of laws and other normative acts issued by the local bodies; and c) to analyse the legality of draft governmental decisions initiated at the local level. The apparatus also supervises the activities of decentralised public bodies and, in cases of conflicts with the local bodies, acts as a mediator. It makes studies and reports on the application of normative acts and proposes solutions for improving them. Its other functions relate to the programmes for European integration, including the harmonisation of local regulation with European standards.

Decision 44/March 3, 1997 on the organisation of the Ministry of Transports[137] establishes the Ministry of Transport as the state organ in charge of national policy concerning transport and the elaboration of policies of development and harmonisation of transport.

Decision 16/January 31, 1997 on the reorganisation of the National Committee for Child Protection as a department within the Government's structure[138] specified the most important functions and prerogatives of the Committee. They are essentially in the areas of monitoring children's rights, the elaboration of governmental policies, proposals for harmonisation of domestic legislation with international standards and participation in humanitarian programmes. Perhaps the most important provisions of the law are connected with the Romanian Child Adoption Committee, now supervised and co-ordinated by the National Committee.[139]

Decision 17/January 31, 1997 on the establishment, organisation and functioning of the Department for the Protection of National Minorities[140] was a result of the last general election. The success of the opposition in the November elections meant the inclusion in the governing coalition of the parties of national minorities, primarily the Democratic Union of Hungarians from Romania. This decision is part of the measures taken by the new Government concerning national minorities. The Department is under the direct supervision of the Prime Minister and is headed by a delegate minister with the rank of a member of the Government. Among the most important powers of the Department are the drafting of statutes, the approval of bills with the assent of the Council of National Minorities,[141] and the organisation of programmes with the aim of maintaining and expressing the language and culture of minorities and monitoring of minority rights in Romania. The Department can also grant financial assistance, with the Council's approval, to organisations of national minorities.

2. SUBSTANTIVE REGULATION

2.1 Privatisation

During the period under review, the Government took a number of decisions in order to speed up and finalise the privatisation process. For example, Decision 26/January 19, 1996 amending some decisions of the Government adopted for the implementation of Law 55/1995 on the acceleration of the privatisation process;[142] Decision 30/January 23, 1996 on measures taken for the implementation of Law 55/1995;[143] and Decision 1174/November 13, 1996 on measures taken for the finalisation of the mass privatisation process established by Law 55/1995.[144]

These decisions demonstrate the Government's efforts to compensate for Romania's delay in the introduction of economic reforms. Since the initial time limits and goals in the sphere of privatisation have not been met, the Government attempted to create a favourable legal framework for successful completion of this important aspect of economic reform.

2.2 Agricultural lands

1996 was marked by serious natural disasters (mainly floods) in Romania. Therefore, the Government adopted a number of decisions designed to compensate the losses of the farmers. The compensations took the form of a direct state subsidy covering a certain percentage of the interest on credits given to the farmers by the commercial banks. Some of the most important decisions were Decision 564/July 12, 1996 on the subsidy in proportion of 75 per cent of the interest of credits given by commercial banks to farmers for the foundation and recovery of orchards and vineyards;[145] and Decision 727/August 23, 1996 on the subsidy in proportion of 60 per cent of the interest of credits given by commercial banks to farmers for the agricultural work of fall 1996.[146] Despite this state intervention the agricultural sector has remained in crisis.

2.3 Finance

Statutory Order 15/January 23, 1996 on the strengthening of the financial discipline,[147] approved and amended by Law 131/October 28, 1996,[148] was adopted as a result of one of the transition crises. This was not uncommon in other Eastern European countries as well. The high prices of utilities (electricity, gas, water) cause both citizens and legal persons to delay payments, which causes huge losses to the suppliers. In order to face this problem, the statutory order stipulates the obligation to pay for utilities using the hard currency (if any) the economic agent has in his bank account. Furthermore, wage payments may be stopped by the banks if a citizen has not paid his debts to the suppliers of utilities. Other provisions regulate the modality of payment between economic agents and the maximum amount of cash a legal person can withdraw daily from banks.

Statutory Order 39/August 29, 1996 on the establishment and functioning of the fund guaranteeing citizens' deposits in the banking system[149] was adopted as a result of another crisis: the insolvency of several commercial banks, which led to serious public discontent. The act establishes the Guarantee Fund as a legal person in public law. The internal statute is approved by the National Bank. The fund aims to guarantee the repayment of the deposits open at any bank by physical persons. All banks that received deposits from physical persons have the obligation to participate in the formation of the Fund and to make an annual contribution to it. The Fund is headed by a three-member Council of Administration appointed by the National Bank. The vice-governor or prime vice-governor of the National Bank is the head of the Council. The other two members represent the Ministry of Finance and the Ministry of Justice. The Fund makes an annual report, which is published, to the National Bank.

2.4 Customs

Decision 147/March 12, 1996 on the organisation and functioning of the General Customs Office,[150] amended by Decision 1127/November 8, 1996[151] set up a public body entrusted with elaborating the customs policy of the government and supervising its implementation. A General Director (secretary of state in the Ministry of Finance) represents and heads the Office and is accountable before the Finance Minister for the activity of the Office and the whole customs system. The main functions of the Office are the organisation, co-ordination and control of customs, the supervision of customs legislation and its observance in the whole country and the prevention of customs offences and crimes. The Office is also in charge of the control and investigation of trafficking of drugs, arms, valuable historical objects, explosives, and money laundering.

2.5 Communication, media

Decisions 285/April 23, 1996 and 2/January 11, 1997 on the temporary exemption from customs duties of newsprint[152] was a response to accusations that the previous government had tried to hamper the freedom of speech through financial means.[153]

2.6 Territorial organisation, planning and construction

Decision 525/June 27, 1996 on the approval of the general regulation of town planning[154] established the general regulative framework of town planning as a unitary system consisting of technical and legal requirements. The regulation introduces comprehensive rules on construction starting from the procedure of authorisation to begin construction and finishing with the normative requirements for buildings. The jurisdiction on decision-making in this area is shared by central and local administration. Conflicts arising from the Decision are to be solved in conformity with the Law on Administrative Contentions 29/1990.

2.7 Education

Decision 301/April 30, 1996 on the organisation of doctoral studies[155] harmonised the Romanian educational system with the European standards for graduate studies. Under the Decision, doctoral programmes are organised only by accredited universities or research institutes and have a duration of either three to four years (full time) or four to five years (part time). The decision on granting a doctoral title is taken after a public defence of the thesis by a commission composed of professors and researchers. The decision can be contested at the Ministry of Education. The decision of the Ministry is final.[156]

Also in this area, Decision 735/August 28, 1996 on the approval of the regulation for scientific research grants[157] established a public system of research grants. The main institutions responsible for the administration of grants are the Ministry of Technology and Research, the Romanian Academy and the Ministry of Education.

2.8 Health care

Decision 382/May 24, 1994 on the approval of norms and regulations for the production, distribution and control of pharmaceutical products,[158] amended by Decision 608/July 26, 1996,[159] made the Ministry of Health responsible for the control of pharmaceutical activities. The pharmaceutical inspectorate, a technical organ in the structure of the Ministry, supervises their production, quality, storage, internal and external commercialisation, as well as the publication of information of public interest.

2.9 Residence of foreigners, refugees

Decision 1182/November 13, 1996 for the application of Law 15/1996 on the status of refugees[160] was adopted for the implementation of Law 15/1996, the 1951 Geneva Convention on Refugees' Status, and the 1967 New York Protocol. The

Decision recognises the necessity of reaching European standards stipulated by the asylum procedure of the Council of Europe and the European Union Resolution from July 1995 concerning the minimum asylum guarantees. Other provisions stipulate that foreigners and stateless persons can be granted refugee status if they come from zones affected by internal conflicts, or if they need temporary protection from humanitarian reasons. Collective requests are not accepted. The Decision establishes the procedure to be followed, the obligation of the public official to inform the petitioner of the relevant rules, and possibility of access to court in case of rejection.

The chapter has been prepared on the basis of information provided by Mihaela Şerban

NOTES

1 The sources used in the first part of the chapter are the Constitution, statutes and standing orders, the relevant jurisprudential commentaries and cases, as well as the most authoritative textbooks in constitutional and administrative law, currently used at the Law School of the University of Bucharest.

2 Emil Cernea, Emil Molcut, *Istoria statului si dreptului romanesc*, Casa de Editura si presa "Sansa", Bucuresti, 1991, pp. 172–173.

3 Antonie Iorgovan, *Drept administrativ, tratat elementar*, Editura Atlas Lex, Bucuresti, 1994, vol. II, pp. 150–158.

4 The most important laws were the law for the reorganisation of the Court of Cassation from July 1, 1906, March 25, 1910 and February 17, 1912; the 1923 Constitution, especially Article 107; the Law on Administrative Contentious from December 23, 1925; the Law on the Committees of Revision from April 20, 1933; the Law on Administrative Courts from March 15, 1939.

5 Monitorul Oficial.

6 Constantin Crisu, Nicorina Crisu Magraon, Stefan Crisu, *Codul Juristului*, Editura Argessis, Curtea de Arges, 1994, p. 421.

7 *Official Gazette* 177/July 26, 1993.

8 *Official Gazette* 147/July, 1993.

9 *Official Gazette* 289/November 14, 1996.

10 *Official Gazette* 122/November 7, 1990.

11 Ioan Muraru, *Drept constitutional si institutii politice*, Editura Actami, Bucuresti, 1995, vol. II, p. 196–197.

12 The term "Government" is used as defined by Article 101, 3 of the Constitution to include only the Prime Minister, ministers and "other members named by an organic law".

13 Article 81, 1 of the Constitution.

14 Muraru, *op. cit.*, vol. II, pp. 210–213.

15 Article 77 Const.

16 Article 144, a, Const.

17 Article 88.

18 Article 86.

19 Article 87.

20 Article 90.

21 Arts. 85 and 102.

22 Article 85, 1.

23 Article 85, 2.

24 Article 140, 2.

25 Article 89.
26 However in "exceptional cases" (a term not clarified by the Constitution) he can ask for the Parliament's approval post facto, in maximum five days after mobilisation (Article 92).
27 In this case, if the Parliament is not in session, it will have to assemble ex officio in 24 hours (Article 92, 2, last thesis).
28 Article 93.
29 Article 91, 1.
30 Article 91, 2.
31 Article 94, a, d.
32 Article 101, 1.
33 Article 102, 2.
34 Article 108, 1. The law on ministerial responsibility has not been adopted yet, although it has been pending in the committees for years now.
35 Article 110. Whenever asked, the Government is obliged to present any information or document requested by any of the Chambers or parliamentary commissions. If a legislative initiative implies the modification of the state budget or the state insurance budget, requesting information is mandatory.
36 Article 111.
37 Article 112.
38 Art. 113.
39 The Standing Orders of the Chamber of Deputies was passed in February 1994 and published in the *Official Gazette* 50/February 25, 1994. The Standing Orders of the Senate was approved in June 1993 and was published in the *Official Gazette* 178/July 28, 1993.
40 Muraru, *op. cit.*, vol. II, p. 116.
41 The Standing Orders of the Senate.
42 This procedure is not the same as a motion of censure as established by art.112.
43 Article 112 para. 1 and 2.
44 Article 112, 4.
45 Article 113, 1.
46 Arts. 113, 2 and 3.
47 Article 3 of the Constitution divides the territory of the country, from an administrative point of view, into three types of units: the commune, the city and the county.
48 Antonie Iorgovan, *op. cit.*, vol. IV, p. 221.
49 "The authorities of public administration exercising local autonomy in communes and cities are the local councils, as deliberative bodies, and the mayors, as executive organs ..." Law 69/November 26, 1991, on local public administration, published in the *Official Gazette* 238/November 28, 1991.
50 Article 120.
51 Iorgovan, *op. cit.*, vol. IV, p. 223.
52 Article 121.
53 Article 122.
54 Article 122, 4.
55 Article 99,2. Conclusion of international treaties, accreditation and recalling of diplomatic envoys and status of diplomatic missions, mobilisation of the armed forces and organisation of the national defence in case of sudden attack, declaration of state of emergency and siege, conferring of decorations and titles of honour, promotions to the ranks of marshal, general and admiral, and the grant of individual pardon.
56 Muraru, *op. cit.*, vol. II, p. 219.
57 Iorgovan, *op. cit.*, vol. IV, p. 86.
58 Iorgovan, *op. cit.*, vol. IV, p. 169.
59 According to Article 72 of the Constitution, there are three types of laws which can be adopted by the Romanian Parliament: constitutional laws, organic laws and ordinary laws. There are procedural and substantive differences between these three types. The constitutional laws are adopted for the revision of the Constitution. They require a two-thirds majority in each Chamber, plus a final approval through referendum. The organic laws are reserved to deal with the specific issues enumerated in

Article 72, 3: a) the electoral system, b) the organisation and functioning of political parties, c) the organisation of referendum, d) the organisation of the Government and of the Supreme Council of National Defence, e) the regime of the state of siege and state of emergency, f) crimes, punishment and the regime of their execution, g) the granting of collective pardon and amnesty, h) the organisation and functioning of the Superior Council of Magistrates, courts, Public Minister and the Court of Audit, i) the status of the public servant, j) the regime of administrative disputes, k) the general legal regime of property and inheritance, l) the general regime of labour relations, syndicates and social protection, m) the general organisation of the educational system, n) the general regime of the religious cults, o) the organisation of the local administration, territory and the general regime of the local autonomy, p) the way of establishing exclusive economic zones, r) other domains for which the Constitution provides to be regulated by organic laws. The organic laws have to be adopted by the majority in each Chamber (absolute majority). All the other laws are ordinary laws. They have to be adopted by the majority of the members of each Chamber actually present (simple majority). Muraru, *op. cit.*, vol. II, pp. 168–169.

[60] Article 114 para. 4.

[61] Article 107, 4.

[62] Iorgovan, *op. cit.*, vol. IV, pp. 209–210.

[63] Instructions, orders, decisions, dispositions.

[64] Law 29/1990, Article 4, 6, 14, 15, 17, and the Code on Civil Procedure, Article 2/1/c, Article 3/1 and Article 4.

[65] Article 1, 2 of the Code on Civil Procedure. For example, Article 11 of the Law 18/February 19, 1991, published in the *Official Gazette* 37/February 20, 1991, which set out the procedure for the establishment of the right of property, either by constitution or by restitution. In this context, the law provides for the establishment of special local commissions, under the supervision of the local mayor. The decisions of these commissions can be attacked in the lowest-level courts. The procedure is a special one, and the decision of the court is final.

[66] Law 29/1990 Article 4 and the Code on Civil Procedure, Article 2.

[67] Iorgovan, *op. cit.*, vol. II, p.158.

[68] Law 29/1990, Article 14.

[69] The Code on Civil Procedure, Article 3/1.

[70] Article 1, 2 of the Code on Civil Procedure.

[71] Iorgovan, *op. cit.*, vol. II, pp. 282–283.

[72] Iorgovan, *op. cit.*, vol. II, p. 158.

[73] Contenciosul administrativ, *Legea nr. 29 din 7 noiembrie cu comentarii si practica judiciara*, Editura Lumina, Bucuresti, 1992, p. 3.

[74] Article 47, 3.

[75] Its binding character is undisputed, though its utility has been questioned by some authors – Iorgovan, *op. cit.* vol. II, p. 210.

[76] Iorgovan, *op. cit.*, vol. II, p. 167.

[77] These are administrative acts having the characteristics and the legal force of jurisdictional decisions, both due to their object–the establishment of vested rights and situations of fact, and their effects–they have the authority of res judicata (*Contenciosul administrativ*, p. 42). Those acts are issued as solutions to conflicts within the administration, based on the principles of case and controversy, and the independence of decision-making. They are exceptions from the general regime of the administrative acts. Iorgovan, *op. cit.*, vol. II, pp. 147–148.

[78] Iorgovan, *op. cit.*, p. 272.

[79] Article 6, 2.

[80] Article 8.

[81] Article 9.

[82] Article 2, a) 1st thesis.

[83] Iorgovan, *op. cit.*, pp. 226–230.

[84] *Contenciosul administrativ*, pp. 23–25.

[85] Article 2/a)/2nd thesis.

[86] Article 2/a)/3rd thesis. This last exception has come under serious attacks by administrative

law scholars and in the jurisprudence. This provision, as many others, was copied almost verbatim from the 1925 Law on Administrative Disputes, despite the present-day conditions and the evolution of international law. C. G. Rarincescu, *Contenciosul administrativ roman*, ed. a IIa, Bucuresti, 1936.

87 The concept of state of necessity cannot be found in the Constitution, which speaks only of states of siege and states of emergency. Therefore, the law implicitly modified the Constitution in this respect. Iorgovan, *op. cit.*, vol. II, pp. 242–248.

88 Article 2/b.

89 Article 2/c.

90 Article 2/c.

91 Article 2/d.

92 There were 142 laws adopted in 1996.

93 *OG*, 150/July 17, 1996.

94 The ombudsman.

95 *OG*, 48/March 20, 1997.

96 As mentioned before, one of the most debated constitutional arrangements in Romania is the almost identical character of the two parliamentary chambers. The election of the ombudsman by the Senate is one of the few distinctions between them.

97 The candidates must be law graduates with high professional competence and at least 18 years experience in juridical or academic activities in law (Article 140 Constitution).

98 An advisory expert body of Parliament, which approves draft normative acts, for the purpose of a systematic unification and co-ordination of the whole body of laws. It also keeps the official record of legislation (Article 79, Constitution).

99 It nominates judges and public prosecutors and performs the role of disciplinary council for judges (Article 133 Constitution).

100 *OG*,77/April 13, 1996.

101 *OG*, 140/July 5, 1996.

102 *OG*, 273/November 1, 1996.

103 The five PPF funds and one SPF were set up by Law 58/1991, the Privatisation Law. They are in charge of the transfer of state property into private hands. There are two methods of privatisation: by free-of-charge transfer and by sale. The free transfer is done through the distribution to the population of property certificates. They represent the stock of the PPF, organised as companies of financial character. The certificates can be sold, exchanged for shares of the companies that are in the process of privatisation, or changed for shares of the PPF, which become companies of financial investment in five years' time. The SPF is in charge of the management and sale of the State's stock or parts. The PPF have 30 per cent of the social capital of the companies that are in a process of privatisation. The 30 per cent have to be split between the five regional PPF, by the National Agency for Privatisation. The PPF have the following functions: to issue property certificates, to try to maximise the profits to be distributed to the owners of the certificates, to ensure brokering services for exchanging the certificates with shares, to make new investments, and to initiate measures for the acceleration of the privatisation process. The members of the PPF and SPF are nominated by the Government and approved by the two chambers. The privatisation strategy was set up with and fulfils the requirements of the international financial institutions (mainly the IMF and EBRD).

104 *OG*, 93/May 8, 1996.

105 *OG*, 244/September 8, 1996.

106 Law 29/1990.

107 *OG*, 152/July 17, 1996.

108 *OG*, 264/October 28, 1996.

109 The banks did not recover, and recently the National Bank withdrew their authorisations of functioning and the judicial liquidation procedure began. It is only one of the corruption scandals occurring in recent years.

110 *OG*, 268/October 30, 1996.

111 Interception and tapping of phone calls can take place only in cases stipulated by law, upon a public prosecutor's authorisation.

[112] *OG*, 156/July 22, 1996.

[113] This is the only requirement of the law. The law allows a large margin of discretion for the Ministry of Communications, with few possibilities for the licenses' owners.

[114] *OG*, 254/October 21, 1996.

[115] For example young persons under the age of 35.

[116] This can be considered an important amendment to the 150-years-old Civil Code.

[117] *OG*, 259/October 24, 1996.

[118] *OG*, 71/April 9, 1996.

[119] For example, 100 years for medical documents, 75 for personal files, 40 years since death for private life, 100 years for national security, and 50 years for foreign policy.

[120] *OG*, 74/April 11, 1996.

[121] *OG*, 120/June 11, 1996.

[122] Only religious motives are accepted.

[123] In light of the constitutional provisions, this stipulation of the law should be interpreted as final in administrative contexts, but not as precluding access to court. The lack of a specific provision in this respect could open the way to unconstitutional interpretations.

[124] *OG*, 237/September 30, 1996.

[125] *OG*, 282/November 11, 1996.

[126] *OG*. 69/April 5, 1996. To be read together with Government's Decision 1182/1996 on the application of this law.

[127] *OG*, 61/March 26, 1996.

[128] The basic record is divided into three parts: a description of the building, inscriptions concerning the property right, and inscriptions concerning all other rights linked to the property.

[129] *OG*, 87/April 29, 1996.

[130] *OG*, 133/June 26, 1996.

[131] Reading these provisions, it should be kept in mind that Romania has one of the largest national minorities in Europe, the Hungarian minority from Transylvania. While political parties based on nationality are not forbidden, the provisions of the law could be interpreted as outlawing the parties of the national minorities from Romania.

[132] A provision inspired by the Communist Party's history. Another provision inspired by the same fear of the past is the one that forbids the organisation of structures of political parties in the workplace.

[133] *OG*, 289/November 14, 1996.

[134] Article 145 defines now the term "public" as everything concerning the public authorities, the public institutions, the institutions and other legal persons of public interest, the management, use or exploitation of public property, services of public interest, as well as any other goods which are defined by law as being of public interest. Article 147 defines as "civil servant" every person who exercises permanently or temporarily, with any title and regardless of the mode of appointment, any task, paid or not, for an institution as defined in Article 145 (as public).

[135] Statutory orders, emergency statutory orders, decisions. In 1996 there were 44 statutory orders, 13 emergency statutory orders, and 1567 decisions adopted.

[136] *OG*, 259/October 24, 1996.

[137] *OG*, 38/March 7, 1997.

[138] *OG*, 17/February 5, 1997.

[139] The Adoptions Committee gained a shumeful reputation, being surrounded by corruption scandals. Some of them ended up in court and were given extensive internal and international media coverage (1994–1995).

[140] *OG*, 17/February 5, 1997.

[141] The Council is a consultative body made up of representatives of all the organisations of national minorities, legally registered until September 27, 1992.

[142] *OG*, 20/January 29, 1996.

[143] *OG*, 20/January 29, 1996.

[144] *OG*, 291/November 18, 1996.

[145] *OG*, 163/July 25, 1996.

146 *OG*, 202/August 29, 1996.
147 *OG*, 24/January 31, 1996.
148 *OG*, 264/October 28, 1996.
149 *OG*, 206/August 30, 1996.
150 *OG*, 71/April 9, 1996.
151 *OG*, 285/November 13, 1996.
152 *OG*, 85/April 26, 1996, *OG*, 14/January 14, 1997.
153 Like many other state-owned companies, the main producer of paper in Romania, despite the huge market request, early ment bunkrupt. As a result, paper had to be imported, and its high price caused some very difficult problems for the great majority of newspapers. Strong accusations against the Government followed.
154 *OG*, 199/August 26, 1996.
155 *OG*, 102/May 20, 1996.
156 The question here would be whether the candidate should have access to court, given the highly specialised character of the conflict. Is a court entitled to judge an academic decision of this sort? The inter-war jurisprudence and doctrine in Romania answered this question in the negative.
157 *OG*, 208/September 3, 1996.
158 *OG*, 113/June 3, 1996.
159 *OG*, 168/July 29, 1996.
160 *OG*, 307/November 26, 1996.

CHAPTER TEN
RUSSIA

I. GENERAL DESCRIPTION OF THE ADMINISTRATIVE LAW SYSTEM

1. ADOPTION OF THE MAJOR ADMINISTRATIVE LAW ACTS

The basic norms regulating the contemporary administrative law system in Russia were laid down by the Constitution adopted in 1993. However, the system is far from established and is subject to constant change.

One of the basic sources of administrative law, the Decree of the Presidium of the Supreme Soviet ("On the Procedures for Consideration of the Proposals, Submissions, and Complaints of the Citizens"),[1] although adopted on April 12, 1968, is still in force. It regulates the internal administrative appeal in disputes between citizens and the administration.

The (external) judicial review of disputed administrative decisions is regulated by a newly adopted law: "On the Court Appeal of Actions and Decisions Violating the Rights and Liberties of the Citizens" from April 27, 1993.[2]

In addition to these two major normative acts, a number of other laws and legal codes touch on administrative law issues. These include the Code of the RSFSR on Administrative Offences;[3] the Customs Code of the RSFSR; the Air Code of the Russian Federation; the Criminal Code, the Criminal Procedural Code of the RSFSR; the Civil Code, the Civil Procedural Code of the RSFSR; the Criminal Enforcement Code of the RSFSR; the Labour Code of the Russian Federation; the Family Law Code; the Forest Code of the RF; the Housing Code; and the Agricultural Code.

2. THE STRUCTURE OF THE EXECUTIVE BRANCH

According to the Constitution of the Russian Federation (RF) of 1993, the executive power is vested in the Government of the RF (Article 110). The basic act currently regulating the structure of the bodies of the executive branch is the Decree of the President of the RF "On the System of the Federal Organs of the Executive Power" of August 14, 1996.[4] Paragraph 1 of this Decree rules that the system of federal executive bodies includes the Government of the RF, the ministries of the RF, and some other federal administrative organs falling generally into the following categories: federal committees, federal commissions, federal services, federal agencies, and federal supervisory bodies. A special federal executive body is the Governing Body of Presidential Affairs.

2.1 The President of the Russian Federation

Article 80 of the Constitution of the RF defines the position of President as head of state. According to the Russian constitutional doctrine the President is not a representative of any of the three branches of power: the legislative, the executive, or the judiciary. Despite this specific feature of his position in the system of separation of powers, a constantly increasing number of administrative bodies are directly subordinated to the President. These bodies are predominantly related to the army, police, and security services. The President has his own administration (separate from the Government of the RF) and enjoys a number of prerogatives typical of the executive branch. All this has led some constitutional and administrative lawyers to question the general doctrine and define the position of President as a "special organ of the executive power".[5]

2.2 The Government

The Government of the Russian Federation consists of the Chairman of the Government, his first deputy, 11 deputy prime ministers, and federal ministers. The structure of the Government is set out in the law "On the Council of Ministers–the Government of the Russian Federation".[6] However this law is obsolete and is in contradiction with the Constitution of 1993, which has a number of articles on the formation and the prerogatives of the Federal Government.

After the re-election of President Yeltsin as head of state in 1996, a new Government was formed under the same Prime Minister, Viktor Chernomyrdin.

2.3 Federal ministries and other federal organs

The creation of federal organs of executive power, and their organisation and abolition are carried out by the President of the RF upon a proposal by the Prime Minister. The federal executive organs have their local bodies organised either in accordance with the administrative division of the country or the specificity of their function.

The organs of local government are defined by the Constitution of 1993 as not falling into the category of "state organs". Therefore, they are not a part of the administrative hierarchy and are not subordinated to any administrative state organ. In practice, a number of central administrations of the subjects (member states, and regions) of the Russian Federation simultaneously act as heads of the local government. In June 1997, President Yeltsin became the head of the newly formed Council on Local Government.

The structure of the state organs of the Russian Federation is represented in the following table.

Table 1. (Russia) Russia's Administrative Structure

Administrative Division	Administration of the President of the RF	Representative bodies	Executive bodies	Judiciary	Local government
Russian Federation	The President and his administration	Federal Assembly	Government	Supreme Court, Arbitrage Court, Constitutional Court	Council on Local Administration
The Subjects of the Russian Federation	Presidential representative (pleni-potentiary)	Local Dumas	Government, Administration	Courts of general jurisdiction, courts of arbitration	
Cities, Districts, administrative regions			Directorates, departments	Courts of general jurisdiction	Elected organs of local government, assemblies
Villages, and other small populated areas			Administration	Administrative Commissions	Elected organs of local government, assemblies

Parliament exercises control over the executive when it adopts the budget drafted by the Government and when it ratifies international treaties affecting vital issues. In most other cases the different branches legally act independently.

Article 132/2 of the Constitution grants the federal organs of the RF the right to transfer certain federal prerogatives to the bodies of local government, and to provide them with material and financial resources necessary for carrying out their duties.

A special case of delegation of prerogatives took place on August 10, 1996, when the State Duma was supposed to hear the presidential proposal for a candidate for Chairman of the Government of the Russian Federation. Some of the MPs insisted that the President should attend the sitting of the Duma.[7] The Chairman of the Duma, G. Seleznev, told the deputies that, in response to the request to attend the sitting, the President proposed that the Chairman of the Duma present Viktor Chernomyrdin as a presidential candidate.

The Government can delegate prerogatives to the ministries. An instance of such a delegation occurred when the Government passed the ordinance "On the Empowerment of the Ministry of Finance of the RF to Guarantee Credits Given by Commercial Banks to the Pension Funds of the RF" in 1996.[8] This ordinance gives the Ministry of Finance the right to guarantee credits on behalf of the Government: the credits are used for paying out the population's pensions.

2.4 Publication of the acts of the administration

According to Article 15 of the Constitution, "All normative legal acts affecting rights, freedoms, and the duties of the people and the citizens cannot be implemented unless they are officially published and open to the public". The Decree[9] of the President of the RF of May 23, 1996, regulated the procedures for official publication and enforcement of all normative acts. The most important provision of the Decree concerns publications where normative acts can be officially published. These publications are: *Rossiiszaya Gazeta, Sobranie Zakonodatelstva, Rossiiszie Vesti, The Bulletin of Normative Acts of the Federal Organs of the Executive Power,* and the electronic database of Systema, the scientific centre for legal information.

2.5 Rules on procedural fairness in administrative decision-making

The rules of procedural fairness concerning administrative procedures are elaborated in the Decree of the Presidium of the Supreme Soviet of April 12, 1968. Article 4 of the Decree prescribes that the officials authorised to decide on a particular issue forward complaints against their activity not later than five days after receipt to the relevant appeal body and notify the complainant of this. When the complainant has filed the complaint in person, notification and an explanation of the procedure should take place immediately. Article 7 rules that the officials must notify the persons concerned in written or oral form of the adoption of decisions: the officials must also explain the procedures of appeal to the citizens.

There are no provisions for the participation of citizens in the process of administrative decision-making. There is an obsolete provision (Article 12) to the effect that members of the public, people's controllers, outstanding workers, kolkhoz workers, and officials could be involved in certain decisions. Further, according to the Decree, the results of the consideration of complaints on issues of public importance must be discussed at the meetings of the labour collectives. Neither of these provisions has been particularly effective, and both are now definitely obsolete and systematically disregarded.

3. THE SYSTEM OF ADMINISTRATIVE COURTS

3.1 Structure of the judicial branch

The status of the judicial branch is determined by the Constitution and the Federal law "On the Judicial System of the Russian Federation".[10] In Russia there are federal courts, constitutional courts, and local courts of the subjects of the Russian Federation: all of them comprise the Russian legal system. The federal courts include:

a. the Constitutional Court of the RF;
b. the Supreme Court of the RF;
c. the supreme courts of the republics (member states), the regions, and the areas;
d. the courts of the autonomous cities and regions;
e. the district courts;
f. the martial courts and the specialised courts;
g. the Supreme Court of Arbitration of the RF;
h. the federal courts of arbitration of the regions and the courts of arbitration of the subjects of the Russian Federation, which fall into the system of federal courts of arbitration.

The courts of the subjects of the RF include:

a. the constitutional courts of the subjects of the federation;
b. the district judges, who serve as judges of general jurisdiction in the RF subjects.

3.2 Jurisdiction of the courts

The jurisdiction of the different types of courts is defined in the Constitution, which rules that judicial power is exercised in the processes of constitutional, civil, administrative, and criminal adjudication (Article 118). The division of power between courts of general jurisdiction and courts of arbitration is not clearly defined, which leads to practical problems. These two types of court have historically dealt with different types of cases: the general courts have adjudicated cases concerning individuals, while the courts of arbitration have dealt with cases involving organisations. In other systems built on the principle of duality, this division is reflected in the division of legal departments into civil law and commercial (corporate) law. However, as mentioned above, the Russian legal system is ambiguous on the status of courts of arbitration. At present, some administrative scholars argue that this division is a remnant from the Soviet past and a compromise of the principles of modern law. Their arguments are based on the fact that Article 118 of the Constitution of the RF and Article 1 of the law "On the Judicial System of the RF" prescribes that judicial power is exercised through the constitutional, civil, administrative and criminal jurisdictions: special procedures of arbitration are not mentioned, and this is interpreted as a ground for the abolition of courts of arbitration. However, during 1996 the role of the courts of arbitration in the resolution of administrative law disputes increased significantly.[11]

3.3 Quasi-judicial bodies

The majority of administrative lawyers consider that in Russia there are no special administrative jurisdictions. The 1993 Law "On the Judicial System" explicitly prohibits the establishment of bodies exercising judicial functions apart from the courts. However, such special administrative jurisdictions do exist and continue to be established. For example, the Judicial Chamber of media and information conflicts and a number of departmental commissions are adjudicative bodies designed to resolve conflicts on issues depending on specialised professional expertise.

With this in mind, it could be concluded that there are a number of quasi-judicial bodies in the RF. Some further examples are the Scientific-Technological Commission on Metrology and Measurement Technology; the ad hoc Commission on Anti-Monopoly Legislation operating in the framework of the GKAP; the City Housing Commission established by a governmental ordinance (May 6, 1997, No. 321); and the Interdepartmental Commission examining citizens' complaints on alleged violations of the right to leave the RF.

Some of the questions about the jurisdiction of the courts of arbitration are regulated by Joint Ordinance No. 6/8 of the Plenum of the Supreme Court of the RF and the Supreme Court of Arbitration of the RF of July 1, 1996.[12] According to this document, disputes involving citizens registered as private entrepreneurs are under the jurisdiction of the courts of arbitration. Once the registration of the entrepreneur expires or is repealed, the case is transferred to the jurisdiction of ordinary courts, unless the dispute has started before the expiry or repeal.

4. APPEAL AND JUDICIAL REVIEW OF ADMINISTRATIVE ACTION

The major legal sources of administrative procedural law in the Russian Federation are the Civil Procedure Code and the Code on Administrative Offences: together with these there are other subordinated (delegated) legislations. The most important are the Rules for Consideration of Cases Involving Violations of the Anti-Monopoly Legislation,[13] and the Temporary Instruction on the Procedure of Consideration and Resolution of Proposals, Claims, and Complaints of the Citizens by the Organs of the RF.[14]

4.1 Internal administrative review (appeal)

The procedures for appealing administrative acts of the different administrative bodies and agencies differ from one another. The differences involve time limits and persons who have standing to challenge the act. Sometimes collective and even anonymous complaints are admissible.

According to paragraph 2 of Article 231 and Article 232 of the Civil Procedural Code of the RSFSR, the complaints against administrative violations are to be considered following the general procedures of civil law adjudication determined by the CPC (Chapter 24) and the Code of Administrative Offences. However, special legislation may alter the general procedures depending on the specificity of the regulated matter. The major differences depend on whether the complaint has been filed following the Code of Administrative Offences or the Law "On the Appeal before Court of Administrative Action or Decisions Violating Citizens' Rights and Liberties".

4.2 Judicial Review

The acts of all administrative bodies are subject to judicial review, but to a differing extent. Article 46 of the Constitution rules that all administrative decisions and actions can be challenged before court if the law sets down no other method of appeal.

A problem of special interest in the administrative process of the RF is the burden of proof (*onus probandi*) in cases of adjudication of conflicts of administrative law. There is a judicial doctrine according to which the burden of proof lies with the administration: it must prove that the requirements it imposes on citizens are grounded and justifiable.[15]

In accordance with Article 3 of the Law "On the Appeal before Court of Administrative Action or Decisions Violating Citizens' Rights and Liberties," every administrative act is subject to judicial review except those acts that fall under the jurisdiction of the Constitutional Court of the RF or acts for which the legislation prescribes another form of judicial appeal.

5. OMBUDSMAN AND OTHER FORMS OF CONTROL OVER THE ADMINISTRATION

The legal status of the ombudsman in the RF is determined by the Law on the Commissioner on Human Rights of the RF.[16]

The Code of Administrative Offences of the RSFSR contains a list of approximately 40 inspectorates that have the prerogative to give binding orders both to citizens and officials. Among others, these bodies include the State Automobile

Inspectorate and the State Nuclear Energy Supervising Agency (Gosatomenergonadzor).

The State Prosecutions Office (Prokuratura) exercises "general supervision" for the lawfulness (legality) of administrative action. At present, the prosecutors are especially active in relation to arbitration cases, where they defend the interests of the state, the companies, and physical persons.

6. THE ROLE OF THE COMMITTEES IN PARLIAMENT IN THE CONTROL OVER THE ADMINISTRATION

The State Duma and the Federal Council have a number of bodies designed essentially to draft documents and papers in the different spheres of legislative activity which come into contact with the organs of the executive power. However, they have no prerogatives to control the administration.

II. DEVELOPMENTS IN ADMINISTRATIVE LAW IN THE RUSSIAN FEDERATION DURING 1996-1997

INTRODUCTION

The major theoretical issue concerning developments in administrative law during the last year was the problem of its subject matter. Nowadays, the majority of lawyers in Russia consider administrative law to be a department of law regulating the activity of the executive branch.[17] However, in the document prepared by the central state-law directorate (Upravlenie) of the President of the RF "General Classification of the Legislative Departments",[18] administrative law does not figure at all.

The courts in the country are also affected by this ambiguity concerning the status of administrative law. Thus, in the Ordinance[19] of the Presidium of the Supreme Court of the RF on the conflict over jurisdiction, the Court held that the subjects of the Russian Federation (member states, regions, etc.) have no right to grant licences, since the list of the activities which require authorisation and licensing is determined in the Civil Code of the RF and is therefore the concern of civil law. On the other hand, the Constitutional Court, when examining the constitutionality of the activity of the tax police,[20] drew a sharp distinction between public and civil law.

In 1996 the major development affecting the entire Russian administration was the re-election of President Yeltsin to the office of head of state: the election was held in two rounds, and 108 million enfranchised citizens had to choose among 11 candidates. In addition to the presidential election, in 1996 most of the subjects of the RF elected their heads of administration (governors).

The major contradiction of the current period in Russia is the collision between the socialist system of law and the introduction of elements from other legal systems.[21] The lack of consistency in the development of the country is also reflected in developments in legal theory: concepts such as a legal system based on the rule of law, or division between public and civil law, have not yet received a clear definition.

A. THE CONSTITUTION

The Constitution entrenched a very rigorous amendment mechanism and therefore there have been no constitutional amendments to date. The only instance of change in the constitutional text concerned an interpretation of the Constitutional Court of the Russian Federation of November 2, 1995.[22] In connection with the change of the name of the Ingushskaya Republic and the Republic of Severnaya Osetiya, which was approved by the subjects of the RF, the question was raised as to who was authorised to incorporate the new names into the text of the Constitution, since the basic law was silent on this issue. The ordinance of the Constitutional Court prescribed that the President should incorporate such changes into the text of the Constitution.[23]

B. FEDERAL LEGISLATION, PRESIDENTIAL AND GOVERNMENTAL DECREES

1. PROCEDURAL ACTS

1.1 Acts on the reform of the judicial system

In organisational terms, the courts in the RF were subordinated to the Ministry of Justice, i.e. the executive branch. The new conception for reform in the legal system prescribes that the Ministry of Justice should essentially enforce the decisions of the courts, rather than take care of the organisation of the judicial system. This conception was introduced by a number of normative acts of the President and the Federal Government. Among those, the most important are the Decree of the President of the RF of May 2, 1996 and the Ordinance of the Government of October 7, 1996.[24]

The Federal Law "On the Judicial System of the Russian Federation"[25] introduced a new feature to the judicial system of the RF: two new bodies, the All-Russian Congress of the Judges and the Supreme Qualification Collegium of the Judges, were established. Along with those two bodies, the Law established the Judicial Department at the Supreme Court of the RF, which is responsible for the organisation of the judicial system and the community of the judges. All these bodies are designed to accommodate the new concept of independence of the judicial branch and the self-administration of the legal profession and judges in particular.

Aside from the above legislation, one of the major acts regulating the procedures of judicial review of the administrative acts is the Ordinance[26] of the Plenum of the Supreme Court of the RF of April 14, 1988: it was amended in 1993 and 1996.

1.2 Acts on the organisation of the administrative organs and agencies

The structure of the federal organs of the executive power, which was regulated by Presidential Decree No. 1177 of August 14, 1996, incorporates the Government of the RF and the federal organs of executive power.

In connection with the local government, a new feature was introduced by Presidential Decree No. 531 of August 14, 1996,[27] which set out the basic structure of the Council of Local Government of the RF. The President himself headed the Council.

1.3 Delegation of power

The most significant instance of delegation of power to the administration occurred in 1991, when the deputies in the Congress of the People's Deputies of RSFSR passed an ordinance "On the Legal Guarantees of the Economic Reform".[28] This ordinance granted President Yeltsin exceptional prerogatives to carry out reforms, including power to issue normative acts with the force of law in the sphere of banking and finance. When, after a year, the Supreme Soviet asked the President to give an account of the exercise of these extensive prerogatives, Yeltsin refused to appear before the representative body. The conflict was resolved by the dramatic events of 1993, which ended with the dissolution of the Supreme Soviet.

At present, many scholars believe that "the Russian legal doctrine reveals a negative attitude towards (delegation of power from the representative bodies to the administration) and is based on a strict interpretation of the principle of separation of powers. Under this principle legislation is an exclusive prerogative of the representative bodies."[29]

2. SUBSTANTIVE ACTS

2.1 The management of economy

2.1.1 PRIVATISATION

On April 1, 1996, the Government adopted an ordinance on the Procedures for Realisation of Projects of Privatisation of Federal Property.[30] In addition, procedures for keeping records of the privatisation deals were elaborated by the departments of Russian State Property (Goskomimushtestvo Rossii)[31] and the Russian Archives (Posarhiv).[32]

Difficulties in the privatisation process generally arise from the fact that most of the enterprises undergoing privatisation have subdivisions designed to provide social welfare services or facilities for cultural activities (known as the "soc-cul-facilites")[33] to their employees. Private entrepreneurs are usually not interested in these particular subdivisions of the enterprises. The difficulties arising from this conflict are illustrated by the following case.

The joint-stock company "Gnezdovo", which produces construction materials, filed an action with the court of arbitration of the Smolensk Oblast against the local administration and the Government of the RF, demanding compensation from them for the losses the corporation incurred in maintaining the housing facilities and the soc-cul-facilities of the Gnezdovo residential area in the city of Smolensk.[34] The case was dismissed by all judicial instances, since the action of the enterprise requires appropriation of compensation funds from the national budget, which is not within the jurisdiction of the judiciary. Moreover, the Presidium of the Supreme Court of Arbitration of the RF observed that, according to the present legislation, there is no adequate opportunity for judicial defence of the financial interests of the entrepreneurs. Further, according to the Presidium, the Code of Administrative Offences does not include under the jurisdiction of the courts of arbitration the conflicts concerning budget appropriations.

2.1.2 PROPERTY

In 1996 the Government took measures to revalue the assets of the enterprises and organisations in order to increase the basis on which property tax is calculated. This was done by Governmental Ordinance No. 1142 of December 7, 1996.

As regards the ownership of agricultural lands, the agency responsible, Roskozem, passed a normative act regulating the contracts for the rent (lease) of agricultural lands.[35] The contracts should be concluded for a period of at least three years and must be registered with the Committee on Agricultural Resources and Land Development. This committee passed a normative Regulation on the Form of State Registration of the Rights to Real Estate Property[36]: according to the regulation, the register (cadastre) number of the plot of land, any buildings or other facilities on it, its exact location, its surface in square measurement units, the owner, and the servitutes (rights of persons other than the owner which burden a given property) imposed on the property have to be recorded.

2.2 Environment

In the sphere of environmental protection, the Law "On State Regulation of Gene Engineering"[37] was passed in 1996. The law established four categories of risk concerning a potentially dangerous impact of gene engineering on human health. For the categories of activities involving a higher degree of risk (III and IV), the law prescribed a licensing procedure.

The Government of the RF also adopted a number of normative acts designed to enhance protection of the environment. The regulation on the Procedures of State Environmental Impact Assessment[38] was among the most important of these acts. Further, the Government adopted an ordinance prescribing some measures for the protection of forests from fire and parasites.[39]

1997 brought a symptomatic change in the status of the officials of the State Committee of the RF on Environmental Protection: officials from the central office and the local organs of the committee were allowed to carry firearms and special protective devices.[40] This change was a result of the growing criminalisation of society and the increasing number of crimes in the sphere of environmental protection.

The courts also had to rule on environmental matters on several occasions during 1996 and the first months of 1997. A case of special interest occurred before the Supreme Court of the Russian Federation. A group of citizens challenged the Presidential Decree "On the Restructuring and Conversion of the Nuclear Industry in the Town of Zheleznogorsk in the Krasnoyarsk Area".[41] The citizens claimed that the import of used nuclear fuel from foreign nuclear power stations in the Zheleznogorsk enterprise, authorised by the presidential decree, was unlawful since the plant did not have the necessary equipment for processing and recycling this fuel. The necessary installations were still under construction when the presidential decree was passed. In this case, the claimants held, the import would constitute a long-term disposal of radioactive materials, which is prohibited by the law and violates the rights of citizens to a healthy environment. The Civil Law Collegium of the Supreme Court declared the presidential decree null and void in the part related to the authorisation of the imports in question.

2.3 Finance

In 1996 a number of normative acts of extreme importance for the financial system of the country were passed: the Law "On the Budget Classification of the RF";[42] the Law "On Accountancy";[43] the Law "On the Stock Market";[44] and the Law "On the Procedures of the Establishment of the Value of the Units Used in the Calculation of the Debts of the RF".[45] The last Law established the "necessary amount of basic products per citizen for a year." These include basic foods (for instance, 26.6 kilogrammes of meat) and basic social services. In addition, the law established the unit "debt ruble" (DOR) as a unit for the calculation of the Russian debt.

The Federal Government of the RF also introduced a number of normative acts affecting the financial system. One of the most important decisions was the prohibition on purchasing gold bars. In accordance with Ordinance No. 1527[46] of 1996, the system of issuing state guaranteed obligations giving the owners the right to receive gold bars was abolished. The reason given for doing so was the "state of the financial market and the inappropriateness of the emission of such obligations".

The President of the RF adopted an act listing the most urgent measures which the Government of the RF recommends to the Federal Assembly.[47] This list in practice includes the basic principles of the policies of the RF. Paragraph 11 of the act prescribes that the local system of bodies of the federal treasury (exchequer) should be fully accomplished by the end of 1997. In addition, the federal budget should be administered solely by the bodies of the federal treasury and not by authorised banks as it is at present. This transition has to be accomplished during 1998, according to this act.

2.4 Management of Natural Resources

The Federal Supervisory Body on Industry (Gornoi i Promishlenoi Nadzor) adopted an instruction (No. 35) in 1996 on the procedures for authorising the exploration and exploitation of oil and gas resources in mountainous areas.[48]

The CAO of the RSFSR was amended to accommodate new sanctions in cases of violation of the rules concerning the exploitation of the resources in the national shelf waters. Similar amendments were also introduced in the Penal Code.

2.5 Transport

1996 brought changes in the regulation of civil aviation. The Government adopted an ordinance[49] prescribing new procedures for licensing pilots. Further, the Ministry of Internal Affairs adopted an order[50] with which it set out the rules for registration of vehicles with the State Automobile Inspectorate.

2.6 Mass Communication Media

By the Presidential Decree "On the Measures for Strengthening the Discipline in the System of State Bodies," the heads of the bodies of the executive branch were obliged to consider within three days any publication in the mass media concerning violations of law by their subordinates. However, until February 1997 not a single head of an administrative body had been prosecuted for non-compliance with the Presidential Decree. This indicates that enforcement of the Decree is questionable, since it is commonly acknowledged that there are numerous violations of it.

2.7 Legislation on education and science

In 1996 the process of accreditation of educational institutions was normatively regulated by the adoption of the Ministry of Education of Order No. 27.[51] Because of the short deadlines for the implementation of the order, the Ministry decided to recognise the accreditation of all existing and accredited state and municipal educational establishments in the system of the Ministry of Education.

In December 1995, the State Committee on Higher Education of the RF adopted "Procedures for the Admission of Students in the Higher Education Establishments"[52] which began to be implemented in 1996. In addition, the Committee adopted procedures for the admission of foreign students to Russian educational establishments.[53] There are special funds appropriated from the federal budgets for scholarships granted to foreign students participating in the programs of the International Co-operation Directorate of the Committee on Higher Education (Goskomvuz).

The Law "On Science and Technological Policy"[54] adopted in 1996 was a general law of enormous importance because it was designed to regulate comprehensively the complex problems of science and technology in Russia. The chairman of the Governmental Commission on Science and Technology Policy approved two policy documents setting out basic policy priorities in the development of science and technology in the country.[55] However, these documents do not concern the humanities.

2.8 Health care

Last year the Ministry of Health Care of the RF passed a normative act concerning obligatory medical check-ups of prospective employees and periodical medical examinations of employees.[56] It also adopted an instruction[57] on the implementation of the list of professional illnesses, approved by the Agency of the Ministry of Health Care responsible for the supervision of the medical industry (Minzdravmedprom).[58] The list included categories of illnesses caused exclusively or predominantly by the impact of hazardous and dangerous substances and industrial factors.

One of the most important governmental regulations passed by the Government in 1996 was Ordinance No. 567 "On the Approval of a List of Social Factors Justifying Artificial Interruption of Pregnancy." The regulation is relatively liberal and recognises social hardship as a ground for abortion: for instance, if one of the partners is unemployed, abortion is automatically authorised.

2.9 Protection of the cultural heritage

The Law "On the National-Cultural Autonomy,"[59] passed in 1996, was one of the major legislative acts of the Federal Assembly. The law grants cultural autonomy to ethnic and national minorities and provides for the establishment of self-governing bodies responsible for the administration of the cultural autonomy. In accordance with this law, the Jewish community has already carried out the first congress of the Jewish National-Cultural Autonomy of the RF (ENKA RF).[60]

The President of the Federation continued to add to the list of cultural monuments enjoying special protection from the state. However, taking into account the poor tax collection during the year, the President adopted Decree No. 452[61] excluding 1060 monuments from those of federal and local importance. Most of these monuments were tributes to Vladimir Lenin; there were also a number of tombs, churches, and museums.

2.10 The Army, the Police, the National Security

A number of important laws related to the system of national defence were passed during 1996. First, the Federal Assembly passed the Law "On Defence"[62] and the Law "On Weapons".[63] Among other things, these laws established procedures for authorising citizens to carry firearms. The Assembly also passed the Law "On Mobilisation Preparation in the Russian Federation".[64] Along with this new legislation, the Parliament amended the Law "On Military Service and Conscription".

In 1996, the RF established its own bodies for co-operation with Interpol. The President passed Decree No. 1113,[65] which set up a National Central Bureau of Interpol as a division of the Ministry of Internal Affairs.

2.11 Meetings, demonstrations, and industrial action

The major laws[66] regulating the right to freedom of assembly were passed in 1995: they amended many provisions of the CAO, the Criminal Code, and the Law "On the Status of the Capital of the RF". All this legislation introduced sanctions for violations of the regulations concerning the freedom of assembly. There was no new legislation on this matter in 1996.

The courts had to deal with conflicts over the right to industrial action on several occasions in 1996. For instance, the industrial action committee of the power station in Arhangelsk challenged a provision of an administrative normative act determining the minimal necessary activity that cannot be interrupted even in cases of industrial action, particularly strikes. The committee claimed that the formulation of the provisions of the administrative act contradicts the Law "On the Settlement of Collective Labour Conflicts"[67]and restricts the rights of the workers' collective of the power station. The judges of the Arhangelsk district court denied the action of the committee. In their opinion, the action was inadmissible since the federal law prescribed that only the establishment of the unlawfulness of industrial action was to be decided judicially. The Civil Law Collegium of the Supreme Court of the RF reversed this decision.[68] The Supreme Court held that every decision of the executive power or local government for which the law does not provide a concrete procedure of appeal can nevertheless be appealed before court. The judges based their judgement on Article 46 of the Constitution.

2.12 Citizenship

The President adopted a Decree "On the Basic Identification Documents of the Citizens of the RF"[69] in December 1996. The Decree regulated the identification that Russian citizens are obliged to carry on trips abroad. Four types of identification were set out by the Act: passport, diplomatic passport, official's passport, and sailor's passport.

In addition, the Law "On Travelling Abroad and Returning to the RF"[70] was passed by the Federal Assembly. The Law entrenched the basic right of the citizens to travel abroad and to return to the RF.

The status of citizens was affected by a number of normative acts granting to particular groups of the population the right to carry firearms for the purposes of self-defence. The Government of the RF adopted an order[71] that set out a procedure for registering officials' and citizens' firearms and ammunition.

2.13 The status of foreigners

In general, the status of foreigners is revealed most clearly in the "Overview of the Practice of the Courts of Arbitration on Cases Involving Foreign Persons."[72] This is a comprehensive source of information and exhausts all the aspects of the legal status of foreigners including questions of administrative law.

The Government of the RF issued an order[73] by which funds from the federal budget were appropriated for the operation of the Russian Centre for Support of Foreign Investment at the Ministry of Economy. Up until January 1, 1997, 9000 branches and subsidiaries of foreign companies were recorded in the tax registers of the RF: more than 3000 of them were registered in 1996.[74] At present, the RF implements 26 bilateral agreements and two multilateral agreements for avoiding double taxation in relation to income and property.

C. REGULATION (GENERAL OVERVIEW)

1. NORMATIVE ACTS OF THE HEAD OF STATE

In 1996 the President of the RF adopted 1792 decrees and 600 orders (*razporyazheniya*); in 1995 their numbers were respectively 1344 and 560. The President has the right to make official addresses to the Federal Assembly and to the Russian citizens on the radio. The President exercises control over whether something is lawful by means of his powers of veto over laws passed by the Federal Assembly.

2. NORMATIVE ACTS OF THE GOVERNMENT AND THE DEPARTMENTS

In 1996, the Government adopted 1592 ordinances and 1955 orders (*razporyazheniya*); in 1995 there were 1309 ordinances and 1390 orders. The ministries and the departments of the RF issue commands (*prikaz*), instructions, orders, and letters of instruction; the Central Bank adopts telegrams. All of these acts have a normative character. In order to enter into force these acts have to be published. However, the "Bulletin of Normative Acts of the Federal Organs of the Executive Power" contains only 220 such acts for 1996. Despite the provisions of the Constitution and the President's decree, some acts are expressly exempted from official publication although they still have normative force and affect the rights, freedoms, and duties of the citizens.

The Ministry of Justice of the RF exercises control over the correctness of published acts. The following case is revealing of the practice in this sphere: The Federal Law "On the Amendment and Supplementation to Paragraph 2 of Article 855 of the Civil Code of the RF" established the order for recovering and compensating for citizens' money held in accounts in banks undergoing bankruptcy. However, in practice, the Ministry of Finance, the Central Bank, and the Federal Tax Office ignored the provisions of the law and sent a letter[75] to that effect to the Ministry of Justice. The Ministry of Justice held that the decision of the Ministry of Finance and the other two bodies was lawful and in compliance with the new amendments. In response to this the State Duma adopted an ordinance[76] stating that the decision of the Ministry of Finance was a "gross violation of the Civil Code of the RF". The Duma made a proposal to Prime Minister Chernomyrdin to "carry out official investigation...of the institutions that have issued the letter in question". However, no measures have been taken to date in order to remedy the situation.

3. INFORMAL RULE-MAKING BY THE ADMINISTRATION

Not all departments are willing to subject their normative acts to the legal scrutiny of the Ministry of Justice. As a result, some departments adopt normative acts that have not been approved by the Ministry of Justice; moreover, sometimes acts that have been expressly denied approval are being adopted.

The existence of informal rules can be illustrated by the case involving the head of the Group on Co-operation of OSCE in Chechnya, T. Guldiman. Guldiman asked the Government of the RF to allow the duty-free import of radio equipment for use in Chechnya. The customs practice of the RF provides a number of examples in which similar exemptions have been granted. The deputy head of the Foreign Ministry asked the State Committee on Customs to exempt the import in a letter of December 12, 1996. In response, the Committee held that there is no legal ground for the asked exemption. However, with respect to the request from the Foreign Ministry, the committee allowed the duty-free import of the equipment. The answer came in a letter dated March 4, 1997: by that time the elections in Chechnya had long been finished and the mission of the Group of Co-operation had been accomplished.

D. JUDICIAL CASES

1. THE SYSTEM OF REPORTING JUDICIAL DECISIONS

The judicial system of the Russian Federation is not based on the principle of stare decisis, and the courts are not bound by precedents. Therefore, the publication of judicial decisions serves more as an educational device to raise the legal culture of the population. Of course, the publication of judicial decisions could serve the purposes of judicial involvement in the political process as well.

Despite the civil law character of the legal system, the Supreme Court of the RF and the Supreme Court of Arbitration of the RF were granted the right to give interpretations and clarifications of cases, which have legal effect (binding character) on the lower courts. This is done for the purposes of consistency and integrity within legal practice.

2. DECISIONS OF THE CONSTITUTIONAL COURT

In 1996, the CC of the RF decided on 21 cases (17 in 1995): each of these cases concerns the operation of the administration, although to a different extent.

On several occasions the Court ruled on the electoral rights of the citizens and the character of the electoral process. For instance, the Court rejected the request of a group of deputies from the Federal Assembly to examine the constitutionality of a number of provisions of the Federal Law "On the Election of Deputies to the

State Duma of the RF".[77] The claimants considered that the Law violates the equality of citizens before the law and their electoral rights and thus violates a series of constitutional provisions (Articles 3, 15, 18, 19, 32, 35, 55, and 94). The Court refused to consider the case on its merits and held that "judicial intervention in the course of the electoral campaign, immediately before the election, can unjustifiably complicate the electoral process, have a negative impact on the opinions of the electorate, and, as a result, influence the outcome of the election. The Constitutional Court would in fact turn into a participant in the political process and the electoral campaign, which is in contradiction with its purpose and principles of operation".

One of the constitutional justices, E. M. Ametistov, disagreed in a dissenting opinion and argued that the decision in this case was based "to a great extent on arguments of political appropriateness, rather than on legal criteria of the admissibility of the claim established by the Constitution of the RF and the Law on the Constitutional Court".[78]

3. THE SUPREME COURT AND THE SUPREME COURT OF ARBITRATION

The functions of a supreme administrative court in Russia are carried out by the Supreme Court of the RF and the Supreme Court of Arbitration of the RF in accordance with the division of power between them. In 1996, 82 courts of arbitration and 10 federal district courts of arbitration operated in Russia.[79]

In the same year, the Supreme Court of Arbitration published some statistics related to its jurisprudence and the jurisprudence of the courts of arbitration in general.[80] The number of cases on which the courts of arbitration have decided increased in 1996 in comparison to 1995: 237,291 (1995) and 290,094 (1996). In all, 23,629 cases, or 10 per cent of the total caseload in 1995, concerned issues of administrative law. In 1996 this percentage increased to 15 per cent or 44,272 cases.

The Supreme Court of the RF considered a very important case of administrative law in 1995. On the basis of this case the Civil Law Collegium of the Supreme Court derived the principle that not only administrative acts but also denials to issue an administrative act by an executive body, which affect citizens' rights and interests, are subject to judicial review under the general clause of Article 46 of the Constitution.[81]

The case was initiated by a citizen–a Mr. Shupanko–who filed an action with the St. Petersburg city court. He asked the court to order the municipal government to pay him damages, because he was not able to make use of his right to reduced transport tickets as a veteran of the Second World War. The problem was that the municipal government had not passed the necessary regulations to implement the provisions of the Law on Veterans that granted the disputed transport reductions. The court in St. Petersburg ruled that the case was inadmissible because there was no administrative act to be judicially challenged.

The Civil Law Collegium of the Supreme Court repealed this decision. It held that the municipal government's lack of action could also be challenged when it affects the legal rights of the citizens. Since the Constitution (Article 46) prescribes that not only acts but also lack of action can be subject to judicial review, Mr. Shupanko was unlawfully denied the right to appeal.

The Supreme Court of Arbitration also ruled on a number of issues of general importance for administrative law. In one of its decisions[82] the Court implemented Article 46 of the Constitution, according to which all administrative decisions can be appealed before a court unless a different order of appeal is prescribed by the law. The Court held a complaint by the Foreign Trade Bank of the Russian Federation against a decision of the state criminal investigation bodies on the arrest of an official accused of abuse of powers in the stock market to be inadmissible. It ruled that this issue be regulated by the criminal procedural laws of the country, which exclude administrative review by a court of arbitration.

4. DECISIONS OF ADMINISTRATIVE QUASI-JUDICIAL BODIES

In accordance with Ordinance No. 302[83] of the Government of the RF, the Interdepartmental Commission, which considers complaints of citizens in connection with restrictions on the right to leave the country, adopts decisions binding on all administrative bodies. The decisions of the Commission are to be implemented within a month after their adoption unless a different time is specified by the decision. The decisions are taken in an open voting procedure: a decision is adopted if more than half of the members of this body vote in the affirmative. A protocol of every sitting is to be kept: the chairman and the secretary of the commission have to sign the protocol at the end of the sitting.

A typical body of administrative jurisdiction is the Judicial Chamber of Information Disputes at the Presidential Institution of the RF.[84] The Chamber was designed to serve a variety of purposes, including adjudication of conflicts over the allocation of air time for the various political parties and factions in the Federal Assembly, and elaboration of instructions for the correction of errors affecting the public interest in mass media coverage.

The Chamber enjoys significant autonomy in its operation: it has the discretion to adopt its own standing orders. The initiation of proceedings is very democratic: the Chamber can consider cases both on complaints of interested persons and on its own initiative. The state organs and the officials to whom the decisions of the Chamber are addressed must report within two weeks of receipt about its implementation. The Chamber can send out material about alleged violations of rights and freedoms in the sphere of mass communication. The officials have to carry out their own investigation and report the results to the Chamber within a month after the receipt of the material.

E. THE WORKINGS OF THE OMBUDSMAN, THE ACCOUNT CHAMBER, STATE PROSECUTORS, INSPECTORATES

There are no published data on the workings of the ombudsman under the new legislative arrangement.

The status of the Accounts Chamber is of special interest. The Chamber lacks any judicial prerogatives characteristic of similar bodies in the Western states. It enjoys the status of a typical administrative body with controlling functions.

To a certain extent, the state prosecutors exercise control for legality over the normative acts of the administration in the framework of the procedure called "general overview for lawfulness". The prosecutors are sufficiently active in the courts of arbitration as well. Out of the 593 cases published in the Gazette of the Supreme Court of Arbitration in 1996, 50 cases have been initiated and supported by state prosecutors (or around 8 per cent).

The role of the prosecutors as defenders of the public interest is demonstrated by a case of the Presidium of the Supreme Court of Arbitration of the RF considered and decided on June 25, 1996.[85] The state prosecutor of the Yamalo-Nentzkii autonomous area asked the Supreme Court of Arbitration of the Udmurtskaya Republic to award damages of 200 billion rubles in favour of the autonomous area against the Udmurtgeologiya geological corporation. The claim was that the corporation had unlawfully appropriated agricultural lands on the territory of the autonomous area. However, the Supreme Court of Arbitration of the Udmurtskaya Republic held that the application was inadmissible since according to Article 41 of the Arbitration Procedural Code of the RF a state prosecutor from a given subject of the RF has no standing in a court of arbitration in another member state of the RF. In the opinion of the judges, only the prosecutor of the Udmurtskaya Republic or some of his deputies could address the Court.[86]

The Presidium of the Supreme Court of Arbitration of the RF repealed this decision, finding it in contradiction with Article 65 of the Constitution and Article 41 of the Arbitration Procedural Code. The judges held that all state prosecutors have equal standing in the courts of arbitration.

Article 194 of the Code of Administrative Offences of the RF authorises five types of state bodies to consider cases of administrative offences and violations: administrative commissions; local administration; commissions on cases involving juvenile offenders, people's (ordinary) courts; and inspectorates (around 40 in number).

In 1996, litigation in the Supreme Court of Arbitration predominantly concerned disputes over the legality of individual administrative acts and administrative sanctions issued to or imposed on the citizens and the organisations by the inspectorates. There were 21 cases involving a challenge of individual administrative acts (9 per cent of the total number of administrative law disputes); 42 cases, or 8 per cent, concerned appeals against imposed administrative sanctions.

F. CORRUPTION

Among the effective devices designed to curb corruption in Russia two are noteworthy: the rules on conflict of interest of official positions and the declaration of the income of the officials. Paragraph 2 of Article 11 of the Federal Law "On the Basis of the Public Administration of the RF"[87] prohibited the members of the public administration from becoming members of the representative legislative bodies of the subjects of the RF or of the local government. Measures to introduce a declaration of officials' incomes were introduced only in 1997 by Presidential Decree No. 484.[88] The decree sets out a list of officials in the state administration and the local government whose incomes are to be declared.

ANNEX 1

List of the Federal Organs of the Executive Power

The following classification was introduced by Presidential Decree No. 1177 "On the Structure of the Federal Organs of the Executive Power", adopted on August 14, 1996.

1. FEDERAL MINISTRIES

Ministry of Nuclear Power
Ministry of International Economic Relations and Commerce
Ministry of Internal Affairs*
Ministry of Civil Defence, Emergencies, and Elimination of the Results of Natural Calamities
Ministry of Nationalities and Federal Relationships
Ministry of Health Care
Foreign Ministry*
Ministry of Culture
Ministry of General and Professional Education
Ministry of Defence Industry
Ministry of Defence*
Ministry of Natural Resources
Ministry of Industry
Ministry of Roads
Ministry of Communication
Ministry of Agriculture and Food Supply
Ministry of Co-operation with the CIS Countries
Ministry of Construction

Ministry of Fuels and Energy
Ministry of Transport
Ministry of Labour and Social Development
Ministry of Finance
Ministry of Economy
Ministry of Justice
Ministry of Science and Technology

2. OTHER FEDERAL ORGANS OF THE EXECUTIVE BRANCH

State Committee on Attestation (of educational establishments and holders of academic degrees)
State Committee on the Anti-Monopoly Policy and the Support for New Economic Structures
Committee on the Development of Northern Regions
State Committee on the State Reserve
State Committee on Youth
State Committee on Forests, Paper- and Wood-Processing Industry
State Committee on Land Resources and Land Development
State Committee on Cinematography
State Committee on Protection of the Environment
State Committee on the Press
State Committee on the Support for and the Development of Small Businesses
State Committee on Fishing
State Committee on Standardisation, Metrology, and Certification
State Committee on Statistics
Sate Committee on Customs
State Committee on the Management of State Property
State Committee on Physical Culture and Tourism
Federal Energy Commission
Federal Commission on the Stock Market*
Federal Commission on Real Estate Property and Its Evaluation
Federal Aviation Service
Federal Archives Service*
Federal Roads Service
Federal Service on Migration
Federal Service on Taxes*
Federal Service on Borders*
Federal Security Service*
Service of Foreign Intelligence*
Federal Service of Geodetics and Cartography
Federal Service of Rail-Transport Troops*
Federal Service of Forests Management

Federal Service of Tax Police
Federal State Guard Service*
Federal Service of Hydrometeorology and Monitoring of the Environment
Federal Service of the State Monopoly on Alcoholic Drinks
Federal Service on the Regulation of Natural Monopolies
Federal Service on Radio and Television*
Federal Service on Hard Currency and Export Control
Russian Agency on Patents and Trademarks
Russian Space Agency
Federal Agency on Governmental Relations and Information*
Federal Control over Industry in Mountain Areas
Federal Control over Nuclear and Radiation Safety*
Directorate on Presidential Affairs

* Federal organs of the executive power subordinated directly to the President

ANNEX 2

List of the Independent Subdivisions of the Administration of the President of the RF

Administrative-Managerial Directorate at the Presidential Administration
Apparatus of the Security Council of the RF
Apparatus of the Council on Foreign Policy
Apparatus of the Defence Council
Apparatus of the Presidential Aides
Archives of the President
Library of the Presidential Administration
Main Public Law Directorate
Main Control Directorate
Main Directorate of the Cossack Troops
State Heraldic Department
Presidential Office
Organisation Directorate of the Presidential Administration
Database Division
Administrative Division Servicing the Commission on the Problems of Citizenship
Administrative Division Servicing the Commission on State Awards in Literature and Art
Administrative Division Servicing the Commission on Drafting of Treaties between the Federal Organs and the Subjects of the Federation
Administrative Division Servicing the Commission on Human Rights

Administrative Division Servicing the Commission on Rehabilitation of the Victims of Political Repression
Administrative Division Servicing the Council on Local Government
Division on State Secrets
Apparatus of the Representative of the President in the State Duma
Apparatus of the Representative of the President in the Constitutional Court
Apparatus of the Representative of the President in the Federal Council
Apparatus of the Judicial Chamber on Information Disputes
Secretariat of the Head of the Presidential Administration
Territorial Directorate
Directorate on Pardoning
Directorate on Case Processing
Recruitment Directorate
Directorate on Recruitment Policy
Directorate on the Question of Co-operation with Political Parties, Social Alliances, Factions, and Deputies from the State Duma and the Federal Assembly
Directorate on Co-ordination of the Activity of the Representatives of the President in the Subjects of the Federation
Directorate on Public Addresses
Directorate on Public Relations
Directorate of Protocol
Centre of Presidential Programmes

ANNEX 3

The Structure of the Apparatus of the Government of the RF

The structure of the Governmental Apparatus at present is determined by Order No. 484 - r of April 8, 1997 (*Rossiiskaya Gazeta*, April 22, 1997, p. 4).

Leadership of the Government Apparatus
Secretariat of the Chairman of the Government of the RF
Secretariat of the First Deputies of the Chairman of the Government
Secretariat of the Deputies of the Chairman of the Government
Secretariat of the Head of the Apparatus of the Government of the RF
Economic Department
Finance Department
Social Development Department
Department on Property and Regulation of Natural Monopolies
Department of Science, Education, and High Technology
International Co-operation Department
Department on the Questions of CIS

Administrative Department
Department of Co-operation with the Subjects of the RF and the Relations with the Federal Council
Department of Co-operation with the State Duma and Public Organisations
Department of State Positions and Staff
Department on the Reform in Housing, Construction, and Industry
Department on the Reform in the Agro-industrial Complex and the Protection of the Environment
Department of Industrial Reform and Conversion
Department on Culture and Information
Directorate on Case Processing
Legal Department
Governmental Archives
Directorate on Organisational and Social Security
Directorate of the Chief Military Expert
Directorate of Protocol
Secretariat of the Expert Council
Secretariat of the Plenipotentiary of the Government in the Chechen Republic
Secretariat of the Plenipotentiary of the Government in the Republic of Severnaya Osetiya-Alaniya and the Republic of Ingushetiya

The Chapter has been prepared on the basis of information contributed by Alexey Afanasyevich Demin

NOTES

1 *Svod Zakonov SSSR*, M., Izvestiya, v. 1, 1980, pp. 373–376. The decree is published as amended on March 4, 1980.

2 No. 4866-1, *Vedomosti Suezda Narodnyih Deputatov Rosiiskoi Federatsii i Verhovnogo Soveta RF*, 1993, No. 19, p. 685.

3 Kodeks RSFSR ob administrativnyh pravonarusheniyah, Vedomosti Verhovnogo Soveta RSFSR, 1984, N. 27.

4 Ukaz Presidenta RF N. 1176, August 14, 1996, "Ob systeme federalnyh organov ispolnitelnoi vlasti".

5 See Alehin A. P., Karmolitskiy A. A., Kozlov U. M. *Administrativnoe Pravo RF, (Administrative Law of the RF)*, Moscow, Zertzalo, Teis, 1996, p. 136.

6 O Sovete Ministrov - Pravitelstve RF, December 22, 1992, N. 4174 -1.

7 See Gosudarstvennaya Duma: Stenogramma zasedanii, 1996, No. 43, p. 3

8 O predostavlenii Ministerstvom finansov RF poruchitelstv po kreditam kommercheskih bankov, privlekaemym Pensionnym fondom RF, SZ RF, 1997, No. 1, st. 162.

9 Decree No. 763, *Rossiiskaya Gazeta*, May 28, 1996, pp. 1–3.

10 Law No. 1 - FKZ, SZ RF, 1997, No. 1, p. 1.

11 Gazette of the Supreme Court of Arbitration of the RF, 1997, No. 4, pp. 131–135.

12 *Bulletin of the Supreme Court of the RF*, 1996, No. 9, pp. 1–10.

13 *Bulletin of Normative Acts of the Federal Organs of the Executive Power*, 1996, No. 4, pp. 46–59.

[14] *Bulletin of Normative Acts of the Federal Organs of the Executive Power*, 1996, No. 7, pp. 18–28.

[15] This judicial doctrine is most explicitly demonstrated in the determinations of the Judicial Collegium on Civil Law at the Supreme Court of the RF. See especially the decision of the Court quashing the verdict of the Petropavlovsk-Kamtchatka City Court regarding the Russian fleet in the bases of Severokurilsk (*Bulletin of the Supreme Court of the RF*, 1996, No. 5, pp. 4–5.

[16] Law No. 1 -FKZ, SZ RF, 1997, No. 9, p. 1011.

[17] See Alehin A. P., Karmolitskii A. A., Kozlov J. M. *op. cit.* p. 31.

[18] Obshteotraslevoi klassifikator otraslei zakonodatelstva, SZ RF, 1997, No. 1, p. 119.

[19] *Bulletin of the Supreme Court of the RF*, 1997, No. 5, pp. 1-3.

[20] Vestnik Konstitutsionnogo Suda RF, 1996, No. 5, pp. 22–29

[21] David R. *Osnovnye pravovye systemyi sovremennosti* (Major Contemporary Legal Systems), Moscow, Progress 1988, pp. 150–256.

[22] Postanovlenie No. 15–P, SZ RF, 1995, No. 49, p. 4868.

[23] The new names of the two subjects of the federation are Republic of Ingushetiya and Republic of Severnaya Osetiya–Alaniya. The President incorporated the new names by Decree No. 20 of 1996, SZ RF, 1996, No. 3, p. 152.

[24] Decree No. 642 and Ordinance No. 1117.

[25] Law No. 1 - FKZ, SZ RF, 1997, No. 1, p. 1.

[26] "O nekotoryh voprosah rassmotreniya sudami v porydke sudoproizvodstva zhalob na postanovleniya po delam ob administrativnyh pravonarusheniyah", *Sbornik Postanovlenii Plenumov Verhovnyh Sudov SSSR i RSFSR po grazhdanskim delam* - M.: Spark, 1996, pp. 269–275.

[27] *Rossiiskaya Gazeta*, June 10, 1997, p. 4.

[28] *Vedomosti Suezda narodnyh deputatov RSFSR I Verhovnogo soveta RSFSR*, 1991, No. 44.

[29] Troitzkii V. S., Morozov L. A., "Delegated Legislation", *Gosudarstvo I Pravo*, 1997, No. 4, p. 91. These authors suggest that delegation of legislative powers should be introduced in the RF as a legal experiment.

[30] Ordinance No. 363, SZ Rf, 1997, No. 14, p. 1532.

[31] Razporyazhenie No. 1131-r, 1996, *Bulletin of Normative Acts*..., No. 11, 1996, pp. 36–40.

[32] Prikaz No. 54, 1996, *Bulletin of Normative Acts*..., No. 11, 1996, pp. 36–40.

[33] The Russian term for such subdivisions is "obiektyi sotzkulbyta".

[34] The big enterprises in Russia used to provide housing, child-care facilities and various other welfare and cultural services to their employees.

[35] *Bulletin of Normative Acts*..., No. 1, 1996, pp. 38–40.

[36] *Bulletin of Normative Acts*..., No. 8, 1996, pp. 28–29.

[37] Law No. 86 - FZ, *Vedomosti Federalnogo Sobraniya RF*, 1996, No. 21, p. 894.

[38] Ordinance No. 698, SZ RF, 1996, No. 40, p. 4648.

[39] Ordinance No. 16, January 12, 1996, SZ RF, 1996, No. 3, p. 190.

[40] Ordinance No. 643 of the Federal Government, May 26, 1997, *Rossiiskaya Gazeta*, June 10, 1997.

[41] Decree of the President of January 25, 1995. The decision of the Court was published in *the Bulletin of the Supreme Court*, No. 5, 1997, p. 23.

[42] Vedomosti Federalnogo Sobraniya, 1996, No. 26, p. 1121.

[43] O buhgalterskom uchete, SZ RF, 1996, No. 17, p. 1918.

[44] SZ RF, 1996, No. 17, p. 1981.

[45] *Vedomosti Federalnogo Sobraniya RF*, 1996, No. 21, p. 895.

[46] SZ RF, 1997, No. 1, p. 172.

[47] Decree No. 278, 1997, "O pervoocherednyh merah po realizatsii Poslaniya Presidenta RF Federalnomy Sobraniyu "Poryadok vo vlasti - poryadok v strane".

[48] *Bulletin of Normative Acts*..., 1996, No. 9, pp. 8–16.

[49] Ordinance No. 996, of August 13, 1996, SZ RF, 1996, No. 37, p. 4289.

[50] *Bulletin of Normative Acts*, 1997, No. 2, p. 20–52.

[51] *Bulletin of Normative Acts of the Ministries and the Departments of the RF*, No. 6, pp. 57–61.

[52] *Ibid.*, 1996, No. 6, p. p. 62–65.

53 *Ibid.*, 1996, No. 5, pp. 26–28.
54 SZ RF, 1996, No. 35, p. 4137.
55 "Prioritetnye napravleniya razvitiya nauki i tehniki", and "Kriticheskie technologii federalnogo urovnya", *Rossiiskaya Gazeta*, August 8, 1996, p. 6.
56 *Bulletin of Normative Acts of the Federal Organs...*, Ordinance No. 405, 1997, No. 2, pp. 52–58.
57 *Ibid.*
58 Order No. 90, March 14, 1996.
59 SZ RF, 1996, No. 25, p. 2965.
60 *Mezhdunarodnaya evreiskaya gazeta*, 1997, No. 11–12, p. 2.
61 "Ob utochnenie sostava obiektov istoricheskogo i kulturnogo naslediya obshterossiiskogo znacheniya", SZ Rf, 1997, No. 19, p. 2219.
62 Law no. 61–F3, SZ RF, 1996, No. 23, p. 2750.
63 SZ RF, 1996, No. 51, p. 5681.
64 SZ RF, 1997, No. 9, p. 1014.
65 SZ RF, 1996, No. 32, p. 3895.
66 Law No. 105 - FZ, 1995, Law No. 106 - FZ, 1995, Law No. 107, 1995 (SZ RF, 1995, No. 30, pp. 2861, 2862, 2863).
67 This law was adopted on October 20, 1995.
68 *Bulletin of the Supreme Court of the RF*, 1997, No. 2, pp. 2–3.
69 SZ RF, 1996, No. 52, p. 5914.
70 SZ RF, 1996, No. 52, p. 5914.
71 *Rossiiskaya Gazeta,* August 24, 1996, p. 9.
72 *Vestnik VAS*, 1997, No. 3, pp. 87–101.
73 Rasporyazhenie, No. 94–r, SZ RF, 1996, No. 6, p. 617.
74 *Finansovaya Gazeta, Regionalny Vypusk*, 1997, No. 20, p. 7.
75 Letter No. 1154 of August 27, 1996.
76 Ordinance No. 683–11 GD, SZ RF, 1996, No. 43, p. 4871.
77 Federal Law of June 21, 1995.
78 *Vestnik Konstitutzionnogo Suda RF*, 1995, No. 6, p. 26–30.
79 *Vestnik VAS*, 1997, No. 4, p. 133.
80 "O rabote arbitrazhnyh sudov v RF v 1995 i 1996", *Vestnik VAS RF*, 1997, No. 4, p. 131–135.
81 *Bulletin of the Supreme Court RF*, 1996, No. 5, pp. 2–3.
82 Ordinance of the Presidium of the Supreme Court of Arbitration of July 9, 1996, No. 1327/96, *Newspaper of the Supreme Court of Arbitration*, 1996, No. 10, pp. 123–124.
83 Ordinance of March 14, 1997.
84 The status of this body is determined by Decree No. 228 of January 31, 1994.
85 Case No. 8661/95, *Vestnik VAS RF*, 1996, No. 100, p. 118.
86 Case No. 2–10/5, October 20, 1996.
87 Federal Law of July 5, 1995.
88 Decree "O predostavlenii litsami, zameshtayushtimi gosudarstvennye dolzhnosti gosudarstvennoi sluzhby i dolzhnosti v organah mestnogo samoupravleniya, svedenii o dohodah i imushtestve", May 15, 1997.

CHAPTER ELEVEN
SERBIA[1]

I. GENERAL DESCRIPTION OF THE ADMINISTRATIVE LAW SYSTEM

1. A BRIEF ACCOUNT OF THE HISTORY OF THE ADMINISTRATIVE LEGAL SYSTEM IN SERBIA

The process of radical institutional reform in the Republic of Serbia started in the beginning of the 1990s with the adoption of a new constitution. Constitution-making in Serbia was an act intertwined with the complex processes of disintegration of Federal Yugoslavia. Of the six constituent republics (Serbia, Croatia, Macedonia, Slovenia, Bosnia and Herzegovina, and Montenegro), Serbia and Montenegro were the only two members that decided to remain in the federation: the rest broke away and established independent states. The new Constitution of Serbia was adopted on September 28, 1990.

2. THE STRUCTURE OF THE EXECUTIVE

2.1 The structure of the major executive bodies

The Constitution introduced a system of separation of powers (Article 9). According to its provisions, the executive power belongs to the Cabinet. The administrative affairs of the state are dealt with by the "ministries and their administrative bodies."[2] The ministries: a) apply the laws and other normative regulations of the Parliament, the Cabinet and the President; b) decide in administrative matters; c) conduct the administrative control; and d) deal with other administrative matters specified by laws.[3]

The highest executive organ, the Cabinet, consists of the Prime Minister, his deputies, ministers, and ministers without portfolio. The members of the Cabinet are elected by the Parliament upon the proposal of the Prime Minister. While performing their ministerial function, the ministers may retain their MP seats (Article 91). The Law on the Cabinet of the Republic of Serbia regulates the duties and responsibilities of the Cabinet as a whole, the Prime Minister, the deputies of the Prime Minister and the ministers without portfolio. Article 5 of the Law on the Cabinet of the Republic of Serbia, in conjunction with Article 5 of the Law on Ministries, regulates the composition of the Cabinet. The Cabinet consists of 23 ministries, which have full departmental duties and powers. With every election of a new Cabinet, the Parliament establishes the number of the deputies of the Prime Minister and the ministers without portfolio. The internal organization and the operational systematization of the Cabinet are set by the Cabinet, such as the scope of jurisdiction of the different ministries, abolition of a government department, and the transfer of functions previously exercised by another department.[4]

The ministerial departments are obliged to coordinate their activities. If one of the departments refuses to co-operate, this fact will be reported to the Cabinet. Along with the ministerial departments, the Constitution (Article 94) provides for the establishment of administrative agencies. The Law on Ministries[5] establishes eight agencies performing special functions in the interest of the Republic.

One of the characteristics of parliamentarism, as established in the Serbian Constitution, is the individual and collective responsibility of the ministers to the Parliament. The Cabinet is accountable to the Parliament. It can initiate a vote of confidence and submit its resignation in the Parliament. The Prime Minister can propose to the Parliament a vote of censure against an individual minister (Article 93 of the Constitution). On the other hand, the Parliament, on the proposal of at least 20 MPs, can pass a vote of no confidence in the Cabinet or individual minister. The representatives of the Cabinet are obliged to respond to interpolations of MPs.[6]

According to the Law on the Cabinet of the Republic of Serbia[7], the Cabinet decides on the general policies of the Republic; implements laws and other regulations passed by the Parliament; passes ordinances, decisions, resolutions and other normative acts; proposes laws and the budget; controls ministries and annuls or invalidates acts of theirs that are not in conformity with the law; gives an opinion to the Parliament about law drafts, proposed by the Cabinet or some other body (in this case, the law has to refer to the policies of the Republic, implementation of laws, the functioning of ministries and administrative agencies or other matter relevant for the functioning of the Cabinet) and suggests the postponement of the adoption of the laws until it gives its opinion on them, for eight days at the most. The Cabinet has the right to start procedures before the Constitutional Court concerning the constitutionality and legality of the regulations and acts of the provinces, the local administrative authorities, corporations of public interest and public services. Until the decision is passed, the Cabinet, upon its own initiative or upon the proposal of the ministry, can stop the implementation of any disputed act. Upon the request of the President, and within the time period set by him, which cannot be less than 48 hours, the Cabinet forms an opinion on certain issues from its competence, and informs the President. The Cabinet also supervises the functioning of ministries, and it sets the general policies of the ministries, with regard to implementation of laws. Directions from the Cabinet cannot refer to acting in administrative matters, in which the ministries enjoy discretion (Article 20).

2.2 Relations between the central and local administration

The local administration consists of municipalities and the city of Belgrade. City municipalities, created on the territory of the city of Belgrade, deal with certain matters of local administration, specified in the Statute of Belgrade.[8] Among the functions of municipalities, through which the local administration is being manifested (Article 22), some are of special administrative importance. These include a) determining the program of development of the services for which the municipality is in charge, urban plan, budget, and the financial balance. (subarticle 1); b) implementing certain laws and other regulations; c) securing the implementation of the municipality's regulations (subarticle 7); d) providing legal aid to the citizens in the exercise of their rights (subarticle 8); e) forming bodies and services necessary for the functioning of the municipality (subarticle 9).

There are several forms of relationship between the central and the local administration. Among these are the central government's control over the constitutionality and legality of municipal regulations and the control over the work of the local administration. Direct control is exercised by the relevant ministry, and the second level of control is conducted by the Cabinet. The control consists of review of legality of regulations, and review of cases of silence of the administration. Along with the control of legality, the central government has the power to look into the compliance of the municipal regulations with the relevant statute, as well as into the compliance of individual legal acts, against which judicial review is not provided, with the municipal regulations. This form of control was introduced for the first time by the Law on Local Administration of 1991.

Each respective ministry has the power over the local administration in the implementation of municipal regulations and other acts related to constitutional rights and freedoms. In the event of a natural catastrophe (e.g. earthquake), when the municipality does not adequately prevent the major damages, the respective ministry acts on behalf of the authority of the local administration and at the same time starts the procedure for establishing the responsibility of the officials of the local administration.

An important prerogative of the central government over the local administration in the field of their competence is the so-called substitution of competence. It derives from two statutory provisions (Article 45): when the authorities of the local administration do not perform their functions longer than three months (subarticle 1); or when, in the process of performing those functions, the constitutional rights or the public interest have been endangered.

According to the Law on Administration of 1992, the ministry cannot assume the functions of the municipal authorities, the city of Belgrade, or the cities or provinces (Article 16, subarticle 1). However, under Article 58, this can happen when 1) the adequate authority of the local administration does not implement its regulations relating to the performance of rights, freedoms and duties of the citizens; 2) when the adequate authority has not acted, after the warning, within a period of one month. Such acquired competence can last only up to three months.

The second type of relationship between the central and local administration is manifested in the cooperation between the ministries and the authorities of the local administration through common initiatives, asking for opinions and submission of suggestions. The ministries can ask for reports, facts and information from the local administration. At the same time they should provide professional help and information about the measures in the implementations of the laws, which are of direct interest to citizens, firms and institutions founded by the municipalities.

2.3 Normative regulations of the President and the Cabinet

The President can adopt normative regulations in two kinds of situations: during a war or an impending state of war, and in a state of emergency.

The first kind of normative regulation is the legal act of the president, enacted in special, extraordinary situations, in which the legislative body is unable to act. The regulation is enacted instead of the law, but its validity is limited to the duration of the circumstances which occasioned it. Accordingly, the President of Serbia, on his initiative, or on the initiative of the Cabinet, during a war, or an impending state of war, adopts acts within the jurisdiction of the Parliament. He is obliged to submit them for approval to the Parliament, as soon as the Parliament is able to convene. Those acts can limit certain rights and freedoms of and alter the organization, composition, and prerogatives of the Cabinet and ministries, courts and public prosecutors.[9]

The second situation is when the security of the Republic, freedoms and rights of the citizens, or the functioning of the state organs are endangered, and the President, acting on the initiative of the Cabinet, proclaims a state of emergency and adopts the regulations for application of necessary measures.[10]

According to the Constitution, the Cabinet can issue "ordinances, regulations and other acts for the implementation of laws".[11] One of the most important normative acts of the Cabinet is the ordinance which specifies the conditions necessary for the implementation of laws, principles of the inner organization of ministries, and regulates the professional services facilitating the Cabinet.[12]

Regulations of the Government are adopted for certain issues and measures of general importance. The regulation prescribes the measures to be taken by the Cabinet, gives an approval or confirms the legal acts of organs or organizations, if this is required by law, and regulates other matters of significance for the functioning of the Cabinet.[13]

The Cabinet can also issue decisions regulating particular situations. By a decision the Cabinet appoints and dismisses officials, approves and confirms legal acts of organs or organizations, if required by a law, invalidates the rules of ministries, and decides on other particular issues from its jurisdiction. (Article 30, subarticle 3, the Law on the Cabinet of the Republic of Serbia.)

3. THE SYSTEM OF COURTS DEALING WITH ADMINISTRATIVE LAW ISSUES

In Serbia there are no separate administrative courts. Courts are divided into courts of general jurisdiction and commercial courts.[14] The courts of general jurisdiction are municipal courts, district courts and the Supreme Court. The Supreme Court is the highest court in the Republic. The commercial courts are ordinary commercial courts and the Higher Commercial Court.

Jurisdiction in administrative matters is divided among the Supreme Court of Serbia and the district courts. According to Article 17 of the Law on Courts,[15] the Supreme Court of Serbia decides in the cases of challenges against the legality of administrative acts of the organs of the Republic. It also acts as a court of appeal against the decisions of district courts, decides on petitions for revocation of judgment against their decisions, and against the decisions of the courts in the provinces, when the law, which is to be uniquely applied on the territory of the whole Republic, has been violated.

The district courts decide on the legality of administrative acts of the following authorities: regional communities, the city of Belgrade, the Republic Social Security Union, and in all other cases over which no other court has competence.

4. GENERAL PROCEDURAL LAWS IN ADMINISTRATIVE MATTER

4.1 The general procedural laws

The first Administrative Procedure Law was enacted in 1956 and has been amended four times since. The most recent changes were adopted in 1994.[16]

The following authorities have the duty to comply with the procedure established in this act: the administrative organs, the assemblies of the federal units, the executive organs of the assemblies, the judicial branch of the government. Those organs are obliged to do so when "in administrative matters, while applying the regulations, they are deciding on the duties, obligations and legal interests of individuals, legal entities and other parties involved" (Article 1, subarticle 1).

4. 2 Procedure for appeal before administrative agencies

The standing for appeal can fall into two categories. The first one is "private"–i.e. the parties whose legal situation is in indirect or direct connection with the decision which will be reviewed. The second one is "public"–i.e. the public authorities who protect the general legality and the public interest of state organs, such as the public prosecutor and the public attorney.

The right to file an appeal is acknowledged primarily to the individual or the legal entity which was a party in the administrative procedure (Article 223, subarticle

1). This solution is the reflection of the principle of the unity of decision-making and appeal procedure. This principle implies that the right to appeal belongs to those who have not taken part in the decision-making procedure, but were nonetheless entitled to do so. They have rights equal to those of the parties, that took part in the primary procedure.

For the public parties to have the right to appeal, a specific legal authorization must exist for representing the public interest in the administrative procedures. This authorization usually derives from statutes, both federal and republic, which regulate specific administrative matters. The authorization has to be explicitly stated in the provisions of the statute.

According to Article 11 of the Law on Administrative Procedure, the right to appeal is excluded when the decisions of some categories of public authorities are in question:

a. administrative decisions of federal and republic secretariats (Article 11, subarticle 2); the Law provides that even against these decisions the right to appeal can exist, but only in two situations:

- when it is provided for by this Law or by regulation;
- when judicial review in those matters does not exist.

b. administrative decisions of the major executive organs, federal and republic, along with the decisions of their committees and boards. The decisions in the administrative procedure of these organs are final.

c. administrative decisions of the assemblies, federal and republic, along with the decisions of their committees and boards.

The appeal is filed against the decision of the first-instance organ in administrative matters and in the event that the first-instance organ has failed to take any decision within the period of two months (the silence of the administration leads to the legal presumption that the original request has been denied).

The grounds for appeal are the legality and proportionality of the decision in question. The period in which the appeal should be filed is 15 days from the moment when the decision was received by the appellant, except in the cases where a specific statute provides otherwise (Article 230). Despite the fact that the superior administrative organ has the competence to decide on the appeal, the appeal itself is to be filed through the organ which has taken the decision in the first instance (Article 232). There is no ex officio procedure, so the unsatisfied party has to initiate it. Therefore, the appellant may withdraw the appeal until a decision has been reached on it, in which case the procedure stops by a decision of the organ which is in possession of the files. An appeal is not allowed against this conclusion, but its legality can be challenged through judicial review.

The competent organ is not restricted by the appellant's claims in the appeal. According to the law, the second-instance organ may go beyond the appeal in three cases.

a. In the case of flagrant violations of legality, the organ acts ex officio regardless of the appeal and that in the cases:

- when the attacked decision has such errors which make it void according to Article 267 (Article 241, subarticle 1)

- when the decision was taken by a non-competent organ

b. *Reformatio in meius* is allowed with two limitations (Article 244, subarticle 1):

- not to go beyond the party's original request in the primary procedure

- not to violate the rights of a third party acquired by the decision in the first instance

c. In principle, *reformatio in peius* is forbidden, but not absolutely. For example, it is allowed on the ground of fairness.

The procedure of appeal can be resolved with the rejection of the appeal or invalidation of the attacked decision, in total or in its parts. The superior administrative authority can decide the matter on its own, return the case to the lower organ which took the decision in the first instance to repeat the procedure, change the attacked decision, and annul the decision. In the case of invalidity on the ground of lack of jurisdiction, the superior administrative authority forwards the case to the competent organ.

4.3 The procedure for seeking judicial review

The procedure before the court is initiated by filing a lawsuit. The plaintiff can be an individual, legal entity or other party which holds that by the administrative act its legal right or legal interests have been violated. A trade union can file an action as well, if it holds that the rights or the legal interests of its members have been violated by the administrative act. The time limit for filing a lawsuit is 30 days from the day of the submission of the administrative act to the party which seeks judicial review. The administrative act, in terms of the Law on Judicial Review, is the act by which the state organ and the company exercising public authority decide on a certain right or duty of the individual, the legal entity or another party.

According to the Law on Judicial Review, judicial review can be requested only against a final administrative act, i.e. against an appealed administrative act or an act against which an appeal is not permitted (Article 7). From this general formula the Law provides two exceptions. First, it specifies acts against which judicial review is excluded. Secondly, it specifies requirements for judicial review in administrative matters in which the administrative act has not been enacted (the case of "silence of the administration"). Such is the case when an administrative act, against which an appeal is not permitted, has not been enacted upon the request of the party, or when there was no decision on the appeal.

The Law on Judicial Review prescribes two time limits for the lawsuit. The first is 60 days, starting from the moment of the submission of the party's request or of the appeal. The second is seven days, starting when a renewed request of the party, after the first time limit has expired, is filed. Apart from the expiry of time limits the

Law prescribes the fulfillment of two basic procedural conditions: that the silence of the administration is final, i.e. that the appeal has been exhausted or it was not permitted, and that judicial review in the respected matter is allowed.

4.4 Administrative acts excluded from judicial review; grounds for applying for judicial review

The administrative acts, which are excluded from judicial review, are enumerated in Article 9 of the Law on Judicial Review. It provides that judicial review is excluded in the following cases:

1. Acts enacted in matters for which the ordinary courts have competence. This competence has to be established and regulated by a law.[17]
2. Acts enacted in matters for which there is an explicit statutory provision for the exclusion of judicial review. Generally, these acts are excluded from any kind of judicial control, except when the organ in the process of issuing has acted ultra vires, in which case judicial review is permitted. In this case, the court decides only on the existence of this technical error.
3. Acts enacted in matters for which, according to the constitutional provisions, the Federal Parliament, the President of the Republic of Yugoslavia, the parliaments of the federal units or the presidents of federal units have jurisdiction.

The grounds for applying for judicial review can be substantive and procedural. Article 10 of the Law on Judicial Review provides the following grounds for judicial action:

1. when the law, other regulation or general acts have been improperly or not at all applied.
2. when the act was enacted by an organ that did not have the jurisdiction.
3. when the enacting of the act has not been conducted according to the rules of the relevant procedure, particularly when facts were not correctly established, or when incorrect conclusions were drawn from established facts.

There is no ground for judicial review when the act was enacted within the scope of the discretionary power granted to the authority by a statute.

4. 5 Judicial remedies

The procedure before the court finishes with a court decision by which the claim can be rejected or upheld (Article 41, subarticle 2). If the court upholds the claim, the attacked administrative act will be annulled. In such a case, if the nature of the matter allows and if the established facts provide a reliable ground, the court can resolve the case on its merits. Such decision replaces in toto the annulled act (Article 41, subarticle 3). If established facts provide a reliable ground, the court may decide upon the request for restitution and award damages in the same decision. In contrario, the court will direct the claimant to seek relief in the ordinary civil procedure (Article 41, subarticle 4).

4. 6 Exceptions from the general procedure

The Law on Judicial Review of 1996 does not provide for any exception from the general administrative procedure. Previously, there were two exceptions according to the Law on Judicial Review of 1994. Judicial review was provided for the cases of violation of constitutional rights and freedoms by an administrative act or official conduct. In the first case, certain provisions of the Law on Judicial Review would have been applied in the appropriate manner accordingly. In the second case, the application for judicial review could have been filed only during the contested official conduct, and not only by the individual effected by the conduct, but by his or her spouse, child, parent or other close relatives. The procedure in this matter was urgent, and the district court was the court of first instance. The Supreme Court of Serbia had the jurisdiction in the case of appeal. As mentioned, those exceptions have been abolished by the Law on Judicial Review of 1996.

5. OMBUDSMAN

In Serbia, there is no ombudsman or any similar institution.

6. FORMS OF SUPERVISION OVER THE ADMINISTRATION

In Serbia, there are two forms of supervision over the administration: internal and external. The internal control is conducted through the administrative inspectorates and by superior administrative organs in the administrative hierarchy.

The ministry competent in administrative matters is responsible for administrative inspections. Mere inspection is conducted by administrative inspectors. Control in this form consists of supervision of the following areas: application of laws and other regulations by the administration, application of the part of the Law on Administrative Procedure which deals with efficiency and promptness in deciding in administrative matters, professional qualifications of the employees involved in the administrative procedure, announcement of the names of officials competent for deciding in administrative matters.[18] In those matters, the inspectorate is supervising the functioning of the administrative organs, companies and organisations, which perform administrative functions and provide services to the President, the Parliament, the Government, the Constitutional Court, the courts, the public prosecutors, as well as the prisons and institutions for juvenile delinquents. If, in the course of control, the inspector discovers a deficiency, he or she will issue a decision to order its removal and set a time period for it. Against this decision an appeal can be filed within eight days, but it does not delay the execution of the decision.

External control takes three forms: parliamentary, judicial and public prosecutor's control. Judicial control, in the form of judicial review, we analyzed earlier.

The right of the public prosecutor to control the administration derives from the general competence of the public prosecutor according to the Law on Public Prosecutors.[19] The public prosecutor is an independent state organ that prosecutes offenders and uses the instrument of "legal aid" to control the constitutionality and legality of administrative acts. If the issue of constitutionality and legality appears in the course of public prosecutor's scrutiny, then he or she can initiate a procedure before the Constitutional Court to decide on the constitutionality of the act.[20]

Since in administrative procedures the public prosecutor has the competence to represent public interests, then he or she has rights and duties of a party to the proceedings.[21] If the public prosecutor finds that because of the breach of the law or an international treaty there is a ground to file an extraordinary "legal aid" against the decision in the administrative procedure, he or she can request the execution of the decision to be suspended or interrupted.[22] The request is submitted to the court, which has the jurisdiction to permit the execution. The suspension lasts until the decision upon the legal aid of the public prosecutor is taken. The decision on deferment or ceasing of the execution ceases to be valid if, within 30 days of the reception of that decision, the public prosecutor does not file the legal aid.

In administrative procedures, the public prosecutor has the right to appeal to a decision which has violated the law benefiting an individual or legal entity but damaging public or community interest.[23] The public prosecutor only has the competence to file a request for the protection of legality (Article 262) against the decision of the administrative authority for which judicial review is excluded. The administrative organ of the Republic, competent for the subject matter under which the decision falls, decides upon the request. It can reject or admit the request and annul the decision, but with the effect only pro futuro. The competent organ is not empowered to decide the same matter differently.

The public prosecutor has the right to request the annulment or the abolishment of the decision of an administrative organ in the process of supervision exercised by the superior administrative organ. The superior administrative organ, who is competent to decide on the appeal, is ex officio controlling the legality of final administrative decisions of inferior organs. It can annul or abolish the decision depending on the reasons for that action. The superior organ can annul the decision if the decision is enacted by an organ that lacked jurisdiction in that matter; if there is another irrevocable decision on the same matter; if the decision required, but did not receive the agreement, confirmation or opinion of another organ; and if the decision is enacted under duress, blackmail, or extortion (Article 263, subarticle 1). The decision on the annulment is enacted by the superior administrative organ ex officio, but also upon the request of the party or the public prosecutor. The superior organ can abolish the decision if there is an obvious violation of the substantive law (Article 263, subarticle 2). In this case, the decision on the abolition is enacted by the superior administrative organ ex officio and also upon the request of the public prosecutor. Against the decision either for annulment or abolition an appeal is not allowed, but a legal remedy is provided in the form of judicial review.

The public prosecutor, as well as the party, can suggest to the administrative organ which enacted a decision, or to a superior organ, to declare the decision void, in toto or in part, for the following reasons (Articles 267 and 268):

- If a matter decided falls under the competence of ordinary courts, or the matter was of such a nature that administrative procedure was not allowed in the first place.
- If the execution of the decision would constitute an offense or the execution is impossible
- If the decision is taken without a prior request of the party, when this request is necessary, and the party has not given ex post consent explicitly or implicitly
- If a special statute cites a certain deficiency as a reason for declaring a decision void.

Against a decision which declares a certain decision void, or which refuses the request of the party or of the public prosecutor, an appeal is allowed. If no superior organ can decide upon the appeal, a legal remedy is provided in the form of judicial review (Article 268, subarticle 4).

In the process of judicial review, the public prosecutor can file an action when the violation of law benefits an individual or legal entity, or when the violation of law damages the State, the local administration and other organ whose interests the public prosecutor represents.[24]

7. PARLIAMENTARY CONTROL OVER THE ADMINISTRATION

As for the parliamentary control, the Constitution explicitly provides for the supervising function of the Parliament over the functioning of the Cabinet, other organs and high civil servants responsible to it (Article 73, subarticle 11). The state administrative organs have the duty to provide MPs, upon their request, with information and data concerning their activity.[25]

II. DEVELOPMENTS IN ADMINISTRATIVE LAW DURING 1996-1997

A. THE CONSTITUTION

No constitutional amendments have been adopted since the Constitution was adopted in 1990.

B. LEGISLATION

1. PROCEDURAL AND GENERAL ORGANISATIONAL LAWS

1.1 The organisation of the judicial system

The Law on Courts was passed in 1991, and was amended in 1991 and twice in 1992. The changes affected the position of judges. According to the current text, the office is tenured and incompatible with the position of Member of Parliament and other political and administrative functions.[26]

1.2 Public institutions

The Law on the Federal Public Institutions[27] was promulgated on September 27, 1996. It regulates the legal status of public institutions established by the Federal Republic of Yugoslavia for the purpose of conducting their activities, e.g. services of interest for the realization of the competencies of the federal state. Military services are not subject to this law. Article 2 gives a definition of "public institution", mentioning in paragraph 2 that they are non-profitable orgnizations, e.g. scientific institutes, research and other centres, and agencies.

Public institutions are, as stipulated in Article 3, legal entities financed from the federal budget (Article 16). Other sources of revenue are income realized from given services and grants or other revenues realized in compliance with this law. Article 17 regulates the way public institutions are financed from the federal budget–for the activities of public interest for which the institution is established, the public institution determines the yearly program at the latest until the end of the current year, to which the federal government is giving its consent. According to this program, the public institution is to sign a contract with the competent federal organ or organization, which regulates the scope of services of the public institution, the time periods and the level of remuneration. For long-term services, a general contract is to be signed, upon the consent of the federal government. The federal government also gives its consent regarding the tariffs of the services. The public institution may own real estate and movable property, commercial papers, bonds, etc. All assets are considered as state property. The management of these assets is left to the organs of the public institution, but preliminary consent of the federal government is needed.

The public institution is established by the federal government (Article 5, subarticle 1) for the following purposes: expert and technical services in relation to the fulfillment of the obligations of the federal state originating from federal laws, other federal regulations and legal acts and ratified and published international treaties; conducting scientific and other research in the interest of the federal organs and organizations; providing of public information about the situation in the

FRY and the world, and other forms of public information; creating conditions for protection and usage of cultural historical property, etc. (Article 4.)

An act of incorporation is adopted by the federal government and contains all necessary data for the functioning of such an institution: firm name and seat of registration; list of activities; rights, obligations and accountability of the establisher to the institution and vice versa; organs of the institution; representation of the institution; acquisition of initial capital; ways of financing of the institution; ways of supervision and inspection, etc. (Article 5). The institution is registered in the court register. The act of registration is published in the *Official Gazette of FRY:* with this the institution acquires the status of a legal entity.

The organs of the public institutions are the council, director and supervisory board. The chairman of the council and the council members, the director, the chairman of the board and the members are appointed by the federal government. The term of office is five years (Articles 7–13).

In the case of a financial loss, the federal government is obliged to secure the financial balance of the public institution, especially when the federal government refuses to give its consent to the opening of bankruptcy proceedings (Article 26). The liquidation of the public institution may happen according to the general provisions of liquidation of enterprises or upon the decision of the federal government (Article 27). In both cases the public institution ceases to exist.

The public institution is obliged to present an annual report to the federal government. As a form of control and supervision the federal government may order the public institution to perform in accordance with the federal law and its act of incorporation, and ultimately annul acts adopted by the institution, et cetera, (Article 29).

Other laws regulating the status of the public institutions are the Law on the Enterprises,[28] or laws adopted by parliament of the respected unit if they regulate the activities i.e. services performed by public institution (Article 30).

2. SUBSTANCE

2.1 Management of the economy

2.1.1 LAWS ON PRIVATISATION

The Law on the Principles of Transformation of Social Ownership [29] stipulates the rules of ownership transformation. In 1994, the Law on the Republic Agency for the Evaluation of Social Capital[30] established an Agency, which was given basic prerogatives in the process of privatisation (Article 3). Its main prerogatives are evaluation of state and socially owned capital of all participants in the processes of privatisation, bankruptcy and liquidation. It also gives professional and administrative support to the activities in privatisation of the state-owned enterprises, their restructuring, buying, selling and establishment. The Agency may delegate its powers of evaluation to companies, institutions or other organisations (Article 3a).

The Agency is responsible to the Cabinet and submits its report at least once every two months (Article 4). The Cabinet is obliged to report to the Parliament at least twice a year about the functioning of the Agency. The Agency is managed and represented by its Director, appointed by the Cabinet.

By the *Law on the Conditions and Procedure of Transformation of State Owned Property into other Forms*[31] privatisation of state enterprises is conducted with the participation of a special agency and the Fund for Development of the Republic of Serbia. The enterprises decide independently on the transformation of the ownership (Article 1), but are obliged to submit the decision and the estimate of the value of the enterprise to the agency. If the agency finds that the estimate has not been done in accordance with this law, it sets a time period within which the situation should be remedied. Against this order, the enterprise has the right to file an action with the commercial court. In the event that the enterprise or its part are sold, the Fund for Development sets the conditions of sale and signs the contract with the buyer.

If an enterprise is privatised through the process of selling shares, the Law provides for the right of the employees to purchase shares with a discount (Article 14). The remaining amount of shares is sold to domestic and foreign legal entities or individuals. The enterprise is obliged to make a public offer, containing all of its substantial elements.

Other laws related to the topic are *The Law on Enterprises*[32]; *The Law on Classification of the Fields of Activities of Enterprises and on the Register of Numerated Classification*[33]; *and The Law on the Procedure of Registration of Enterprises.*[34]

2.1.2. LAWS ON THE OWNERSHIP AND MANAGEMENT OF AGRICULTURAL LANDS

By the *Law on Transformation of the Socially Owned Agricultural Land into Other Forms of Ownership*[35] the Fund for protection, use, advancement and regulation of agricultural land is given basic prerogatives in the process of privatization of agricultural lands (Article 2, subarticle 2). The Fund concludes contracts on selling the land and suggests to the Cabinet to give the land for use to other enterprises. If an enterprise is not using the land in accordance with the law or programs of the Fund, the Fund manages the land until the processes of selling or bankruptcy are finished. The Fund has the right of first refusal in the process of selling socially owned agricultural land.

2.1.3 LAWS ON THE ENVIRONMENT

The Law on the Protection of the Environment[36] stipulates in Article 6 that enterprises and other subjects are obliged to keep records on types and quantities of dangerous and harmful substances which are used during the conduct of their activities. The law further obliges the enterprises to keep records on the types and quantities of dangerous and harmful substances which their factories release into the water, air or soil and to deliver those data to the relevant competent organs. The enterprises are subject to control whether they are complying with their obligation: a high financial penalty is stipulated (Article 102). The municipalities deliver plans on improvement of the quality of air (Article 22), and the relevant ministry is a supervisor since the ministry sets the criteria for defining the areas of protection according to the type and quantity of pollution (Article 22, subarticle 8).

2.1.4. LAWS ON FINANCE

The Law on National Bank of Yugoslavia, adopted by the Federal Parliament in June 1993,[37] broke with the unusual experimentation in central banking, practiced for more than two decades in the former Yugoslavia. The adoption of this law was preceded by a year-long discussion in academic and professional circles, as well as in competent parliamentary bodies. The new law on the National Bank of Yugoslavia (NBY) incorporates the approaches and solutions characteristic for central banks in the countries with developed market economies.

First, monetary power is now centralized at the federal level as in other federations. This means that the NBY, as a legal entity, is the only institution of issue in the FRY, which has a network of main branch offices and branch offices in the administrative centers of the federal units and the provinces. However, branch offices do not have the status of a legal person and, accordingly, can only implement the decisions taken by the highest management body of the NBY.

Second, the basic task of the NBY is to ensure the stability of the national currency. This means that in conducting the monetary policy, it should not attach much importance to the realization of developmental and other economic policy objectives in relation to the achievement of price stability.

Third, the NBY enjoys a high degree of institutional independence from the legislative and executive power, which is reflected in the following: 1) it has the power to set the monetary policy and undertake measures for its implementation; 2) the governor and other six members of the NBY Council are elected for a term of five years, so the overlapping of this term and that of parliamentary elections is avoided; 3) NBY Council members must be experts and highly qualified specialists in the area of monetary, credit and foreign exchange system; 4) the NBY and the FRY Government cooperate in establishing the basic economic policy objectives, particularly in setting the exchange rate policy of the dinar: the NBY proposes the policy and the Government fixes the exchange rate 5) the FRY and the republics may borrow from the NBY to bridge the time gap between the inflow of revenues and outflow of expenditures on account of obligations; such borrowing may be up to a maximum 10 per cent of the planned annual budgetary revenues (on the condition that the amount of such credits do not exceed 15 per cent of the NBY's placements in dinars). The borrowing must be repaid until the end of the budget year, at the latest (only in the transitional 1993–1994 period was the permitted proportion of state borrowing set higher).

Fourth, in regulating the money supply the NBY needs, pursuant to the Law, to resort to open market operations, and only then to the rediscount of domestic and foreign securities, credit refinancing on the basis of specific short term securities, etc.

Fifth, to allow for efficient payment operations in the country and to introduce the financial discipline, the NBY is given the right to set the criteria that potential payment operation users are bound to observe.

Sixth, the control function is centralised. The NBY thus controls the legality in carrying out financial operations, and checks the creditworthiness of banks and other financial organisations.

Centralisation as a principle of organisation of the NBY is evident in the new organisation of the NBY's bodies. The organs of the NBY are the Council and the governor. The FRY Constitution stipulates that the governor manages the Bank and that he or she is elected by the Federal Parliament at the proposal made by the President of FR Yugoslavia, for a five-year term (Article 114). The Council has seven members. They are: the governor of the NBY, ex officio, and six members appointed for a five-year term by the Federal Parliament. Three Council members are appointed at the proposal of NBY governor, and three at the proposal of the FRY Government. The Law on NBY explicitly states that any NBY Council member "must have a specific and thorough technical knowledge in the area of monetary, credit and foreign exchange system" (Article 12, subarticle 3 of the Law). The Council meetings are chaired by the NBY governor who is, by his function, chairman of the Council. The Council decides by the majority of votes of all Council members. The competences of the NBY Council are:

a. to take decisions in connection with the establishment of the monetary policy and the policy of NBY interventions on the foreign exchange market;
b. to adopt monetary policy projections;
c. to make proposals to the Federal Parliament relating to legal projects and other regulations in the area of monetary, foreign exchange and credit system;
d. to enact statutes, financial plan and the annual balance sheet of the NBY;
e. to provide general guidelines for NBY activity;
f. to enact the rules of procedure.

The Law on Banks and Other Financial Institutions[38] regulates the establishing, organization, functioning and managing of banks and other financial institutions. The main competence in this area is given to the Central Bank, which gives and withdraws authorisation to commercial banks and other financial institutions.

According to Article 8 the governor of the Central Bank authorises the operation of a bank. This decision is final. The Central Bank also authorises the selling of shares of a financial institution by which the buyer acquires more than 15 per cent of the investment capital. The Central Bank further gives approval for the founding acts, for the statute of a bank and changes to it, for the establishing of a bank and its branches in a foreign country and for the change of the name and domicile of a bank. Article 28 provides for the opinion of the Central Bank on the appointment of bank directors. By Article 29 banks are obliged to inform the Central Bank on the new emission of shares, loans, change in the managing and control boards, opening of new branches in the country and on the sale of shares by which the buyer acquires more than 10 per cent of the investment capital.

2.1.5. LAWS ON THE MANAGEMENT OF NATURAL RESOURCES

The Parliament of the Republic of Serbia passed a new *Concession Law* on May 12, 1997.[39] This law regulates concessions over the property and resources of the Republic of Serbia. Concessions may be granted to a domestic or foreign entity (legal or natural). In broad terms, the law divides concessions into three general groups: a) concessions on natural resources, b) concessions on using public resources, and c) concessions on performing public services. A foreign or domestic entity (legal or natural) may construct, manage and transfer the subject of concession under conditions specified in the permit for a period not exceeding 30 years. Upon the expiration of a granted concession, the subject of a concession becomes the property of the Republic of Serbia. Foreign entities are not to be granted concessions for activities in which state and federal laws prohibit the formation of companies with foreign ownership (e.g. arms production, forestry and wildlife).

Under the federal concession law, concessions may be granted by an authority defined by federal and/or state law. Because of the weak federal government it was common practice to have concessions granted by the governments of Serbia or Montenegro. The new law creates an Agency for Investment in Areas of Special Interest for the Republic of Serbia. It is unclear when the Agency will be formed since the law does not establish a procedure or deadline for its formation. The Agency will be responsible for selecting and promoting concession programs, preparing documentation and concession plans and preparation and implementation of concession auctions. Also, the Agency will be responsible for the supervision and control for the duration of the concession. The provisions concerning the supervision rights of the Agency contain broad and undefined terms and may develop in practice as vehicles for governmental interference with the management of the concession enterprise.

Concessions may be granted only if making use of them will a) reasonably utilize natural resources and public property, b) provide for more efficient operation, and c) enable rational resource management and preserve the natural environment.

All concession proposals shall be submitted to the Government of the Republic of Serbia through the Agency. Concession proposals may be submitted by any state ministry, local governments or other interested parties (including foreign entities).

All concession proposals shall contain clear definitions of 1) the subject of the concession and the reason why a concession should be granted; 2) the time needed to complete preparatory operations; 3) the time of making actual use of a concession; 4) the methods and time limits of providing concession financing; 5) conditions of using natural resources; 6) fees for using concessions and the payment terms; 7) rights and obligations regarding environmental protection; and 8) estimates of the number of new jobs to be created.

In the event that a concession proposal is approved, the government of Serbia passes a special concession draft act, which is then published in the Official Gazette of the Republic of Serbia. The Agency is then responsible for auctioning the approved concession through a specially constituted Commission. The Commission shall, within 30 days from the expiration of the auction deadline, submit the results to the Agency. The law prescribes a minimum of two bidders for the auction to be valid. The Government, upon a review of the received submissions, makes the final decision, which is then published in the Official Gazette of the Republic of Serbia. Presumably, the bidding for the concession is "with reserve", allowing the Government discretion in the assessment of the offers. Auction participant(s) alleging illegality of the auction process may lodge a complaint with the government within 15 days from the government's final decision. The law contains a provision specifically guaranteeing the right of foreign concessionaires.

After obtaining the concession permit, the concessionaire is obliged to form a concession company, in full accordance with the laws of the FR Yugoslavia and the Republic of Serbia. Foreign concessionaires may legally transfer their concessions to other parties, in whole or in part, only with the explicit agreement of the other party in the contract. Any contracts without such an explicit agreement will be void. The law contains a provision specifically guaranteeing the right of foreign concessionaires in this respect as well.

Concession contracts must be registered with the Federal Trade Ministry–the Federal Secretariat for Economic Relations with Foreign Countries. The concession application must be accompanied by the contract text in Serbian (including all changes and/or supplements) within 30 days from the day of signing of the contract. If the Ministry finds these documents to be legally unacceptable, it will refuse registration by an administrative decision. The Ministry is obliged to make its decision within 30 days from receiving the valid request. If no decision is made within 30 days, the contract is deemed to be in full accordance with federal laws. Foreign concessionaires may lodge complaints against the decisions made by the Federal Trade Ministry with the federal government within 15 days from receiving the decision. The federal government's decision is final.

2.1.6. LAWS ON TRANSPORT

The Law on Road Transport[40] regulates the "public and private transport of persons and goods, conditions for construction, managing and operation of bus stations, and other conditions concerning the road transport" (Article 1). The Law provides for the supervisory function of the inspectorate for road traffic. The inspector controls all forms of transport, transport timetables, necessary documentation, identity of persons managing and involved in transport. He has the right to order remedying of defects, to forbid transport conducted against the rules and remove vehicles from the road, along with the seizure of driving licenses and plates (Article 44). Against a decision of the inspectorate the appeal to the Cabinet can be filed.

The Law on Roads[41] regulates the construction, maintenance and protection of roads. For conducting the maintenance, protection, development and managing of roads the Law establishes the Office for Roads. The Office enacts the long-term plan, which is confirmed by the Parliament, while its annual plan is enacted with the consent of the Cabinet. (Article 47). The Office is responsible for damages to users suffered due to the omition of undertaking of necessary measures in the maintenance of roads (Article 50).

The Ministry of Traffic supervises the execution of the law and relevant regulations. The supervision of the execution of laws and regulations, the state of public roads, measures of protection, the application of technical measures, construction and reconstruction of public roads is conducted by the Inspector for Public Roads (Article 60). Against the decision of the inspector enacted in those matters, an appeal to the relevant ministry can be filed.

2.1.7 LAWS ON CUSTOMS

The Law on Customs is a federal law and was passed in 1992. The last amendments regarding the base of custom duties were made in 1996.[42]

The Law on Duty-free Zones[43] was passed in 1994. The Federal Ministry of Finance has discretionary power in granting the permission for the establishment of a free zone. The managing agency submits the request for the establishment of a duty-free zone to the Federal Ministry of Finance, which is obliged to decide on the matter within 30 days. The Law was amended in 1996 regarding Article 43, which introduced fines for customary offenses.

2.2 The management of socio-cultural processes

2.2.1 LAWS ON TERRITORIAL ORGANISATION, PLANNING AND CONSTRUCTION

The Law on Construction[44] was passed in 1995. *The Law on Planning and Territorial Organisation* was passed in 1995 (OG RS, 44/95).[45] Since then there have been no new amendments.

2.2.2 LAWS ON EDUCATION

The Law on Universities was passed in 1993.[46] Since then there have been no new amendments.

2.2.3 LAWS ON HEALTH CARE

The Law on Records in the Field of Health Care[47] stipulates in Article 1 that in the field of health care, records of interest to the whole state have to be kept, in particular the records on regular and periodical medical examinations of citizens; conditions and means of protection and advancement in environmental protection; health standards of food and goods of general usage; births and abortions; statistics on family planning; immunization against infectious diseases; usage of medicines; usage of narcotics; and drug addicts and employees in the medical institutions. Further, the Law specifies the institution responsible for keeping particular records and the fines in the case of non-performance or violation.

The Law on the Protection of the Citizens from the Infectious Diseases Which May Endanger the Whole Country[48] provided for protective measures against the spread of infectious diseases.

The Law on Health Care[49] regulates the health-care organization of and the system of medical institutions. For the foundation, management and control of the legality of functioning of medical institutions and their abolition, the provisions of the Law on Public Services apply, if it is not stated otherwise in the Law on Health Care (Article 19). By Article 15 of the Law on Health Care, a medical institution can be established by any physical and legal person, if not stipulated otherwise by this act. The Cabinet establishes medical institutions, which provide a number of essential medical services determined by this law (Article 15, subarticle 2). When other entities (legal or physical persons) are founders of the medical institution, the regulations of the Ministry for Health and the provisions on the necessary conditions for establishing of medical institutions of this law have to be observed. The necessary conditions relate to the number of doctors, equipment and devices, medicines and other means for medical treatment (Article 16). The Ministry for Health gives the authorization for medical institutions when the necessary conditions are fulfilled.

The Law establishes three types of control over medical institutions: control of legality of conduct, control over the medical profession, and control over the implementation of laws, regulations and prescribed measures. The director of the medical institution is responsible for the legality of the institution, while the Ministry for Health controls the legality of all medical institutions. The control over the medical profession takes two forms: external and internal control. The Ministry for Health conducts the external control through outstanding medical experts and medical academics, while the internal one is conducted by experts from the given medical institution. The experts are responsible to the director (Article 52–55). The control over the implementation of laws, regulations and prescribed measures is conducted by the Health Inspectorate (Article 60). For the advancement of the medical and pharmaceutical profession the Law provides the grounds for the establishment of Medical and Pharmaceutical Chambers (Article 77a).

Other laws in the area are *The Law on Sanitary Inspection*[50]; *Health Insurance Law*[51]; and *The Medical Supervision of Food and Goods of Public Usage.*[52]

2.3 The management of political processes

2.3.1 LAWS ON NATIONAL SECURITY

The Law on National Security, outlining the defense doctrine of the country and the status of the armed forces, was passed in 1990 and amended the last time in 1991 (44/91). The Internal Affairs Act, regulating the police forces, was amended for the last time in the same year.[53]

2.3.2 LAW ON MEETINGS, MANIFESTATIONS AND STRIKES

The Law on Meetings[54] was passed in 1992 and was amended[55] in 1994. In 1996, *The Law on Strikes*[56] was passed. This law defines "strike" as a suspension of the working process organized by workers for the protection of their professional and economic interests in relation to their job (Article 1). The strike can be organized in a company, in an economic branch, as an "ordinary" strike or as a warning strike, which can last for only an hour. The organ of the union or the majority of the employees decides on the beginning of the strike. This decision establishes requests, starting time and the strike's council, which represents the interests of the employees. The strike is announced to the employer five days before its start The strike's council and the employer are obliged to try to settle the dispute through an agreement. If the strike is organized in an economic branch that is of public interest or whose suspension may endanger lives and the health of the people, or cause a damage of great proportions, the strike can start if a minimal process of work is provided. In this case the strike is announced to the employer, the supervising state organ and the competent organ of local administration 10 days before it is to start (Articles 9–11).

The organization of and the participation in a strike do not present a violation of working duties and cannot be a ground for the initiation of a procedure for establishing of disciplinary and material responsibility. It cannot result in the dismissal of the employees either. Participation in the strike can result in dismissal if the participant is a professional member of the army or the police, or is employed by a state organ (Article 18). During the strike, the employer cannot employ new workers to replace the ones in the strike, prevent the worker from participating in it, use force to terminate the strike or provide higher salaries or privileges to those who do not participate in it (Article 15). The supervision over the implementation of this Law is conducted by the relevant competent federal organ, which in that process enacts the decision for ordering the remedying of established violations. The Law also provides for monetary penalties for violations of its provisions (Article 19–20).

2.3.3 LAWS ON CITIZENSHIP AND ADMINISTRATIVE STATUS

The Law on Citizenship was passed in 1983.[57] Since then it has not been amended. *The Law on Domicile and Residency* was passed in 1977.[58] The last amendments were passed in 1994.[59]

2.3.4 LAWS ON THE RESIDENCE OF THE FOREIGN NATIONALS; REFUGEES

The Law on Refugees was passed in 1992.[60] *The Law on the Residence of the Foreign Nationals*[61] was passed in 1980 and was last amended in 1994.[62]

C. REGULATIONS

1. PRIVATISATION

The following major governmental decrees and other regulation have been enacted in the sphere of privatization since 1995: Decree on the Principles of Methodology of Evaluation of Capital, Revalorization of Evaluated Capital and on the Ways of Displaying Capital in Shares or Quotas;[63] Rules on the Ways of Revalorization of the Value of the Social Capital Which Was Established through the Process of Transformation of Social Capital into Other Forms of Ownership and the Value of Shares and Quotas;[64] Decree on the Organization of the Branches of the Enterprises Whose Seats of Registration are on the Territory of Bosnia and Herzegovina, Slovenia and Croatia;[65] Decree on Registration in the Court Register of Enterprises.[66]

2. FINANCE

On of the major sub-legislative acts of 1996 in the sphere of finance was the Resolution on the actions which the National Bank of Yugoslavia undertakes: a decision on the withdrawal of the permission for operation of a bank, a decision on liquidation of the bank, a decision on the fulfillment of the conditions for opening of bankruptcy proceedings.[67]

3. HEALTH CARE

The following governmental decrees and decisions have been adopted in the sphere of healthcare since 1995: Decree on Integrated Preventive Health Care of Citizens against Chronic Illnesses;[68] Decision on the Establishment of the Clinical Center of Serbia for Laboratory Analyses and Control of Medical Materials;[69] Decision on the Adjustments of Medical Costs,[70] Book of Regulations on Number, Structure and Way of Operation of the Ethical Committee in Medical Institutions;[71] Book of Regulations on the Required Documents Enclosed with the Request for Issuance of Sanitary Certificates;[72] Book of Regulations on the Expenses and Evaluation of Incurred Expenses during Inspection Control Requested by a Party;[73] Book of Regulations on Conditions of Performing Medical Services in Medical Institutions;[74] Program of the Integrated Preventive Health Care of Citizens from Chronic Non-Infectious Diseases.[75]

D. JUDICIAL DECISIONS

The information included in this part is based on the "Survey of the performance of the Serbian Supreme Court and the lower general jurisdiction courts": this is an official report, prepared to be presented in the Parliament. It has not been published. According to this source, more than 118,000 cases were decided upon during 1996. The caseload was kept at previous levels. There are 169 general jurisdiction courts in Serbia of which 138 are municipal, 30 district and the Supreme Court of Serbia. The registered inflow of administrative law cases was 2,183 during 1996: the workload of the Supreme Court was heavier than the one of the district courts. As for efficiency, the adjudication of an administrative dispute has taken an average of 8.6 months: in comparison with previous years this constitutes a deterioration of efficiency.

During 1996, district courts and the Supreme Court accepted 12,010 administrative contentious matter cases, which is 1,624 cases more compared to the previous year. The Supreme Court accepted 7,977 and all district courts 4,033. Together with the unsolved cases from the previous years, the workload for 1996 was 19,174 cases which had to be solved in the first instance out of which the Supreme court acted as a first instance court in 14,109 cases and the district courts - in 5,065 cases.

Most of the cases in the district courts fall into the area of retirement and disability insurance, whereas the cases of the Supreme Court are predominantly in the area of taxation, inspection services, restitution of land, expropriation, and building in urban areas.

At the end of 1996, an increase was registered in complaints against the decisions of election committees during the elections for organs of local government. The municipal courts received 1,346 complaints. The report concludes that the proceedings were quick and efficient and the election process was not impeded.

The report registered inconsistencies in the normative framework of administrative law, which in some respects hampers the operation of courts. Further, in the report an emphasis was given to the time period the courts have to wait for the requested documentation to be delivered to them by the sued administrative organ, which affect the length of the pretrial procedure. Such delays have been noticed especially in Kosovo–Metohija, where the documentation from health and other institutions is generally very hard to obtain. For this reason the courts were forced in compliance with Article 33 of the Law on Judicial Review (*Official Gazette FRY* 46/96) to decide on certain cases without the proper documentation.

The Chapter has been prepared on the basis of information provided by Danica Kilibarda and Snežana Rajšić

NOTES

[1] Serbia is a unit of the Federal Republic of Yugoslavia. According to the Federal Constitution, the unit independently regulates the organisation of the government by its Constitution (Article 5, para. 1-2 Constitution of the Federal Republic of Yugoslavia). Therefore, federal and republic executive organs are organisationally and functionally separated. There is no hierarchy among them. However, all federal legal norms have priority over the norms of the federal units, and all federal legal norms are binding on the executives of the units.

[2] Article 1, subarticle 1, The Law on Ministries, *Official Gazette RS*, 44/91.

[3] Article 94, subarticle 4. of the Constitution.

[4] Article 38 of the Law on the State Administration, *Official Gazette RS*, 48/93.

[5] Article 276, *Official Gazette RS*, 67/93.

[6] Article 12, subarticle 4, The Law on the Cabinet.

[7] Article 2-4, *Official Gazette RS*, 45/93.

[8] The Law on Territorial Organisation and Local Administration, *Official Gazette RS*, 47/91, Article 16, subarticle 1-2.

[9] Article 83, subarticle 7 Constitution of Serbia.

[10] Article 83, subarticle 8 of the Constitution.

[11] Article 90, subarticle 2 of the Constitution.

[12] Article 30, subarticle 1, The Law on Cabinet of Republic of Serbia, *Official Gazette RS*, 5/91.

[13] Article 30, subarticle 2. The Law on the Cabinet of the Republic of Serbia.

[14] Article 8, Chapter 2 of the Law on Courts, *Official Gazette of the Republic of Serbia*, 71/92.

[15] *Official Gazette RS*, 7/92.

[16] *Official Gazette of the Republic of Yugoslavia*, 24/94-272.

17 Decision of the Supreme Court of Vojvodina, No. U-315/77, of 21. IV 1977.
18 Article 34, The Law on the State Administration, *Official Gazette, Republic of Serbia*, 48/93.
19 *Official Gazette RS*, 43/91 and 71/92.
20 Article 128, subarticle 2 of the Constitution of the Republic of Serbia.
21 Article 52, The Law on the Administrative Procedure, *Official Gazette of Yugoslavia*, No. 24/94
22 Article 14, The Law on the Public Prosecutors.
23 Article 223, subarticle 2 of The Law on the Administrative Procedure.
24 Article 2, subarticle 2, 3 of The Law on Judicial Review.
25 Article 28, subarticle 5 The Law on Ministries.
26 Article 5, *OG RS*, 71/92.
27 *OG FRY*, 46/96.
28 *OG FRY*, 29/96 and 33/96.
29 *OG FRY*, 29/96.
30 Article 1 and 2, *OG RS*, 71/94.
31 *OG RS*, 51/94.
32 *OG FRY*, 29/96 and 33/96.
33 *OG FRY*, 31/96 and 34/96.
34 *OG FRY*, 80/94.
35 *OG*, 49/92.
36 *OG RS*, 66/91 last amended in 1995. *OG RS*, 53/95.
37 *OG FRY*, 32/93, last amended Article 60 *OG FRY*, 28/96.
38 *OG FRY*, 28/96.
39 *OG RS*, 20/97.
40 *OG RS*, 46/95.
41 *OG RS*, 52/91.
42 Article 42, *Official Gazette*, 28/96.
43 *OG RS*, 81/94.
44 *OG RS*, 44/95.
45 *OG RS*, 44/95.
46 *OG RS*, 67/93.
47 *OG FRY*, 28/96.
48 *OG FRY*, 46/96.
49 *OG RS*, 25/96.
50 *OG RS*, 34/94 and 25/96.
51 *OG RS*, 17/92 last amended 25/96.
52 *OG RS*, 25/96.
53 *OG RS*, 79/91.
54 *OG RS*, 51/93.
55 *OG RS*, 48/94.
56 *OG FRY*, 26/96.
57 *OG RS*, 13/83.
58 *OG RS*, 42/77.
59 *OG RS*, 48/94.
60 *OG RS*, 18/92.
61 *OG SFRY*, 56/80.
62 *OG FRY*, 24/94.
63 *OG FRY*, 44/96.
64 *OG RS*, 17/95.
65 *OG RS*, 53/95.
66 *OG FRY*, 1/97 and corrections 5/97.
67 *OG FRY*, 54/96.
68 *OG RS*, 32/96 with included program.
69 *OG FRY*, 59/96.
70 *OG RS*, 29/96.

71 *OG RS*, 30/95.
72 *OG RS*, 5/95.
73 *OG RS*, 41/96 and 44/96.
74 *OG RS*, 49/96 and 50/96.
75 *OG RS*, 32/96.

CHAPTER TWELVE
SLOVAKIA

I. GENERAL DESCRIPTION OF THE ADMINISTRATIVE LEGAL SYSTEM

1. HISTORY OF THE ADMINISTRATIVE LEGAL SYSTEM[1]

1.1 The establishment of the major institutions of the administrative legal

System in their present form is primarily connected with the adoption of the Constitution[2] of the Slovak Republic on September 3, 1992, and the establishment of the Slovak Republic as an independent state on January 1, 1993. The structure and organization of the Slovak Government were determined by Constitutional Act No. 143/1968 CL on the Czechoslovak Federation: this Act set up the republic's ministries and defined their exclusive competencies as well as the competencies they shared with the federal government.

1.2 Major administrative acts

The major administrative procedural code is the Code of Administrative Procedures (hereinafter CAP), adopted in 1967, which is still in force.[3]

2. THE STRUCTURE OF THE EXECUTIVE

2.1 Government

The supreme executive body is the Government, which consists of the Prime Minister, Vice Prime Ministers and Ministers.[4] The Government is collectively responsible for the exercise of its powers to the National Council of the Slovak Republic (hereinafter the Parliament), which may take a vote of confidence in the Government at any time (Article 114, paragraph 1). Members of the Government are individually accountable to the Parliament (Article 116, paragraph 1). The Parliament may pass a vote of no confidence in any individual member of the Government (Article 116, paragraph 3). The Parliament may ask a report from the Government, heads of administrative agencies, the President of the Fond of National Property of the Slovak Republic and higher state officials in matters within their official jurisdiction: they are obliged to answer within 30 days or other term but not less than 15 days.[5] The Members of Parliament may interpellate the Government, any member of the Government or any heads of administrative agencies in matters within their official powers. The members of the Government and the heads of administrative agencies are obliged to answer within 30 days to the MP in written form (Article 80 of the Constitution and Article 129 and 130 of the SO). The Parliament expresses its opinion to a rejected answer to interpellation with a resolution. On the proposal of the Government or the interpellated body or at least one-fifth of the MPs the voting on the resolution may be connected with a vote of no confidence in the Government or one of its members [6]. Another form of the Government's accountability before Parliament is the hour of questions, when together with the General Prosecutor and the head of the Supreme Audit Office, the members of the Government, are obliged to answer the questions of the members of the Parliament.[7]

2.2 Local government

Currently, due to important new laws concerning the administrative territorial division of the country[8] and the local state administration,[9] the territorial and administrative division of the state and the status and competencies of the regions (kraje) and districts (okres) have changed substantially. As a result of these changes, 448 first level and 128 second-level administrative divisions have been replaced by 79 district (okres) and eight regional (kraj) offices. The laws reflect the goal to weaken local administration and subordinate it to the control of the state administration. The laws define the interrelation between the state administration and the Ministry of Internal Affairs, as well as the relations in this field between the Ministry of Internal Affairs and other ministries.[10] The branches of the Regional and District Offices (bodies of the local state administration) act and decide independently in a particular field of administrative matters (Article 9); they are entitled to issue generally binding ordinances (Article 3, paragraph 2). The principals of regional and district offices are nominated by the Government (Article 8, paragraph 1,2) and they act and are responsible for their work to the Government. On the other hand, the ministries direct the implementation of state administrative policies on the regional and district level by issuing generally binding legal norms, guidelines, directives, etc. (Article 11).

The municipality is the basic territorial administrative entity according to the Constitution (Article 64, paragraph 1). Higher territorial administrative entities and their bodies, as predicted by the Constitution (Article 64, paragraph 3.) have not been elected yet. The law defining their competencies is also lacking. In matters concerning local government the municipality decides independently: any restriction on this principle may be imposed only by a law. Local administration is carried out by local assemblies of citizens, referenda or through the executive authorities of the municipalities (Article 67). The municipalities pass generally binding ordinances in matters of local government. The municipality may be authorized by law to exercise some of the powers of the state administration. When exercising the powers of the state administration the municipality may, within its territorial jurisdiction, pass generally binding ordinances, which can be controlled and supervised by the Government (Article 71).

2.3 Acts of the administration

The President of the Republic is not entitled to issue normative regulations: he may return passed laws to the Parliament once, with remarks for reconsideration (suspensive veto, Article 102)n) of the Constitution). He is the chief commander of the army (Article 102)j), and as such is empowered to issue orders to the army.

The Government has power to issue decrees for the implementation of laws (Article 120, paragraph 1 of the Constitution). The ministries and the other administrative agencies may issue generally binding normative regulations only if they are empowered by laws, according to the laws (Article 123). If, according to a bill discussed in the Parliament, a decree is required for its implementation, the President of the Parliament may ask the drafter to submit a proposal for a decree. The drafter is always obliged to submit a draft decree if it will enter into force concurrently with a particular bill.[11] The Parliament need not approve the Government's or the ministries' decrees or generally binding normative regulations. The Parliament is not entitled to delegate its legislative power to the Government or to the President. The Government is not entitled to delegate its power to issue decrees to administrative authorities or empower ministries to issue normative regulations for the implementation of government decrees.

3. THE SYSTEM OF COURTS DEALING WITH ADMINISTRATIVE LAW ISSUES

3.1 Structure of the judicial system

There are not separate administrative law courts. Judicial power is exercised by the Constitutional Court of the Slovak Republic and the system of general courts that consists of the District (Okresne), Regional (Krajske) Courts and the Supreme Court of the Slovak Republic. The District and Regional Courts are instances of judicial review of administrative acts (Article 142, paragraph 1 of the Constitution). In connection with the new territorial and administrative division[12] new seats of courts have been established (eight regional courts, and 56 district courts, while there are 79 administrative districts).

3.2 Scope of jurisdiction of the courts

The Code on Civil Procedure (hereinafter CCP)[13] regulates the scope of courts' jurisdiction in administrative law issues (Articles 244 to 250). Generally, the courts scrutinize the legality of the decisions taken by bodies of the State administration, the bodies of the territorial governments, as well as the bodies of interest organisation authorities and other legal entities, empowered by law to decide on rights and duties of physical and legal persons in matters of public administration (Article 244, paragraph 2). There are two main forms of judicial jurisdiction in administrative issues: 1) deciding on actions brought against decisions of public authorities, 2) deciding on the remedies against the decisions of the public authorities. In the first case (Article 247) an action is brought before the court against an effective decision of public authority, while in the second one the action is brought against a non-effective decision of public authority (Article 250). The Supreme Court decides on competence disputes between courts and public authorities (Article 8a). The regional courts are general courts for judicial review of administrative decisions (Article 246). The district courts, if they are empowered by law, decide in cases of administrative offences (Article 246, paragraph 3).

3.3 Special quasi-judicial administrative bodies

In Slovakia, there are special quasi-judicial bodies for adjudicating cases requiring professional expertise in professional self-governments. The Law of the Slovak National Council No. 9/1992 on Commercial and Industrial Chambers sets up an arbitration court as an independent quasi-judicial body for the decision of cases on financial disputes (Article 16). The Supreme Court has subject competence to decide on remedies against decisions on professional self-government bodies (Article 246 paragraph 2)d) CCP). Law No. 218/1995 CL on arbitration decisions stipulates in Article 25 the method of cancellation of arbitration decision by the Court.

4. GENERAL PROCEDURAL LAWS AND CODES OF ADMINISTRATIVE LAW

The general administrative procedural law is Act No. 71/1967 CL on Administrative Procedures (CAP), which regulates the procedure on the rights, legally protected interests or duties of physical and legal persons affected by acts of the state administration unless a specific law provides otherwise (Article 1.1). This Code has not been directly amended; the indirect changes reflected only developments in the organization of the central and local state administration.

4.1 Internal administrative appeal

The procedure for appeal before administrative agencies is regulated by Articles 53 to 61 of the CAP. A party to the administrative proceedings has the right to appeal, unless a law provides otherwise. The party has to submit an appeal to the administrative authority which has issued the contested decision within 15 days of the delivery of decision. This body may reconsider its own decision, if it fully accepts the claims of appeal, if reconsideration does not affect another party to the proceedings, or if the parties to the proceeding agree to it. If this body does not reconsider its decision, it is obliged to submit the whole material with the appeal to the administrative authority deciding on the appeal, which is the "closest superior administrative body to which the body that issued the contested decision is subordinated" (Article 58)1) within 30 days since it received the appeal. Unless stipulated otherwise, the appeal has a suspensive effect. The appeal in administrative proceedings is generally in two instances.

The Regional State Authority decides in the cases of appeal against the district administrative body's decisions, while the right to decide in the cases of the appeal against the Regional State Authority's decisions belongs to the central body of state administration. Generally, the vast majority of administrative decisions can be appealed within the administrative hierarchy. The situation is different if: 1) the CAP does not apply and there are other specific laws, which do not provide for the right to appeal; 2) a specific law provides for appeal directly to the Court.

4.2 Judicial review of administrative acts

The Constitution of the Slovak Republic in Article 46, paragraph 2 regulates that "any person who claims to have been denied his or her rights through a decision made by a public authority may turn to a court of law to have the legality of the decision reviewed, unless otherwise provided by law. The review of decisions in matters of fundamental rights and freedoms shall not be excluded from the jurisdiction of courts of law." The procedure for seeking judicial review against valid decisions of an administrative body begins by an application for judicial review, which has to define the applicant's claims regarding which part of the decision or the whole of it is alleged to be "illegal" as well as what the applicant's proposal is.

The applicant can be a physical or legal person who claims, as a party to some administrative procedure, to have suffered a violation of his or her rights. The applicant has to be represented by a lawyer, if he himself has no legal education. The application for the judicial review has to be submitted within two months since the delivery of the administrative body's decision in the last instance. The application has no suspensive effect for the implementation of the decision of the administrative body unless stipulated otherwise by a law. If the matter of fact defined by the administrative body is correct, the court can decide without trial. For the court, it is of primary importance to determine the matter of fact in the time of issuing the administrative decision in scrutinizing the decision's legality. The procedure is somewhat different in cases when the court is empowered to decide as first instance on non-effective administrative decision.[14] Parties in the litigation are the parties to the administrative proceedings under dispute and the administrative body. The application has to be submitted to the court within 30 days after the issuing of the administrative decision. According to a party's proposal the court can decide to postpone the implementation of the administrative decision. In both cases the ground for invoking judicial review is the "illegality" of the administrative decision.

4.3 Acts excluded from the scope of judicial review

The categories of administrative acts excluded from judicial review are enumerated in Article 248 of the Code of Civil Procedure (CCP). 1) Courts do not scrutinize administrative decisions which do not have the nature of decision on rights and duties of physical or legal persons, especially generally binding normative acts, decisions of organizational nature and decisions regulating internal relations within the issuing body. 2) Furthermore, courts do not have jurisdiction over 10 categories of cases enumerated in Article 248, paragraph 2, such as decisions to be examined according to the general provisions of the CCP; decisions of administrative bodies in civil and commercial matters, when an administrative body acts in the name of the state as an owner; decisions of the military administration during a state of emergency; commands by army officials; decisions of administrative authorities that are of preliminary, procedural or disciplinary nature; decisions on disciplinary punishment of members of the armed forces; decisions on rejection of professional abilities for physical or legal persons; decisions on applications for benefits if there is no right to them, etc. 3) Annex A to the CCP, which is part of the Code, enumerates cases in which judicial review of decision of administrative bodies is excluded. A reasons for the exclusion from judicial review in these cases among others is the discretionary nature of the administrative decisions. 4) Decisions whose review is prescribed by specific laws are also excluded from judicial review.

4.4 Judicial remedies

In the case of judicial review against valid administrative decisions, if the court concludes that the administrative decision is legally incorrect or that the matter of fact in file does not accord with reality or is insufficient, it cancels the administrative decision and returns the file to contested administrative body for further proceedings. The administrative authorities are bound by the court's legal opinion. There is no further appeal against the court's decision (Article 250,1). In cases when the court is empowered to decide as a first instance on non-effective administrative decisions, if the administrative body issues a new decision accepting the applicant's proposal the court stops its procedure by resolution. The court can order a retrial and ask for the proof necessary for the judicial review of the contested decision. The court decides on the appeal by confirmation or cancellation of the decision. In the second case it returns the case to the administrative body for further proceedings: the body is bound by the court's legal opinion.

4.5 Exceptions from the general procedures

Except for the Code on Administrative Procedure, which serves as a general administrative procedural norm, there may be a specific law establishing specific administrative procedure in particular cases. Such laws establishing specific administrative procedures include the Law of the Slovak National Council (SNC)[15] on the Administration of Taxes and Fees, which establishes a specific procedure to be followed by the financial bodies in taxation disputes; and the Law of the SNC[16] on the Service Relations of the Employees of the Police of the Slovak Republic, which contains provisions on administrative procedure in matters of service relations etc. In several norms there are provisions referring to the implementation of CAP in certain cases, along with particular procedural rules in other cases such as the Code on Territorial Planning and Construction,[17] Law No. 100/1988 CL on Social Security, the Law on Offenses,[18] etc. There are also specific procedural rules for complaints and petitions by citizens set out by Government Order No. 150/1958 of the *Official Journal*. The territorial and professional self-governments are also governed by specific procedural rules.

5. THE OMBUDSMAN

The institution of ombudsman has not been established in the Slovak Republic.

6. OTHER FORMS OF SUPERVISION OVER THE ADMINISTRATION

The system of supervision of public administration is regulated by Law No. 10/1996 CL[19] on Supervision over the State Administration. This law gives supervisory prerogatives over the administration to the Government Office, the ministries, other bodies of state administration, bodies of the local state administration, and other bodies of state administration established by law. The law determines the structure of the organs. Yet it does not define clearly the competencies of the specific bodies (Article 4), and gives the Government Office broadly and vaguely defined competencies. The current system of supervision in the Slovak Republic consists of the National Council of the Slovak Republic (Parliament), the Government, the Supreme Audit Office, the central bodies of the state administration, the bodies of the local state administration, inspectorates, other specialised administrative agencies, town and village municipalities.

The Supreme Audit Office (Articles 60 to 63 of the Constitution) is "an independent agency supervising the auditing of, and control over, budgetary funds, public property, public property rights and public debts." The Supreme Audit Office submits annual reports to the National Council of the Slovak Republic. According to the Law on the Supreme Audit Office,[20] it is bound only by law, and it is responsible for its functioning only to the National Council. The Office prepares a statement on the governmental proposal for state final balance, and upon a request by the Council, a statement on the proposal for state budget, and submits them to the National Council. The Office has no right to impose sanctions; it only informs the supervisory bodies about violations of rules and unreasonable policies discovered during its supervision. It informs the ministry concerned and the Government. The supervised body is obliged to solve the problems within a given term, and inform the Office about it. If it fails to do so, the Office informs first the Government and then the National Council.

The inspectorates are independent budgetary organisations subordinated to the ministries concerned and act in narrowly specified fields. Their concrete competencies are regulated by specific laws. There are inspectorates on commercial, agriculture and food industry, environment, energetic, inspectorate on schools, spas and natural resources, etc. Further, there are other specialized administrative agencies for the supervision of veterinary issues, health, security and protection of health in labor, etc.

Other groups of state authorities are empowered by a specific law to supervise the administration, e.g. the state norm and test offices. The role of the public prosecutors in supervising the administration is defined by a law.[21] The Prosecutor's Office is an independent state body that protects the legal rights and interests of the physical and legal persons and the state. Its role in supervising the administration concerns primarily the implementation of laws and other generally binding legal norms, where the personal freedom of citizens is endangered by the decisions of state authorities (Article 4)1)b). Also, prosecutors supervise the implementation of laws and generally binding legal norms in proceedings and decisions of the bodies of the state administration and the bodies of local governments (Article 4)1)e). The prosecutors are empowered to examine the legality of generally binding legal norms, generally binding orders of villages, guidelines and resolutions issued by the bodies of the public administration, as well as to scrutinize the legality of the proceedings and decisions of the public administration in concrete cases. The prosecutors are also empowered to control the implementation of laws within the bodies of the public administration. If they find a violation of laws or generally binding legal norms, they can send a protest to the authority that issued this decision or to its superior organ. The issuing body can change its own decision accepting the protest of prosecutor or send it to its superior body in the administrative hierarchy. In cases governed by CAP, the minister decides on the supreme level about the protest of the prosecutors. If there is no specific term defined by the prosecutor, the administrative body has to decide on the protest within 30 days. If the protest is accepted, the administrative body concerned has to remedy the violated rights. The bodies of the public administration have to inform the prosecutor about the measures taken by them to implement his proposal and restore legality.

7. PARLIAMENTARY COMMITTEES

According to Article 92)1) of the Constitution, the National Council establishes committees composed of its own members as initiative and supervising bodies. The procedures governing the debates and deliberation in the Parliament and the Committees are regulated by Law on the Standing Orders.[22] The National Council, according to the Standing Orders (Article 45 1,2,3)b), sets up a committee on mandate and immunity, on conflict of interest and a constitutional committee; other committees are established on demand. The purpose of the committees concerning the supervision of the administration is to examine the implementation of laws and control whether decrees issued for their implementation are in conformity with them. The National Council also establishes special supervisory committees (Article 60) for the supervision of administrative activities implemented according to special laws (such as the Law on the Slovak Intelligence Agency,[23] and the Law on Military Intelligence Agency[24]). The National Council and the committees can set up permanent or temporary commissions for consultations or preparation of statements. Members cannot only be members of Parliament but others as well. Only MPs, however, can be elected as presidents of such commissions.

II. DEVELOPMENTS IN ADMINISTRATIVE LAW DURING 1996-1997

INTRODUCTION

One of the most important developments in administrative law during the discussed period was the attempt of the third Meciar Government (after winning the election in October 1994) to endorse cronyism through privatisation, centralise its power in the administration, increase the control of the executive towards the Parliament, local governments, and the other branches of power. In this respect for the erosion of constitutionalism brought by some government steps, the disregard of public interest in favour of political and personal interests, and the lack of respect for the rule of law demonstrated by government coalition officials gave grounds for a sharp internal criticism (by the opposition) and external criticism (by the European Union, the United States, and others). It was primarily this "democracy deficit" that caused the exclusion of Slovakia from the first round of NATO and European Union enlargement, despite its being a member of the Visegrad Four.

The government's approach to the exercise of power was demonstrated beginning on the night of November 3–4, 1994, when the government coalition–composed by the Movement for Democratic Slovakia (HZDS), the Slovak National Party (SNS) and the Association of the Workers of Slovakia (ZRS)–restricted the minority representation in parliamentary committees, excluding the opposition from the supervision committees over key state functions (e.g., secret police, media, etc.). The coalition further changed the governing bodies of the National Property Fund and staffed them with its own members: the ruling coalition acted according to the majority rule in a proportional electoral system. This resulted in a delegative rather than representative notion of authority, weak accountability and a number of authoritarian practices. There were further attempts to change the rules of the game, exercise confrontational power politics, replace the parliamentary form of government with a presidential one, and even change the Constitution itself. The main aim of these steps was to ensure the ruling coalition control over all political life in the country.

The continued conflict between the President and the Prime Minister has caused further external and internal problems in such areas as the adoption of laws, lack of co-operation on the government side, and mutual verbal attacks. Politically motivated violence remained one of the main public concerns, coupled with the lack of subsequent investigation by the responsible bodies and lack of opposition control in the committees supervising the secret police. This resulted in substantial public suspicion concerning the participation of the state secret police in some of these actions (e.g. the kidnapping of President Kovac's son to Austria, and the murder of Robert Remias, who helped to hide a witness of the kidnapping of a former secret service agent).

The most disputed laws between the government and the opposition in 1996 and 1997 were two amendments to the Penal Code, the laws on administrative territorial division, on prosecutors, on universities, on foundations, and the new standing orders of Parliament. The Law on State Language (adopted in November 1995) and its implementation caused–in education, in local governments and other fields–further tension between the Government and the ethnic Hungarians, which make up to 11 per cent of the population.

The unfinished investigation of the President's son's kidnapping, the withdrawal of parliamentary mandate of Member of Parliament Gaulieder against his will, and the thwarting by the Minister of Internal Affairs of the referendum on NATO and the direct election of the President were among the most controversial acts of the governing coalition. The unconstitutional vote of no confidence in the President by the Parliament, and the cronyism and etatism endorsed by the Government mainly through the establishment of new administrative bodies also became a matter of serious public concern. Several cases were raised addressing constitutional and administrative issues. In many of them the Constitutional Court has played an essential role. For example, in 1996 the Constitutional Court ruled in eight cases on the unconstitutionality of some laws passed by the Parliament. The real impact of the Constitutional Court's decision was diminished by the fact that it was not possible to change retrospectively the results of the unconstitutional decisions of the state administrative bodies (as in the case of FNM; see section D), or that the decisions of the CC were clearly ignored (the continuation of FNM practice in sales, or the refusal by the parliamentary majority to give MP Gaulieder back his mandate).

Scholarly discussion has taken place on Slovakia's present situation, which can be characterised as unconsolidated unstable democracy, with fragile democratic institutions. The implementation of democratic procedures is often thwarted, and the continuing struggle over the rules of the game has led to legal and political uncertainty. In this respect, most scholars share the view that Slovakia still has a democratic regime: "Despite the political setbacks of November 1994, the current political problems of Slovakia remain problems of democratic consolidation rather than of authoritarianism. The establishment of an authoritarian regime, however, would be possible if the democratic forces fail to mount effective resistance to the current authoritarian tendencies. Consolidation remains an open-ended process... Regime transition in Slovakia remains an open-ended process".[25]

Relations between the independent, local governments and the centrally controlled local administrations have been consistently tense. Three major controversies dominate the conflict. First, the independent local governments and the Government-controlled state and local administrations are locked in a tight contest over financing and the division of rights and responsibilities. Second, there is an ongoing dispute over the appropriate boundaries of the administrative and electoral units. Finally, there is a conflict over the creation of a second set of regional authorities.

Efforts by the Government of Prime Minister Meciar to increase its control over Slovakia's regions has shaped policy on three issues since it took power at the end of 1994. First, the Meciar government has made a concerted effort to centralise and consolidate the power of the local state administration at the expense of the local governments. Second, there has been a constant threat that it could gerrymander administrative and electoral boundaries to maximise electoral advantage—particularly over Slovakia's Hungarian minority. Third, it has delayed and complicated the process of creating a new, regional level of independent local governments that might compete with the state's regional administrations."[26]

The period under discussion has also been characterised by the increasing tension between the Government and the ethnic Hungarians. The Government passed several laws, especially on the proposal of the SNS, aiming at the restriction of the rights of the Hungarian minority in Slovakia directly, such as the Law on State Language, and the Standing Orders of Parliament, or indirectly such as the amendments to the Penal Code, the Law on Administrative Territorial Division, the Law on Foundations, etc. Several administrative steps of the Ministry of Culture and the Ministry of Education caused further direct restriction of minority rights (e.g. in the sphere of education, the prohibition of bilingual school report cards, and the dismissal of those school directors and teachers who opposed it; in the sphere of culture, the drastic reduction of state subsidies for cultural organisations of Hungarians, denial of the capacity of legal entities of Hungarian cultural institution [two theatres], and others.). The irony of the situation is that these severe restrictions happened after the signature of the Hungarian-Slovak Treaty on Neighbourliness and Co-operation on March 19, 1995.

Generally, this period has been characterized by sharp political disputes between the Government, the opposition and the political parties of the ethnic Hungarians over the nature, content and exercise of power in the state administration, the role and competencies of the administrative bodies, administrative division of the country, the criteria for redistricting, the relationship between local administration and state administration, as well as the scope of the principle of separation of powers.

A. THE CONSTITUTION

There were no constitutional amendments with a direct impact on administrative law in the period under review. The only Constitutional Act adopted in this period is CA No. 47/1996 CL, regarding border changes with the Czech Republic, which has only confirmed the agreements between the Slovak and the Czech government.

B. LEGISLATION

1. PROCEDURAL AND GENERAL ORGANISATIONAL LAWS

1.1 Laws on the judicial system

The general procedural law has not been amended during this period. In connection with the law on new territorial-administrative division, Law No. 328/ 1996 CL established new seats of courts and court districts. According to this Law eight regional courts and 56 district courts were established: that means there are fewer court districts than administrative ones (79). According to Article 145) 1) of the Constitution a judge shall be elected by the National Council on the advice of the Government for a four-year term. Upon the completion of this term, the National Council, on the advice of the Government, shall re-elect the judge for the same tenure. This enabled the Government to veto unwanted candidates every four years by law. However, after strong protests from the Association of Judges and the media, the Government approved all candidates that fulfilled the requirements (except in two cases).

1.2 Laws on the structure of the Government

There have not been changes in the structure of the central government bodies in 1996–1997. The last change occurred in mid–1995 when the Ministry of Privatisation was dissolved and its competencies were transferred to the Fund of National Property.

Substantial changes were introduced in the structure of basic executive institutions and local administration by the adoption of the Law on the Organisation of Local State Administration[27]. This Law established regional and district offices and defined their competencies.[28] By this Law, the local state administration assumed the powers of some specialised agencies, which were independent before. Agencies such as the District Agency on Environment, the Regional Forest Agency, and the School Agency were abolished. This law established a two-level system of state administration; the corresponding legislation for two-level self-governing bodies is not in place yet.

The finding of the Constitutional Court published under No. 352/1996 CL held that Law No. 369/1994 CL on Amendments to the Law on the Conditions for Transfer of State Property to Other Persons, which transferred the competencies (in privatisation by direct sales) of the Government to the Fund of National Property, is contradictory to the Constitution. In its reasoning the Court stated that the Constitution defines the government's competencies, which could not be implemented if they are transferred to the competency of other bodies, especially if another body renders the final decision and the government only gives an unbinding opinion on it.

Also in this area, Law No. 10/1996 CL on the Supervision over the State Administration established a system of bodies for supervision.

1.3 The Standing Orders of Parliament

The Standing Orders of the National Council of the Slovak Republic[29] establishes the rules of deliberation and the functioning of the Parliament and its committees. After a long preparation the Law was adopted in September 1996. The President exercised his suspensive veto and returned it to the Government with remarks. The Government had also asked the President to do so for formal and substantive reasons. The President requested to include additional provisions in the Standing Orders, e.g. his right to be present in closed sessions of the Parliament, and the right of national minorities to use their mother tongue in the sessions of the Parliament. The President further insisted on having at least eight days to decide whether to return a bill to the Parliament. The Government has asked to have the right to issue its own legislative rules, and that the Parliament would not have the right to determine concrete and scheduled tasks for the Government.

The Parliament passed the Standing Orders, leaving out the presidential suggestions. According to Article 69)1) of the Standing Orders the Parliament adopted Resolution No. 519 on December 18, 1996, on Legislative Rules for the Creation of Laws. The Standing Orders introduced new method of deliberation of bills in three readings, which can improve the quality of legislation. On the other hand it restricted the President's constitutional powers with defining the date for the return of bills to the Parliament. Article 18 of the former Standing Orders that guaranteed MPs the right to use their mother tongue in Parliament was repealed, breaking a long-standing tradition of tolerance.

2. SUBSTANCE

2.1 Management of the economy

2.1.1 PRIVATISATION

No laws on privatisation have been adopted since 1994. The last amendment[30] to the privatisation law was in 1994, which abolished voucher privatisation and introduced the bond method, and transferred the powers of direct sales of the Ministry of Privatisation to the Fund of National Properties (FNP).[31] Several rulings of the Constitutional Court, however, concerned laws on privatisation or their parts. Besides the finding mentioned above, Finding No. 4/1996 CL concerning the constitutionality of the issue whether the replacement of the voucher method of privatisation by a bond method is in compliance with the constitution was a matter of significant public attention. The Court admitted the possibility of changing the rules of privatisation of state property by the state. In the view of the Court, Article 20 of the Constitution only guarantees the protection of property of the owner: it is not a ground for demanding property. It is fully within the legitimate power of the state to decide the method of privatisation of its property.

2.1.2 LAND AND PROPERTY ISSUES

In another finding (No. 135/1996 CL) the Constitutional Court dealt with the equal position of the state with other parties in property issues. The Court did not accept as constitutional the "special" position of the state concerning property relations under Article 6 of Law 192/1995 CL on the safeguarding of state interest in privatisation of strategically important state enterprises and shareholding companies. Law No. 180/1995 CL on some measures for arrangement of land properties regulates the procedure in renewal for the land register and renewal of the registration of the land owners. It establishes the competencies of the Slovak Land Fund in the case of unknown owner. The goal of the law is to eliminate the creation of small pieces of land. A group of MPs brought an action before the Constitutional

Court claiming contradiction of some provisions of this law with the Constitution. The CC, in its Finding No. 131/1996 CL, held that the provision stipulating that agricultural land smaller than 20 ars (1 ar equals 10x10 m) and forest smaller than 50 ars, should be transferred to the state in return for adequate compensation, if the ancestors cannot agree on the distribution of property rights among themselves, is contradictory to the Constitution.

2.2 Resolution of commercial disputes

The adoption of the Law on Arbitration[32] aimed to speed up and simplify the work of commercial courts and make easier the development of commercial relations. According to this law, by the arbitration contract parties can agree that disputes between them will be solved by an arbiter.

2.3 Environment

In 1996 legislation on the fees for waste storage was passed. According to Law No. 222/1996 Cl, article 3)1)f), regional and district offices exercise state power in the field of environment. The District Office is an appeal body deciding on complaints against the decisions of the municipalities. The regional offices are second-level appeal bodies if the district bodies decide as a first instance.

2.4 Finance

The most important laws on finance were the Law on Banks,[33] which introduced the institute of hypothecate (mortgage) banking. According to this law (Article 38), hypothecate business consists in offering of hypothecate loans and issuing of hypothecate bonds, as well of communal bonds by banks. The Law on Concessional Procurement[34] established rules of procurement of construction of public interest. The procurement concerns construction of buildings owned by the state or a municipality by private firms. Aside from legal definitions of construction of public interest, aquisitor, concessionaire and concession, the law defines the rules in concessional procedure, where the general rules of the Code of Administrative Procedure are not applicable.

2.5 Transport

The Law on Road Transport[35] regulated the conditions of running an enterprise in road transport and the jurisdiction of the bodies of the state administration in this field. According to this law, it is possible to start an enterprise only with the permission of an administrative body, issued on the ground of compliance with professional requirements. It is in the jurisdiction of the municipalities to issue and cancel licences for town and road transport firms, to supervise transport in the municipal territories.

2.6 Customs

The Law on Customs[36] regulated the jurisdiction of the bodies of the state administration in the field of customs and the organisation of the custom administration, the rights and duties of the custom authorities, declarants and other persons in custom control matters. Furthermore it defined criteria for the imposition of custom duties, restrictions in importing goods from abroad. The law also defined the principles and condition for the determination of custom debts, custom offences, custom deposits and the collection of back payments.

2.7 Media

The Law on Audiovisual Media[37] regulates some conditions of the production, use and distribution of audiovisual products. It defines an audiovisual product and regulates the rights and duties of the producers, distributors and users of audiovisual products. It permits the participation of the Ministry of Finance in the financing of the production and the distribution of domestic audiovisual products through the state cultural fund Pro Slovakia. The Law on Advertisement[38] regulates the general requirements concerning the advertisement and relationship between associations established for the protection of advertisement ethics and the bodies of administrative supervision. There is no specific law on the press, in spite of years of preparation of drafts on the issue. One of the main reasons are the disputes between the government and the Journalists' Association on the scope and content of the law. There is a dual system of broadcasting (public and private) regulated by the Law on Operating Radio and TV Broadcasting,[39] and Law No. 294/1992 CL. Law No. 321/1996 CL amended the Law on TV and Radio Broadcasting. Among other amendments, it redefined some functions of the Council on TV Broadcasting and the Council of Radio Broadcasting, as well as the rights and duties of their members.

2.8 Management of socio-cultural processes

The management of socio-cultural processes in territorial organisation has been modified by Law No. 221/1991 CL on the Territorial and Administrative Division and Law No. 222/1996 CL on the Organisation of the Local State Administration

(See Part I.)2)2.2). According to Law No. 222/1996 CL the district office (*okresny urad*) has competency (Article 5)3)a) to represent the state in deliberations of territorial planning of the municipalities, except for Bratislava and Kosice, where the regional offices have this prerogative.

One of the most disputed laws of this period has been Law No. 30/1997 CL on Higher Education (on universities), which amended Law No. 172/1990 CL. Broad professional discussions and sharp confrontations preceded the adoption of this law: the President vetoed the law, but his veto was overruled by Parliament. The Law stipulates the condition for the establishment and abolition of universities, the conditions for licensing of establishment and abolition of non-state universities. The Law further changes the role of some academic bodies, enhances the powers of the Ministry of Education toward universities, regulates the approval of academic decrees, teachers' qualifications, etc. This Law has caused substantial changes by weakening the universities' autonomy and worsening their economic situation. The position of the Ministry of Education became stronger toward universities, as reflected e.g. in Article 14 (on its prerogatives to intervene in academic matters) and Article 34 (on the process of decision in habilitation procedure for docents and the inauguration procedure of professors; the Law on Administrative Procedure is applicable). Other change is that until now the university government consisted of two chambers (employees and students), with the right of student veto in certain cases. Now the Law establishes a separate University Student Council only for students. In the ministry's opinion the Law empowered the ministry to allocate means from the budget "in accordance with the state policy of employment, and the state policy in the field of the development of universities, state policy in the field of the development of science and technology" Article 15)1)c). The cancellations of the provision that guaranteed tax-free income from other than budget sources for the universities worsened their economic situation. Positively evaluated regulations are the provisions on Ph.D. programs, scientific preparation, awarding academic degrees to graduates, etc.

The reorganisation of the local state administration resulted in changes in the field of education as well. Law No. 222/1996 CL in Article XXIII specified the bodies that exercise state supervision in education (directors of school, district and regional offices, and the Ministry of Education). According to these modifications the regional offices have under their jurisdiction the secondary schools, while the district offices have the elementary schools.

Law No. 222/1996 CL modifies Law No. 277/1996 CL on Health Care in conjunction with the reorganisation of the local state administration. It enumerates the health-care institution (Article XX), and establishes time limits for asking authorisation of establishments from the ministry. The annex to this law also lists the powers of the Regional Offices in the field of health care (points 153 to 174). While the Ministry of Health (among others) specifies the structure of the health care institutions, professionally direct medical service, the regional offices professionally guide the state district health inspectorates, direct and exercise state health supervision, and establish a wide range of medical institutions.

Finally, the Ministry of Environment in its Regulation No. 293/1996 CL published the list of protected areas and natural reserves: they have been declared as national natural reserves and granted special protection.

2.9 Management of political processes

A number of new legislative acts have been adopted in this area. First, the President of the National Council by Decree No. 25/1996 CL promulgated the full text of Law No. 3/1993 CL, as amended, on the establishment of the Army of the Slovak Republic. This law regulates the essential structure of the army and its main hierarchy. Secondly, the Ministry of Internal Affairs has passed Regulation No. 303/1996 CL on Securing Preparation for Civil Protection: in it the Ministry determined the scope of competence of the Regional and District Offices in this field.

Further, the Parliament has passed a Law on Slovaks Abroad,[40] which defines the status of the Slovak abroad as a person "who is not a citizen of the Slovak Republic, if he/she has Slovak nationality or Slovak ethnic origin and Slovak cultural-linguistic consciousness" (Article 2)2). The Ministry of Foreign Affairs is empowered to decide on granting the status of Slovaks abroad: it registers those with this status, directs and co-ordinates the creation and implementation of state foreign policy in relation to the Slovaks abroad and elaborates the concept of state policy toward the Slovaks abroad in co-operation with other central bodies of state administration.

The Ministry of Culture co-ordinates and provides aid to state and non-state institution of Slovaks abroad aiming to maintain their Slovak identity and co-ordinates and provides documentation concerning the Slovaks abroad. A person with this status has a right to ask for acceptance for studies, ask for a job without any specific further permission, ask for citizenship, own and buy real estate in Slovakia, etc. Under this definition, former non-ethnic Slovak citizens of Slovakia living abroad are not covered by this law.

The Law on Foundations[41] regulated this issue independently for the first time. Before it was covered by provisions of the Civil Code. The content and nature of this law have been discussed broadly internally and internationally. The law defines the concept of foundation; it regulates the requirements for the establishment and abolition of foundations, their governing bodies and competencies, and the management of a foundation. It has introduced several essential modifications to the previous principles of regulation. The law transferred the registration of foundations from the district offices to the Ministry of Internal Affairs, it made obligatory re-registration for each already existing foundation within 12 months. If they are not ready to comply with the requirement of this law, they are to be abolished. It has also increased the amount of required founding capital to establish a foundation. The law increased the state control over the foundation's property and its management by state administration. The main source of criticism against this law by the representatives of NGOs has been that it increases the role of the state, the possibility of state interference with its management, and the broadening of discretionary powers of central state administrative bodies in the registration procedure. It has been argued that the law would lead to the disappearance of smaller foundations and restricted possibilities of the citizens for participation in the activities of civil society.

Another controversial bill proposed by the Government has been the amendment to the Penal Code, which is also known as Bill on Protection of the Republic. The Government's bill focused on the solution of two issues–acts against the state and its constitutional arrangement and offences directed against financial regulation. The Government's bill was adopted in March 1996, but the President exercised his right of suspensive veto and returned the adopted bill with remarks to the Parliament. He argued that the adopted bill was undemocratic, violated the freedom of expression, freedom of assembly, freedom of information, equality before the law and equal protection of different forms of property. What happened next was an oddity, from a constitutional point of view: the President of the National Council did not propose the returned bill for a second deliberation and voting. Furthermore, at the end of 1996 MPs from the Government coalition proposed their own bill on the same subject. Although slightly modified, the new bill still contained undemocratic and unconstitutional parts. This bill did not receive a majority, but the whole process violated the procedure for adopting legislation prescribed by the Constitution and the Standing Orders of Parliament, according to which two bills on the same subject cannot be put simultaneously before the Parliament. These bills were perceived as a vehicle against the opposition, the journalists and the ethnic Hungarians, which caused a substantial loss of international respect for the country.

Probably the most controversial dispute between the Government and the political parties of the ethnic Hungarians causing tensions in everyday life was the Law on State Language,[42] which entered into force on January 1, 1996, together with regulation concerning fines, which entered into force on January 1, 1997. This law stipulates that the Slovak language is the state language on the territory of the Slovak Republic and enjoys precedence over all other languages. The law, at least as it declares in Article 1)4), does not regulate the use of national minorities' languages. The law regulates state language and its protection, the use of state language in official communication, in education, mass media, the army, judicial and administrative procedure, the economy, social services and health care. The Ministry of Culture is empowered to supervise the implementation of the law. It can punish the violation of language law by imposing high fines. The main criticism against this law emphasised the following problems:

This law cancelled Law No. 428/1990 CL on the Official Language, which allowed for the use of minority languages in official communication. In this situation there is a lacuna, because according to the Constitution (Article 6.2) the use of other languages in official communication shall be determined by a law. The law by some of its provisions intrudes into the sphere of private life, freedom of speech, culture, and media. The discretionary power of the Ministry of Culture in imposing fines, the vague criteria of evaluation, and the ambiguous role of language inspectors are further controversial characteristics of this piece of legislation.

In accordance with the law, the Ministry of Culture issued on September 2, 1996, a statute on linguistic adviser,[43] responsible for supervising and proposing sanctions against language offenders. This led to further tension, legal uncertainty, minority language oppression, and possibilities of abuse. Citing the law on state language, the Ministry of Education introduced the Slovak school report cards, replacing the former bilingual report cards in Hungarian language schools. Those directors refusing to do so were dismissed. Thirty-three MPs of the Hungarian Coalition and the Christian Democratic Movement brought an action before the Constitutional Court regarding the unconstitutionality of several provisions of this law.

The Constitutional Court in its Finding No. 260/1997 CL on August 26, 1997, said that Article 3)5), in conjunction with Article 12 of the Law on State Language, contradicts Article 34 of the Constitution. This means that by the cancellation of the former Law on Use of Official Language (which permitted the use of minority languages in official communication) the provisions according to which the citizens have to prepare all written submissions to public bodies in the state language contradicts the provision of the Constitution guaranteeing the right to use a minority language in official communications (Article 34)2)b).

Another issue of significant controversy was the legal regulation of an institution, Matica Slovenska, designed to protect the national identity and culture of Slovakia. The very specific status of this institution is reflected in the Law on Matica Slovenska.[44] According to this law, Matica is a public institution and legal entity that has a set of tasks given to it by the state (Article 2)1), including to strengthen Slovak patriotism, deepen the relation of the citizens to Slovak statehood, participate in the development of local and regional culture, increase national consciousness of the Slovaks in nationally mixed areas, and strengthen the relations of national minorities and ethnic groups with Slovak national culture. Furthermore it co-operates with the state bodies and the bodies of local government in the development of culture and social life and co-operates in the preparation of school books for elementary and secondary schools, as authorised by the Ministry of Culture. Matica Slovenska contributes to the realisation of the tasks of the state in the field of culture and science.

The Law regulates the organisation of Matica, the competence of its bodies, and its economic management. Matica manages its own property and state property, and it receives subsidies from the state budget for the fulfillment of its tasks. Critics argued that such legal protection for Matica Slovenska, which undoubtedly was a historically and culturally important organisation for the Slovaks in the period of statelessness and oppression, is anachronistic in an independent Slovak state. Moreover, it takes some of the competencies of the Ministry of Culture and other ministries, along with subsidies from the state budget, without clear mechanisms of accountability and transparency. The minorities regard the present policies of Matica Slovenska as nationalistic, aiming at the forced assimilation of non-Slovaks through culture, education, media and laws with the government's political, legal and financial support. Matica has been the initiator of the exclusionist "Only Slovak" language law bill and organiser of a mass demonstration in support of it.

C. REGULATION

1. THE PRESIDENT

The President of the Slovak Republic is not empowered to issue normative acts.

2. NORMATIVE ACTS OF THE GOVERNMENT AND THE DEPARTMENTS

See the discussion on legislation.

D. JUDICIAL DECISIONS

INTRODUCTION

The Code on Civil Procedure[45] regulates the procedural and substantive criteria for judicial judgements in Articles 152–175, which also apply to the decisions within the judicial review of administrative acts.

All judgements have to be declared publicly. A judgement contains a decision on the merits of the case with reasoning, information on the right to appeal, and on the execution of the judgement (Article 156)1). The most relevant decisions for further practice are published in the Supreme Court's "Collection of the Judicial Decisions and Opinions".

The Administrative and Standing Orders of the Constitutional Court[46] regulate the form of the decisions of the Constitutional Court in Articles 25–31. The Constitutional Court decides in three forms: 1) on the merits of a case generally by findings; 2) on the case of treason allegedly committed by the President of the Slovak Republic, by decisions; 3) in other cases, by resolutions (Article 25)1). All findings of the Constitutional Court are published annually in the Collection of Findings and Resolutions of the Constitutional Court of the Slovak Republic. Resolutions dealing with the interpretation of constitutional provisions or other resolutions decided by the Constitutional Court are also published in the Collection (Article 31)1). From all findings and resolutions, only the part of the decision on the merits and the part of the reasoning from which the legal opinion of the Court is clear are published.

The written form of the decisions is standardised. After the words "In the name of the Slovak Republic" must appear the name of the court, whether it decided in plenary session or in Senate, the names of judges, the subject, the parties in case, the names of their representatives, the decision on the merits, the reasoning, the date and the place of declaration (Article 25)2). As mentioned above, a part of the decision on the merits is published in the Collection of Laws (Article 27).

1. CONSTITUTIONAL COURT

The Constitutional Court has played an important role in guaranteeing constitutionality and the rule of law. Many of its rulings are essential for the development of administrative law. In 1996, for example, the Constitutional Court ruled eight times that some laws or parts of laws adopted by the Parliament did not comply with the Constitution. We have already referred to some relevant rulings of the Constitutional Court: here we offer some of the other relevant findings, resolutions or interpretations of the Constitutional Court.

The existing tension between the President and the Government has caused a set of cases before the Constitutional Court dealing with the relations between the constitutional actors, the prerogatives of the government, and interpretation of constitutional provisions on separation of powers. Finding No. 153/1996 CL concerned the constitutionality of the amendment to the law on referendum[47] article I.)1 and 3). The President of the Republic complained against this amendment because it deprived him from the power to declare a referendum upon citizens' petition. According to this amendment, citizens have to submit their petition on referendum not to the President of the Republic, but to the President of the Parliament. The Court ruled that according to Article 95 of the Constitution, the President of the Republic is not only empowered, but also obliged to declare a referendum if two constitutional requirements are fulfilled. Firstly, the petition must be signed by more than 350,000 citizens or voted by the Parliament; secondly, the question of referendum should not concern basic human rights and freedoms, taxes, revenues and the state budget as it is stipulated by Article 93)3) of the Constitution.

Resolution No. 139/97 CL of May 21, 1997, gives an interpretation of Articles 72 and 93)2) of the Constitution concerning the question whether it is possible to amend the Constitution by referendum. In the resolution, the Court held that legislative power is regulated in two forms: it does not belong just to the National Council but also directly to the citizens. The Constitution does not contain any prohibition to declare referendum according to Article 93)2 on matter of the amendment of the Constitution or its part by referendum.

Two other resolutions offered an interpretation of the President's powers according to Article 102)r and i) toward the Government and toward the bodies acting in criminal proceedings. According to Resolution No. 229/1996 CL of July 11, 1996, the President's prerogative to ask for a report from the Government or its members does not empower him to determine the method and procedure of its preparation: these belong to the exclusive competency of the Government. The President is not empowered to define a deadline for the submission of the Government's report. The period for the preparation of report depends on the constitutional principle of co-operation between the two bodies of executive power. Its length is conditioned by the time objectively necessary for the Government to collect the necessary data.

In the second case, Resolution No. 88/1997 CL, the Court, on the request of the General Prosecutor, interpreted the relevant constitutional provisions and held that the President is empowered to ask for the co-operation of the bodies involved in criminal procedure, if their co-operation is necessary for the presidential decision on a request for pardon, and if the President considers such a co-operation proper, effective or necessary.

There have been several findings of the Constitutional Court concerning controversial issues in privatisation. These include Finding No. 352/1996 CL on non-compliance of Law No. 369/1994 CL on the conditions of transfer of state property to other persons with the Constitution. According to this law the competence to decide on direct sale in privatisation has been transferred from the Government to the Fund of National Property. The Constitutional Court ruled that all direct sales within the privatisation process approved by the Fund of National Property since the end of 1994 until the Constitutional Court's finding in mid–1996 were unconstitutional. In the reasoning it argued that the Constitution regulated certain competencies of the Government, which cannot be exercised if, for matters in its exclusive competence, the Government gives only an unbinding opinion, while the final decision is in the power of another body, the Fund of National Property. With this decision the Government voluntarily gave up part of its competence over the economy of the country in the area of privatisation by transferring it to a non-state body, without any control or democratic accountability. As a result of this step, billions of crowns in state property have been privatised without any direct control by the Government and Parliament. This finding further stated that all direct sales approved by the FNP between the end of 1994 and the date of issuing the finding were unconstitutional, but it was not possible to change the unconstitutional situation created by the practice of FNP. As a result, the Fund of National Property continued its unconstitutional practice of privatisation decisions even after the Constitutional Court's ruling in 1997.

Finally, a group of MPs brought a complaint before the Constitutional Court against Articles 29)5) and 55)a) of the former Standing Orders of the Slovak National Council[48]. The main point of the complaint was the unconstitutionality of the named provisions which authorised the Parliament to establish investigative commissions empowered to take certain procedural measures, including the use of forms of legal coercion toward witnesses. The Court, in its Finding No. 2/1996 CL, declared the unconstitutionality of these provisions. In the reasoning it argued that Parliament can regulate legal and other relations in society only within limits and by methods in compliance with the Constitution. Thus the Parliament can investigate but only within the frame of the Constitution. Further, the Constitutional Court argued that the Constitution does not permit connecting the supervisory competency of the Parliament with sanctioning and obliging other citizens except for the major constitutional actors. The Parliament cannot establish investigatory commissions outside the framework of the Constitution; the commissions cannot oblige citizens to give evidence.

A short list of other cases before the Constitutional Court: In September 1996 the Court proclaimed the unconstitutionality of the presence of prosecutors in civil procedure after the amendment of the Code of Civil Procedure. In November 1996 the Court confirmed the President's powers to nominate the chief of general staff of the army and declared unconstitutional the provision of the regulation to the law on the army passed in 1995 that took it away from the President. On the other hand, the Court confirmed the amendment, which took the power of the President to nominate the head of the secret intelligence service, because his status has been defined as not "higher state functionary" according to Article 102 of the Constitution, but only "state functionary". In September 1996 the Court declared that the constitutional right of citizen Kovac Jr. (the kidnapped son of the President of the Republic who, at the time, was in Austria) to enter the Republic had been violated: his entry was made impossible by non-action of the Ministry of Foreign Affairs.

Finally, in the middle of 1997 the Court ruled in the case of MP Gaulieder (who left the fraction of the ruling party of HZDS, and after this was stripped of his mandate against his will by the parliamentary majority) that this decision was unconstitutional. The parliamentary majority openly refused to cancel its own resolution and comply with the Court decision. The mandate of MP Gaulieder was not restored.

The Chapter has been prepared on the basis of information provided by Ivan Gyurcsik

NOTES

1 The development of the major institutions of state administration in the present territory of the Slovak Republic in this century was a complex and dynamic process. Originally the territory of present-day Slovakia constituted the northern part of the Hungarian Kingdom and was under the jurisdiction of the central executive and administrative bodies of the Hungarian Kingdom and the Hungarian system of counties as administrative units. After the First World War Slovakia became a province of the Czechoslovak Republic with a special Ministry for Slovakia, later called the Provincial Office. In 1938 Slovakia became an autonomous republic. In 1939, an independent Slovak state was established, which existed until 1945. After the Second World War Slovakia again became part of the unitary Czechoslovak Republic (1945–1968) without a separate administrative legal system. In 1969, however, Slovakia was granted the status of a federal republic (1969–1992), with Slovak government and central administrative bodies enjoying limited autonomy.

2 No. 460/1992 of the Collection of Laws, hereinafter CL.

3 Law No. 67/1967 CL.

4 Articles 108 and 109 paragraph 1 of the Constitution.

5 Article 128 of the Law No. 350/1996 CL on Standing Order of the National Council of the Slovak Republic, hereinafter SO.

6 SO Article 130, paragraph 6

7 Article 131, SO.

8 Law No. 221/1996 CL on territorial and administrative division.

[9] Law No. 222/1996 CL on local state administration.
[10] Article 11, of the Law No. 222/1996 CL.
[11] Article 68, paragraph 4. Standing Orders No. 350/1996 CL.
[12] Law No. 328/1996 CL.
[13] No. 38/1995 CL.
[14] Articles 250l to 250s, CAP.
[15] No. 511/1992 CL.
[16] No. 410/1991 CL.
[17] No. 50/1976 CL.
[18] No. 372/1990 CL.
[19] No. 372/1990 CL.
[20] No. 39/1993 CL.
[21] No. 314/1996 CL.
[22] No. 350/1996 CL.
[23] No. 46/1993 CL.
[24] No. 198/194 CL.
[25] Vladimir Krivy, "Slovakia's Regions and the Struggle for Power", ***Slovakia: Problems of Democratic Consolidation, The Struggle for the Rules of the Game,*** Slovak Political Sciencc Association, Friedrich Ebert Stiftung, Edited by Sona Szomolanyi and John A. Gould, Bratislava 1997, Szomolanyi, p. 12.
[26] "Slovakia's Regions and the Struggle for Power " by Vladimir Krivy, ***Slovakia: Problems of Democratic Consolidation, The Struggle for the Rules of the Game***, Slovak Political Science Association, Friedrich Ebert Stiftung, Edited by Sona Szomolanyi and John A. Gould, Bratislava 1997, p. 113 9 Slovensko 1996, Edited by Martin Butora, IVO, Bratislava, 1997, p. 48
[27] No. 222/1996 CL.
[28] See Part I.2.2.2.
[29] No. 350/1996 CL.
[30] Law No. 352 CL.
[31] See Part II. B.1.2.
[32] No. 218/1996 CL.
[33] No. 58/1996 CL.
[34] No. 119/1996 CL.
[35] No. 168/96 CL.
[36] No. 180/96 CL.
[37] No. 1/1996 CL.
[38] No. 220/1996.
[39] No. 468/1991 CL.
[40] No. 70/1996 CL.
[41] No. 207/1996 CL.
[42] No. 270/1995 CL.
[43] No. MK-2952/96-1.
[44] No. 68/1997 CL.
[45] No. 38/1995 CL.
[46] No. 114/1993 CL.
[47] No. 269/1995 CL.
[48] No. 44/1989 CL.

CHAPTER THIRTEEN
SLOVENIA

I. GENERAL DESCRIPTION OF THE ADMINISTRATIVE LEGAL SYSTEM

1. THE HISTORY OF THE ADMINISTRATIVE LEGAL SYSTEM

Slovenia is a very young state. It declared its independence on June 26, 1991, and most countries recognised it by 1992. It has been a member of the United Nations since May 21, 1992. Prior to independence, Slovenia was one of the six republics of the former Socialist Republic of Yugoslavia. Since the former Yugoslavia was a strongly decentralised federal state, the republics had considerable autonomy in the field of administrative law. As such, prior to independence, Slovenia had its own Parliament, Government, and various government agencies, as well as its own judicial system.

In April 1990 the first free elections to the Slovenian Parliament (National Assembly) and to the municipal councils were held. The elections were won by a coalition of rightwing parties. The newly constituted Parliament decided on June 13, 1990, to start a procedure for the adoption of a new Constitution of the Republic of Slovenia.[1] This new constitution would be based on democratic principles. The Constitution was adopted on December 28, 1991.[2] It established the main governmental bodies–the National Assembly, the National Council, the Government and the President of the Republic–and provided the basic procedures for the operation of those institutions. The Constitution is the highest legislative act in Slovenia.

More detailed provisions were provided by separate statutes: the Constitutional Court Act,[3] the Government Act,[4] and the Council of State Act.[5] Other administrative and judicial institutions are established and regulated by special legislation. The most important statutes are the Judicial Service Act,[6] the Public Administration Act,[7] and the Act on Local Self-Management.[8]

Slovenia has inherited from the former Yugoslavia two types of administrative procedures: *judicial review* of administrative acts ("administrative dispute"), and decision-making in administrative matters, including *administrative review* of administrative decisions ("administrative procedure"). The procedural rules of former Yugoslavia, the Administrative Disputes Act and the General Administrative Procedure Act of 1952[9] and 1956, respectively, are still in force. New draft legislation has already been discussed in the parliamentary committees.

2. THE STRUCTURE OF THE EXECUTIVE

2.1 The central administration

The highest executive body in the country is the Government. The Government is composed of the Prime Minister and the Ministers of State. It is accountable to the National Assembly.[10] The Government is constituted in the following manner: The President of the Republic proposes, after consultations with the leaders of the various political groups within the National Assembly, to the National Assembly a candidate for the office of Prime Minister. The Prime Minister is then chosen by the National Assembly by a majority of the votes of all Deputies.[11] If the Prime Minister is elected by the National Assembly, he makes a proposal for all the other Ministers of State, who have to be appointed by the National Assembly.[12]

The National Assembly may, upon the motion of no less than 10 Deputies and by the vote of the majority of all Deputies, elect a new Prime Minister. Such a vote shall be deemed to be a vote of no confidence in the Government carried out by the National Assembly (the so called "constructive vote of no confidence"). Where such a vote is carried out, the outgoing Prime Minister is deemed to have been relieved of his official duties. The Prime Minister may combine the vote on a motion of confidence in his Government with a vote on a particular statute or some other matter by the National Assembly. If such a vote is lost, it is deemed to constitute a vote of no confidence in the Government. No less than 48 hours must elapse between the initiation of a motion of no confidence and any vote on such a matter.[13]

An interpellation with respect to the work of the Government or of an individual Minister of State may be required by no less than 10 Deputies of the National Assembly. If, following such an interpellation, a majority of all elected Deputies carries out a vote of no confidence in the Government or in an individual Minister, the Government or the Minister, as the case may be, shall be dismissed by the National Assembly.[14] The National Assembly may bring the Prime Minister or any Minister of State before the Constitutional Court to answer charges relating to breaches of the Constitution or of statutes committed during the performance of official duties.[15]

2.2 The relations between the central and the local administration

Slovenia is divided into communes, the number of which is not fixed. The communes are regulated by the Local Government Act.[16] The executive body of the commune is the Mayor, who is assisted by deputy-mayors. Their number varies. The Mayor is accountable to the council of the commune.

The range of duties and functions performed by a commune includes local matters affecting only the people of that commune, as the commune may independently determine. The State may, statutorily, vest such duties and functions falling within its jurisdiction in the communes and the larger self-governing local bodies,[17] subject to the prior consent of the communes and the other bodies concerned and to the provision of the means (funds) for the performance of such duties and functions. The State supervises the proper and efficient performance of the functions and duties of the municipalities and larger self-governing local government bodies.[18]

The communes can merge with other communes and establish larger self-governing local government bodies or regional local government bodies to exercise administrative powers and to deal with matters of wider common interest. The State may, upon an agreement with such larger bodies, vest within the original jurisdiction of such bodies specific duties and functions otherwise falling within the state jurisdiction.[19]

The state authorities supervise the performance of the duties and functions of the local government bodies.[20] Article 145 of the Constitution provides for the right of the citizens to form other self-governing local bodies to pursue their common interests. Specific matters falling within the jurisdiction of the State may be statutorily vested in such local bodies as well.

2.3 Normative regulations adopted by the president, the government and the departments

The head of state does not have the power to adopt normative acts. The Government and the ministries do have such power. Their power to adopt such acts is regulated by the Government Act.[21] In addition, a statute can provide that the Government or a ministry shall adopt more detailed regulations in order to execute the provisions of that statute. All normative acts of the Government and the ministries have to be based on a statute.[22] Such acts do not have to be approved by the parliament. Their legality and constitutionality can be examined by the Constitutional Court through a constitutional complaint procedure.

3. THE SYSTEM OF COURTS DEALING WITH ADMINISTRATIVE LAW ISSUES

There are no separate administrative law courts in Slovenia. However, plans call for the establishment of special administrative courts. A limited possibility of judicial review of administrative acts is exercised by the Supreme Court. In some cases, it is also possible to file a constitutional complaint with the Constitutional Court. There are also special quasi-judicial bodies, Courts of Honour, for adjudicating cases requiring professional expertise for professionals, such as lawyers, doctors, architects, and journalists.

4. THE CONSTITUTIONAL COURT

Slovenia has had its own Constitutional Court since 1963, but the Constitution of 1991 has expanded its role and importance. The Constitutional Court is the highest body performing judicial review and protection of constitutionality, legality, and human rights. It has, according to Article 160 of the Constitution, jurisdiction over the following matters: the conformity of statutes with the Constitution; the conformity of statutes, regulations, and by-laws with international agreements adopted by the State, and with the general principles of international law; the conformity of regulations with the Constitution and the statutes; the conformity of local government by-laws with the Constitution and the statutes; the conformity of the proclaimed regulatory measures of statutory authorities with the Constitution, statutes, and regulations; the complaints of breaches of the Constitution involving individual acts infringing human rights and fundamental freedoms; the jurisdictional disputes between the State and local government bodies as well as the jurisdictional disputes among such local government bodies; the jurisdictional disputes between the courts and other State bodies; the jurisdictional disputes between the National Assembly, the President of the Republic, and the Government; unconstitutional acts and activities of political parties.

On the initiative of the President of the Republic, the Government, or of no less than one-third of the Deputies of the National Assembly, the Constitutional Court must provide an opinion as to the conformity of an international treaty in the process of ratification with this Constitution. The National Assembly is bound by any such opinion.

The Constitutional Court shall only decide upon a constitutional complaint when all other legal remedies have been exhausted. The Constitutional Court shall decide whether to adjudicate upon a constitutional complaint according to the criteria and procedures prescribed by statutes.

If the Constitutional Court determines that a statute (a regulation, a by-law or any other regulatory measure) is unconstitutional, it shall abrogate that statute wholly or partially. Such an abrogation takes effect immediately or within a period of time determined by the Constitutional Court.[23]

5. THE GENERAL PROCEDURAL LAWS OR CODES OF ADMINISTRATIVE LAW

Both types of administrative procedure mentioned above are regulated by specific codes of procedure: the General Administrative Procedure Act of 1956 (revised in 1965, 1976, 1978 and 1986[24]) and the Administrative Dispute Act of 1952 (revised in 1953, 1965 and 1976[25]). The General Administrative Procedure Act applies to decision-making and administrative review of administrative acts, unless a specific statute provides for a special procedure. The right to appeal is regulated by Article 11. When an administrative body of first instance renders an unfavourable individual administrative act,[26] individuals have the right to appeal before an administrative body of second instance.[27] The right to appeal also exists if the administrative body does not make a decision within the prescribed period of time.[28] An act cannot be appealed within the administrative hierarchy in the following two cases: a) if the right to appeal is explicitly denied by statute, (this right can only be denied when the protection of the rights of the individual, and the legality of administrative action are ensured by other means[29]); b) if an administrative body of second instance does not exist, unless another form of appeal within the administration is statutorily provided for.[30]

Decisions rendered in appeal are not further appealable.[31] Such decisions are subject only to judicial review, as well as acts rendered by an administrative body of first instance, where there is no possibility of appeal within the administration. The judicial review is regulated by the Administrative Disputes Act. The following administrative acts are excluded from judicial review[32]: acts against which other means of judicial protection are open; if the review is denied by an explicit statutory provision; in cases, where the decision is taken by the Parliament, the Government, the President, or other major institutions of the State.

Judicial review is possible on grounds of legality only. The court decides whether the administrative act is in accordance with the statutes and/or with the by-laws.

If the court ascertains illegality, it will abolish the administrative act.[33] The court may substitute its own decision, if the nature of the case and the facts needed to make the decision allow. The court can also ascertain damages to be paid by the administration. In most cases, however, the administrative body that has taken the appealed decision is required to produce a new act, taking into account the decision of the court.

5.1 Exceptions from the general procedure

One of the main principles[34] of the General Administrative Procedure Act is the principle of subsidiarity, stated in Article 3. This principle means that the General Administrative Procedure Act applies only when there are no rules of procedure provided by a specific administrative statute. Specific procedural rules exist mainly in the following fields: acquisition and loss of citizenship, regulated by the Citizenship Act;[35] public procurements, regulated by the Public Procurements Act,[36] and taxation, regulated by the Taxation Procedures Act.[37] In most cases, those specific procedural rules establish specific bodies, which take the decisions and/or decide upon an appeal. Specific procedural rules, for example, rules protecting the interests of the individual, also apply in those procedures.

6. OMBUDSMAN

The institution of the ombudsman was introduced in Slovenia by the Ombudsman Act.[38] The ombudsman is established in order to protect the human rights of individuals, against the public administration, central and local, and to carry out other public functions.[39] The ombudsman is elected by the National Assembly, upon the proposal of the President of the Republic.[40] He has at least two, but not more than four deputies, appointed by the National Assembly upon his proposal.[41] The mandate of the ombudsman and his deputies lasts six years, with the possibility of an extension.[42] The ombudsman has to submit an annual report to the National Assembly.[43]

All public institutions are obliged to provide the ombudsman any information that he requests.[44] The ombudsman is entitled to address proposals, criticisms, opinions or recommendations to the public institutions. The public institutions are obliged to discuss such acts and to give an answer within a period of time set by the ombudsman.[45]

Anyone may request that the ombudsman initiate an investigation. The ombudsman may also initiate an investigation on his own.[46] The investigation is confidential and free of charge.[47] The ombudsman can decide not to investigate an initiative, if he deems it to be anonymous, delayed, insulting or abusive.[48] He can also turn down an initiative for the following reasons, set out in Article 30: in case it is beyond any doubt that there was no violation of human rights nor any other violations; in case the initiative is incomplete and it is, upon the request of the ombudsman, not completed with the necessary information and data; if there is a judicial procedure pending in that case, if the case falls within the jurisdiction of the parliamentary investigatory committees; if legal remedies have not been exhausted; in cases of minor importance where the investigation, even if concluded, could not result in an appropriate remedy.

In both aforementioned cases the decision is final.

The ombudsman or his or her representative has access to the premises of every administrative body and the prisons. The ombudsman has the right to talk to the prisoners in private.[49]

After an investigation is concluded, the ombudsman sends a draft of the report to all parties for comment.[50] After comment has been received, he makes a final report. In the report, the ombudsman issues his or her opinion with respect to the alleged violation. If a violation is found, he makes a proposal for removing the irregularity (e.g. by new proceedings, compensation of damages, etc.).[51] If an administrative body complies with his recommendations only partially, or not at all, the ombudsman can report the case to a higher body, to the ministries, or to the National Assembly, or can make the case public.[52]

7. OTHER FORMS OF SUPERVISION OVER THE ADMINISTRATION

7.1 State Audit Agency

The present Slovenian audit service is modelled after a similar institution in the former Yugoslavia. In the former Yugoslavia, the Public Audit Service was a constitutional, autonomous and independent organisation, which carried out public auditing and supervision over domestic payment operations between the socially (publicly) owned enterprises and other users of public funds[53]. The Agency of the Republic of Slovenia for Payment Operations, Control and Information (APOCI) has become its legal successor and taken over its tasks.[54] The tasks of the APOCI are[55] payment operations in the country, tax control, collecting, elaborating, and providing of statistical information, other statutorily provided control functions, auditing in connection with the transformation of ownership of legal entities, control of the legality and proper implementation of regulations, the governing of financial and material transactions of legal entities, and the disposition with socially owned property of legal entities, in accordance with the Ownership Transformation Act.

The last two functions are already, by their nature, temporary and will only be performed until the ownership transformation is complete. The control, payment operations, information, statistics and provision of information will be performed by the APOCI, as long as they are not entrusted to other institutions. After the sanation of the commercial banks, they will probably take over the payment operations; meanwhile the auditing (and related services) in private enterprises will be taken over by registered accountants.

Slovenia has also a Court of Auditors,[56] which is the highest body to supervise the state budget, the expenditures of public legal persons and the expenditures of other institutions, which are (co-) financed from the budget.

7.2 Public prosecutors

Unlike the other communist states, former Yugoslavia did not have the institution of *"Prokuratura"* (prosecutor's office). The public prosecutor did not have any functions with respect to the supervision of the administration. His task was and still is in Slovenia the prosecution of criminal offences.

A special institution, however, the so-called *"Federal Social Attorney of Self-Management"* (Article 374 of the old Constitution of the Federal Republic of Yugoslavia), existed as a kind of Public Attorney who supervised the persons and legal entities with respect to rights of self-management and the socially owned property. After the legal and political reform of 1989-90, this institution was transformed into the institution of the Public Attorney, who at present represents and provides legal advice to the State, its agencies and other public bodies having legal personality in the courts of law in Slovenia and abroad.

8. THE ROLE OF THE SYSTEM OF PARLIAMENTARY COMMITTEES IN THE SUPERVISION OVER THE ADMINISTRATION

The Parliament has the power to establish a parliamentary investigation, regulated by the Parliamentary Investigation Act and by the Regulation of the Procedure.[57] On the basis of a parliamentary investigation, the National Assembly can issue decisions regarding the political responsibility of bearers of public authorisation and other issues that fall within the scope of its jurisdiction. The Assembly may also amend legislation.

In the case of absence of specific provisions, the procedure applied is similar to the criminal procedure, whose rules apply by analogy.[58] The courts are obliged to provide all the assistance that is requested by the Committee (Article 13). Article 14 of the Act obliges the Government, the administrative bodies, and public services to provide access to all the requested documentation.

The regulation governing the procedure gives more detailed provisions regarding the initiation and conduct of the investigation. Such investigation may be requested by each deputy. If one-third of the Deputies or the Council of State requests an investigation, then the National Assembly must initiate one.[59] After the investigation is concluded, the committee must submit a report to the National Assembly detailing the committee's findings and proposals.[60]

II. DEVELOPMENTS IN ADMINISTRATIVE LAW DURING 1996-1997

INTRODUCTION

The elections to the National Assembly, which took place on November 11, 1996 in Slovenia, occupied enormous attention with difficult negotiations on the formation of a new Government. The Government was finally appointed in March 1997 after an unexpected coalition was formed between the Liberal Democratic Party and the Slovene People's Party. The most controversial issues, such as denationalisation,[61] privatisation, the issue of property rights of foreigners, and the relations between the State and the Church (including the question of religious education in public schools), remain unresolved.

One of the most discussed issues of administrative law in 1996 has been whether to ease the limit on the denationalisation of forests in favour of foreigners and of the Catholic Church. The Constitutional Court has framed the issue in terms of whether "feudal property" of foreigners is subject to denationalisation.

A. THE CONSTITUTION

No constitutional amendments were passed during the last year. In June 1997, the Government tabled a much-discussed proposal to modify Article 68, paragraph 2 of the Constitution, which forbids acquisition of land by foreigners, except in case of inheritance. This provision is not in accordance with the requirements of the European Community. Slovenia already (in 1996) promised to change that provision to gain acceptance as an associated member of the EC.

B. LEGISLATION

Slovenia adopted new legislation on the most important issues of government and administration from 1991 to 1994, after its declaration of independence. In general, during the following two years legislation has addressed less controversial and decisive issues.

Slovenian legislation has a strong tendency towards overregulation, most likely inherited from the days of "socialist self-management". This tendency translates into very long statutes and attempts to micromanage almost everything, leaving little space for subordinated regulations and even less space to the judiciary applying the law in practice. This excessiveness of regulation, voluminous statutes passed within a relatively short time, also results very often in a need to modify a recently enacted statute as a result of flaws, detected shortly after the statute's passage. This haste explains why the statutes in Slovenia, and before in the former Yugoslavia, have been so often amended purely on technicalities.

1. PROCEDURAL AND GENERAL ORGANISATIONAL LAWS

1.1 The organisation of the judicial system

There was no new legislation with respect to the organization of the judicial system. The only amendment of note was the *Amendment to the Judicial Service Act.*[62] The main goal of this amendment was to make the judicial profession more attractive, since a considerable demand for judges exists with not enough qualified lawyers available to fill the vacancies. The amendment provides for a limited liberalisation of the eligibility conditions and for an increase in the salaries of judges.

1.2 The structure and the prerogatives of the government and the basic executive institutions

There were two main changes in the area of the structure and prerogatives of the Government and the basic executive institutions during the period under discussion. First, *The Law on the Establishment of New Communes*[63] granted citizens the right to decide about the formation of new communes. Article 2 makes it possible, for example, to split an existing commune into two new ones, to merge two communes into one, to detach part of an existing commune and merge it with another commune, or to detach parts from existing communes in order to form a new one. The only condition that limits the variety of combinations is that the decision must be made by a referendum. The statute regulates such referenda in Articles 16–24. Every qualified voter[64] residing in the territory in which the status could change has the right to vote in the referendum. Following the referendum a special statute must be enacted to regulate the establishment of the new commune.[65]

Second, *The Law on the Administration of Taxes*[66] was passed regulating the organisation of the fiscal administration. Under the law, a special body of the Ministry of Finance, the Tax Administration, has been established to handle the collection of taxes. The Tax Administration has a director, who is appointed by the Government.[67]

The Tax Office consists of a main office and regional tax offices. The government determines both the number and the territory of regional tax offices.[68] The main office organises the work of regional offices, supervises their work, takes care of a uniform tax register, and issues decisions in taxation matters in second instance.[69] The regional offices assess and collect the taxes and maintain records of collected taxes and fines.[70] This statute also regulates the fiscal supervision of taxpayers by inspectors[71] and enacts provisions about the tax register.[72] This statute has also introduced fiscal numbers for all potential taxpayers. Information about each citizen is kept in the register. This information includes personal data such as the numbers of bank accounts, investments of capital, and employment. Article 58 provides that persons, with access to such information, cannot use this information for any other purpose or disclose such information to third persons. However, the statute does not provide for any sanctions in case of an unauthorised or unlawful disclosure of information.

1.3 The general procedures for appeal and judicial review of administrative action

New legislation regarding the general procedures for appeal and judicial review of administrative action is proposed to the Parliament. Enactment can be expected in 1998.

2. SUBSTANCE

2.1 The management of the economy

2.1.1 TAXATION

In 1996 the National Assembly passed the new *Taxation Procedures Act,*[73] which regulates the taxation procedures, and a *Law Regulating a Special Tax on Wages*[74] (LRSPW). Both amendments were introduced to accommodate a new tax in the tax system of Slovenia. The employer must pay this tax for each of his employees. The size of the tax depends proportionally on the size of the employee's salary. The highest percentage possible is 15 per cent of the gross salary. The Taxation Procedures Act regulates the procedure for the assessment and the collection of taxes. General procedural rules are given in Articles 1–29 of the LRSTW. Articles 30–35 of the same law contain provisions with respect to the duty of banks, financial, and other institutions to provide the Tax Office with all the required information. Articles 36–40 regulate the secrecy of the information that is disclosed to the Tax Office. Furthermore, the statute provides for the collection of tax debts[75] and sets out detailed provisions governing the manner of collection of different types of taxes.[76]

In addition to these changes, there was an amendment to the *Gross Sales Tax Act.*[77] Slovenia still has a turnover tax system. The seller has to pay turnover tax for every item sold and for every service rendered. Introduction of the value-added tax system, as used in Western Europe, is expected in 1998 and is required by the EU in order to harmonise Slovenian legislation with the legal arrangements of the EU.

2.1.2 PRIVATISATION

Two new statutes were enacted in the field of privatisation. The first one is the *Act on Transformation of Ownership of Tourism Enterprises, Owning Moveables in the Triglav National Park,*[78] and the second is the *Privatisation of the Loterija Slovenije Act*[79]. The first statute regulates two topics: the protection of the Triglav National Park (TNP) and the transformation of ownership of tourist enterprises on the territory of the TNP.

First, the statute provides for the foundation of a special fund (the Fund for Stimulation of the TNP) to co-finance and stimulate the development of the TNP. This fund is organised as a joint-stock company (Article 3), founded by the State, who would take all the shares of the first emission (Article 6). The communes, situated within the territory of the TNP (five per cent per commune maximum, up to a total of 25 per cent for all the communes) and Slovenian citizens (0.2 per cent per citizen, up to a maximum of 24 per cent) qualify as shareholders of the Fund. The State will transfer the originally acquired shares to the communes and offer them to the citizens.[80]

With respect to the ownership of the enterprises in the TNP, the statute provides that the capital of such companies must be held as follows:[81] 10 per cent by the Pension and Disability Insurance Fund, 10 per cent by the Slovenian Compensation Fund, and 20 per cent by the Fund for the Stimulation of the TNP. The remaining 60 per cent can be offered to the employees of the companies, to the members of their families, and ultimately to the public.

Article 29 regulates the ownership of immovables that will be moved to the Fund, the State, the Slovenian citizens, and domestic legal persons after the transformation of ownership. The owners are forbidden by Article 29(3) to sell those immovables to foreigners, since foreigners are not allowed to acquire ownership of such properties.[82] The same applies to domestic legal persons directly or indirectly owned by foreigners.

The second statute regulates the transformation of the Slovenian Lottery into a joint-stock company. The capital of the company must be divided as provided by Article 1: 25 per cent to the Pension and Disability Insurance Fund, 15 per cent to the Slovenian Compensation Fund, 40 per cent to the Fund for Financing of Disability and Humanitarian Organisations, 10 per cent to the Fund for Financing of Sport Organisations in the Republic of Slovenia, and 10 per cent to (ex-) employees of the Slovenian Lottery.

The Fund for Financing of Disability and Humanitarian Organisations and the Fund for Financing of Sport Organisations are new funds, established according to the provisions of Article 10 of this statute. The Funds are administered by councils of 21 and 11 members, respectively, who are appointed by the National Assembly.[83]

2.1.3 MANAGEMENT OF AGRICULTURAL LANDS

The *Agricultural Lands Act*[84] passed by the National Assembly regulates the protection, use, sale, and lease of agricultural lands, including forests (Article 1). In accordance with Article 5, the owner, the lessee, or other user, of uncultivated agricultural lands must permit access, movement, recreation, hunting, harvesting, and other related activities by third persons. The statute provides in Article 8 limitations for the change of purpose of high-quality agricultural lands. Articles 11–16 provide the terms of compensation, which the owner has to pay if he wants to change the purpose of agricultural lands (e.g. to housing). The compensation goes to the State (70 per cent) and to the commune (30 per cent).

Sale or other disposition of agricultural lands is limited by the provisions of Articles 17–25. One can acquire ownership of such lands only upon the consent of the commune or municipality.[85] The statute provides for appeal to the Ministry of Agriculture.[86] The statute lists the persons who have the right of pre-emption. These persons include the co-owner, the lessee who is a farmer, the neighbouring farmer, other farmers, the State, and the commune. Only if none of these persons wants to purchase the agricultural lands is the seller entitled to sell to a non-farmer.

Articles 26–38 give special provisions as to the lease of agricultural lands. The statute requires long-term contracts of a minimum of 10–25 years, which vary depending on the purpose to which the lands are put, for example, not less than 25 years for vineyards.

2.1.4 SOCIAL (EMPLOYEES') PROTECTION

In 1997, the *Law on the Guarantee Fund of the Republic of Slovenia*[87] was enacted. The Fund is established, in order to fulfil the obligations of employers to their employees in case of insolvency.[88] Insolvency for these purposes means either that bankruptcy proceedings have been initiated against the employer or that a forced settlement of the employer has been finalised.[89]

The fund is a public legal entity founded by the State,[90] with the government regulating its status.[91] The Fund is managed by a Director and a Managing Committee.[92] The Managing Committee is composed of nine members including the President of the Committee. Three members are appointed by the organisation of employers, three by the trade unions, and three by the Government. The President is always one of the members appointed by the Government.[93]

The Fund is financed by the contributions of the employers and from the State Budget.[94] An employee is entitled to the benefit if his employment contract is terminated due to insolvency and he has been employed by the same employer for at least six months immediately prior to the termination.[95] The benefit cannot be larger than the statutorily guaranteed minimum wages for the last three months before the insolvency crisis and the minimum compensation for termination.[96]

The benefit has to be requested by the employee. The Fund takes the decision in first instance and the Ministry of Labour in appeal. In case of an unfavourable decision, the employee can initiate the proceedings in the labour court.

2.1.5 PUBLIC PROCUREMENT

A new *Public Procurement Act*[97] was passed in 1997. It regulates the procedure according to which a public body is obliged to act in cases of public investment. This procedure applies in case of acquisition of goods, ordering services, and in case of construction contracts.[98] The bodies which are obliged to follow this procedure are all bodies entitled to funds of the state budget; public commercial institutions and public enterprises and other legal entities that are (co-) founded by the State or by a local community (such as a commune). The investor has the obligation to inform the potential tenderers,[99] and the conditions of the competition must be made public.[100]

The Statute[101] allows the favouring of Slovenian tenderers, for example, by contracting with them on the basis of higher remuneration for the same services as offered by a foreign tenderer, except in cases where Slovenia has the obligation imposed by international law not to discriminate against foreign tenderers. This is the case with the EU countries. In practice, some construction works, such as roads and bridges, are performed by foreign companies. One case has granted concessions for service stations next to new motorways in 1996. Foreign companies were not excluded from the competition because they were foreigners, but because the tenderer had to meet some other conditions that could only be met by domestic tenderers. This case caused a strong informal reaction from Brussels.

The decision is taken by a special committee appointed by the principal of the investing organisation. The committee has to grant the project to the most suitable, not necessarily the cheapest, tenderer. The decision, together with the grounds upon which it is based, has to be published in the *Official Gazette*.[102]

A tenderer who is not satisfied with the decision may file a complaint seeking its revision.[103] A special revision committee, which is appointed by the National Assembly, performs the revision on a proposal submitted by the Government.

The rules of the General Administrative Procedure Act apply to this procedure.[104] This decision is final. After it is taken, there is still a possibility of a damage claim being brought before the regular courts, but the decision of the court cannot affect the decision about the granting of the project.

2.2 Environment

The *Law Regulating the Economic Exploitation of Certain Rivers*[105] was adopted in 1997. This statute regulates the possibility of granting the concession for building and exploitation of small power plants on certain smaller rivers. The concession is granted in a public competition.[106] The applicant must be a Slovenian citizen and must own the premises where he wants to build the plant.[107] The concession can be granted for a period of 30 years.[108] The statute also contains provisions as to the protection of the environment, the amount of water such a plant is allowed to use, etc.[109]

2.3 Transport

The Public Roads Act[110] regulates the classification, the construction and the maintenance of public roads. Public roads are, according to Article 2, public goods and thus *res extra commercium*, excluded from the commercial turnover of goods. They are owned either by the State, e.g. State roads, or by the communes, e.g. communal roads. The roads are further classified in Article 14. The Minister of Traffic is empowered to issue detailed regulations, containing technical, ecological, and other standards, specifications, etc.[111] In accordance with statutory provisions, concessions may be granted by the Government, or by a commune respectively, for the construction of roads and other infrastructural projects in the proximity of roads.[112]

The State and the communes are responsible for the management of the roads. On behalf of the State, the Directorate of the Republic of Slovenia for Roads has been established to take care of the construction, maintenance, and protection of State roads.[113] The statute provides for the possibility of establishing a special company to be in charge of the organisation and management of the construction and maintenance of public roads. The setting up of such a company must be, however, regulated by a special statute.

The statute also contains provisions with respect to the protection of environment[114] and to the nationalisation of lands necessary to construct a road. The lands can only be nationalised in accordance with statutory provisions and if no agreement between the owner and the investor can be reached.[115]

2.4 The management of socio-cultural processes

The Law on the Reparation of Injustices[116] was enacted to compensate former political prisoners imprisoned between May 15, 1945 and July 2, 1990, and the relatives of the post-war victims of political persecution. The statute provides for the possibility to claim damages and receive a pension and/or disability insurance. This statute represents one of the few measures taken in order to give some compensation to the victims of the communist terror.

The claimants, whose applications are accepted, are entitled to a compensation that will be established in accordance with the legislation regulating the war damages.[117] According to Article 6, the time that the claimant has spent in unjust imprisonment will be calculated towards his or her pension years.

The Government must appoint a special commission of nine members that will deal with the claims.[118] The procedure is regulated in Articles 10–16. The decision of the commission is not appealable, but there is a possibility of judicial review by the Supreme Court, following the rules of the "administrative dispute" procedure.[119] The statute provides also for a possibility of revision of the criminal proceedings in which the persons in question were convicted.[120]

2.5 Health care

The *Medicaments Act*[121] was an innovation in the area of health care. The statute regulates the production and distribution of medicaments and other medical goods, as well as the measures to guarantee their efficiency and quality. The statute also applies to the distribution of drugs and other related substances.[122] Articles 2–6 give a definition of and classification scheme for medicaments and medical goods. The medicaments are basically classified in three categories: medicaments obtainable only in a pharmacy and with a prescription a); medicaments obtainable only in a pharmacy, but without a prescription b); and medicaments obtainable in pharmacies and specialised shops, such as drugstores, without a prescription c).

Articles 11–31 relate to the testing of medicaments, and Articles 32–56 regulate the permit for the distribution of medicaments issued by the Bureau of the Republic of Slovenia for Medicaments. Furthermore, the statute regulates: a) the production of medicaments that require a permit issued by the Bureau for Medicaments;[123] b) the establishment of the prices of medicaments, which is within the jurisdiction of the Minister of Health Care;[124] and c) the informing of the public about medicaments.[125]

The statute provides in Article 84–94 for three stages of quality control: the internal control by the producers and the sellers, the expert control, provided by the Institution for Pharmacy and Testing of Medicaments, and administrative control, which is provided by the Ministry of Health Care.

Also new in this area was the law, rigorously *restricting the consumption of tobacco products.*[126] It forbids smoking in all public places, including schools, universities and health-care institutions. Restaurants, pubs, cafés, etc., have to provide a non-smoking area.

2.6 The management of administrative-political processes

There were no new legislation or amendments of importance in this field in 1996. In 1997 the following statutes were enacted:

The *Temporary Asylum Act*[127] provides for the conditions and the procedure to be followed in case of an application for a temporary asylum. The application must be submitted at the border to the border police. The applicant is taken to a reception centre. The decision is taken by the office in charge of internal affairs of the administrative unit, where the reception centre is situated.[128] The statute provides for a possibility of appeal at the Ministry of Internal Affairs, and the decision of the Ministry is final.

The *Public Attorney Act*[129] regulates the position of the Public Attorney. The Public Attorney represents the state and other public bodies which have legal personality in the courts in Slovenia, abroad, and in the international courts as well. The Public Attorney also gives legal advice to those institutions, especially with respect to rights *in rem* on immovables, real estate property rights.[130]

The office of the Public Attorney is headed by the Public Attorney General, and consists of public attorneys and deputy public attorneys. The Public Attorney General is appointed by the National Assembly, upon a Government's proposal for six years; the others are appointed by the Government, for eight years. After that period has expired, they can be appointed again.[131]

The statute provides also for the duties of other persons with respect to the Public Attorney. Administrative bodies, local communities, and bearers of public authorisation are obliged to provide the Public Attorney with all the information he needs.

If a third party, e.g. a citizen or a company, wants to sue an institution that is represented by the Public Attorney, he or she first has to propose an out-of-court settlement. Only if a settlement cannot be reached can judiciary proceedings be commenced.[132]

C. REGULATION

As already stated, Slovenian legislation has a strong tendency towards overregulation. The statutes are often very detailed leaving little room, for regulations, by-laws, etc. If such regulations are passed, they are very detailed. Still, the important issues are, as a rule, regulated by the statute, itself.

1. NORMATIVE ACTS OF THE GOVERNMENT

One of the more important regulations adopted by the Government during the discussed period, was the regulation regarding the *electronic access to judicial documentation.*[133] According to this regulation, the right of direct electronic access to judicial documentation and registers, is granted to the following groups: notaries, administrative bodies, the central bank (the Bank of Slovenia), the Agency in Charge of the Stock Market and legal persons bearing public authorisation. A major drawback of this regulation is that it does not address the protection of persons whose names and other data figure in such judicial documentation.

2. NORMATIVE ACTS OF OTHER PUBLIC INSTITUTIONS

The Agency in Charge of the Stock Market has issued an amendment to its decision regarding the *publicity of the operations of investment funds,*[134] the bodies which are administering the privatisation vouchers. According to Article 9a, the companies managing such funds must submit to the Agency a monthly report containing information or changes of the existing information about the persons, connected with such companies. Those qualifying as persons connected with such companies are the members of the board of directors, the members of the supervisory board, close relatives (spouse, life partner, children or adopted children) of the members of both boards, legal persons, of which at least 20 per cent belongs to the company, persons directly or indirectly holding at least 10 per cent of the capital of the managing company. The information has to be submitted in a special written form to the Agency. The information is then published in the *Official Gazette*.

3. A NOTE ON "INFORMAL RULES" OF THE ADMINISTRATION

Due to the overregulation mentioned above, little space remains for self-imposed informal rules of the administration. Some informal rules exist, but they are not published nor publicly discussed. Because judicial review of administrative acts is very limited and inefficient, such rules have not yet arisen as problems in the Slovenian jurisprudence.

D. JUDICIAL DECISIONS

Judicial decisions are not systematically published, with the exception of the decisions of the Constitutional Court. All decisions of the Supreme Court are, however, available on-line. In addition, twice a year the Supreme Court publishes a few of the opinions it has handed down during its common session, which takes place twice a year. Furthermore, some judicial decisions are selected by scholars and published as separate books or as appendices in law books. Those decisions are published not in full, but only in excerpts.

1. CONSTITUTIONAL COURT

There were 750 constitutional complaints filed with the Constitutional Court in 1996. The Court has decided on 612[135] cases, 66 of which were published in the *Official Gazette*. Unconstitutionality, illegality or non-conformity with international law was established in 36 cases. In three cases only partial non-conformity of the legal acts examined was established. Six cases concerned conflits of jurisdiction, mainly in the field of the denationalisation procedures.

Two recent decisions are of special interest. The first one[136] was a decision upon a complaint of a member of the Yugoslav royal family against Article 87 of the Denationalisation Act, which denies the right to denationalisation to the members of the royal family. The complaint was filed on grounds of discrimination,[137] and the right to property and inheritance.[138] The Constitutional Court held that the disputed provision of the Denationalisation Act is not unconstitutional. The main goal of the denationalisation process is to remove the historical injustice done by nationalisation. Confiscation of property of royal families when the monarchies are abolished cannot be seen as a historical injustice, but as a common practice of new republics.

Second, the Constitutional Court was asked to give an opinion with regard to the constitutionality of the association agreement between Slovenia and the EU.[139] This agreement gives foreigners the opportunity to acquire land in Slovenia. The Constitutional Court held that this agreement is unconstitutional, since the Constitution prohibits acquisition of land by foreigners.[140] This decision has postponed the ratification of the association agreement, which may hinder Slovenia's chances to become a full member of the EU.

2. ADMINISTRATIVE COURTS (THE SUPREME COURT)

As mentioned above, no special administrative courts exist. A limited possibility of judicial review is provided by the Supreme Court. In the publication of the opinions mentioned in the introduction to the section, nine opinions in 1996 were classified as concerning administrative law issues, with one of them actually concerned the law of industrial property. Of the remaining eight decisions, five concerned denationalisation issues, with one of them actually a question about the interpretation of the law of citizenship, two concerned urban planning, and one taxation. Only two of the decisions included the grounds upon which the decisions had been taken.

The protection provided by the Supreme Court is highly ineffective. The Supreme Court started 1996 with 3,374[141] unresolved cases. During the year 2,458 new cases were filed, so the caseload of the Court reached 5,832 cases for 1996. It solved 1,611; 4,221 cases were deferred to 1997. This amounts to approximately a 25 percent increase in unresolved cases. The average duration of an administrative procedure before the Supreme Court is already about two-and-a-half years.[142]

There were 1,130 appellate decisions in Administrative Dispute (judicial review of administrative acts), out of the 1,611 resolved cases. There were 1,104 appeals against acts of the central administration, and 26 appeals against acts of communal and other local administration. Most cases concerned the process of denationalisation (169), customs (143), taxes (121) citizenship (111), construction and real estate property documentation (94), and the rights of foreigners (30). In most of the cases (71.2 per cent) the appeal was dismissed.

E. WORKINGS OF OMBUDSMEN, INVESTIGATORY PARLIAMENTARY COMMITTEES, PUBLIC PROSECUTORS, ETC.

The Ombudsman[143] has received 2,513 requests for investigation in 1996. Most of them (30.3 per cent) concerned the work of the judiciary and the police, administrative matters (20.7 per cent), social security (12 per cent), limitations of personal freedom (5.8 per cent), and housing (5.6 per cent). Together with 447 initiatives deferred from the previous year and 991 reopened cases,[144] the Ombudsman has dealt with 3,981 cases. In all, 3,282 investigations were concluded in 1996, and 699 were deferred to 1997; 535 of the deferred investigations are already pending. A comparison with 1995 shows that the number of cases has risen by 69 per cent.

The report of the Ombudsman for 1996[145] focuses on the following general problems related to administrative law and procedures: The administration often does not provide individuals with sufficient information about their rights; sometimes the individuals are not even heard before a decision affecting them is made; the grounds for the decisions are provided only in part, or not at all; in most cases the individuals have to provide the needed documentation, in spite of the statutory provision that such documentation can also be provided by the administrative body itself; and the administration does not respect the statutorily regulated time limits for decision-making.

According to the report, one of the major problems in Slovenia is the question of citizenship.[146] Most cases concern former Yugoslav citizens of non-Slovene origin, who have already lived for a long period in Slovenia. The naturalisation procedures are much too long and complicated. There is no specific time limit for decision-making prescribed; as a result, in May 1997 the applications filed in May 1993 were still being processed! The applicants often lose their jobs, because they are foreigners and because they do not have a job, they do not meet the conditions for naturalisation. A special problem is the condition that the applicant must not represent a danger to the defence of Slovenia. This vague condition is often misused by the administration as a pretext to refuse citizenship to former soldiers.

Another problem exposed by the Ombudsman[147] is the implementation of the legislation, regarding foreigners (in most cases again former Yugoslav citizens of non-Slovene origin). The policy of admitting foreigners is very strict. The administration is, according to an "opinion of the legislation department of the Government of January 12, 1995," analogously applying the rules regarding the process of naturalisation. This means, that a person applying for a residence permit must meet the same requirements, as for naturalisation. Here again, applications are turned down if the applicant has no regular job[148] or if a vaguely defined "potential danger for the State defence" is perceived.

1. THE PARLIAMENTARY COMMISSIONS OF INQUIRY

The National Assembly has established several commissions of inquiry. The commissions have been investigating their cases for several years, and have heard many witnesses, but to date they have not ascertained any irregularities. It seems, that there is not much political will to provide evidence for possible criminal investigations.

The Chapter has been prepared on the basis of information provided by Matjaz Tratnik

NOTES

1 *Official Gazette of the Republic of Slovenia*, 29/90. The first number represents the number of the issue of the *Official Gazette* and the second is the year of publishing. Several legislative acts are published in one issue. Sometimes a third number is placed between them, indicating the consecutive number of the legislative act, published in that year (for example: 33–1409/91). Legislative acts are not usually referred to by any date (either parliamentary approval, promulgation or entering into force).

2 *Official Gazette* 33/91.

3 *Official Gazette* 15/94.

4 *Official Gazette* 4/94.

5 *Official Gazette* 44/92.
6 *Official Gazette* 19/94, amended by 8/96.
7 *Official Gazette* 67/94.
8 *Official Gazette* 72/94.
9 *Official Gazette* 23/52 and 52/56.
10 Article 110 of the Constitution.
11 Article 111 of the Constitution.
12 Article 112 of the Constitution.
13 Article 117 of the Constitution.
14 Article 118 of the Constitution.
15 Article 119 of the Constitution.
16 *Official Gazette* 72/94.
17 For a definition of "a larger self-governing body", see the next paragraph.
18 Article 140 of the Constitution.
19 Article 143 of the Constitution.
20 Article 144 of the Constitution.
21 *Official Gazette* 4/94.
22 "Statute" here means a normative act adopted by the Parliament.
23 Article 161 of the Constitution.
24 *Official Gazette SFRY* 10/1965, 18/1965, 24/1965; 4/1977; 11/1978, 32/1978; 9/1986, 16/1986, 47/1986.
25 *Official Gazette SFRY* 15/1953; 16/1965, 21/1965; 4/1977, 60/1977.
26 General administrative acts can only be subject to a constitutional complaint before the Constitutional Court.
27 Paragraph 1.
28 Paragraph 3.
29 Paragraph 1.
30 Paragraph 2.
31 Paragraph 4.
32 Article 9.
33 Article 42 (1).
34 Stating the main principle of a statute in its first provisions was a typical style of Yugoslav legislation.
35 *Official Gazette* 33/91.
36 *Official Gazette* 24/97.
37 *Official Gazette* 18/96.
38 *Official Gazette* 71/93.
39 Article 1.
40 Article 2.
41 Article 15.
42 Articles 12, 16.
43 Article 5.
44 Article 6.
45 Article 7.
46 Article 9.
47 Article 8.
48 Article 28.
49 Article 42.
50 Article 38.
51 Article 39.
52 Article 40.
53 According to the Act on Public Audit Service in the SR Slovenia, *Official Gazette* 1/85.
54 Article 72(1) and Article 73(2) of the Act on the APOCI, *Official Gazette* 48/94, 58/95, 18/95 and the decisions of the Constitutional Court, published in the *Official Gazette* 73/95, 27/96.

55 Article 4(1), 73(1).
56 Regulated by the Court of Auditors Act, *Official Gazette* 48/1994.
57 Both published in *Official Gazette* 63/93.
58 Article 9 of the Act.
59 Articles 1–4 of the Regulation.
60 Article 22.
61 For an expalantion of the meaning of this term see the next paragraph in the text.
62 *Official Gazette* 19/94, amended by 8/96.
63 *Official Gazette* 44/96.
64 Slovenian administrative law recognises two types of residence, permanent residence and temporary residence, but it does not recognise habitual residence. Many Slovenes have their permanent residence in places where they have not lived for many years (for example, where their parents live). Also the Slovenes living abroad are generally considered to have their temporary residence abroad and their permanent residence in Slovenia, even if they have no intention of returning to Slovenia.
65 Article 3.
66 *Official Gazette* 18/96.
67 Articles 11, 12.
68 Articles 5, 6.
69 Article 8.
70 Article 9.
71 Articles 13–24.
72 Articles 28–53.
73 *Official Gazette* 18/96.
74 *Official Gazette* 34/96.
75 Articles 99–119.
76 Articles 120–181.
77 *Official Gazette* 16/96.
78 *Official Gazette* 24/96.
79 *Official Gazette* 44/96.
80 Articles 8, 9.
81 Articles 22–25.
82 Article 29 (2).
83 Article 11.
84 *Official Gazette* 59/96.
85 Article 19.
86 Article 20.
87 *Official Gazette* 9/97.
88 Article 2.
89 Article 17.
90 Articles 3, 4.
91 Article 5.
92 Article 7.
93 Articles 8, 9.
94 Article 13.
95 Article 16.
96 Article 19.
97 *Official Gazette* 24/97.
98 Article 2.
99 Article 6.
100 Article 7.
101 Article 11.
102 Article 42.
103 Article 63.

104 Article 70.
105 *Official Gazette* 23/97.
106 Article 14.
107 Article 3.
108 Article 6.
109 Article 4.
110 *Official Gazette* 29/97.
111 Articles 6, 7.
112 Article 12.
113 Article 19.
114 Article 26.
115 Article 30.
116 *Official Gazette* 59/96.
117 Article 5.
118 Article 9.
119 Article 18.
120 Articles 21-35.
121 *Official Gazette* 9/96.
122 Article 1.
123 Articles 57-76.
124 Articles 77-78.
125 Articles 79-83.
126 *Official Gazette* 57/96.
127 *Official Gazette* 20/97.
128 Article 12.
129 *Official Gazette* 20/97.
130 Article 8.
131 Article 29.
132 Article 14.
133 *Official Gazette* 10/97.
134 *Official Gazette* 8/97.
135 According to the President of the Constitutional Court, in an interview for *Mladina,* May 6, 1997.
136 *Official Gazette* 5/97.
137 Article 14 of the Constitution.
138 Article 33.
139 The decision has not been published yet.
140 Article 68 (2).
141 All the figures were published in: "Sodna Statistika za leto 1996", *Judiciary Statistics for 1996,* Ljubljana 1997, ISSN 1318-4326, p. 106, 109.
142 *The Annual Report of the Ombudsman for 1996,* p. 110.
143 *The Annual Report of the Ombudsman for 1996,* pp. 166-169.
144 "Reopened" means that an investigation has already been concluded but the authorities did not comply, so the individual has filed a new complaint at the ombudsman.
145 *The Annual Report of the Ombudsman for 1996,* pp. 78-80.
146 *The Annual Report of the Ombudsman for 1996,* pp. 81-86.
147 *The Annual Report of the Ombudsman for 1996,* pp. 86-90.
148 Which he cannot have, because he does not have a residence permit.

CHAPTER FOURTEEN
UKRAINE

I. GENERAL DESCRIPTION OF THE UKRAINIAN ADMINISTRATIVE LAW SYSTEM

1. BRIEF HISTORY OF THE ESTABLISHMENT OF THE UKRAINIAN ADMINISTRATIVE LAW SYSTEM

1.1 The process of legal separation from the USSR

After the Verkhovna Rada (Parliament) of the Ukrainian Soviet Socialist Republic passed the Declaration on the State Sovereignty of Ukraine on July 16, 1990, in order to avoid a legal vacuum and to create the preconditions necessary for the adoption of the Constitution and the new laws regulating the transition from a totalitarian administrative system to a democratic social legal state, the Laws "On the Application of the Laws of the Former Soviet Union in Ukraine" were passed. The Law "On the Implementation of International Treaties on the Territory of Ukraine" was passed on December 10, 1991. According to this law, "International treaties concluded and appropriately ratified by Ukraine are an integral part of the national legislation of Ukraine and are used in the order specified for the norms of international legislation."[1] Thus, at present the administrative and legal regulation in Ukraine is comprised of four groups of laws: international treaties; the laws of the former Soviet Union[2]; laws passed in Ukraine when it was still a part of the Soviet Union;[3] and new laws, passed by Ukraine as an independent state.[4]

Practical life requires both that new laws be created and existing laws amended. Difficulties determining which law is presently applicable are common. The laws and normative acts that existed prior to the passage of the Constitution[5] and are not contradictory to the present Constitution, are still in force either wholly or in part. Each edict issued by the President contains in its final clause a list of normative acts that lose their force pursuant to it, and a proposal to the Cabinet of Ministers to bring their decisions in accordance with the new edict.[6]

During the Soviet period a state monopoly on foreign trade existed that contradicted several international norms and standards and subsequently became an obstacle for Ukraine's integration into the international economic community. This situation made it necessary to pass a law liberalising foreign trade.[7] The liberalisation of foreign trade activities underlined the need to simplify the procedures of customs control in order to bring the customs registration into accord with international standards.

Similar circumstances were characteristic of other areas and institutions of administrative legislation.[8] In all, 385 such bodies and institutions introduced appropriate changes and additions into the legislation in force. The distribution of the laws passed in different fields of legislation was as follows (the number of new laws are given in brackets): constitutional - 94 laws (44), administrative - 139 (61), financial - 104 (44), civil - 47 (21), economy - 56 (23), labour 64 (18), criminal - 33 (7), criminal procedure - 54 (13), civil procedure - 10 (1), and some others. One hundred and sixty international treaties were ratified.[9]

1.2 Extent of codification of administrative law

Administrative legislation in Ukraine has not been formally codified because of the great diversity of existing administrative legal norms. Nevertheless, in some fields codification is being carried out. For instance, the legislation on administrative responsibility (administra-tive offences) has already been fully codified. Also, on December 7, 1984, the Enactment of the Verkhovna Rada put the Code of Ukrainian SSR on Administrative Offences in force from July 1, 1985;[10] presently a new project of enacting the Administrative Offences Code is being worked out.

Several acts in Ukraine have already been codified.[11] In some cases codification has been carried out not by the passage of a code, but instead by the issuance of laws that in their generalised form contain norms, regulating state administration in certain fields.[12] In general, the first years of independence were characterised by very extensive legislative activity.

2. STRUCTURE OF THE EXECUTIVE POWER

In compliance with the Constitution, Article 5: "The people are the holders of state sovereignty and the only source of power in Ukraine. The people exercise power directly and through the bodics of state government and local government".[13] State power in Ukraine is executed on the basis of its separation into legislative, executive and judicial branches.[14] The structure and activities of the executive power in Ukraine are enumerated in the Constitution, the Law on the Cabinet of Ministers, the Law on Local Administration, the Law on Local government and also the Decrees of the President.

2.1 The Cabinet

The Cabinet of Ministers is the highest body within the executive branch[15] and consists of the Prime Minister, the First Vice-Prime Minister, three vice-prime ministers, and ministers. The Prime Minister is appointed by the President with the consent of more than one-half of the constitutional membership of the Verkhovna Rada.[16] The president may also suspend the authority and dismiss the Prime Minister.[17] The Cabinet of Ministers is responsible to the President, under the control of and accountable to the Verkhovna Rada.[18] Article 87 of the Constitution provides:

The Verkhovna Rada of Ukraine, upon the proposal of no less than one-third of the People's Deputies of Ukraine from its constitutionally determined membership, may consider the issue of responsibility of the Cabinet of Ministers of Ukraine and take a vote of no confidence in the Cabinet of Ministers of Ukraine by the majority of its membership. The issue of responsibility of the Cabinet of Ministers may not be considered by the Verkhovna Rada of Ukraine more than once during one regular session, as well as within a year after the adoption of the Ukrainian Cabinet of Ministers' program of activity.[19]

The Law on the Regulations of the Verkhovna Rada of Ukraine was passed on July 27, 1994.[20] Under it, the Verkhovna Rada executes control over the ministries.[21] The Cabinet of Ministers, being accountable to and under the control of the Verkhovna Rada, must present to it the programme of its activities for its entire term in office within a month of its formation. The Verkhovna Rada then examines this programme and issues an appropriate decree.[22] The Cabinet of Ministers, at least once a year, reports on its work to the Verkhovna Rada. The Verkhovna Rada can make a decision at any time about an extraordinary report.[23] During its sessions the Verkhovna Rada can hear from any member of the government regarding his activities.[24]

Upon the submission of the Prime Minister, the President may appoint members of the Cabinet of Ministers, heads of central bodies of executive power, and heads of local state administrations as well as suspend or withhold their authorisation.[25] In order to do so, the Prime Minister must submit a proposal to the President on the creation, reorganisation and liquidation of ministries and other central bodies of executive power within the funds allocated by the State budget for maintaining these bodies.[26] On December 14, 1996 (by decree), the President established the list of ministries.[27] Accordingly, the Ministries of Internal Affairs, Foreign Affairs, Information and Defence must report directly and be responsible to the President on issues which fall within his or her constitutional powers.

The Resolution of the Cabinet of Ministers dated October 17, 1996, carried out the reorganisation and liquidation of some working and consultative bodies of the Cabinet of Ministers. Under the Constitution, the Cabinet of Ministers, as a body of general competence, supervises and directs the work of the ministries and other central bodies of executive power. The governing of specific fields and areas of life is executed by the ministries and other central bodies of executive power–state committees, departments and services.[28] The ministries and central bodies must act on the basis of both a special statute[29] and other laws. Some central bodies of executive power and their local branches act only on the basis of clarifying laws.[30]

Central executive bodies carry out their activities through regional departments and administrations. This power is exercised through the right to approve or reject statutes promulgated by such parties.[31]

At the local level there are two types of departments and units of administrations. While one type is subordinate only to the central executive bodies, the other type is subordinate both to these bodies and to the structural branches of local government. However, the President has determined that the heads of all branches (except the security service) will be accountable to and under the control of the heads of the appropriate local state administrations on the issues, as attributed by the law to the competence of these administrations.[32]

2.2 Local administration

Local state administrations, regional and district ones (*oblast* and *rayon radas*), and the city and district administrations in Kiev and Sevastopol act under Articles 118–120 of the Constitution of Ukraine, the Law "On Local Administration", the "Statute on the Regional, Kiev and Sevastopol City State Administrations" and the "Statute on the Country District and City District in Kiev and Sevastopol Local State Administrations". Both of these statutes were ratified by the President of Ukraine in 1995 but have since been subjected to several amendments. In particular, the President of Ukraine has inserted considerable changes in the structure of these administrations.[33]

In accordance with the Constitution of Ukraine and the above-mentioned Statute, local state administrations exercise executive power in the regions and districts. Heads of local state administrations may be appointed to and dismissed from their position by the President of Ukraine upon submission to the Cabinet of Ministers of Ukraine. The heads of local state administrations are responsible to the President of Ukraine and to the Cabinet of Ministers of Ukraine.

Local state administrations are accountable to and under the control of *radas* (local representative assemblies) with regard to powers delegated to them by the appropriate *rayon* and *oblast radas*. Local state administrations are accountable to and under the control of the bodies of executive powers of higher level. *Oblast* or *rayon radas* can express non-confidence in the head of the appropriate local state administration. Such expression forms the basis for the President's decision to approve the decision or to reasoned reply, if he does not agree. If there is a vote of no confidence in the head of a *rayon* or *oblast* state administration, passed by two-thirds of the deputies of the membership of the appropriate *rada*, the President must make a decision regarding the dismissal of the head of the local state administration.[34]

Bodies of local government may be provided by law with certain prerogatives residing in the bodies of executive power.[35] Prior to the passage of the Constitution, the President of Ukraine granted some powers of the state executive to the bodies of local government, including executing control over the use and protection of the land, mineral resources, water, air, flora and fauna; other natural resources on the appropriate territory in the limits and order, established by law; registration of the property rights to land, right to land lease; organisation and execution of work on the privatisation of land in accordance with the laws; and control over the observance of laws on land tenure and protection of land and natural environment by land users.[36]

The bodies of local government carry out their activities on the basis of Chapter XI of the Constitution of Ukraine and the law "On Local Administration in Ukraine" passed on May 21, 1997.[37] This Law, in compliance with the Constitution, establishes the system and guarantees of local administration, and the posts, organisation and activities, legal status and responsibility of the bodies and officials of the local administration. The general provisions regulate the concept of local administration, the rights of citizens to participate in the local administration, and the main principles of local administration. The system of local administration includes: the territory community; the village, settlement, town and city *rada*; the head of the village, settlement, town and city; the executive bodies of the village, settlement, town and city *rada*; district and regional *radas*, which represent common interests of the territory communities of villages, settlements, towns and cities; and the bodies of self-organisation of the population.[38]

Chapter II provides the organisational and legal basis for the local administration. In accordance with Article 26, the following issues are within the exclusive competence of the village, settlement, town and city Radas and may be dealt with exclusively at their plenary meetings: approval of the Rada's regulations; creation and liquidation of the commissions of the Rada; abrogation of the Rada's executive bodies' acts which do not correspond with the Constitution, existing laws, or other legislative acts or the decisions of the Rada made within the limits of its powers;[39] solving issues on the creation of communal property by the enterprises, joint enterprises, including those with foreign investments;[40] and solving in accordance with the laws issues on the regulation of land relationships.[41] The powers of the executive bodies of the village, settlement, town and city radas include their own powers; preparation of the programs of social, economic and cultural development; and provisions for drawing up the balances of financial, staff, and resources. Delegated powers include considering and approving plans of enterprises, institutions and organisations, belonging to the communal property of appropriate territorial communities, that might cause negative social, demographic, ecological or other outcomes; preparation of conclusions on the plans and making propositions concerning them to appropriate bodies; and statistical calculation of the citizens, and living permanently or temporarily on the corresponding territory.[42]

Chapter II determines the powers of the head of a village, settlement, town or city mayor. In compliance with Article 42, the head, within the limits regulated by law, provides for the execution of the powers of the executive bodies, observance of the Constitution and the laws of Ukraine, and the execution of the acts of the President and other bodies of executive power.[43] The head is also responsible for organising the work of the appropriate Rada and its executive committee.[44] The head must also sign the decisions of the Rada at its executive committee;[45] prepare draft programs for socio-economic and cultural development for examination by the Rada;[46] call together general meetings of citizens in the place of their residence;[47] provide for the execution of the decisions of the local referendum and appropriate Rada and its executive committee.[48]

The head must also distribute the resources allocated for special purposes and use them only for the purpose determined by the Rada.[49] The head is also responsible for appeals to the court concerning the validity of acts issued by other bodies of local administration, local bodies of executive power, enterprises, institutions or organisations, and also for limiting the rights and interests of territory communities or the powers of the Rada and its bodies.[50]

Chapter IV determines the powers of regional Radas. Article 43 provides that the election of the head and the creation and the election and liquidation of permanent and other commissions will be solved exclusively at the plenary meetings. Chapter V determines the order for the formation and the organisation of the work of the local self-administrative bodies and officials. The Radas consist of deputies elected by the population of the appropriate territory. The general composition of a Rada is determined by the Rada in accordance with the Law on Elections forming and the organisation of work of the local self-administration bodies and officials. Village, settlement, town, city, city district, country district and regional radas carry out their work at sessions.[51] Sessions are held when the need arises, but not less than once every three months.[52]

3. LEGAL ACTS OF THE EXECUTIVE

3.1 Acts of the President of the Republic

According to the Constitution of Ukraine, the President is the head of the state, and the highest executive body in the country is the Cabinet of Ministers. The Constitution does not determine to which branch of power the President and his administration belongs. Nevertheless the range of his state administrative powers is most similar in form to executive power.

In accordance with Article 106 of the Constitution the President may issue edicts and decrees; these must be implemented in the whole territory of Ukraine. The President's statements, issued in the framework of the powers, provided for in items 3, 4, 5, 8, 10, 14, 15, 17, 18, 21 and 24 of Article 106 of the Constitution, are to be countersigned by the Prime Minister and the minister in charge of the execution of the regulation. In compliance with item 16 of Article 106 of the Constitution, the President has the right to abrogate the documents issued by the Cabinet of Ministers of Ukraine and the Council of Ministers of the Crimea Republic. The President's statements do not require confirmation by the Verkhovna Rada.

The power to determine whether the President's statements comply with the Constitution resides with the Constitutional Court of Ukraine. This question is considered on the application of no less than 45 People's Deputies of Ukraine, the Supreme Court of Ukraine, a Commissioner of the Verkhovna Rada of Ukraine on Human Rights or the Verkhovna Rada of the Crimea Republic.[53] The decision of the

Constitutional Court is final.[54] The question, however, can be discussed and evaluated in the mass media before the final decision is made.[55]

Chapter XV of the Constitution, "Transitional Provisions", Article 4, provides that:

The President of Ukraine, within three years after this Constitution comes into force, has the right to issue decrees that shall be approved by the Cabinet of Ministers of Ukraine and signed by the Prime Minister of Ukraine on economic issues not regulated by law; the draft decree shall be submitted to the Verkhovna Rada of Ukraine in the order stipulated in Article 93 of this Constitution. Such a decree of the President of Ukraine comes into force if, within 30 days from the date of submission of the law draft (except for the intercession period), the Verkhovna Rada of Ukraine will not adopt a law or will not refuse the submitted law draft by a majority of its members. The decree is to remain in force until a law on these issues is adopted by the Verkhovna Rada of Ukraine.[56]

When speaking about administrative law regulation, it is necessary to mention the activities of the President's Administration, which has a wide range of state authority powers. The commissions of the President, the First Assistant of the President, the Vice-President and the Vice-Head of the Administration of the President in cases defined by the President, and in the issues within their competence, are binding on the bodies of executive power and their officials.[57]

3.2 Acts of the Cabinet of Ministers and the departments

The Cabinet of Ministers, within its competence, issues rulings and decrees, that must be executed.[58] The acts of the Cabinet of Ministers must be signed by the Prime Minister.

The decisions of heads of local state administration, which contradict the Constitution and the laws of Ukraine may be voided by the President or by the head of local state administration of a higher level.[59] Article 144 of the Constitution states:

Bodies of local government within the limits of authority established by law adopt decisions that are binding throughout the appropriate territory. Decisions of bodies of local government which contradict the Constitution or laws of Ukraine are suspended in the order established by the law, with simultaneous appeal to court.[60]

The normative and legal acts of the Cabinet of Ministers of Ukraine, ministries and other central bodies of executive power shall be registered in the order established by law.[61]

The state registration must be carried out in compliance with the President's October 3, 1992, Decree "On the State Registration of Normative Acts of the Ministries and Other Bodies of Executive Power".[62] In conformity with Article 6, the Ministry of Justice of Ukraine carries out state registration of the normative acts of the ministries and other bodies of state executive power and bodies of economic management and control. The Department of Justice of the Council of Ministers of the Crimea Republic, regional, Kiev and Sevastopol state administrative bodies register the normative acts of the administration departments, regional state administrative bodies and some others. They also can refuse to register these documents, particularly if the acts contradict the Constitution or existing laws. Such decisions can be appealed up to the Cabinet of Ministers, and the decisions of the Department of Justice–up to the city state administrative bodies. Amendments and supplements to normative acts are subject to state registration in the general order.

4. THE SYSTEM OF COURTS DEALING WITH ADMINISTRATIVE LAW ISSUES

4.1 Courts and bodies examining administrative cases

There are no special administrative courts in Ukraine. Under Article 124 of the Constitution of Ukraine legal proceedings are carried out by the Constitutional Court of Ukraine and by the general jurisdiction courts.

The system of general jurisdiction courts is organised according to the principles of territory and specialisation. The highest judicial organ in the system of general jurisdiction courts is the Supreme Court of Ukraine. The highest judicial organs of the specialised courts are the appropriate higher courts. Courts of appeal and local courts exist and function. The organisation of extraordinary and special courts is prohibited. The cases on administrative offences are examined by: a) administrative commissions, attached to the district and city executive committees in cities, towns and villages and to the village radas; b) executive committees of town and village soviets of people's deputies; c) district judges and bodies of internal affairs; and bodies of state inspections and other official bodies (officials), authorised to do so by legislative documents of Ukraine.[63]

The bodies in charge of the cases on administrative offences are defined in the Code on Administrative Offences. For example, administrative commissions examine cases on the violation of rights of state property to forests and the animal world, on the pollution and damage of agricultural and other lands, and the illegal use of land belonging to the state forest stock. The executive committees of town and village soviets of people's deputies consider the cases on destroying or damaging young plants in the forests, and damaging the pastures belonging to the state. District courts examine cases on making and using radio broadcasting equipment without special permission and malicious insubordination to a legal demand or order of a militia official. The organs of the Ministry of Internal Affairs consider cases on the breach of the peace and violation of the frontier regime rules. The state fire control bodies examine cases on administrative offences and causing the infringement of the fire safeguarding rules. The railway transport supervision bodies are in charge of the cases on infringement of the rules of this transport.

Administrative cases are also examined by the bodies supervising sea and river transport, the state inspectorates on small vessels, the supervisory bodies of air transport, motor and electric transport, legal and technical inspectorates of labour, trade unions, state techological supervision, state atomic energy supervision, customs, the Ministry of Defence, sanitary inspection, state veterinary inspection, water resources, fish inspection, and forestry, and many others. These bodies carry out their activities on the basis of appropriate legislation, which defines the relationship of the action of the Code on Administrative Offences to the trade legislation.

4.2 Jurisdiction of the Courts

In compliance with the amendments introduced to Articles 236 and 237 of the Civil Procedure Code in 1988, 1990, 1991 and 1993, courts examine the following categories of cases. First, the court examines complaints about errors in the lists of electors and in the lists of citizens who have a right to take part in a referendum; on the applications for issuing a resolution on the existence of grounds for overturning of a decision to register a candidate; and on the complaints on the refusal to register a candidate in presidential elections. Secondly, the courts examine those complaints on the actions of official bodies and officials as to the infliction of administrative punishment. Thirdly, the courts examine complaints on those illegal actions of officials and infringement of citizens' rights that are attributed by law to their competence; on complaints concerning the decisions taken by officials towards religious organisations and on the statements of the public procurator on the recognition of a juridical document as illegal. Lastly the court examines complaints regarding the collecting arrears of taxes from citizens, self-taxation of the farmers, obligatory state insurance and some other categories of cases.

Special laws define other cases which may be appealed. For instance, the refusal of the bodies of executive power to register an enterprise can be appealed by its founders in court.[64] The founders have a right to claim damages resulting from illegal refusal in registration. Article 27 of this law provides that if a state or other body issues an act that does not correspond with its competence or the norms of legislation, or if questions arise as to the result of issuing this act, the enterprise has a right to appeal to a court or submit the question to arbitration and hand in an application to decide whether the act is valid.[65]

Decisions of the Soviet of People's Deputies on disputes relating to land can be appealed to a court or an arbitration court.[66] A decision on the refusal to register a non-governmental organisation or a political party can be appealed.[67] Legislation provides for the same legal defence for religious organisations, educational institutions, and health institutions.

Arbitration courts may examine disputes on the validity of acts in the context of arbitration proceedings, on the bases stated in the laws, except disputes that arise in discussions of standards and technical conditions; disputes on determining prices of products and goods and about the tariffs for different services (work), if these prices and tariffs cannot be established by agreement between the two sides in accordance with the existing legislation; and other disputes, whose resolution is attributed to the competence of other bodies.[68] Enterprises and organisations have the right to submit a dispute not solved by a regional arbitration court to the higher court of arbitration.

Amendments and supplements to the Civil Procedure Code (CPC) of December 15, 1992,[69] regulated the order of handing in and examining complaints on the action of official bodies and officials in connection with imposition of administrative punishment.[70] The law defines the circle of persons who have a right to apply with a complaint and a list of questions to be examined by the court in examining the complaint. Examples of such questions include enquiring whether the punishment was imposed by the competent body, whether the term of prescription was expired,[71] and whether there were demands for decisions on complaints.[72] Chapter 31-A, added to the CPC on April 25, 1988, regulates the examination of complaints on illegal actions of officials and alleged infringements of citizens' rights.[73] The law defines officials' actions and the order of their examination in court. Illegal action involves either the total or partial deprivation of a citizen's ability to enjoy a right, granted by a law or some other normative act, or the illegal imposition of some duty on a citizen.[74]

The law also defines the terms for appealing against a judgement and the order of examination of cases. The rules of the Civil Code govern the appeals against judgements given on citizens' complaints.[75] An appeal may be lodged against the decisions of the state bodies concerning the following issues: exceeding of a legally established term of decision-making on the registration of the charter (regulations) of a religious organisation; refusal to register a charter (regulations); and owning and using religious (cult) buildings and property.[76] A complaint may be lodged by the founders of these organisations within a month, counting from the day on which the decision was taken by the bodies of executive power.

5. GENERAL PROCEDURAL CODES IN ADMINISTRATIVE LAW

The Code of Administrative Offences (1984) regulates the proceedings in the cases of administrative offences; it contains a description of the kinds of administrative offences, procedures of establishing and documenting offences, administrative detention, personal examination, the order of considering the cases, the kinds of remedies and punishment, the rights and order of appeal, and the order of passing a resolution considering the imposition of an administrative punishment. It also indicates the bodies that may carry out administrative proceedings. The legislative acts passed in the field of departmental regulation on the issues of administrative offences are based on the principles stated in the Code. If some questions concerning a concrete group of administrative offences are not regulated by a specific legislative act, the norms of the Code of Administrative Offences apply.

The Customs Code of Ukraine (1991) regulates the proceedings in cases regarding the violation of customs rules, and includes procedures of establishing and documenting offences, questioning of persons, rules of customs examination, expert examination, the terms of imposition of punishment, appealing against the decisions, and the responsibility of customs bodies and their officials. Issues not regulated by the Customs Code are governed by the Code of Administrative Offences and other administrative legislation.[77]

The bodies executing proceedings on administrative cases, such as the bodies of the State Fire Inspectorate and the bodies of railway transport supervision, follow the regulations or statutes of these branches and the Code of Administrative Offences. The actual correlation of the Code of Administrative Offences and the trade laws can be shown in the following examples. The Forestry Code of Ukrainian SSR (1980), Article 141 defines the kinds of violations of the forestry legislation, such as infringement of the fire safety measures in the forests and destruction or damages inflicted upon the forest and forest flora. For these offences people bear criminal, administrative and other kinds of responsibility, according to the law. Article 241 of the Code of Administrative Offences provides that the forestry bodies may examine the cases of administrative offences, concerning the infringement of the fire safety measures in the forests: Article 77 of the Code of Administrative Offences provides sanctions for the violation of fire safety measures in the forests in the form of a fine.

The Land Code of Ukraine (1992), Article 115 establishes sanctions for violation of land laws, such as unwarranted occupation of a land lot and pollution or damage of agricultural or other land. The guilty parties bear civil, administrative or criminal responsibility. For pollution or damage of agricultural or other land the guilty party bears administrative responsibility in the form of fine.[78] This category of offences is considered by administrative commissions.[79] Thus, a trade law (in this case, the Land Code) establishes the kinds of violations of the land laws, while the Code of Administrative Offences defines the concrete administrative sanctions for those offences and regulates the administrative proceedings of examining the cases of this category as well as the administrative body in charge of their resolution.

Some trade laws, such as the Customs Code (1991), regulate the administrative proceedings in the area in greater detail, defining the proceedings to be followed by the officials in imposing administrative penalties. But even in this case the Code itself contains a direction to follow the Code of Administrative Offences on issues unregulated by the Customs Code. District judges are to examine the following categories of administrative offences: petty theft of state property; evasion of paying compensation for property damage, petty profiteering, and unauthorised making and using of radio transmitting equipment.[80] These categories of cases are examined by the courts in administrative court proceedings.

6. PROCEDURES OF APPEAL AND JUDICIAL REVIEW OF ADMINISTRATIVE ACTION

According to Article 16 of the Law on Citizens' Appeal (1996):

> Complaints on the actions and decisions of a body of state power, a body of local administration, institution, organisation, association of citizens, enterprise, mass media or official are lodged with a higher body or official in the order of administrative subordination. This does not prevent citizens from appealing to court in accordance with the laws in force; in the absence of a higher administrative body or if the citizen does not agree with the decision issued on his or her complaint recourse to court is also permitted.[81]

Thus, the Law recognises the citizen's right to appeal the actions or decisions of a subordinated body to a higher one.

Decisions of an administrative commission can be appealed to the executive committee of the appropriate Rada of People's Deputies or to the district court, whose decision is final; resolutions of an executive committee of a village or settlement Rada can be appealed to the executive committee of the district, city or city district Rada of People's Deputies, or the (city) district court, whose decision is also final.[82]

Decisions of other bodies (or officials) in cases involving imposition of fines may be appealed to a higher official or to the court. In cases involving other administrative sanctions, the appeal can be addressed first to the higher official and only then to the court.

Complaints regarding decisions of a body of internal affairs (police), or the state inspectorate on small vessels in cases where an administrative punishment in the form of a warning is given at the time and where the offence was committed without drawing up a report, are not subject to examination in court. These decisions may be appealed to a higher body.[83] Resolutions of military automobile inspectorates with respect to cases on infringement of traffic regulations are not subject to examination in court. In these cases complaints are addressed to the higher official, who has a right to examine the complaint.[84] Thus the Law defines which bodies' resolutions may be appealed to a higher body or to the court. That means that the Law establishes two procedures of appeal against these resolutions. An appeal against a resolution to a body does not prevent a simultaneous appeal to the court. The court is not bound by the decision of the higher body and is instead free to take its own decision. The existing practice demonstrates that complaints are usually sent first to the higher body, and if they are not granted, they are further addressed to the court.

6.1 Internal review of administrative action (appeal)

The Code on Administrative Offences, Articles 289–293, regulates the order of handing in a complaint to a higher body. The time limit for appeal is 10 days.[85] If it is missed for legitimate reasons, it can be extended by the body, who has a right to consider the complaint.

Besides appeals lodged against a decision on imposing administrative punishment by a private person or organisation, the Law provides the procedures for the procurator's (public prosecutor's) appeal.[86] As well as lodging a complaint, the procurator's appeal suspends the execution of the decision.[87] The time limit for examining an appeal or a complaint is 10 days. The Law regulates the powers of the body, which makes a decision on the appeal. It may make one of the following decisions: leave the act unchanged; repeal it and remand the case for re-examination; repeal the decision and discontinue the case; and change the measures of punishment within the limits provided by the Act on Responsibility for Administrative Offences: the punishment should not be more severe. If it is established that the decision was issued by an official body that had no right to decide on this case, it may be repealed and the case sent for examination to a competent body. This procedure applies if the decisions are appealed to a higher body.

6.2 Judicial Review of Administrative Action

Article 244 of the Civil Procedure Code provides that an act on the imposition of an administrative punishment, other decision of an administrative body or an official on a case of administrative offence, can be appealed to court either by the person whom the decision concerns or by the alleged victim. The complaint must be lodged to the court where the official body is located or where the official works, within 10 days of the decision being taken; if the decision on this kind of administrative offence was subject to previous appeal to an administrative body, within 10 days of the day on which the decision on the complaint was issued. If "good reasons" are established, then the time limit may be restored.

On receiving the complaint the judge may demand and obtain the materials on the case from the appropriate body or official. The complaint is then examined in the presence of the plaintiff, although his absence does not prevent the trying of the case. While examining the complaint, the judge must resolve the following questions: whether the punishment was imposed by a competent body; whether the actions of the person whom the resolution concerned amounted to the offence for which administrative responsibility was determined; whether the punishment was imposed within the time limits established by the law; whether the term fixed for imposing a punishment has expired; and whether the nature of the committed offence, the personality of the offender, the extent of his guilt, his property position, and the circumstances extenuating or aggravating his guilt were taken into account in the establishment of the form of punishment.

The court then pronounces one of the following judgements on the complaint: a refusal to satisfy the complaint; repeal of the decision and re-direction of the case for repeated examination, if the body (official) which passed it did not consider circumstances important for the case or if the case was illegally discontinued; direction of the case for examination by the competent body (official) if the decision was passed by an incompetent body (official); repeal of the decision and discontinuation of the case, if circumstances which, according to the law, prevent the proceedings on the case have been revealed; or, finally, change of the punishment within the limits provided by the Act on Responsibility for Administrative Offences: the punishment should not be more severe. The decision of a city district court on a complaint is final and is not subject to cassation appeal, although it can be appealed on general grounds.[88] The court must send a copy of its judgement on the case to the body whose act was appealed.[89]

6.3 Judicial Remedies

The courts examine cases arising on the grounds of administrative legal relationships using Chapter III, Part B of the Civil Procedure Code of Ukraine. When granting a complaint against an action or inactivity of state official bodies, juridical persons or officials in the field of administration, the court: (a) obliges them to satisfy the demand of the applicant and eliminate violations of his or her rights; (b) releases the person from a duty, with which he or she is illegally entrusted; (c) abrogates the measures of punishment imposed on him or her; or (d) restores his or her violated rights and freedoms in some other way.[90] The execution of the court's judgement is carried out by the state body, judicial person or official under procedures provided for in Article 248.9. In a case in which the judgement is not executed, the state body, juridical person or official, or any other guilty party is made responsible for this under Article 417 of the Civil Procedure Code, and if they intentionally fail to execute it–under Article 176.4 of the Criminal Code of Ukraine. Thus, the powers of the court to provide remedies consist in obliging state bodies, juridical persons or officials to carry out certain actions. While examining a complaint, the court considers the case in essence, according to the rules of civil proceedings.

7. OMBUDSMAN

At present the law regulating the activities of the Authorised Representative on Human Rights (Ombudsman) of the Verkhovna Rada has not been adopted. Nevertheless the Constitution provides for the creation of such a institution, the procedures for its establishment and its basic powers.

According to Article 55 of the Constitution, every person has a right to appeal for the protection of his or her rights to the Authorised Representative on Human Rights of the Verkhovna Rada.[91]

Article 85 of the Constitution provides:

The powers of the Verkhovna Rada include the following: Paragraph 17–to appoint to position and discharge from position the Authorised Representative on Human Rights of the Verkhovna Rada of Ukraine; to hear his or her annual reports on the situation with protection of human rights and freedoms in Ukraine.[92]

Article 150 provides that the Authorised Representative on Human Rights of the Verkhovna Rada can appeal to the Constitutional Court concerning the resolution of issues on the constitutionality of laws and other legal acts of the Verkhovna Rada of Ukraine, acts of the President of Ukraine, acts of the Cabinet of Ministers of Ukraine and legal acts of the Verkhovna Rada of the Autonomous Republic of Crimea. The Law on the Constitutional Court, adopted on October 16, 1996, determines that the forms of appeal to the Constitutional Court are constitutional complaints and constitutional appeals.

The Authorised Representative has the right to appeal with constitutional complaints.[93] The Authorised Representative has the right to raise issues of official interpretation of the Constitution and laws of Ukraine.[94] The Authorised Representative on Human Rights of the Verkhovna Rada, in accordance with his powers, executes control over the observation of laws on the appeals of citizens.[95] Most likely, the Law on the Authorised Representative on Human Rights of the Verkhovna Rada of Ukraine will be adopted in the near future: at present, although this institution is established by the Constitution of Ukraine and by the Law on the Constitutional Court, it is not in operation.

8. OTHER FORMS OF CONTROL OVER THE ADMINISTRATION

Chapter VII of the Constitution of Ukraine regulates the institution of the Procurator's (Prosecutor's) Office. Article 121 provides:

The Procurator's Office of Ukraine is a unified system performing the following functions:

1. state prosecution in court;
2. representation of the interests of citizens or the State in court, in cases envisaged by law;
3. overseeing of the compliance with the law by bodies which conduct investigations, inquiries, and preliminary inquests;
4. overseeing of the compliance with the law during the enforcement of court decisions on criminal cases, as well as during the implementation of other coercive measures related to the restriction of the personal freedom of citizens.[96]

Article 122 determines that the Procurator General shall be appointed with the consent of the Verkhovna Rada of Ukraine and dismissed by the President of Ukraine.[97] The Verkhovna Rada of Ukraine may pass a vote of no confidence in the

Procurator General of Ukraine which shall cause his or her resignation from the office. The term of office of the General Procurator is five years.

The Law of Ukraine "On the Procurator's Office" was adopted on November 5, 1991.[98] It is still in force, with amendments and supplements. According to this Law the highest form of supervision over the observance and correct use of laws by the Cabinet of Ministers, ministries and state committees, departments and other bodies of state and economic administration and control, the Government of the Autonomous Republic of Crimea, local Radas of People's Deputies, their executive and administrative bodies, military units, political parties, public organisations, mass movements, enterprises, institutions, organisations, irrespective of their forms of property, and the citizens is executed by the Procurator General of Ukraine and procurator's offices which are subordinated to him or her.[99]

The procurator's office consists of the Procurator's Office General of Ukraine, the Procurator's Office of the Republic of Crimea, regions, Kiev and Sevastopol (having the rights of regions), city, district, inter-district procurator's offices, and also the military procurator's office. The procurator's office executes general supervision.[100] The object of general supervision is: (a) the observance of acts which are adopted by all the bodies, enterprises, institutions, organisations and officials, and are requirements of the Constitution and laws in force; (b) the observance of the laws on personal immunity, social, economic, political, personal rights and freedoms of citizens, and the protection of their honour and dignity, if the law does not provide any other order of protection of these rights; (c) and the observance of laws concerning economic and international relations, protection of the environment, customs and external economic activities.

The control over the observance of laws is executed on applications and other reports on the violation of laws that require the procurator's reaction, and also if there are grounds, on personal initiative. The procurator's office may not act as a substitute for the bodies of department administration and control and may not interfere with economic activities which do not contradict the laws in force.[101]

To execute its power of general supervision the procurator's office has a right to: (a) control the decisions, resolutions, instructions, orders and other acts and documents; (b) receive information on the state of lawfulness and measures on its granting; (c) demand that the administrative heads and collegiate bodies execute control revisions of the activities of the enterprises, institutions, organisations and other structures, irrespective of their forms of property, subordinated to them and under their control; (d) appoint specialists to control expert investigations both within and outside departments.[102] Within the limits of his competence a procurator has a right to appeal against the acts of the executive and administrative bodies of local Radas, enterprises, institutions, organisations, public organisations, and also the actions and decisions of officials. He can also put forward a complaint or appeal against the decisions of local Radas, depending on the nature of the violations.[103]

9. PARLIAMENTARY COMMITTEES

The parliamentary committees (formerly commissions) execute control over the executive power as provided by the Constitution, the Law on Permanent Committees of the Verkhovna Rada, and the Law on the Regulations of the Verkhovna Rada. The powers of the committees are established by the Constitution and this Law, and their tasks and competence by the Regulation of the appropriate Permanent Committee, approved by the Verkhovna Rada, the Regulations and the Decree of the Verkhovna Rada.[104] The order of creation, liquidation or reorganisation, election of the heads and their recall is established by the Regulations of the Verkhovna Rada. The organisation of the work is established by this Law and the Regulations of the Verkhovna Rada.

The number of committees and their functional specialisation is established by the Verkhovna Rada depending on the state economic, social and cultural priorities. The Permanent Committees are responsible to the Verkhovna Rada and are subordinate to it. They must study the expediency and effectiveness of the actions of the Government, other bodies of the state executive power, and their officials in the issues that are under their jurisdiction, and also prepare and present appropriate resolutions to the Verkhovna Rada.[105] The functions of Permanent Committees include preliminary discussion of the candidatures of officials, who in accordance with the Constitution and the laws of Ukraine are elected, appointed or commissioned by the Verkhovna Rada, and the preparation of appropriate resolutions on these candidatures. The Permanent Committee carry out control over the observation of the Constitution and the laws of Ukraine by the central bodies of executive power and local government, enterprises and organisations irrespective of their form of property, and also control over the legality and effectiveness of the expenditures from the state budget. All the bodies of the state executive power, enterprises and organisations, and their officials are obliged to grant the requests of the Permanent Committee and present to them all necessary materials. The recommendations of the Permanent Committees are subject to obligatory examination by the central bodies of executive power and local government.[106] In the execution of their functions the Permanent Committees have a right to hear the First Vice-Prime Minister, and vice-prime ministers, the heads of the state committees, departments and other bodies of the state executive power, organisations, trade union bodies, bodies of local government, associations of citizens and private persons.

Information on the sessions of the Permanent Committees is published in the newspaper *Golos Ukraini*. The Permanent Committees present to the Verkhovna Rada their resolutions and recommendations.[107] The resolutions on the supervision and control over the activities of the bodies of executive power or officials must contain concrete referrals to articles of the legislative acts of Ukraine (thus providing the norms which have either been violated or not appropriately observed by this body or official) and present the facts proving the violation.[108]

II. DEVELOPMENTS IN ADMINISTRATIVE LAW DURING 1996-1997

A. THE CONSTITUTION

Ukraine passed its new Constitution on June 28, 1996. The fundamental law determined the structure of state power, human and civil rights, liberties and duties, the powers of the Verkhovna Rada of Ukraine, the President of Ukraine, the Cabinet of Ministers and other bodies of executive power, the administration of justice, the administrative and territorial structure, and the powers of the local government. The administrative legal institutions regulated by the Constitution represent a rather different model of public administration than those provided for by the former Constitution of the Ukrainian SSR.

Presently state power in Ukraine is separated into legislative, executive and judicial branches,[109] whereas in the Constitution of the USSR (1978), Article 2, provided that "the people execute state power through the Soviets of Peoples' Deputies": accordingly, all other state bodies were accountable to and under the control of the Soviets. The organisation and the activities of the Soviet state were based on the principle of democratic centralism, making the decisions of higher administrative levels obligatory for lower ones.[110] This principle has been replaced by the "Rule of Law" principle, in which public officials must act in accordance with and restrained by constitutional and legal norms. As such, a public official has no authority except for that set forth in some duly enacted legal or constitutional act.

Article 1 of the new Constitution proclaimed Ukraine a sovereign and independent, democratic, social, and legal State. The legislative transition from the administrative totalitarian system to a democratic system of government began only after 1995. Several laws were passed and some changes were inserted into the Constitution, which established new administrative law institutions, as well as new procedures.[111] Therefore the Constitution passed on June 28, 1996, besides having several other important aspects, has recapitulated the development of the administrative legal institutions at present and has determined their development for the future.

The passing of the Law "On the Constitutional Court of Ukraine" on October 16, 1996, was an important stage in the development of the provisions of the new Constitution.[112] This Law provides that the Constitutional Court has the authority to resolve issues on the correspondence of laws and other legal acts by the Verkhovna Rada of Ukraine, acts of the President, acts of the Cabinet of Ministers and the legal acts of the Verkhovna Rada of the Autonomous Republic of Crimea to the Constitution. The Court is also empowered to interpret officially the Constitution and the laws.[113]

Thus, the Law "On the Constitutional Court" regulates the order for executing constitutional control over the correspondence to the Constitution of the listed legal acts. These issues are considered upon complaints by: a) the President; b) no less than 45 People's Deputies; c) the Supreme Court; d) the Authorised Representative on Human Rights of the Verkhovna Rada of Ukraine; or e) the Verkhovna Rada of the Autonomous Republic of Crimea.[114] The jurisdiction of the Constitutional Court covers also the conformity of Ukrainian legal acts with the international treaties in force and those, which are presented to the Verkhovna Rada for ratification.[115] The Court can decide on the constitutionality of acts adopted before the passage of the new Constitution as well.

B. LEGISLATION

Some laws were passed during the period of democratisation of the governmental sphere and the development of an economy based on free enterprise which, despite certain amendments and supplements, are still in force. They include the laws on large and small privatisation, the laws on property (1991), on enterprises in the Ukrainian SSR (1991), on enterprise (1991), on prices and price formation (1990), on the state tax service (1990), on securities and fund exchange (1991), and on economic associations (1991). In the field of nature preservation legislation, the Law "On the Nature Reserves Fund of Ukraine" (1992) and some others were passed the period.

In the field of finance, the Law "On Banks and Bank Activities" was issued. In the sphere of mass media laws "On Information", "On Publishing Resources of Mass Media", and "On Television and Radio Broadcasting" were passed. Overall, a serious legislative effort is underway to reform the major institutions in the country and the administrative system in particular. This was also the most important feature of legislative activity during 1996–1997.

1. GENERAL PROCEDURAL LAWS

1.1 The Code on Administrative Offences

In 1996 considerable changes were introduced into the Code on Administrative Offences. Some administrative offences were revised (for instance, infringing on property, violation of state property in forests or the animal world, administrative offences in the field ofnatural resources preservation, and use of natural resources or preservation of historical or cultural relies).[116] Changes were also introduced to the administrative offences in the field of trade, public catering, various public services, finances and economic activities.[117] Changes to the Chapter "Administrative Offences against the Established Order of Government" were introduced as well.[118] The Chapter "Jurisdiction over Cases on Administrative Offences" was seriously amended.[119] The amendments concerned mainly the competence of the bodies in examining cases regarding administrative offences. The competence of the district courts in this regard was expanded. All cases on administrative offences committed by persons aged 16 to 18 years are to be heard in court. Under the new provisions,[120] the bodies of the state tax service consider cases on administrative offences connected with the sale or taking of commission, or storing with the purpose of selling of alcoholic drinks and cigarettes without the stamps of excise for the established brand.[121] The competence of the bodies and institutions that carry out sanitary inspection and that of some other bodies were changed as well.

The chapter "Proceedings on the Cases of Administrative Offences" was also amended.[122] It now provides that the court decisions on the cases of administrative offences committed by people between 16 and 18 years of age can be repealed or alleviated by the judge on the protest (prosecutor's complaint) of the public procurator; and irrespective of the existence of the procurator's protest, by a representative of a higher court.[123]

1.2 The Code on Civil Procedure

Since March 13, 1996, a new wording of chapter 31-A of the Civil Procedure Code has been in force defining the judicial order for examining citizens' complaints on the decisions, actions or inactivity of state bodies, judicial or official persons. In accordance with Article 248.1 of the Civil Legal Procedure Code of Ukraine, a citizen has the right to lodge a complaint to the court (in the case of a military servant, to the military court), if he or she considers that the activities of a state body, a judicial or an official person in execution of their administrative functions, infringe upon his or her rights and freedoms. Public organisations or the staff of an enterprise can also appeal to court in the interests of an individual. The Law also defines the range of people whose activities can be appealed: a) the bodies of the state executive power and their officials; b) the bodies of local government and their officials; c) heads of institutions, enterprises and organisations, irrespective of their form of property; and d) officials entrusted with administrative economic duties or other duties related to the exercise of administrative powers.

The objects of the judicial appeal are decisions, actions or inactivity of the subjects of appeal, in connection with which a citizen considers that: a) his rights or freedoms are infringed; b) obstacles are created for the exercise of his constitutional rights or freedoms, or the measures taken for the realisation of his rights or freedoms are inadequate; c) duties imposed on him are not provided for by legislation; d) he is considered responsible for an action not provided for by the law; e) some form of penalty has been imposed on him without legal grounds.[124]

The Law also defines decisions and actions, the complaints against which are not within the jurisdiction of the courts. These include the acts of the bodies of legislative and executive power, subjected to examination as to their compliance with the Constitution; the acts concerning the defence of the state, state security, external political activities of the state, state and military secrets; the acts and actions of officials and bodies instituting inquiries and preliminary investigations, if another procedure of appeal has been established by a law; and the acts of citizens' associations that, according to law and the statute, belong to their internal or exceptional competence.[125] Complaints may be lodged either directly with the court or with preliminary appeal to the official or body of the higher level. If a complaint is lodged with the court, the execution of the act appealed will be suspended.

The Law establishes the terms and the procedure of examining complaints, making and execution of court decisions, and the responsibility for the execution of the judgement in the form of fines. Cases of deliberate non-execution of judgement or obstruction of execution by an official result in criminal prosecution in accordance with Article 176.4 of the Criminal Code and punishment in the form of a fine.

1.3 Law on appeals of citizens

In accordance with the Verkhovna Rada Decree No 394/96 VR dated October 2, 1996, "The Law of Ukraine on the Appeals of Citizens" was brought into force. The new Law provides a wider range of citizens' rights to appeal to the bodies of state power or local government, associations of citizens, institutions and organisations (public or private), enterprises, mass media, and officials. Citizens may file a number of different forms of appeal: "remarks", "complaints" and "proposals" in relation to the work of these officials and bodies, "petitions" or "applications" as to the realisation of social, economic, political and personal rights and legal interests of the citizens, or "complaints" against infringement of rights. In general, citizens have the right to make proposals on the improvement of the activities of public authorities and appeal against actions of officials and state or public bodies.

The law provides the citizens of Ukraine with possibilities to participate in the government of the state and in social activities, and to influence the improvement of the work of the government and local government, as well as other institutions and organisations (public or private). Applications are addressed to the bodies of state power and local government, institutions which have powers to resolve the relevant issues.[126]

Article 7 forbids the sending of citizens' complaints for examination to the bodies or officials whose actions or decisions are appealed. Complaints on the actions or decisions of a body of state government or local government must be addressed to a higher body or official. This does not deprive the citizen of the right to appeal to the court. If the complaint is satisfied, the body or the official who had issued the illegal decision compensates him or her for any monetary loss, such as the costs of lodging the complaint or necessary travel expenses.[127]

1.4 Law on the Account Chamber

The Law on the Account Chamber of the Verkhovna Rada of Ukraine was passed in 1996, pursuant to the provisions of the Constitution. This Law establishes the legal basis for the activities of the Account Chamber of the Verkhovna Rada of Ukraine, its status, functions, powers and the order of their execution.[128]

The Account Chamber is a permanent acting highest body of state financial and economic control, created by, accountable to and under the control of the Verkhovna Rada.[129] The main task of the Account Chamber is executing control over the appropriate use of the income and expenditure parts of the state budget.[130] The functions of the Account Chamber include control over the observation of the laws of Ukraine, the financing of national programmes, the keeping and using of state property by the bodies of executive power or officials elected, appointed or assigned by the Verkhovna Rada.[131] Upon a request of the Verkhovna Rada and the Committees of the Verkhovna Rada of Ukraine, the Account Chamber executes control over the functions governing the financing of the national programmes of ecological, social, national and cultural development, and the preservation of environment and other programmes approved by the Verkhovna Rada of Ukraine. The field of powers of the Account Chamber include the right to present to the Verkhovna Rada, the President or the bodies of executive power petitions for the initiation of proceedings against officials who have caused material damage to the state.[132] The Account Chamber must regularly publish information on its activities in the mass media.[133]

2. *SUBSTANTIVE LEGISLATION*

2.1 Laws on privatisation

The Law "On the Privatisation of Small State Enterprises" establishes the new legal mechanism of market privatisation of small state enterprises.[134] The Law establishes that the field of its action is industrial and economic branches subject to immediate privatisation: processing and local industry, production of construction materials, light and food industry, construction, some kinds of transport, trade and public catering, everyday repairs and other services, as well as housing and communal services.[135] Chapter III concerns selling of establishments by way of redemption (debt for property), and Chapter IV is about selling at open auctions (tenders).

The Law "On the Specific Features of Privatisation of Property in the Agricultural and Industrial Complex" (July 10, 1996) defines the order of privatisation of enterprises, processing agricultural raw materials, and providing different services for the agricultural commodity producers;[136] as well as privatisation of the property of enterprises and organisation of the fishing industry,[137] or processing raw materials of forestry.[138]

The Law "On Introducing Amendments into Some Legislative Acts in the Field of

Lease Relationship" provides that the privatisation of leased state property is carried out under the same procedures, as these established by the legislation on privatisation. If the lease contract provides the right of the lease-holder to privatise the leased property granted, privatisation must be executed under the terms of the contract.[139]

According to the new arrangement established by the Decree of the Cabinet of Ministers of Ukraine "On the Privatisation of Leased Complexes of State Enterprises and Their Structural Parts" (1993): "Decisions on the privatisation of state enterprises leased under contracts allowing for privatisation by the lessee are made by the state organs in charge of privatisation only with the consent of the lessee. In other cases the decisions on privatisation of leased property are taken without the lessee's agreement."

2.2 Laws concerning land reform

The Decree of the Verkhovna Rada of the Ukrainian SSR "On Land Reform" (December 18, 1990) defined land reform as a component of the transition to market economy. Under this reform agricultural lands were restructured and simultaneously transferred into permanent and hereditary ownership of citizens, enterprises, institutions or organisations.[140]

In September 1996 a Decree of the Verkhovna Rada of Ukraine was passed providing for the coming into force of the Law "On the Entering of Changes and Additions to the Law of Ukraine on the Payment for Land Dated 1992" on January 1, 1997. In compliance with the Decree, the Law the "On the Payment for Land" has now been issued in a new wording. The new law defines the procedure for and amounts of payment for using land; it also determines the using of financial resources, received as the payment for land, the responsibilities of the payers and the control over the correct calculation and collection of land taxes.

Article 12 of the Law establishes certain privileges in relation to the payment for land. The following institutions are free of land taxes: nature reserves, botanical gardens, natural experimental farms, research institutions, bodies of state government and local government, public organisations of the disabled, registered non-profit charitable and religious organisations, and some others.

Finally, changes were made in the Law on the Collective Agricultural Enterprise (1992). The new arrangement introduced the right to create confidential societies that carry out representative activities with securities.[141]

2.3 Laws on education

In the field of governing the socio-cultural processes, the Decree of the Verkhovna Rada of Ukraine (March 23, 1996) enforced the Law "On Entering Amendments and Supplements to the Law of Ukraine on Education (1991)." The Decree provided that the Cabinet of Ministers of Ukraine should present to the Verkhovna Rada proposals for bringing the legislative acts of Ukraine into conformity with the new Law. The Cabinet of Ministers must also prepare and present by 1998 to the Verkhovna Rada draft laws on the professional training of teachers, on higher education, on high school education, on pre-school education, and on the state support for the extra-curriculum education in Ukraine. The reworded "Law of Education" provides that the state policy in the field of education is defined by the Verhovna Rada of Ukraine and is executed by the bodies of state executive power and the bodies of local government.[142]

A system of state and public authorities has been created to govern and regulate education: the two major organs responsible for this area are the Ministry of Education and the Higher Certifying Commission. The Ministry of Education is responsible for establishing the state standards of education, executing inspections and supervision, carrying out accreditation of higher and professional technical educational institutions (public or private), and giving licences for operation and graduation certificates.[143]

Licences are given under procedures established by the Cabinet of Ministers of Ukraine.[144] Appointments in the educational institutions must be carried out in accordance with Article 54. Teachers are subject to certification on the basis of which they are categorised: the different categories depend on the pedagogical qualifications of the teachers. Article 13 defines the competence of the Higher Certifying Commission of Ukraine, which is responsible for organising and carrying out the certification of the scientists and teaching personnel: it also confers scientific degrees.

2.4 Laws on financial groups and competition

The Law "On the Industrial Financial Groups in Ukraine" establishes the procedure of starting, reorganising and liquidating industrial financial groups as well as the financial economical conditions for their activities.[145] Control and supervision of Industrial Financial Groups activities is executed by the Cabinet of Ministers, the bodies of the State Tax Inspectorate, the National Bank of Ukraine, the Anti-Monopoly Committee of Ukraine, and other state bodies.

The Law "On the Protection Against Unfair Competition" defines the legal basis of protection of economic subjects (owners of a business) and consumers against unfair competition.[146] The Law aims at the establishment, development and promotion of commercial and other kinds of competition in the conditions of market economy.[147] Chapter 4 of the Law defines some types of violations, e.g. illegal use of information and disclosure of commercial secrets. Chapter 5 regulates the sanctions in cases of unfair competition. Chapter 6 provides the legal instruments for protection against unfair competition and the procedural basis for examining cases of unfair competition by the Anti-Monopoly Committee.

2.5 Laws on media and advertisement

The Law "On Advertising" defines the main principles of commercial advertising in Ukraine, regulates the legal relationships in the process of creation of advertisements, and governs the spreading and receiving of advertisements.[148] In accordance with Article 6, the language of the advertisements is defined by the laws "On the Languages in the Ukrainian SSR", "On Information", "On Print Mass Media (Publishing) in Ukraine", "On Television and Radio Broadcasting" and some others.

The control over the observation of the laws on advertisement is exercised by the Ministry on Press and Information, the State Committee on Protection of Consumers' Rights (in the field of consumers' protection), the Anti-Monopoly Committee (in accordance with the anti-monopoly laws), the National Board of Ukraine on Television and Radio Broadcasting (concerning broadcasts of all the forms of property).[149] Associations of citizens in the field of advertising have the right to execute independent examinations of advertisements as to their compliance with the law; to present materials on the violations of the laws on advertising to the procurator's offices and the bodies of executive power; and to appeal to courts and courts of arbitration in the interest of advertisers, owners of businesses, and distributors of advertisements.

2.6 Law on Insurance

The Law on Insurance concerns the field of insurance and serves the purpose of creating a market of insurance services; another purpose is to increase the insurance protection of the property interests of enterprises and other institutions, organisations and private individuals. The scope of this law does not cover state social insurance.

The Law regulates the insurance bodies (agencies), the kinds of insurance, insurance contracts, and the licensing of insurance activities. The state control over insurance activities[150] is executed by the Committee on Control over Insurance Activities, set up pursuant to a Decree of the Cabinet of Ministers. Articles 36 and 37 define the functions and the rights of this Committee.[151]

2.7 Laws on finance

The Law "On the State Regulation of the Securities Market" provides the legal basis for the execution of state regulation of the securities market and the state control over the issuing and circulation of securities in Ukraine.[152] The state regulation is executed by taking comprehensive measures of structured control and supervision over the securities market and their derivatives and prevention of abuse and violations of law in this field.[153]Article 14 regulates criminal prosecution. Disputes arising in the process of application of this law are solved in courts of arbitration.

Amendments introduced to the Law "On the Securities and the Stock Exchange"[154] included: a) Article 22 "The procedure of issuing bonds and shares of enterprises and the information on their issuing is defined by the State Commission on Securities and the Stock Exchange". Further, complaints on the actions of the local branches of the State Commission on Securities and the Stock Exchange are examined by the State Commission itself.[155] The decisions of the State Commission can be appealed against in courts and the courts of arbitration.

Amendments were made to the Law "On the Budget System of Ukraine":

If the indices of expenditures from the State budget are subject to further detailing in accordance with the "Rules of Registering the Draft Law on the State Budget" in the supplements to this Law, these supplements are an inalienable part of the Law on the State Budget. Changes, specifications and additions to them during the budget year can be made only by a decision of the Verkhovna Rada.[156]

2.8 Laws on transport

The Law "On Pipeline Transport" defines legal, economical and organisational aspects of the management of pipeline transport and the system of pipeline transport.[157] This area is also regulated also by the Law "On Transport" and some other legislative acts.[158] Privatisation and changes of ownership of major state enterprises involved in pipeline transport is prohibited.[159]

Activities associated with planning, construction, repairs and exploitation of pipelines are carried out on the grounds of special permissions (licences) and are subject to obligatory certification. Licences are given by the appropriate bodies of state power under procedures established by the Cabinet of Ministers.[160]

The Law "On the Railway Transport" defines legal, economical and organisational aspects of the management of railway transport of communal use, its role in the economy and social life. The law regulates the relationships between the railway authorities with the bodies of state executive power, and the bodies of local government. It also specifies the kinds of railway transport, the rights and duties of passengers, senders and receivers of loads, luggage management, and post while taking into account the specific features of the functioning of this type of transport as a united industrial and technical complex.[161]

Article 3 provides that the legislation on railway transport consists of the Law "On Transport", the Regulations of Railway Transport ratified by the Cabinet of Ministers, and some other laws. The adoption of the Regulations of Railway Transport is executed by the Ministry of Transport on the agreement of the Ministry of the Economy and the Anti-Monopoly Committee.[162] The administration of railway transport is executed by the State Administration of Railway Transport ("Ukrainska Zaliznitsya"), and is under the jurisdiction of the Ministry of Transport.[163]

2.9 Laws on customs

The Law on Introducing Amendments to the Law "On the Unified Customs Tariff"[164] rules that: "Changes of the tariffs of customs duties, with the exception of the import duty for excisable goods, are executed by the Cabinet of Ministers. The amounts of the import duty for excisable goods are established and changed by the Verkhovna Rada of Ukraine."[165]

2.10 Laws on the environment

In the field of nature preservation, the Law "On Introducing Amendments and Additions to the Legislative Acts on the Preservation of Natural Environment" was passed on March 6, 1996.[166] The act introduced amendments to the Code on Administrative Offences and The Law of the Ukrainian SSR "On the Preservation of Natural Environment".[167] In particular, amendments were made to Article 20: "The officials of Special Departments of the Ministry of Preservation of Natural Environment in the field of fire prevention are subject to obligatory personal insurance in case of death at the expense of the state budget, in the amount of 10 times their yearly salary." In case of injury, an official receives an extraordinary allowance in the amount of his yearly salary.

2.11 Laws on health care

In the field of health services the Law "On Medicines" was passed. It regulates the creation, registration, production, control over the quality and sale of medicines. It also defines the rights and duties of the enterprises, institutions and persons involved in the production and distribution of medicines. The law further defines the powers of the bodies of executive power and their officials in this field. State registration of medicines is regulated in Article 9. State control is executed by special bodies of executive power.[168] The powers of the officials and bodies of state control are established by Article 15.[169]

2.12 Other laws

Several amendments and additions were made into other important acts as well, such as, to the Law "On the Universal Conscription and Military Service";[170] to certain acts of Ukraine on the sanctions for offences in the field of communication;[171] and to the Criminal Procedural Code of Ukraine on Administrative Offences, in particular an increase of the penalties for violation of the right to life, health and property of judges, officials of the judicial bodies, persons taking part in the protection of the public law and order and citizens.[172]

The Chapter has been prepared on the basis of information provided by Eugeniya Dodina

NOTES

[1] "On the Implementation of International Treaties on the Territory of Ukraine", December 10, 1991.

[2] *See e.g.* "The Railway Regulations" and "The Rules on the Export of Valuable Works of Art".

[3] *See e.g.* The Resolution of the Soviet of People's Commissars of June 4, 1933, "On Holding More than One Position or Job of Relatives at Institutions, Enterprises and Organisations of the Collectivised Sector"

[4] *See e.g.* the Code of the Merchant Navy, passed by the Verkhovna Rada of Ukraine on December 9, 1994, No 277/94-VR

[5] The Constitution was passed on June 28, 1996.

[6] Thus, when the President's Edict No. 1228/96 "On the Composition of the Cabinet of Ministers of Ukraine" was passed on December 14, 1996, the President's Edict No. 707 of August 17, 1996, "On Some Issues in Forming the Cabinet of Ministers of Ukraine" was considered invalid; the Act of the Cabinet of Ministers of Ukrainian SSR of June 13, 1991, No. 25 "On the Presidium of the Cabinet of Ministers of Ukrainian SSR" and the act of May 23, 1993, No. 293 "On the Composition of the Cabinet of Ministers of Ukraine" were abrogated as not corresponding to Article 114 of the Ukrainian Constitution.

[7] No. 959-XII "On the Foreign Trade Activities", dated April 16, 1991.

[8] According to information provided by the Institute of Legislation of the Verkhovna Rada of Ukraine, published in an interview with the Director of the Institute V. Oprishko, from the day when the Declaration of State Independence was passed to the end of December 1996, 808 laws were passed.

[9] Newspaper *Golos Ukraini*, February 18, 1997. No. 29 (1529).

[10] *Vedomosti Verkhovnogo Soveta USSR* 1984, Appendix to No. 51, p. 1123.

[11] *See e.g.* Merchant Navy Code (1995), Customs Code (1991), Air Code, Railway Regulations, Land Code (1992) and about 20 other trade laws.

[12] *See e.g.* "On the Mineral Wealth" & "On Veterinary Medicine"

[13] Article 5, Constitution of Ukraine.

[14] Article 6, Constitution of Ukraine.

[15] Article 113, Constitution of Ukraine.

[16] Article 114, Constitution of Ukraine.

[17] Article 106, Constitution of Ukraine.

[18] Article 85, Constitution of Ukraine.

[19] Article 87, Constitution of Ukraine.

[20] No. 130/94 VR No. 35 p. 338.

[21] Chapter 8.2, "Execution of Control Functions Concerning the Executive and Judicial Power".

[22] Article 8.2.1.

[23] Article 8.2.2.

[24] Article 8.2.4.

[25] Article 106, clause 10, Constitution of Ukraine.

[26] Article 114, clause 5, Constitution of Ukraine.

[27] "On the Membership of the Cabinet of Ministers of Ukraine", December 14, 1996.

[28] *See e.g.* The State Comity on the Protection of the Consumers' Rights.

[29] "General Statute on the Ministry and Other Central Body of Executive Power of Ukraine", approved by the President's Decree, of March 12, 1996.

[30] For instance, the status of the militia is determined by the Law "On Militia", of December 20, 1990; the status of the frontier troops is established by the Law "On the Frontier Troops". There also exist specialised bodies, such as the Foundation of State Property (p. 36), or the Anti-Monopoly Committee.

[31] March 12, 1996, Statute.

[32] Decree of November 5, 1996, "On the Measures, Increasing the Effectiveness of Work and Responsibility of the Local Branches of the Ministries and other Central Bodies of Executive Power and Promoting Their Interaction with the Local State Administrations".

[33] Decree of September 12, 1996, "On the Regulating of the Structure of Local State Administrations".
[34] Article 118, Constitution of Ukraine.
[35] Article 143, Constitution of Ukraine.
[36] Decree of December 30, 1995, "On the Delegation of Powers of the State Executive Power to the Heads and the Staff of Executive Committees of Village and City Radas".
[37] No 280/97 VR and published in the newspaper *Golos Ukraini* on June 12, 1997.
[38] Article 5, Constitution of Ukraine.
[39] Paragraph 15.
[40] Paragraph 33.
[41] Paragraph 34.
[42] Article 27.
[43] Paragraph 3, item 1.
[44] Item 2.
[45] *Id.*
[46] Item 9.
[47] Item 11.
[48] Item 12.
[49] Item 13.
[50] Item 15.
[51] Article 46.
[52] *Id.*
[53] Article 150.
[54] *Id.*
[55] For example, the Speaker of the Verkhovna Rada O. Moroz at the press conference on April 24, 1997, characterised the President's edict "On the Land Lease" as unconstitutional (*Golos Ukraini*, April 25, 1997, No. 75).
[56] Article 5, Chapter XV of the Constitution of Ukraine.
[57] Decree of the President of Ukraine "On the Administration of the President of Ukraine" of December 14, 1996, paragraph 5.
[58] Article 117 of the Constitution.
[59] Article 118, paragraph 8 of the Constitution.
[60] Article 144 of the Constitution.
[61] Article 117 of the Constitution.
[62] "On the state registration of normative acts of ministries, other bodies of state executive power and bodies of economic management and control, that concern rights, liberties and legal interests of citizens or have interdepartmental nature" was ratified by the Decree of the Cabinet of Ministers of Ukraine on December 28, 1992, No. 731. The proposal contains the list of items, regulated by the normative acts, subject to state registration.
[63] Article 213 of the Code on Administrative Offences.
[64] Article 6 of the Law "On the Enterprises in Ukrainian SSR" (1991).
[65] Article 27.
[66] Article 112 of the Land Code of Ukraine (1992).
[67] Law of Ukraine "On the Associations of Citizens" (1992), Article 16.
[68] Article 12 of the Arbitration Proceedings Code of Ukraine (1992).
[69] *Golos Ukraini*, January 16, 1993.
[70] Chapter 31 of the Code.
[71] Article 257 of the CPC of Ukraine.
[72] Article 248.
[73] *Vedomosti Verkhovnogo Sovieta Ukrainskoi SSR*, 1988, No. 19, p. 480.
[74] Article 248.2 CPC of Ukraine.
[75] Article 248.9 CPC of Ukraine.
[76] April 23, 1992, Article 248.11 CPC of Ukraine.
[77] Article 121.

78 Article 52 of the Code of Administrative Offences.
79 Article 218 of the Code of Administrative Offences.
80 Code of Administrative Offences in Article 221 in 1985, 1986 and 1987.
81 Article 16, paragraph 1.
82 Article 288 of the Code on Administrative Offences.
83 Article 289, paragraph 4, of the Code on Administrative Offences.
84 *Id.*
85 Article 289.
86 Article 290.
87 Article 291.
88 Article 248, Paragraph 2.
89 *Id.*
90 Article 248.7 of the Civil Procedure Code.
91 Article 55 of the Ukrainian Constitution.
92 Article 85 of the Constitution of Ukraine.
93 Article 40 of the Ukrainian Constitution. This subject is described in Article 13, paragraph 1 of this Law (its content is the same as Article 150 of the Constitution of Ukraine).
94 Article 41.
95 Article 28 of the Law of Ukraine "On the Appeals of Citizens".
96 Article 121.
97 "The Procurator's Office of Ukraine is led by the Procurator General of Ukraine".
98 No. 1789-XII, *Vedomosti Verkhovnoi Radi Ukraini* No. 53, p. 793.
99 Article 1 of the Law in the wording of March 21, 1995, *Golos Ukraini* March 29, 1995).
100 Chapter I, Part III.
101 Article 19 in the wording of November 26, 1993.
102 Article 20, paragraph 2, 3 in the wording of November 26, 1993.
103 Article 20, paragraph 2 in the wording of November 26, 1993.
104 Law on Permanent (Standing) Commissions (April 4, 1995, No 116/95-VR *Vedomosti Verkhovnoi Radi,* 1995, No. 19, p.134).
105 Chapter II "The Functions and Powers of the Permanent Commissions", Article 5, item 2.
106 Article 8, item 6.
107 Article 36.
108 Article 39.
109 Article 6.
110 Article 3 of the Constitution of USSR, 1978.
111 *See e.g.* "The Law on the President of Ukraine".
112 No. 422/96, *Vedomosti Verkhovnoi Radi,* No. 49, p. 272.
113 Article 150 of the Constitution.
114 Article 150 of the Constitution.
115 Chapter IV of the Law on the Constitutional Court - "Final and Transitive Provisions" - Article 3.
116 *Vedomosti Verkhovnoi Radi Ukraini,* 1996, No. 15, p. 70) - changes dated March 6, 1996.
117 *Vedomosti Verkhovnoi Radi Ukraini,* 1996, No. 44, p. 216) & *Golos Ukraini*, 1996, No 238-239, December 19.
118 *Vedomosti Verkhovnoi Radi Ukraini*, 1996, No. 15, p.70, *Vedomosti Verkhovnoi Radi Ukraini*, 1996, No. 46, p. 247 & *Vedomosti Verkhovnoi Radi Ukraini*, 1996, No. 25, p. 104.
119 March 6, 1996, April 26, 1996, October 1, 1996.
120 *Golos Ukraini,* 1996, No. 145 - August 7.
121 Article 234.2 of the Code on Administrative Offences.
122 March 6, 1996, July 12, 1996, October 1, 1996, November 13, 1996.
123 Article 294 of the Code on Administrative Offences.
124 Article 248.2 of the Civil Legal Procedure Code of Ukraine.
125 Article 248.3.
126 Article 5.
127 Article 25.

128 July 11, 1996, *Vedomosti Verkhovnoi Radi Ukraini* No. 315/96 - VR, No. 43, p. 212.
129 Article 1.
130 Article 2.
131 Article 6.
132 Article 7.
133 Article 40.
134 May 15, 1996, No. 189-96, *Vedomosti Verkhovnoi Radi* No. 34.
135 Article 1.
136 Chapter II.
137 Chapter IV.
138 No. 209/96, *Vedomosti Verkhovnoi Radi Ukraini* No. 41 p. 188.
139 May 13, 1996, No. 485/96, *Vedomosti Verkhovnoi Radi Ukraini* No. 52, p. 303.
140 In accordance with this, several laws were passed, including the Land Code of Ukraine (1992), the Decree of the Verkhovna Rada of the Ukrainian SSR "On the Forms of State Acts" (1991), Regulations on the Order of Allotment and Withdrawal of Land Plots (1991) and some others.
141 October 31, 1996, No. 456 *Vedomosti Verkhovnoi Radi Ukraini* No. 50. p. 280.
142 Article 4.
143 Article 11.
144 Article 18.
145 Article 5, May 21, 1995 No. 437/95 VR.
146 June 7, 1996, No. 236/96, *Vedomosti Verkhovnoi Radi Ukraini* No. 36.
147 The protection against unfair competition is also regulated by the Law of Ukraine "On the Limitation of Monopolism and Prevention of Unfair Competition in the Business Activities"; the Law "On the Anti-Monopoly Committee of Ukraine"; the Law "On Foreign Economic Activities" and some others.
148 July 3, 1996, No. 270/96, *Vedomosti verkhovnoi Radi Ukraini* No. 39.
149 Article 26.
150 Article 35.
151 March 7, 1996, No. 85/96 VR, *Vedomosti Verkhovnoi Radi Ukraini* No. 18, April 30, 1996, was to come in force July 1, 1997.
152 October 30, 1996, No. 448/96, *Vedomosti Verkhovnoi Radi Ukraini* No. 51, p. 292.
153 Article 1.
154 July 9, 1996, No. 283, *Vedomosti Verkhovnoi Radi Ukraini* No. 40.
155 Article 40.
156 May 6, 1996, No. 171/96, *Vedomosti Verkhovnoi Radi Ukraini* No. 27.
157 May 15, 1996, No. 192/96, *Vedomosti Verkhovnoi Radi Ukraini* No. 40.
158 Article 3.
159 Article 7.
160 Article 13.
161 July 9, 1996, No. 283/96 VR, *Vedomosti Verkhovnoi Radi Ukraini* No. 40.).
162 Article 4.
163 Article 4.
164 February 6, 1996, No. 29/96.
165 *Id.*
166 No. 81/96 VR, *Vedomosti Verkhovnoi Radi Ukraini* No. 15, p. 70.
167 *Vedomosti Verkhovnogo Sovieta Ukraini* No. 41, p. 546.
168 Article 13.
169 April 4, 1996, No. 123/96 VR.
170 April 19, 1996, No. 129/96 VR.
171 Articles 144-148 of the Administrative Code, October 1, 1996, No. 387/96 VR, *Vedomosti Verkhovnoi Radi Ukraini* No. 46, p. 247-248.
172 Article 185 of the Code on Administrative Offences , October 2, 1996, No. 388/96 VR, *Vedomosti Verkhovnoi Radi Ukraini* No. 46 p. 250.

LIST OF CONTRIBUTORS

EDITORS

Denis James Galligan (BCL, MA) is Professor of Law at the Law Department and Director of the Centre for Socio-Legal Studies at the University of Oxford, and Recurrent Visiting Professor at the Legal Studies Department of the Central European University, Budapest.

Daniel Mihaylov Smilov (LLM, MSt, MA) is a DPhil student at the Law Department of the University of Oxford and a PhD student at the Legal Studies Department of the Central European University, Budapest.

Bulgaria

Katya Hristova is a PhD student at the Department of Political Science of the University of Sofia. She holds degrees in Political Science and Public Administration from the Sofia University (MA) and the Sorbonne (MA).

Croatia

Alexander Dordević is a practising lawyer from Rijeka, Croatia. He holds law degrees from the Central European University, Budapest (LLM) and the University of Rijeka, Croatia.

The Czech Republic

Andrea Baršova is legal adviser at the Department for Refugees at the Czech Ministry of the Interior. She holds law degrees from the Central European University (LLM) and the Masaryk University in Brno.

Estonia

Piret Lappert is a graduate student at the University of Tartu. She has worked as a senior legal expert at the Ministry of Finance and as Deputy Director at the Consumer Protection Fund. Since October 1995 she has been a legal adviser at the Estonian Translation and Legislative Support Centre in Tallin.

Ellen Valter is currently a law student in her final year at the University of Toronto, Canada. During 1995-1997, she took a leave of absence from her studies to be Translation Legal Counsel at the Estonian Translation and Legislative Support Centre in Tallinn, Estonia.

Hungary

Maria Bordás (JD, PhD) is lecturer at the National School of Public Administration Law and researcher at the College of Public Administration in Budapest.

Latvia

Dr. Anita Usacka is Judge of the Constitutional Court of the Republic of Latvia and Associate Professor of Law at the University of Latvia.

Lithuania

Ramunė Dulevičienė (LLM, the University of Chicago) is a senior lawyer of the Lithuanian branch of the law firm Bishop and Robertson Chalmers UAB.

Audrius Bukaveckas is Assistant Professor at the Administrative Department of the Lithuanian Law Academy.

Antanas Bukaukas is Director of the Centre for Police Reforms at the Ministry of Interior of the Republic of Lithuania.

Poland

Justyna Stencel is a law researcher at the Adam Mickiewitz University, Poznań, Poland.

Romania

Mihaela Şerban is a PhD student at the Central European University, Budapest. She holds law degrees from the Central European University (LLM) and the University of Bucharest Law School.

Russia

Dr. Alexey Afanasyevich Demin is a senior lecturer at the Law Department of the Moscow State University.

Serbia

Danica Kilibarda is a DPhil student at the Department of Law, University of Oxford. She holds law degrees from the University of Oxford (MSt), the Central European University, Budapest (LLM), and the University of Belgrade.

Snežana Rajšić is a practising lawyer from Belgrade. She holds law degrees from the Central European University, Budapest (LLM), and the Belgrade University.

Slovakia

Ivan Gyurcsik is a PhD student at the Legal Studies Department of the Central European University, Budapest. He holds law degrees from the Central European University, Budapest (LLM) and from the Bratislava University.

Slovenia

Dr. Matijas Tratnik is Professor of Law at the Institute for Civil, Comparative, and International Business Law at the University of Maribor, Slovenia.

Ukraine

Eugeniya Dodina is a practising lawyer from Odessa and a PhD student at the Odessa State Academy of Law. She holds law degrees from the Central European University, Budapest (LLM) and the University of Odessa, Ukraine.

INDEX

For Product Safety Concerns and Information please contact our EU representative GPSR@taylorandfrancis.com Taylor & Francis Verlag GmbH, Kaufingerstraße 24, 80331 München, Germany

Batch number: 10725853

Printed by Printforce, the Netherlands